Medicine & Society
In America

Medicine & Society
In America

Advisory Editor

**Charles E. Rosenberg
Professor of History
University of Pennsylvania**

PUBLIC HYGIENE

IN AMERICA:

BEING THE CENTENNIAL DISCOURSE DELIVERED BEFORE
THE INTERNATIONAL MEDICAL CONGRESS,
PHILADELPHIA, SEPTEMBER, 1876

BY

HENRY I. BOWDITCH, M.D.

WITH

EXTRACTS FROM CORRESPONDENCE FROM THE
VARIOUS STATES

*A*RNO P*RESS* & T*HE* N*EW* Y*ORK* T*IMES*
New York   1972

Reprint Edition 1972 by Arno Press Inc.

Reprinted from a copy in
The Princeton University Library

LC# 70-180557
ISBN 0-405-03937-9

Medicine and Society in America
ISBN for complete set: 0-405-03950-1
See last pages of this volume for titles.

Manufactured in the United States of America

CENTENNIAL DISCOURSE

ON

PUBLIC HYGIENE AND STATE PREVENTIVE MEDICINE.

"I look for the time when our courts of law shall punish cities and villages, for permitting any of the sources of bilious and malignant fevers to exist within their jurisdiction." — BENJ. RUSH.

"There are people who think that every thing may be done, if the doer, be he educator or physician, be only called in season. No doubt; but *in season* would often be a hundred or two years before the child was born, and people never send so early as that." — O. W. HOLMES.

"In a wide sense, the science of public hygiene enlists the services of the people themselves, in continuous efforts at self-improvement; of the teachers of the people, to inculcate the best rules of life and action; of physicians, in preventing as well as curing disease; and of law-givers, to legalize and enforce measures of health preservation." — WILSON, *Handbook of Hygiene*.

PUBLIC HYGIENE

IN AMERICA:

Being the Centennial Discourse delivered before
the International Medical Congress,
Philadelphia, September, 1876.

BY

HENRY I. BOWDITCH, M.D.

WITH

EXTRACTS FROM CORRESPONDENCE FROM THE
VARIOUS STATES.

TOGETHER WITH A DIGEST OF AMERICAN SANITARY LAW,

BY

HENRY G. PICKERING, Esq.

BOSTON:
LITTLE, BROWN, AND COMPANY.
LONDON: TRÜBNER AND COMPANY.
1877.

Copyright, 1877,
By Henry I. Bowditch.

Cambridge:
Press of John Wilson & Son.

TO THE MEMORY OF

MY BELOVED MASTER IN MEDICINE,

LOUIS,

Whose noble example will always lead every honest scholar to a reverent regard for scientific truth; whose works have been to me a stimulus to patient labors in my profession, and whose friendship was to me a life-long delight; and

TO MY LIVING ASSOCIATES,

My Professional Brethren throughout these United States, without whose courtesy and cordial co-operation it would have been impossible for me to prepare it,

I respectfully and gratefully dedicate this Centennial Discourse.

HENRY I. BOWDITCH.

Boston, March, 1877.

PREFACE TO THE AMERICAN EDITION.

THE Discourse which I delivered before the International Medical Congress, held in Philadelphia, in September, 1876, was the following, very much abridged. In its present condition, it would have been too long for a public address. In its abridged form, by a vote of the Congress, it has been already printed, and sent to the Governors of these States, to those of the various provinces of the Dominion of Canada, and to the Presidents of the State Medical Societies of this country.

In the Appendix will be found some of the data on which the Discourse is, in part, founded. I have deemed it well to publish them, as confirmatory of the statements contained in the Discourse. I have thought they would be of value to some future investigator; for they will enable him to know, more definitely than he could without them, the precise status of public opinion, in different parts of the country, upon Public Hygiene and State Preventive Medicine, — topics which are destined, in the future, to have such powerful influence on the duration of life, and the preservation of the public health.

The data from the colleges I have condensed, so as to show, approximatively, the amount of instruction on

these topics, now given by the seminaries of learning in America.

I owe to the kindness of my young friend, Henry G. Pickering, Esq., the digest on American, National and State, Sanitary Law, which he, at my request, has prepared.

My thanks are due to Drs. C. F. Folsom, Secretary of the State Board of Health of Massachusetts, E. H. Bradford, G. Stedman, and E. H. Brigham, for valuable assistance, given during the preparation of the work.

To my various professional and lay correspondents throughout the Union, I cannot, by mere words, express my gratitude, for the trouble they have taken for me. I have admired their loyalty to scientific truth, while narrating facts, at times, apparently little creditable to their respective governments, either of State or of township.

HENRY I. BOWDITCH.

CONTENTS.

PAGE

CENTENNIAL DISCOURSE: —

PART I. Historical Account of the Gradual Evolution of the Idea of State Preventive Medicine during the Centennial Period . . . 1

PART II. Present Status of the Country in Reference to Public Hygiene and State Preventive Medicine, as shown by an Analysis of Answers to Various Questions, submitted to Correspondents resident in all Parts of the Country 39

SUMMARY 120

OUR PRESENT DUTY 121

APPENDIX.

I. Circular to Correspondents, with a List of their Names 125
II. Extracts from their Letters 135
III. Returns from Universities and Medical Colleges, on the Amount of Attention given to Instruction in Public Hygiene and Preventive Medicine . . . 279
IV. Digest of American Sanitary Law, by Henry G. Pickering, Esq., Counsellor-at-law 299
V. Louis's Estimate of James Jackson, Jr. 441
VI. Law of Soil Moisture as a Cause of Consumption in Massachusetts and elsewhere 451
VII. Massachusetts Law on Noxious and Offensive Trades 463
VIII. European Sanitary Work 467

INDEX 479

CENTENNIAL DISCOURSE

ON

PUBLIC HYGIENE.

GENTLEMEN OF THE INTERNATIONAL MEDICAL CONGRESS:

I have been requested to speak to you on PUBLIC HYGIENE and STATE PREVENTIVE MEDICINE, as they appear to an observer looking back upon this centennial period of our country which has just closed.

Theoretically, Public Hygiene is the most important matter any community can discuss, for upon it, in its perfection, depend all the powers, moral, intellectual, and physical, of a State. But as a practical measure, in which every citizen of a well-organized community should feel a vital interest, it will be found that no nation has so viewed it. *Public Hygiene neglected.* Nay, more, I take the ground that, in this country at least, though the same may be said of most other countries, it is only within a few years that the people seem awakening from their stolid indifference of centuries to a sense of its importance. Hitherto, little or no attention has been paid to it, except when, under the influence of some frightful epidemic, the panic-struck nations have been aroused from their usual apathy, and have then vainly tried to resist the pest by drugs, by appeals to the gods whose laws they have never studied, or finally, perhaps, by legal enactments, after the days of suffer-

ing have passed. Recently, in this country and in Europe, we seem entering upon a new career; viz., the minute and accurate study of the causes, not only of these occasional scourges of our race, but of all diseases, however trivial. It is, moreover, proposed that this should be done with the full power of the State, directed by experts, professional and scientific, chosen not alone from the medical ranks, but from any class of life in which the requisite scientific or other appropriate knowledge can be found. This leads us to the idea of

Marginal note: State Preventive Medicine.

STATE PREVENTIVE MEDICINE.

What meaning can we attach to this expression? Generally, the terms *state* and *preventive* medicine have been used separately. I shall, in this address, consider them as one, and for the following reasons. It is impossible for any one person to investigate thoroughly the whole domain of the causation of disease. Only the State, with its great resources, with a large corps of able and earnest agents occupied in the observation of the rise and progress of disease, and in the analysis of such observations for many generations, can hope to unravel even a few of the many mysterious causes of the diseases of any nation, especially of one covering so large a portion of the earth's surface as the United States. Hence, preventive medicine must be undertaken by the State, or we shall hereafter go on, as hitherto, somewhat vainly, or perhaps foolishly, struggling, with but little success, against what may be preventable disease. Still further, I hold it to be true that the study of the prevention of disease is the only branch of medical learning which the State can legiti-

mately undertake. The practice of medicine and surgery, and the appropriate use of drugs, must be left to medical schools and to private practitioners of medicine. The State, as a student of the causes of all disease, only supplements, and indeed nobly supplements, them.

These reasons appear to me sufficient to justify my present use of language, and of my combination of the two terms under the expression *state preventive medicine*. To this last, this noblest phase of public hygiene, its gradual evolution during the past centennial period, its present status and future prospects, I ask your attention and candid consideration during the brief period I shall have the honor of addressing you. If, after the termination of my remarks, our foreign associates find that I have given them little information, and my countrymen feel that I have said but little in praise of our country, one and all of you will, I trust, give me credit for sincerity of purpose, and a desire to speak the exact truth, so far as I have been able to learn what that truth is. Moreover, I hope that what I shall say, and still more what I shall give in the appendix to this discourse, but which I shall be able only briefly to allude to at this time, — viz., selections from my correspondents' letters from all parts of our Union, — will become a stand-point by which our descendants of the coming century will know, more definitely than they otherwise would, the precise distance we have already gone in this important direction, at this most interesting year of our nation's life. I hope, also, that the unvarnished history of our shortcomings in this respect, sustained as it is by documentary evidence from all quarters of our country, will stimulate each State government, and the United States authori-

The noblest phase of public hygiene.

ties, to do more thoroughly than they have heretofore done the duty which plainly lies before them.

Before laying down the propositions I intend to defend, let me say that we cannot, in the consideration of the question, confine our view simply to this country. We shall be obliged constantly to refer to ideas prevalent in other countries, as well as to those in our own, and to some of the great men of Europe, as well as to those of this country. For, since the times of Watt, with his steam-engine, Stephenson, with his steam-locomotive, both of England, and Morse, with his telegraph-wire, in America, finely supplemented by Field, with his Atlantic cable, binding continent to continent, there has been a solidarity among the nations of the earth such as never before existed; and much of this has arisen within the memories of numbers of those who now listen to me. Each people acts and is reacted upon now in a manner wholly unknown before. In citing, however, the names of men who may have been prominent, I shall do so without intending either praise or blame, but simply as those of illustrious representatives of great systems of medicine, or as apparent directors of the currents of thought upon which the medical profession, and, of late, the laity, have been *borne, often perhaps almost unconsciously*, along.

Influence of countries upon each other.

Natural Divisions of the Centennial Period.

Three divisions of the Centenary.

The past centennial period may be easily and plainly divided into three unequal epochs.

DIVISIONS OF THE CENTENARY. 5

First Epoch, from 1776 *to* 1832.

This period commences with our political revolution. It arises from the preceding century, and is a fair continuation of it. It terminated with the fall of Broussaisism, about 1832. Benjamin Rush, of America, and Broussais, of France, appear as its leaders. It is the epoch of systems of medicine, wrought out by the imaginations of some few of the great leaders of our profession. These systems have been dogmatically, and often violently, asserted by real geniuses, and as slavishly adhered to by thousands of deluded, and at times foolish, followers. This epoch believes in drugs, and the almost supreme power of our art. It has little or no faith in Nature's ability to cure disease. It comprehends the first *fifty*-six years of the centenary.

<small>First Epoch, 1776–1832.</small>

Second Epoch, from 1832 *to* 1869.

The second period commences with the rise of more exact and scientific methods of study, with most minute observation of facts, and subsequent analysis of such facts, without the least regard to preconceived opinions. It may be said to extend, in this country, from 1832 until 1869, when the first State Board of Health was established. It comprises, therefore, a period of thirty-seven years. Its precise methods have led not only to a thorough overthrow of all the imaginative theories that preceded it, but it has gone still farther; and towards its termination we shall see arise an apparently most unhappy degree of scepticism as to the precise value of the very medical art so haughtily vaunted in the preceding epoch,

<small>Second Epoch, 1832–1869.</small>

and especially as to the use of drugs, while at the same time we shall notice a profound reverence for nature, and a strong belief in its powers of limiting and of curing disease. In other words, medical opinion will take, during this second epoch, a position as completely as possible the reverse of the dogmatism of the first, with its contempt for the *vis medicatrix naturæ*, and its fulsome praise of the power of our art. No two epochs could be more diametrically opposed than these two. Together, they occupy the first ninety-three years of our centennial period. Louis of France, Forbes of England, Bigelow and Bartlett of America, will be seen as the eminent exponents of this period.

Third Epoch, from 1869 to the Far Future.

The third and last epoch, which I believe will be the noblest and most beneficent of all, begins in 1869. Though as yet infinitely small in its influence, and in what it has really done, it promises golden fruits for coming centuries. It is now just opening upon a grand career, such as has never yet, I believe, been seen in the history of medicine. In this period, and immediately preceding it, the laity first come forward prominently as acknowledged and able coadjutors and promoters of medical reform. Lemuel Shattuck, of America, and Edwin Chadwick, of England, appear as pioneers, followed by a host of able men in this country and in Europe. It is supported by the fullest legislative and executive power of mighty States, by the active co-operation of the medical profession, and the good-will of the public generally, all pursuing the same general direction towards *State Preventive Medicine*. This last is the culmination of,

Third Epoch, 1869 to the far future.

State Preventive Medicine, the culmination of the centenary.

FIRST EPOCH.

and the beautiful blossoming out, if I may use the expression, of our centennial period.

Let us now examine more in detail each one of the three epochs, and see if they can be proved to exist.

FIRST EPOCH, OR THAT OF MEDICAL SYSTEM-MAKING,

Filled with an Overweening Confidence in our Art, and with little or no Faith in the Vis Medicatrix Naturæ. It extended from 1776 *to* 1832.

The influences which governed the opinions of the medical profession during this epoch, and during the previous century, may be sketched as follows. The illustrious Boerhaave, with his commanding intellect, began to enunciate his doctrines of disease at Leyden, in 1701. With him, all disease was in the fluids of the system. His doctrines held sway in Europe and America until about 1765; that is, until ten years before the opening of our centennial period. Cullen, of Edinburgh, following Hoffman, proclaimed exactly the reverse; viz., that all disease was in the solids, and that spasm of the vessels was the cause of fever. What Boerhaave prescribed to expel morbific matter, Cullen prescribed to relieve spasm. Both were heroic in their methods of practice. After Cullen, came Brown, of the Edinburgh school; and all disease was either sthenic or asthenic. Darwin followed Brown, and for a short period his Linnæan classification of disease prevailed. With him, irritability and sympathy were the factors in disease. Our ingenious and powerful countryman, Benjamin Rush, in 1790 (that is, fourteen years after our Revolution began), proclaimed his own system; viz., that a convulsive mo-

Side notes: Influences during First Epoch. Boerhaave. Cullen. Brown. Darwin. Benj. Rush.

tion of the arteries is the proximate cause of all fever, and that there is but one fever, however different the causes may be.[1]

Benjamin Rush was one of the most noteworthy men our profession has had during this past century. He had more influence upon medical opinion during the first epoch than any other American. He was regarded by his compeers as the "American Sydenham."[2] It seems, therefore, not improper to mention on this occasion some facts of his history. He was born Dec. 24, 1745, on his father's plantation, fourteen miles from Philadelphia. Consequently he was thirty-one years old, just at the prime of young manhood, in the birth-year of our nation, 1776. Seven years before that, at the age of twenty-four, he had been appointed Professor of Chemistry in the University of Pennsylvania. During the war of the Revolution, he resigned his professorship, and was made Medical Director of the Middle Department of the Continental army, and served with high honor. He was subsequently member of Congress, and was one of the signers of the Declaration of Independence. In 1789 he resumed his professorship of chemistry, and in October, of the same year, became professor of the theory and practice of medicine, which office he held until his death, in 1813. During all this time he energetically and ably defended his own system of medicine, as he had previously upheld Cullen's, and indulged in the most heroic kind of practice. He moreover left descriptions of yellow fever, and many

[1] Medical Inquiries and Observations, by Benjamin Rush. Philadelphia, 1818. Vol. iii. pp. 10, 11.

[2] Review of the Improvement, Progress, and State of Medicine in the Eighteenth Century. Read by David Ramsay, on the first day of the nineteenth century, before the Medical Society of South Carolina. It is dedicated to Benjamin Rush, as "the American Sydenham."

other observations and essays, which are valuable as records of this period, and evidences of his intellectual and moral worth. He was, however, essentially a medical system-maker, like his predecessors. He believed fully in violent remedies, and rather scoffed at Nature.[1] His scholars spread over some of the Eastern, more of the Middle, Western, and Southern States, carrying with them the errors of their great master, — errors always necessarily connected with any theory unsupported by solid facts carefully observed and recorded. He thus had a vast influence upon the medical ideas of the country.

We must readily believe this, when we remember that Dr. Rush held the first professorship of the chief medical school in the country, and that towards the latter part of his career his pupils numbered nearly four hundred, annually drawn by his genius to Philadelphia from every State of this Union.

The reputation of the profession among the laity, when Dr. Rush was in full glory, is thus graphically given by his great political colleague, Thomas Jefferson, who, in writing to his friend Dr. Wistar, of Philadelphia, in 1807, makes use of the following words as applied to medical men: "We have seen the fashions of Hoffman, Boerhaave, Stahl, Cullen, and Brown, succeed one another like the shifting figures of a magic lantern; and their fancies, like the dresses of the annual doll-babies from Paris, becoming, from their novelty, the vogue of the day, and *Jefferson's estimate of the profession.*

---

[1] Dr. Jacob Bigelow, of whose very important influence in another direction I shall speak hereafter, recently informed me that he listened as a student at the feet of Rush, and well remembers that the Professor often used expressions like the following: viz., "Turn nature out of doors, gentlemen, and appeal to art;" and "Cullen's *vis medicatrix naturæ* is a mere delusion."

yielding to the next novelty their ephemeral favor."[1] This certainly is not a very high compliment to the profession of that time. Nevertheless, the violence with which Dr. Rush defended his own views, and the grotesqueness of some of his propositions, were a justification of these remarks by Mr. Jefferson. Both of these citizens were great men. They were colleagues as statesmen, and patriots of the loftiest type. The names of both appear upon our Magna Charta, the Declaration of Independence. Both were earnest defenders of the rights of man, and both alike will descend to fame as long as our country lasts. But Dr. Rush appears in a most ludicrous light, when, in the violent support of his heroic methods of treatment against the opposition shown to them by some of his fellow-physicians, he declares " that the time must and will come when, in addition to the above remedies (viz., air, light, and water, which are used by all, without a physician's advice), the general use of calomel, jalap, and the lancet, shall be considered among the most essential articles of the knowledge and the rights of man."[2]

Dr. Rush's ultraism.

But Dr. Rush's zeal did not prevent his theories and wild propositions, relative to the human rights to venesection and to the use of calomel, from yielding to the influence exerted by the fascinating system-maker, the eloquent and dogmatic Broussais. Broussaisism spread widely in Europe and America, and fastened itself firmly in New York and Philadelphia, and thence spread West and South. It had less influence over New England, which had

Broussaisism spread widely in United States.

---

[1] The Works of Thomas Jefferson, by H. A. Washington. Washington, 1854. Vol. v. 107.

[2] Rush's, as above, vol. iii. p. 176.

been trained more to observation, and less to theory, under the care of those masters in medicine, Holyoke, and his more eminent pupil, the elder Jackson.[1] Broussais was born in 1772, when Rush was already giving evidences of his great powers, and only three years before our centennial period opened. He died in 1838, retaining to the last his ardent zeal for his doctrines. As a controversialist in behalf of his physiological ideas, he was unsurpassed. Doubtless some now before me saw him, as I did, in Paris, in 1834, when his fame was dimmed before the rising glories of a newer and a better school. His ardor and violence in defence of his work were undiminished. It was painful to see him struggling vainly against the inevitable fate, which had crushed the theories of his predecessors, and awaited him.

With him, our first epoch terminates. The whole tenor of it, with its theories and its systems concocted in great minds, was not suited to the growth of any thing like what we understand by *State Preventive Medicine*. Throughout its whole course, we find a tyranny of egotistically proclaimed theory, unsustained by strict observation of fact. We must, however, admit that Dr. Rush and Broussais have recorded many facts in various portions of their works; and Dr. Rush, in one or more of his essays, alludes to the idea of the prevention of disease.

Characteristics of First Epoch.

---

[1] The late Dr. James Jackson, Senior, probably had more influence on medical ideas in New England, from 1808 to 1838, than any other one man. But even he, while Professor of the Theory and Practice of Medicine, allowed himself to indulge at times in what he himself, were he now alive, would admit were most untenable, if not absurd, theories, in reference to the physiological influence of blood-letting. These theories he held, in spite of his usual accuracy in the observation of disease, and his strong tendency not to allow himself or his numerous pupils to pass, in the least degree, beyond what strict fact would permit.

Second Epoch, or that of Observation,

And the Accurate Recording of Facts and Subsequent Analysis of them, with an Extreme Confidence in Nature's Power of curing Disease, and Corresponding Scepticism in regard to Drugs, and finally with Dim Presages of Preventive Medicine. This Epoch extends from 1832 *to* 1869.

Our second epoch presents characteristics precisely the reverse of the first. But, before proceeding to trace the gradual evolution of this period, I must briefly allude to one or more characteristics of the times long previous to the present, but which continued to be seen and felt till far into this second epoch of our centenary: 1st, To the estimate in which the physician's art was held, both by the practitioner and the public; 2d, To the relations existing between the medical practitioner and the public.

<small>Characteristics reverse of the first.</small>

Until very lately, quite within the memory of some of us elders in the profession, the physician held too often the notion that he had the power of life or death of his patient in his own hands, to a much greater extent than is really true. The present juniors of the profession cannot conceive the agony that formerly would, at times, seize upon a young physician, when brought face to face with a severe attack of acute disease He had been told that a certain course must be pursued, at a certain time, and in a certain way, and to a certain amount, and that, according as all these points were attended to by himself wrongly or rightly, either death or recovery would ensue. The venerable

<small>Relations of physician to patient.</small>

<small>Dr. Bigelow's views of it.</small>

Dr. Bigelow, already alluded to, informs me that, when he commenced practice, if he or any other youth had dared to neglect the administration of an emetic at the commencement of a fever, and the patient had died, " he would have been considered by others, and would have thought himself, the murderer of his patient."

So, too, the relations of the physician to his patient were very different from those which now prevail. The community generally believed as the physician did; viz., that in his hands were the issues of life and of death. The family physician, with his gold-headed cane, often armed with its "pouncet-box," with his oracular, despotic sayings, and his dignified and sagacious *looks*, in spite of, at times, a head entirely devoid of knowledge of the subject suddenly brought before him, excited a certain degree of awe. He was regarded as a sort of demi-god. A deep meaning rested upon his every look and word. In his own and his patient's view, he was, for the time being, the vicegerent of Almighty Power. There was little or no frankness on either side; and the existence of a doubt, much less of absolute ignorance, in regard to the case in hand, was never admitted by either party. It was my fortune to commence practice only a year or two after the beginning of this epoch. I had studied under Louis, and had learned to doubt about the plenary powers claimed by the physician, and by the public for him; and I well remember the grave rebuke and sage counsel I received from one of the oldest and best physicians of Boston, one who ranked with the most distinguished, and received the highest honors the Massachusetts Medical Society could bestow. I had, in conversation with him, broached what seemed to me

The "family doctor."

Anecdote.

one of the most reasonable of propositions; viz., that I was willing, and that I intended, during my subsequent practice, to act up to the rule of speaking frankly with intelligent patients, and of telling them. *if they wished to know*, what medicines I intended to use in their cases, and my reasons for so doing, so far as I could give any valid reasons therefor. With a manner I shall never forget, he replied, in what, doubtless, he thought were words of infinite wisdom: "No, that will never do. You will never succeed in your profession, if you do not keep always something secret from your patients." What absurdity is this! and how has the current of modern thought swept away, in the practice of honorable physicians, all these relics of mediæval superstitions existing between the laity and our profession! Hereafter we shall see how necessary for the perfect evolution of the third epoch was this crushing of a blind superstition, and the bringing of the laity into proper relations with our profession. With these preliminary remarks, which I deem, and hope you will think, legitimate, let me now pass to the history of our second epoch. Louis, and his numerical method, will stand prominent in it. Louis was the lineal scientific descendant of such men as John Hunter, Morgagni, and the like. His whole nature rebelled against the dogmatism of the past. The practical results, too, of his early professional experience in Russia, were, in his estimation, deplorable. His inability to gain any foundation for more efficient therapeutics, when he again appealed to the so-called science of medicine of Paris, on his return to that metropolis in search of truth, drove him back to first principles. In 1820, he began again, as a simple, humble scholar, to study for himself, in the wards of his friend Chomel,

Louis.

As scholar.

the laws of diseases, and to learn the exact influence of remedies on all such. All of you know the great works that resulted. *Writer.*

Our second epoch may be said to have commenced in this country when Dr. Gerhard, of Philadelphia, and James Jackson, Jr., of Boston, returned to these two cities and began their honorable careers. Both were endowed with fine mental powers, richly cultivated. Both came back devoted friends and admirers of Louis as a man and as a medical reformer, and steeped with ideas gained from him,[1] whose ardent disciples they had become during their long stay at the brilliant and most fascinating metropolis of France. The Vienna School, of late years so famous, was at that time unthought of or unseen by most medical students, dazzled as they were by the brilliant light given out by the great triumvirate, Andral, Louis, and Chomel, of Paris. *Gerhard. James Jackson, Jr. Andral, Louis, Chomel.*

Broussais, at the time these young men returned, still held his powerful sway in Europe, at Philadelphia, and at the West and South of this country; and similar doctrines, not so thoroughly carried out, prevailed in the North.

Louis was Broussais's able and all-powerful opponent. He became so, not by any new theory or system of medicine concocted out of his own brain, which by his power he had forced upon his pupils, but by his simple and child-like faith in natural law, and in his confidence that, by thorough and close observation of that law alone, could truth be found out. From Louis's pupils, especially Gerhard and Jackson, sprang an influence which extended over the entire country. *Louis opposed to Broussais. Influence of Gerhard and Jackson.*

[1] See Appendix V. for Louis's opinion of Jackson.

It must be confessed that there seemed to be something
unwarrantable and supercilious in the terms
in which some disciples, rather than Louis
himself, spoke of the past. It seemed as if they would,
if they could, wholly ignore it in their desire to build
up medicine on the basis of strictly observed and recorded
fact. "Perpendendae et numerandæ observationes,"
was their motto; but, as observations made in
former times were imperfect in detail, and sometimes
bore marks of the follies of the age they came from, they
were to be wholly ignored themselves, and the observers
and recorders of them were to be summarily cast into
the limbo of useless men and facts of the past. All previous
medicine was to these disciples as a "*tabula rasa.*"
They did not feel as they should have felt; viz., that the
past is always full of bright prophecies of the future.
By this exclusive spirit of many of the numerical school,
while infinite good has been done, an apparent evil has
arisen to practical medicine in our day. I allude
to a more or less complete scepticism on
the part of many of the profession and of the laity in
regard to all medical treatment, save, perhaps, in that
of the art of good nursing. Moreover, by what we may
call an overweening confidence in Nature, we have at
times allowed her wild operations to inflict grievous injury
on our patients, which we might have prevented,
and which I believe our fathers would have
prevented. The common usages and remedies
of our fathers have been often recklessly
thrown aside. For example, our young physicians too
often go out into the world wholly ignoring
that venesection, which, according to Rush,
was to be claimed by every one as a natural right! It is
not even taught in some of our best schools as among, at

least, the minor operations of surgery. Our young men never touch antimony, and generally eschew purging, even if really favorable occasions arise for the use of any of them. As in the past it has always happened, and as in the far future it will always happen, according to the very constitution of the human mind, the pendulum of human thought has swung far beyond the line of exact truth and from a blind faith in the supreme power of our art, noticeable during the first epoch, in the second, physicians fell into an equally blind and fanatical scepticism in reference to it. But, notwithstanding this result, a part of which undoubtedly was evil, I think that all will admit that Louis's school was needed, in order to sweep away all theoretical systems, when unsupported by well-observed, well-recorded, and sufficiently numerous facts. Louis's works on Bloodletting, Phthisis, Typhoid and Yellow Fever, were soon published in America, and they indoctrinated the rising masses of the profession. They were at times vehemently objected to by some of the elders of it, whose lives had been moulded by the doctrines of the previous epoch. Philosophical minds, however, were charmed with the accuracy observable in these writings, and this feeling was enhanced by Louis's use of the numerical method. This last, though not infallible, apparently presented a means for as near an approach to truth as men could hope to obtain in medicine. It is now adopted by some of the best minds as the basis of Public Hygiene.[1] Above all, the pure and high example of the master ennobled each pupil in his own eyes. Each one hoped, and felt himself able, in a certain degree, to arrive at truth by simple observation, and by analysis of a sufficiently large number of accu-

[1] Public Health, W. A. Guy. London, 1874.

rately recorded cases. The consequence has been, that a great number of independent observers and workers have been educated in this country and in Europe to use their own minds and senses for medical observation. Everywhere, in fact, in Europe and America, do we find that influence exerted. No one calls himself a follower of Louis, because the very principles laid down by that great man really forbid a pupil from doing so. Louis himself, by his writings and precepts, takes away such a thought. He directs the pupil to follow truth, and naught else. Witness the following quotation from Rousseau's "Émile," which Louis cites as his motto introductory of his work on Typhoid Fever: " Je sais que la vérité est dans les choses et non dans mon esprit qui les juge, et que moins je mets du mien dans les jûgements que j'en porte, plus je suis sûr d'approcher de la vérité." So, too, the following, which was given out by Louis in his later days, after he retired from active life: " Il y a quelque chose de plus rare que l'esprit de discernement, c'est la besoin de la vérité, cet état de l'âme qui ne nous permets pas de nous arrêter dans les travaux scientifiques à ce que n'est que vraisemblable et nous oblige à continuer nos recherches jusque à ce que nous soyons arrivés à l'évidence."[1]

Has made many observers.

Louis's mottoes.

These two mottoes might be taken as the watchwords of this second epoch. They were never more powerful than they are at the present hour; and they place the profession in the line of progress with all modern science, whose mottoes are virtually the same.

The watchwords of modern science.

Besides Gerhard and Jackson, there were three more

[1] Louis, Panthéon des Illustrations Françaises au XIX. siècle. Victor Froud. Paris, 1865.

men of great influence, who by their writings powerfully assisted in this new reformation. I allude —

1st, To JACOB BIGELOW, of America, by his teachings, and especially by his address on "Self-limited Diseases,"[1] and his volume entitled "Nature in Disease."[2]

2d, To ELISHA BARTLETT, also of America, in his "Essay on the Philosophy of Medical Science."[3]

3d, To JOHN FORBES, editor of the "British and Foreign Medical Review," by his article entitled "Homœopathy, Allopathy, and Young Physic."[4]

Two of them are dead. Dr. Bigelow still lives, at a very advanced age. He entered his ninetieth year some months ago. His life nearly spans our centennial period. As it closely unites the first and second epochs, I feel sure that you will permit me to make some special allusion to him and to his labors towards the evolution of modern medical ideas, as allusion was made to Dr. Rush as the leader during our first epoch. Jacob Bigelow.

Dr. Bigelow was born February 27, 1787; that is, two years before Rush resumed his chair of the professorship of medicine in the University of Pennsylvania. After a most honorable and successful life as a physician, and Professor in Harvard University and Harvard Medical College, Dr. Bigelow has been for years totally blind, and is hopelessly unable to move from his bed, where he has lain for more than eighteen months. To a casual visitor he seems as bright and as witty as ever; while his beautiful submission to His life.

---

[1] Address before the Massachusetts Medical Society, May 27, 1835.
[2] Boston: Ticknor & Fields. 1864.
[3] Philadelphia: Lea & Blanchard. 1844.
[4] British and Foreign Medical Review, vol. xxi. p. 225. 1846.

what most persons would deem a sad fate raises him, in the eyes of all who know him, higher even than he was in the days of his greatest energy and fame. A visit to his bedside affords a delightful sense of repose from the bustle of daily toil. It was my happiness to have a long conversation with him very recently, during which I found that he remembered well the scenes of his youth.[1]

His views of Dr. Rush. He graphically described Dr. Rush and his various colleagues of the Medical School of the University of Pennsylvania, as they discoursed on medicine more than half a century since, and only a few years before Dr. Rush died. He fully sustains me in my position in regard to Dr. Rush's views of Nature and of the medical art. *Influence on American medical opinion.* Dr. Bigelow has had very great influence all through New England, and I cannot but think elsewhere in the country, where his works have been read. That influence went bravely to sustain the seminal principles planted by Louis and his school. In May, 1835, Dr. Bigelow first broached publicly his own views of medicine in his remarkably suggestive address on "Self-limited Diseases," delivered at the annual meeting of the Massachusetts Medical Society, and but three years after the commencement of our second epoch. In it he brings out, in a pointed manner, the inferior position held by the science and art of medicine, when compared with other sciences and arts, most of which were rapidly advancing. *Advocacy of Louis's method.* He advocates Louis's method " as being as near an approach to certainty as

---

[1] One of my friends, a ripe scholar, to whom I gave an account of the interview, quoted Virgil, remarking that, by the substitution of " viro " for " Deo," the following was applicable to Dr. Bigelow's mental estate : —

"Jam senior : sed cruda Deo viridisque senectus."

Æn. vi. 304.

the subject itself admits."[1] Alluding to Louis, he writes that "no previous medical inquirer has apparently submitted to the profession any species of evidence so broad in its foundations, and so convincing in its results, as that which characterizes the great works of this author on Phthisis and Typhoid fever" (page 34).[1] Again he says, speaking of Louis's methods, "And such, it is not difficult to foresee, must ultimately be the only species of evidence on this subject to which the medical profession will pay deference" (page 33);[1] and a little later he remarks (page 37),[1] "In certain self-limited diseases, we can do but little more than follow in the train of disease, and endeavor to follow Nature." In 1852, under the title of "Treatment of Disease," he remarks (page 83), "The modern crying evil of polypharmacy and over-medication is profitable to the druggist, habitual to many physicians, and annoying, if not detrimental, to most patients;" and again (page 84), "The enlightened physician looks for the presence of any deleterious agencies or unremoved causes of disease," — thus hinting at preventive medicine. In his "Practical Views on Medical Education" (1850, page 96), he thunders forth in opposition to views of the great men of our first epoch, in the following severe but just language:

Opposition to Rush and Broussais.

"How much time has been wasted in our seminaries of learning in acquiring the visionary and now neglected theories of Rush and Broussais!" And finally he asserts (1854, page 104),[2] almost in the language of Jefferson, already quoted, "It is a fact much older than the constitution of this Society, that visionary systems of prac-

[1] Nature in Disease. Boston: Ticknor & Fields. p. 34. 1859, p. 45.
[2] Nature in Disease, ib. Report on Homœopathy, p. 107.

tice have replaced each other in the faith of multitudes at least several times in a century." As may be readily believed, such stalwart blows, given by such a teacher, upon the medical practice of the day, had potent influence upon medical opinion, at least of the North. The scepticism caused by Louis was greatly augmented; and not only were Dr. Rush's lancet and heroic remedies recklessly thrown away, but, instead of these, we have had the absurdities of infinitesimal homœopathy sustained by vast numbers of the most intelligent of the laity, and by the States, with a drivelling scepticism or palsied fear on the part of the profession, while administering even the smallest doses of those medicines, which the men of the previous epoch gloried in, and used with powerful effect, — often, I doubt not, for evil, but sometimes, I feel sure, for infinite good, to their patients. Whilst Bigelow was thus sapping our faith in mere drugging, and during the interval between his first and last essays upon the subject, there was sent forth from the chief medical journal of that day (1846) in London, under the sign manual of its editor, one of the boldest and ablest defences of the same views that has ever been written. I allude to the extraordinary article by Dr. Forbes, entitled "Homœopathy, Allopathy, and Young Physic."[1] I well remember the effect produced upon the medical profession in this country; and, from some allusions to the subject, made eighteen months afterward, by Dr. Forbes (October, 1847, p. 594, vol. xxiv), I infer that a similar one was caused in England.

Scepticism augmented.

John Forbes.

Admired by the few, ignorantly and violently opposed or wholly ignored by the many, it has nevertheless

[1] British and Foreign Medical Review, January, 1846. Vol. xxi. p. 225.

stood the test of time, as one of the noblest defences of the claims and powers of Nature in the treatment and cure of disease. Among the passages therein bearing upon our subject, he states that it is one of the besetting sins of English practice to use certain powerful remedies in large doses, in a multitude of different diseases. "Mercury, iodine, colchicum, antimony, also purgatives in general, and bloodletting, are frightfully misused in this manner" (vol. xxi. page 263). Where, under its cogent arguments, were the systems of the past devised by individual men? and this, too, only about fifty years subsequent to the period of the proclamation by Benjamin Rush, that every child would be taught to use these remedies, as they were taught in our republic to read and write! But that which made this assault upon our faith the more galling was that the editor, in his pungency of wit and sarcasm, placed the results of the usual medical practice as nearly, if not quite, on a par with those of homœopathy. Nay, he allowed, what I admit was strictly true, but not agreeable to think of, nevertheless, that homœopathy had conferred the greatest boon possible upon us, by teaching us the powers of Nature and the inefficiency or deleteriousness of polypharmacy. While reading at the present day his arguments in behalf of "allopathy," as Dr. Forbes, most unwisely accepting a nickname put upon us by opponents, calls the regular profession, one cannot but admit that they are exceedingly weak, and apparently damaging to our standing as a profession in the community. Hence, notwithstanding my high estimate of the value of this paper, I think very few youths would enter with enthusiasm upon the study of our profession after the perusal of it. It is too destructive of all

Nature in disease v. polypharmacy.

Forbes's Essay needed, though too destructive.

earnest faith in our art. Nevertheless, it was just what was needed at that time. Polypharmacy then and there received its most deadly blow. Nature was glorified, and no one can doubt that such a blow was necessary previously to our entering upon the new phase of development of medical science and art expressed under the term *State Preventive Medicine*. Under the influence of Drs. Forbes and Bigelow, and others of that stamp, physicians began very generally to ask themselves, in all cases that came before them, these questions: What are the causes of this disease? Cannot we cure the patient by simply removing these causes? Is any medicine necessary? Can we do good by medication? May we not do evil? How little can we give to act efficiently? These are hard questions; and, if we are true to our convictions, we must all admit that at times we are at fault, and more or less incapable of guiding the patient or ourselves through the many doubts and uncertainties in which both patient and physician are enveloped. We can be the kind, thoughtful, and painstaking attendant, not the guardian angels, or arbiters of life and death, our fathers claimed themselves to be.

Dr. Forbes's faith in the future. But amid this darkness even Dr. Forbes sees, with a strong faith, an escape from our difficulties by reformation and regeneration in practical therapeutics. He frequently alludes to the reformation that is impending, which is to be the "result of mature reflection, and of the labor of many years and many hands" (page 262). And in the following words he virtually, though imperfectly, hints at *State Preventive Medicine*. The idea seems to come up naturally to his mind; for one of his articles of faith in the future is thus expressed: "We must direct redoubled attention to hygiene, public

And hints at State Preventive Medicine.

and private, with the view of preventing diseases on a large scale; and individually, in our sphere of practice. Here the surest and most glorious triumphs of medical science are achieving, and to be achieved" (page 263). With these grand words of hope and of faith for the future, I might close this second epoch; but I cannot well do so without reference to another able writer and teacher, who possessed a wide influence upon the Middle, Western, and Southern portions of our country. I allude to Dr. Elisha Bartlett. He was one of the most philosophical men America has produced during the centennial period. He was born 1804, and practised medicine some years in Lowell, Massachusetts, where he was highly respected, as one of our ablest and most accomplished men. He was early called to teach at Pittsfield, Massachusetts, at Woodstock, Vermont, and afterward at the Transylvania School of Medicine in Kentucky, as Professor of the Theory and Practice of Medicine. Subsequently he held the same professorship in the University of Maryland, and at New York. From these chairs, and from his previous residences at the North, he was able to influence widely the North, South, East, and West of our country. He had a clear, well-balanced intellect, with fascinating manners, and early became an eloquent teacher. As he told me, when starting for the West, he felt "called to teach." Though not educated under Louis, he thoroughly appreciated his writings. In both of his works, — viz., that on Typhoid and Typhus, Bilious Remittent and Yellow Fever, published in 1842,[1] and in his "Essay on the Philosophy of Medical Science," published in 1844,[2]

Dr. Elisha Bartlett.

His widespread influence.

---

[1] Philadelphia: Lea & Blanchard, 1842.
[2] Idem, 1844.

— he fully avows his admiration for Louis, and for his method of studying disease. He dedicated his first volume to Drs. James Jackson, Jr., and Gerhard, and his second to Louis himself, returning thanks for the permission granted to dedicate his own work to one " whose various and invaluable researches and publication thereof" "have constituted a new and great era in the history of medical science." In the first, he speaks of Louis's influence on medicine as being analogous to that of Bacon upon all modern science, and aptly applies a couplet from Dryden: —

Admiration for Louis.

> "The world to Bacon does not only owe
> Its present knowledge, but its future too."

Whilst thus bestowing the highest encomiums upon the great Frenchman for teaching students to observe, record, and analyze such records of disease, Dr. Bartlett expresses himself in terms somewhat like contempt for the theorizers and system-makers who preceded him. Among them, Dr. Rush comes in for a full share of condemnation for his propensity to dogmatic theory. He writes thus (page 218): "So far as medical science has any just title to the appellation, and so far as medical art possesses any rules sufficiently positive to be worth any thing, it is owing exclusively to the diligent, unprejudiced, and conscientious study of the phenomena and relationships of disease."[1] And he warns against all those false teachers who, while loudly professing an appeal to facts, constantly bend facts to the vagaries of their own imaginations. He points out the absurdities of heroic remedies used by some such teachers in the West.

Scorns system-making.

Defends the Observation School.

And ridicules heroic practice.

---

[1] Bartlett's Philosophy of Medical Science. Philadelphia: Lea & Blanchard, 1844.

He quotes a case worthy of the satire of Cervantes or Molière (page 239),[1] — criticises with a powerful pen the theories and practice of Tully and Gallup, and finally dares to summon the philosophy of Thompsonianism to stand erect beside that of Rush! He declares that a "spirit of a false philosophy . . . pervades almost the entire science of medicine amongst us" (page 248).[1] Nevertheless, "in casting the destiny that awaits us," he speaks hopefully of "the history of practical medicine during the last twenty-five years, &c., as furnishing us with very positive assurance that many of its most important laws will gradually, but steadily and certainly, be carried forward to their entire and final establishment" (page 283), "and the natural history of diseases shall be made out and written" (page 284).[1] This having been arrived at "in the natural course of events," "the next thing to be done will be to find out the best methods of preventing, of modifying, and of curing them" (page 287). *Prevention, as well as cure of disease.* This is, he claims, the great mission which lies immediately before us; this is to constitute the great work of the next and of succeeding generations. He alludes to the establishment of the "*Modern School of Medical Observation,*" by Louis, as one of the most remarkable epochs in the annals of medical science (page 298).[1]

Only a short time previously, all our American medical opinions had come from London and Edinburgh. But now "our young men have almost entirely ceased to visit British capitals" (page 306),[1] "and the principles of Louis's school have taken deeper root here than elsewhere." "His pupils are scattered through our principal cities, North and East" (page 306).[1] And he

---

[1] Bartlett's Philosophy of Medical Science. Philadelphia: Lea & Blanchard, 1844.

closes (page 310) [1] with an eloquent expression of belief that " hereafter, year by year, there will be a closer and more effective co-operation than has hitherto existed in carrying forward, in their career of illimitable progress and indefinite improvement, all branches of the science of life." Thus closes, with fair prophecies for the future, the second epoch of our centennial period. Although Louis, Forbes, Bigelow, Bartlett, and others of a like stamp of mind, were needed for the proper evolution of events, or, rather, although they may be declared as eminent illustrations of the gradual evolution of medical thought during this part of our centenary, none of them fully saw what we now see opening before the coming century. Their mission was chiefly destructive, or constructive only as to the natural history of disease. The general tendency of their writings, so far as they bore upon medical practice, was to scepticism, not only in regard to the absurdities of our fathers, but likewise in reference to many of the good things suggested by them. Although they sometimes hinted at preventive measures, they did not dream of the close union of the profession with the laity in carrying forward *State Preventive Medicine* in its widest scope, which has already begun in various parts of this country, and in Europe. Their scepticism, like all scepticism, was iconoclastic. We need faith in an idea before we can build it up in practice. Such a faith we shall see breaking out in our third and last epoch. And to that I now turn.

Results of the Epoch.

Chiefly destructive.

And sceptical.

[1] Bartlett's Philosophy of Medical Science. Philadelphia: Lea & Blanchard, 1844.

THIRD EPOCH, OR THAT IN WHICH THE MEDICAL PROFESSION IS AIDED BY THE LAITY, AND STATE PREVENTIVE MEDICINE INAUGURATED.

It began in 1869, when the first State Board of Health was legally organized. It extends from 1869 into the far-off future.

It is with a feeling somewhat allied to regret that I must say we owe more to the laity than to the profession the awakening of the spirit which governs this epoch, and which is to hold sway in the long future of *State Preventive Medicine.* The laity as pioneers of medical reform.

My own professional experience teaches me the truth of this statement. The status of the profession, up to within a very brief period, supports that view; and the present attitude of our medical schools, only one or two of which make any pretence at teaching either public or private hygiene, prove the general lukewarmness of the profession in regard to public hygiene and preventive medicine. The scepticism of those outside of our ranks, and the scepticism of the medical profession, and finally the leadership of philosophical, earnest laymen, proving as they went onward, without our help, the value of their sanitary work, have at length aroused us; and we are now, at a late day, looking earnestly at the idea of the prevention rather than the cure of disease.

In all that tends to the promotion of State Preventive Medicine hereafter, as well as heretofore, the laity will naturally and cordially co-operate with the profession. I infer this: Future co-operation of the laity and of the profession.

1st, From the fact above stated, that the laity first

brought home fully to our minds the idea of Preventive Medicine.

2d, State influence and support will hereafter always be needed; for the laity through its legislative and executive officials, vastly more than the profession in its limited sphere of action, must sustain all efforts for the thorough and systematic study of the causes of disease.

The ruling idea of this epoch is yet in its infancy, but it shows, in what it has already accomplished, its great nascent power. Its objects are vastly grander than all that has been accomplished by its predecessors. Its early manhood, even, will not be reached until far towards the termination of the next century. In its destiny, it undoubtedly will be as permanent as the steam-engine, the telegraph-wire, the locomotive, or the use of anæsthetics. In fact, I cannot foresee or imagine a time when the ideas underlying this epoch will not be held in esteem, and acted upon for the benefit of mankind. Before going into a detailed account of this epoch, it will be necessary to point out some of the influences which were at work many years ago, and which, as shown in the labors of certain noted men, were prophetic of the present hour. Among these stand pre-eminent, in their relation to the English-speaking race, two laymen. One of these, I fear, may be but little known to most of those present, or even to the majority of people in the State where he lived. That one is Lemuel Shattuck, of Boston. The other is Edwin Chadwick, of London, a barrister well known and honored by every civilized nation. In relation to the former, I will take the liberty of quoting from an Appendix to an Address on Public Hygiene delivered by myself, as chairman of a Committee on Public Hygiene,

Third Epoch, 1869 to the far-off future.

Its destiny will be coeval with civilization.

Lemuel Shattuck.

last year, before the American Medical Association, at its meeting in Louisville: "Twenty-five years ago,— viz., in 1850, only six years after Dr. Bartlett's work on Medical Philosophy was published,— a Report of the Sanitary Commission of Massachusetts was printed by order of the Legislature. It was written chiefly, if not entirely, by a layman, Lemuel Shattuck, Esq., an earnest sanitarian of that day. It *His Sanitary Report.* was an admirable and exhaustive statement of what the State had previously done. It gave detailed plans and propositions as to what it was incumbent on the State still further to do. Many of its pages will apply to any State at the present day. Among other recommendations, it suggested the appointment of a State Board of Health. It demanded that Board on similar grounds to those taken when establishing a State Board of Education; viz., the public weal. As I *His labors.* read it now, after a lapse of a quarter of a century since it was written and presented to the Legislature, I wonder at the wisdom of its suggestions, and learn much from them." I remember Mr. Shattuck well. *His confidence in the future.* Calm in his perfect confidence in the future of preventive measures to check disease, he walked almost alone the streets of his native city, not only unsustained by the profession, but considered by *Neglected by the profession.* most of them as an offence, for his earnest defence of what seemed to the majority of us physicians out of a layman's sphere, and, withal, of trifling moment, compared with our usual routine of so-called "practice." The public, ignorant of hygiene, *His advice unheeded by the public.* treated him no better. The report fell stillborn from the State Printer's hands. Its recommendations were ignored. Nevertheless, the ideas contained therein germinated slowly but surely; and

twenty years afterwards, viz. in 1870, Dr. Derby, as Secretary of the State Board of Health of Massachusetts, looked to the book as his inspiration and support. In that year, Dr. Derby brought out the first essay ever published in any one of these United States, under the direction of a permanent body appointed by State authority for the purpose of investigating the causes of disease, and for warning the people in relation thereto. The paper was really the outgrowth of seed planted by a layman twenty years before. And, in saying this, I do not wish to ignore or to undervalue the many and persistent efforts of individuals, and occasionally of the Massachusetts Medical Society, to persuade the State, in its legislative capacity, to sustain the ideas avowed by Mr. Shattuck; but there is no doubt that he, as a layman, did more towards bringing Massachusetts to its present status than all the efforts made by the Massachusetts Medical Society in its corporate capacity, or by members, great as this labor was on the part of one or two of our more zealous associates, prominent among whom appears Dr. Edward Jarvis, of Dorchester.

<small>Ultimate triumph.</small>

The second layman I have named is Edwin Chadwick. All of you know him well as one who, more fortunate than Shattuck, has been able to live and to work for many years, and to see rich fruits everywhere springing up in Great Britain and in other countries, under the power of his writings and of his labors.

<small>Edwin Chadwick, of London.</small>

But there are other influences which have tended to the evolution of the third period. Europe has influenced us as much, if not more than at either of the other epochs. France long since entered upon a career of studies and of publi-

<small>France.</small>

cations upon the public health. The "Annales d'Hygiène Publique," so long and so ably supported, is proof of this.[1] The great labors of Parent Duchatelet all acknowledge. The zeal of Quetelet, of Belgium, has been like a household word in the medical profession of this country. Pettenkofer, of Munich, more recently, has labored in the same field; and still nearer the present hour comes up the extraordinary genius of Virchow, of Berlin, great in every department of science or of state upon which he enters. But by far the greatest influence has been exerted by England, which has been, of late years, steadily working in the direction of *State Preventive Medicine*. Parliament, in 1875, by endeavoring to codify under one law all previous sanitary legislation, and by the establishment of the Local Government Board, made immense strides towards having a perfect system of sanitary guardianship of the realm, carried on by trained assistants and special inspectors. I hesitate not to say that the keenness of investigating powers attained by the body of inspectors in Great Britain, under the direction of Mr. Simon, is wholly unequalled and unprecedented, I suspect, in all past time. And these inspectors are permeated with the enthusiasm and accuracy of modern science. One of my scientific friends said, when reading Vol. 2, New Series, of Mr. Simon's Reports to the Privy Council and Local Government Board, he felt as sure of the results brought out as he would of those derived from "the most careful chemical analysis." The masterly essay on "Filth

marginal notes: Parent Duchatelet. Quetelet. Pettenkofer. Virchow. England. Local Government Board. Inspectors. Mr. Simon.

[1] See Appendix II. Sanitary work in France, and Dr. Varrentrapp's letter on the sanitary work of Europe.

Diseases," by Mr. Simon, sent out as a preface to these reports, applies as well and appeals as strongly to this country as it does to Great Britain.

Among the more recent influences from America tending to help in the development of this epoch, may be named the papers published by the Metropolitan Board of Health of New York, and the establishment of State Boards of Health in various States of this Union. All these have tended powerfully to interest the whole community in the subject of Public Hygiene.

<small>New York.</small>

<small>State Boards of Health.</small>

The reports of those longest established have each contained valuable papers, all tending to the same end; and many of them suggest important hygienic measures. The United States, by its army publications previous to, during, and since the late civil war, has done an immense work in the same direction. Its library and its museum, commenced during the horrors of that contest, are invaluable aids. I think I merely re-echo public opinion when I say that, search the world over, you will hardly find two plans of this nature carried out more thoroughly, or which will contribute more to the public weal. If they be well sustained in the future by the General Government, and the same enlightened judgment and energy be shown by the officers in command hereafter, as have been shown in the past, we may have in them a perennial source of advancement of Public Hygiene. During the Crimean and Italian wars, the world was taught most fearful lessons from neglect of it. The late civil war in this country was the means of bringing into active life many most beneficent institutions, which never before were thought of in war, or, at least, were never before

<small>U. S. army publications.</small>

<small>Library and Museum.</small>

<small>Lessons of war.</small>

carried out on such a magnificent scale; institutions which will hereafter always tend greatly, by their examples, to the alleviation of suffering and the saving of human life.

To the American Sanitary and Christian Commissions, the Western Sanitary Commission, so called in those Northern States, and to similar institutions, the Wayside Hospitals, the State Hospitals at Richmond and in Georgia, and other kindred relief societies in the South, humanity owes all praise. *Northern and Southern Relief Societies in war.* Through these and various private associations, money and assistance of every kind were dispensed without stint to the wounded and sick of both parties in the strife, whenever met and found suffering on the battle-field or in the temporary hospital. We can never know how many were saved or how much torture prevented by the agents of these noble institutions on both sides of the line of battle; their charity being often given to foes as well as to friends. But we can estimate how much the desire to save life and promote health was, under their blessed influences, instilled into the hearts of our people, from Maine to Texas.[1]

National Sanitary Conventions.

The National Sanitary Conventions, so called, were among the pioneers in this movement of Preventive Medicine. They were held in Philadelphia, 1857, in Baltimore, 1858, in New York City, 1859, and the fourth in Boston, 1860, just on the eve of the war. It was the last of the series. No one can doubt the great effect these meetings had, indirectly, at least, upon our present views. We can *National Sanitary Conventions.*

---

[1] See Appendix II. Sanitary and Christian Commissions, and letters from Dr. Turnipseed, &c.

judge this when we look at the published transactions, and note the prominent personages seen either as leaders of the meetings, writers of communications, or partakers in the discussions therein held. The last, in Boston, was presided over by Dr. Jacob Bigelow of Boston, assisted by Dr. R. D. Arnold of Georgia, Dr. Alexander H. Stevens of New York, and others, as Vice-Presidents. The city, by its mayor, welcomed the body to meet within its limits.

Sanitary Work during the War.

During the war there were immense strides made Sanitary work among the people during the war. in public hygiene, owing to the fact that the people outside of the military lines, and the officers and men inside of them, very soon began to learn by dire experience, or by the urgent appeals of experts in sanitary matters, the all-important rules of cleanliness, sobriety, and discipline, in opposition to the distress consequent on filth, intemperance, and chaotic rule. We cannot doubt that every surgeon who served during the war, on either side, became more practically versed in the advantages of the prevention of disease over the cure of it, than he ever was before. To a greater or less degree, the matter of strict "policing" of camps impressed upon all in the army more certain and more definite rules for subsequently governing and arranging their own premises in civil life. Since the war, we find the same ideas, and often the same individuals, appearing in the Social Science and Public Health meetings, which have, within the very few past years, reappeared in different parts of the country.

Public Health Association.

On April 18, 1872, was held the primary meeting whence has sprung the very important association entitled the American Public Health Association. Its first meeting was held in New York, Sept. 13, 1872. Three have been held annually since; viz., at Cincinnati, Baltimore, and Boston. The volumes containing the records of its reports and papers are very valuable, as showing opinions on various sanitary questions; *i.e.*, on the mode of transmission and prevention of various diseases, quarantine, &c., longevity, hospital hygiene, climatology, sanitary architecture and administration, water-supply, &c.[1]

Public Health Association.

American Medical Association.

Among the more strictly professional institutions which have had some weight in helping forward the cause of *State Preventive Medicine* may be named the American Medical Association. In 1847 this Association was instituted; and, from its inception, it has almost annually published papers relating to epidemics, climatology, &c. Still more recently, definite efforts have been made by its members in furtherance of Preventive Medicine. The intermingling of men from all quarters of the Union, at its annual meeting, has also contributed to the same end. But it must be confessed that, judging from the numbers usually attendant on the section devoted to that subject, Public Hygiene seems to afford less interest to the profession than almost any other topic.

American Medical Association.

[1] Reports and Papers presented at the meetings of the American Public Health Association, in the years 1873, 1874, 1875. New York: Hurd & Houghton. Riverside Press, Cambridge, 1875–76.

Public Interest in Sanitary Work.

Notwithstanding the apparent indifference at times still displayed by our profession and by the public at large in reference to Public Hygiene, I may safely assert that during the past three or four years there has sprung up, wherever European civilization holds sway, a thoughtfulness about the necessity and value of hygienic measures. Almost all persons in their various spheres have become more accessible to the protests of the sanitarian. Still further, I think it may be said with truth that during this last epoch, short as it is, More sanitary work lately than for centuries. more practical work has been done among the people tending to crush out disease and prevent its appearance, and more valuable papers have been written illustrating the subject of public hygiene, the world over, than since the opening of the Christian era. Among the subjects discussed in all societies, and in the public journals which all classes of people read, sanitary discussion seems to interest many persons as much as the pages of the novel attract others. A physician said to me the other day, " There seems to be arising among the citizens a kind of panic relative to the drains of their own houses, and they have a great horror of the least odor of sewer gases." I take courage from the remark. The workers are all around us. A Journals and societies discuss them. popular writer sits beside the " Autocrat of the Breakfast Table," and discusses sewerage in the " Atlantic Monthly " with infinite gusto, and apparently to the satisfaction of all readers of this popular monthly. In every State there are active and earnest co-laborers. It would be impossible to name them all. Some of the States, in their corporate capacity, have sustained these laborers for the pub-

lic weal. But I regret to say that a large majority of the States and Territories of this Union are not as yet sufficiently enlightened to appreciate the duty devolving upon them, to be careful of the health of their people.

With these preliminary statements, I pass to the present status of the country on this important subject.

The Present Condition of State Preventive Medicine in the various States, Territories, and the Nation.

Some months ago I sent out a circular,[1] containing several questions bearing upon the above subject, and tending to elucidate it quite as far as I thought as I could do so, with the means at my command. *Circulars to States and Territories.*

Doubtless, to a critical eye, many imperfections and omissions will be observed in the small number, the character, and relevancy of the questions proposed. I thought a few interrogatories, all or most of them answered, even mono-syllabically, from all quarters of the country, would enable me to get at least a glance at the present condition of Public Hygiene and Preventive Medicine better than a larger number, or even a few, requiring elaborate replies, very many of which, I was satisfied, from my experience in similar undertakings, would not be answered at all, if much labor were required of my correspondents. The paper was sent to two hundred and sixty-three[2] medical men living in the

---

[1] See Appendix I.

[2] The main propositions of my circular came before twenty-one more individuals, who answered more or less in detail; making the whole number two hundred and eighty-four instead of two hundred and sixty-three, as mentioned in the text.

thirty-eight States, nine Territories, and the District of Columbia, making, in all, forty-eight different governments. These embrace an area of twenty-five degrees of latitude, — viz., from Maine to Florida, — and fifty-seven of longitude; spanning, in fact, the continent, from the Atlantic to the Pacific Oceans. In the South, some lie almost within the tropics; while, in the North, others are close to the coldest inhabited regions of the earth.

Of the character and ability of these correspondents,

<small>Character of my correspondents.</small> I would remark that I endeavored to select the ablest I could get; as far as possible, those known or supposed to be interested in Public Hygiene, — representative men, in fact, in the various States and Territories. I may not always have succeeded in my effort, and may have omitted many, who would have been willing and most valuable correspondents. But I trust that you will admit that their various reports will, together, constitute as full and as accurate an account of the whole matter as it is possible for any one man, without governmental influence, to obtain; that is, so far as my questions cover the object sought for. Replies have been obtained from one hundred and seventy-nine correspondents, many of whom have not been satisfied by mono-syllabically answering each question. Some have entered cordially, and oftentimes very fully, into detail. Many of these

<small>Replies from every State and Territory.</small> details will be found in the Appendix II. The writers are residents in all the various States and Territories, except Alaska, our newly acquired

<small>Except the Indian Territory and Alaska</small> Russian territory in the North, and the so-called Indian Territory in the South, just north of Texas. The former, we know, is chiefly occupied by Indians. The latter, as its name indicates, is really "an unorganized portion of the

United States." It contains an immense congregation of Indians of the various tribes, collected there, and living separately, each according to its own method, under the protection of the Union; some, like the Camanches, being still in a wild state, while others, as the Cherokees, are comparatively civilized.[1]

ANALYSIS OF CORRESPONDENCE.

FIRST QUESTION.

Does your State, by its Legislation, show a Due Appreciation of the Duty devolving upon a State to be careful of the Health of its People?

I considered this an important, nay, a fundamental, question. That it would cause unpleasant feelings in the minds of most of my correspondents, when called upon to answer it truly and categorically, I was well aware, because I believed that few could reply affirmatively. The loyalty to truth evinced by them, even while oftentimes regretting to be obliged to write what seems derogatory to the character of their native States, has been most honorable. It evinces, likewise, their interest in the cause we all now have at heart. It enhances a hundred-fold the value of their courtesy to me. The answers to the question are as follows, viz.: —

_{Correspondents loyal to truth.}

>   Thirty-four (34) . . . . . No.[2]
>   Eight (8) . . . . Yes.
>   Four (4) . . . . Indefinite.
>   Two (2) . . . . No replies.

[1] *Vide* Appleton's New American Cyclopædia, 1874.
[2] Under each question, I shall give similar returns for the *forty-eight* States and Territories of which this Union is composed. The terms

In other words, of the forty-eight governments in this Union, thirty-four, by their legislative acts, have virtually shown but little care for the health of their people. Among the States which have given these negative replies are two which, as they were the most powerful of the original thirteen colonies, so they bear, by the consent of all at the present time, epithets for which they may well be proud; viz., of the "Empire" and the "Keystone" States. I cite them not in invidious distinction, but simply to show how little any of these confederated governments have done. For even the correspondents from other States, who claim that their States have done all that is required, will be compelled to admit: 1st, That it is only within six or eight years that their States have shown any marked interest in the question of State Preventive Medicine, in its widest sense; and, 2d, That, although this has been gained, the number of deaths from preventable diseases is still frightfully great, which ought not to be the fact if these same States had really shown, for any length of time, this "due appreciation," which is claimed for them by my correspondents.

Little governmental care for the public health.

Large number of preventable diseases.

But those who have followed the course of my previous statements, in regard to the gradual evolution of the idea of State Preventive Medicine during the century, will admit that we have advanced quite as far as could have been anticipated. Remembering the dogmas

---

"yes" and "no" mean that *all* the correspondents in a State or Territory answered *unanimously* "yes" or "no" to the special question. "Indefinite" means that there was a diversity of opinion in the replies, some answering "yes," and others "no." "No reply" suggests its own meaning. It means no reply to that special question, although others in the series may have been answered.

of the imagination which prevailed in the first epoch, the scepticism and utter indifference of the profession and of the community generally to the idea of Public Hygiene during the second, and the present want of real appreciation by most people of the inherent but dormant powers of modern preventive medicine; remembering these facts, we shall cease to wonder at the neglect of Public Hygiene shown by the various States. We may rather rejoice at the present awakening of all civilized nations to the vast importance of the subject; and we can readily conceive of the benefits which will arise in future centuries, when the intellect and conscience of the people shall have fairly and fully grasped the ideas underlying this third and last epoch.

The present is the natural resultant of the past.

Second Question.

Is it willing to expend Money? —
 a. To support State or Local Boards of Health?
 b. To carry out Scientific Investigations as to the Causes of Disease?
 c. To repress Noxious or Offensive Trades?
 d. To prevent Adulteration of Food?
 e. To prevent Cattle Disease?
 f. Or to carry on any other Investigations tending to Public Health, or to prevent Ill-health?

The touchstone which tests the earnestness of an individual and of a nation, in reference to any subject, is a willingness to spend money in furtherance of it. The scientific man clothes himself in rags, if need be, to gain his beloved aim. A great and intelligent State pours out without stint of its abundant means to support what it deems a noble cause.

Money spending a test of earnestness.

This noble, self-sacrificing enthusiasm, which ignores expense, blazed forth to its fullest intensity on both sides of the line of battle during our late conflict. To relieve suffering and prevent death, money was spent by both contending parties, without a thought of its value, save as a means of gaining a wished-for end. Tested by this talisman, how stands our nation in regard to Public Hygiene and Preventive Medicine in these days of peace?

Grandly shown during the late war.

The main question is divided into six specifications. Let us look at each one of them.

a. *To support State or Local Boards of Health?*

The following answers were received to this question, viz. : —

Thirty-six (36) . . . . No.
Ten (10)[1] . . . . Yes.
Two (2) . . . . No reply.

From this table we learn that thirty-six of the forty-eight are *unwilling to expend money to support a Board of Health.*

This fact, I think, marks the very small advancement made by most of the States of this Union in regard to the whole subject. I believe that those who are to follow us in the coming centuries will so regard it. And it is my firm conviction that, ere many generations, the amount of money thus willingly spent by a State to support a board of health, with all necessary agencies to promote the public health, will be an index of the degree of its civilization One of the States, viz., Virginia, has established a board, but refuses to

Small advance by most States of the Union.

Virginia.

[1] Two States have established boards of health since this statement was made up.

STATE BOARDS OF HEALTH. 45

pay any thing to enable its members to perform the duties properly. For the time being, the result has been discouraging to the able and earnest men connected with it. Were it not for the hopefulness of the future on the part of its members, and their interest in the cause, I fear it would expire outright. But, if the exact truth be told, no one of the States at present *duly* appreciates the height and breadth of its duty in this respect, and the great claims it will eventually make on every community, any more than our fathers could anticipate, in 1776, the real grandeur of our territorial limits and of our nation in the matters of commerce, agriculture, textile arts, and manufactures. A glance at what each State, which has established a State Board of Health, proposes to spend to sustain it amply proves this. I place the returns of my correspondents in a tabular form, viz. : — No State does fully its duty.

Amounts paid by various States for health boards.

STATE BOARDS OF HEALTH IN THE UNITED STATES.

State.	Annual Appropriations for Board.	Population 1870.	Value of Taxable Property.
California	$500 (or thereabouts)	560,247	$269,644,068 (1870)
Colorado	500 (1876)	39,864	17,333,101 (1870)
District of Columbia	60,000 (about ?)	181,700	74,271,693 (1870)
Georgia	1,500 (1875), $1,800 (1876)	1,184,109	227,219,519 (1870)
Louisiana	2,000 to $24,000	726,915	253,371,890 (1870)
Maryland	1,500	780,894	423,834,918 (1870)
Massachusetts	7,500 to $17,500 (1876 special)	1,457,351	2,164,398,548 (1874)
Michigan	4,000.	1,184,059	272,242,917
Minnesota	400 to $1,500	439,706	217,427,211
Wisconsin	2,000	1,054,670	

46   CENTENNIAL DISCOURSE.

The larger appropriations are special grants for purposes of drainage, for the laying out of streets, warding off epidemics, &c. But the amounts proposed and annually paid by each State, in proportion to the objects aimed at, — viz., to study all the diseases of the people, and to teach them how to avoid the causes of disease, — are ludicrously small. For example, in Massachusetts, whose annual appropriation is $7,500 for expenses of the Board and the Secretary's salary, it is only about half a cent, *i.e.* 5 mills, annually, to each inhabitant, and only $\frac{1}{28858}$ of the estimated value of the property of the State.

<small>Massachusetts.</small>

Before closing this part of our subject, I will, however, enter a *caveat*. While claiming that the State should pay well its experts who labor for it, I should greatly deplore the fact of any vast sums being submitted to the control of any board of health; because, however virtuously inclined the board might be at first, it is to be feared that, ere many years, its large allowance of money would become the means of corrupting the whole sanitary work of the State. The members of the board should never be paid. The Secretary should be paid *well*, and devote his whole energies to the object. But, so far as I know, no State at present gives enough to induce every man, who is fitted for the office, to accept it. The salaries given require, on the part of those who accept office, a rarely found single-hearted love for the object to be attained.

<small>Large sums demoralize.</small>

<small>But now all pay too little.</small>

A Massachusetts legislative committee proposed, on this very centennial year, to reduce the salary of its Secretary of Health to $2,000, instead of $2,500, which is itself a mere pittance. The proposed sum is but $500 more than what the State pays for a night-watch-

man to guard the State House. Fortunately, the wisdom of the Senate checked the folly, which had passed the House of Representatives, and thus the honor of the State was sustained.[1]

b. To carry out Scientific Investigations as to the Causes of Disease?

The following answers were received to this question, viz.: —

  Thirty (30) . . . . No.
  Twelve (12) . . . . Yes.
  Five (5) . . . . Indefinite.
  One (1) . . . . No reply.

Thirty governments out of the forty-eight are reported as being unwilling to spend money for the scientific study of the causes of disease. Twelve report affirmatively; viz., Arizona, California, Colorado, District of Columbia, Georgia, Louisiana, Maryland, Massachusetts, Michigan, Minnesota, Rhode Island, and Wisconsin. Of these, some report that the State does so rather "unwillingly;" "not much;" when "importuned;" or "to a limited extent." It moreover should be observed that, of the above-named States, Arizona has not as yet established a board of health; that California, Colorado, Georgia, Louisiana, Maryland, and Wisconsin decline to make special grants for special investigations, and that Michigan and Rhode Island, according to two of the most eminent sanitarians of the country, report the same fact. Of Rhode Island, however, it is said that

The majority give nothing for the study of the causes of disease.

Some do so imperfectly.

Others not at all.

[1] For further remarks on the willingness of States to spend money for sanitary purposes, see question 8.

"the State grants as much as has been asked for." This latter reply seems to indicate that the medical profession is unwilling to avail itself of the means within its grasp for promoting State Preventive Medicine. Massachusetts has only moved in the right direction, this centennial year, in its Report on the Pollution of Streams.

<small>Massachusetts only this year.</small>

c. To repress Noxious or Offensive Trades?

The following answers were received to this question, viz. : —

    Twenty-six (26) . . . . . No.
    Fourteen (14) . . . . . Yes.
    Seven (7) . . . . Indefinite reply.
    One (1) . . . . No reply.

A priori, this would seem to be a most legitimate and imperative duty of a State, — to so govern noxious and offensive trades that they should not bring ill-health to the people. Yes twenty-six States are reported as doing nothing. Fourteen, only, are attempting to do something. In this connection, I wish to call attention to a law passed by Massachusetts, which has fortunately had a most benign effect. In every free State, it will often happen that the local boards of health, if any exist, or the selectmen, or mayor and aldermen of cities, where no boards are established, and who therefore act as boards of health, will be unable, from various local causes, political or private, to cope with and manage a local nuisance.

<small>Duty neglected by the majority.</small>

<small>Town boards often inefficient.</small>

Moreover, if such a nuisance is brought before court, a trial is expensive, and a jury's wisdom is very likely to fail at the moment one expects the best result.

NOXIOUS AND OFFENSIVE TRADES. 49

From this general infirmity of human nature, it has happened often in Massachusetts that a town, or portion of a town, has remained powerless to suppress what was a terrible evil to the community immediately around it. What was needed was a body of experts, chosen from the laity and the profession, who should, as far as possible, unbiassed by local prejudice or by favor for either side, decide the question of the sanitary effects of any establishment. If deciding adversely, they should have the power to order the proprietors to "cease and desist" from "the further carrying on of that offensive trade." It happened that a most glaring example of this kind of evil existed in Brighton, Massachusetts, under the very eyes of the Legislature, and almost within reach of the olfactory nerves of its members. This beautiful, undulating country is in close proximity to Boston, and, as such, admirably suited for dwelling-houses for all persons doing business in the city. Only three years ago Brighton was a pestilent and disgusting place, owing to the number of slaughter-houses in it. In no direction, for miles in extent, could one drive without encountering the most sickening of smells. About fifty slaughter-houses were dotted in every direction over the place. No one except a butcher or his family, or one wholly regardless of comfort, could think of purchasing ground for a homestead on any one of its numerous and beautiful hills, because all were reeking with the putrefying blood and offal of slaughtered animals.

Therefore a higher power needed.

Brighton.

Its disgusting condition.

In vain had some of the more offensively conducted premises been indicted. They could not be stopped, and new ones were annually springing up. One of the citizens, a lawyer, saw a way out of the difficulty very

soon after our State Board of Health was established. By his agency, a law was passed, June 16, 1870, authorizing the Board to order any one "to cease and desist from carrying on an offensive trade;" provided the Board, after a full and public hearing, decided that such trade was "contrary to the health, comfort, and convenience" of the inhabitants. At our earliest meeting, many protested against the constitutionality of the law, on the ground of the extraordinary powers conferred by it, in contravention of the Massachusetts Bill of Rights, which allows individuals to conduct their business as they see fit, unmolested, save by the law, in its usual processes. The Board accepted and recorded its protests, but continued their hearing. The Board, either as a whole or by committee, has personally examined, after such public hearing, every establishment complained of, before making a final decision. During some of the hearings, one of which continued daily for three weeks, able lawyers have argued before the Board; and it has been called upon to decide questions vitally involving even the trade of Boston. At times, the judgments of the Board have been defied; but, on the petitioners for the abatement of the nuisance appealing to the Superior Court, the Board's decisions have always been sustained. The records in the case, as sworn to by the Secretary, the court deemed all-sufficient proof; and the party has always been ordered to desist, under the pains and penalties of being punished for contempt of court, if he refused. This latter result once occurred. A butcher, having openly defied the Local and State Boards, refused to obey the orders of the Superior Court; but he was compelled to yield. Last year the last butcher in

Brighton was compelled to give up his local slaughter-house, and to go to work in the newly built and admirably conducted abattoir. Land, only a few years since disgusting and repulsive to all visitors, has become fit for decent human habitations. The price of it has augmented, in certain places, threefold beyond what it was previously to the action of the Board. *Brighton redeemed from filth by its abattoir.*

I have dwelt more on this particular fact, because it is the most important of the practical results obtained thus far in Massachusetts. It will be understood, however, that the authority of the Board extends to the most distant borders of the State; and it has already exercised its power, or has acted as mediator between contending parties in many different portions of the Commonwealth. I therefore heartily commend the provisions of the law to all of our sister States, as one which I am sure, from our experience, will prove most valuable.[1] *Law commended to other States.*

d. *To prevent the Adulteration of Food?*

The following answers were received to this question, viz.: —

      Twenty-three (23) . . . . No.
      Sixteen (16) . . . . . . Yes.
      Seven (7) . . . . Indefinite.
      Two (2) . . . . No reply.

Certainly a most extraordinary result, but one which possibly might have been anticipated, when we reflect on the very wide extent of the system of sophistication and adulterations known, *Food adulteration little cared for.*

---

[1] See Appendix VII. for law about noxious and offensive trades.

and yet allowed to exist among us. Rapidity and quantity of work, rather than excellence, is sought for everywhere. The stimulus of competition leads to deterioration as much as it does to improvement, in all directions. Our articles for the sustenance of life suffer, as almost all others suffer. Years hence, when public hygiene is duly cherished, the adulteration of the food of a people will be considered a most heinous crime.

<small>Europe in advance of America.</small> Now, it is practically allowed to flourish in the majority of these States, even in those who have laws against it. Europe, I think, is far in advance of America in this respect.

e. To prevent the Cattle Disease?

The following answers were received to this question, viz.: —

Twenty-one (21) . . . . . No.
Ten (10) . . . . Yes.
Sixteen (16) . . . . . . Indefinite.
One (1) . . . . No reply.

Upon this subject an unusual number of the States <small>Cattle disease.</small> appear as doubtful. A part of the correspondents report nothing as having been done, and others that efforts have been made. It is, however, an undoubted fact, that about twenty years ago a great panic existed in some of the States in relation to the <small>At time of panic, large sums expended.</small> matter. Large sums of money were voted by the legislatures of some of the Western States. In Massachusetts, some most valuable <small>Diseased cattle killed.</small> imported cattle were slaughtered, and all having the disease were so treated. In the West, still more important and wide-spreading efforts were

made in reference to the diseases brought by the Texan cattle. I refer to the Appendix for further details.[1]

f. To carry on any other Investigations tending to Public Health, or to prevent Ill-health?

The following answers were received to this question, viz.: —

>   Twenty-eight (28) . . . . No.
>   Ten (10) . . . . Yes.
>   Nine (9) . . . . Indefinite.
>   One (1) . . . . No reply.

That is, a little more than one-half say definitely "no;" less than a quarter, "yes." From all that precedes, we can readily admit the above result as a most natural sequence of the present indifference of our people upon the question of Public Hygiene. Our correspondents in Michigan, Louisiana, and Massachusetts, will prove that there has been some active work in this direction. Doubtless also, during the whole centennial period, in every State there have been individual workers. But it will be found, on examination, that during the past few years only have the legal authorities made their chief investigations, generally by means of the town or city authorities, and under the influence of a single idea, or special terror of a fatal epidemic, rather than for a general scientific and calm investigation by chosen agents of the State.

Other sanitary investigations.

Only made under some special fear.

[1] See Dr. S. P. Breed's letter from Princeton, Illinois, &c.

Third Question.

Has your State established a State Board of Health?
  a. If so, when was it established?
  b. What Amount of Annual Appropriation is made for its Support?
  c. Are any Occasional and Extra Grants made for Special Investigations?
  d. Has such a Board any Organized Body of Correspondents or Inspectors throughout the State?
  e. What Executive Powers have been given to the Board with reference to Local Nuisances or Noxious Trades?

a. If so, when was it established?

I have already, elsewhere (*vide* 2d question, *a*), made some general remarks on the main subject. Up to the present time (May, 1876), twelve of the governments have established such boards under the following dates, viz.: —

STATE BOARDS OF HEALTH.

State.	Established.	State.	Established
Alabama	1875	Maryland	1875
California	1871	Massachusetts	1869
Colorado	1876	Michigan	1873
District of Columbia	1870	Minnesota	1872
Georgia	1875	Virginia	1871
Louisiana	1873	Wisconsin	1876

That is, the last decade of the centennial period more than includes the origin of all these boards. And yet this is the initial step, so to speak, in State Preventive Medicine. Without such

_{Only during the last decade.}

a board, according to the spirit of all my previous argument, no State can be said to have really entered upon any definite career of State Preventive Medicine.

In a very few States, a foothold has been gained; and the idea seems healthfully growing in the confidence and respect of the people of these United States. But at present, in some States where State boards have been inaugurated by the earnest labors of certain members of our profession, their States fail to give adequate pecuniary support.

At the first glance, it seems singular that three Southern States — viz., Alabama, Louisiana, and Georgia — should in a body, as it were, seem so much more energetic in the support of State Preventive Medicine than most of their sister States. But the explanation seems to be this, viz.: The frequent incursions of yellow fever and other malignant diseases, supposed to be brought into these States from Havana, Europe, and South America, through the great avenues of commerce, Mobile, Savannah, and New Orleans, have, during the whole century, kept the idea of prevention, at least by quarantine, before the minds of the people. *Yellow fever incursions a stimulus to State action in the South.* Efficient and earnest boards of quarantine have been established in each of these great cities; but, as the fatal disease extended inward, the people of the State have been probably prepared to receive more gratefully the idea of State Medicine than less exposed States. A similar process of education is seen in Pennsylvania and New York, through the influence of Philadelphia and New York City; *New York and Pennsylvania not yet educated by suffering.* but, as these cities have suffered less from virulent epidemics than their Southern sisters, the education of their States has been less, and they have not established

State Boards of Health, although they have very efficient City Boards of Health. But I must remark still further, and I believe I may say so with truth, with some modification for the recent action of Georgia, that, although the more imposing title of "State Board" is given to these arrangements in our three Southern States, these boards are in reality intended chiefly for the three cities above named, and do not extend their influence far beyond the city limits into the State at large.

b. What Amount of Annual Appropriation is made for its Support?

It will be seen, Table I., p. 45, that they vary very much in amount. I have already made some general remarks upon the subject (*vide* p. 46, 2d question) of the willingness or otherwise of a State to appropriate money.

<small>Appropriations vary much in amount.</small>

It must be evident to all who intelligently look at the questions involved under the term Preventive Medicine that, with the exception apparently of the District of Columbia, all the States are still wanting in their appreciation of the importance of the subject. The large sum spent by the District was for a special purpose, not an annual appropriation. As for the others, we may be sure that vastly larger sums will be eventually expended, because self-interest will induce the States to do so. If the boards of health do their duty with thoroughness, and without selfishness, they will gradually so educate the popular mind, that sums which now seem sufficient, will be recognized as quite inadequate to meet all the demands of the future. Certainly this has already been proved to a certain extent true in Massachusetts.

<small>All small.</small>

<small>Will become greater as the people are educated.</small>

There, the annual appropriation for the uses of the Board is five thousand dollars, and twenty-five hundred as salary for the Secretary. But every year new duties have been placed upon the Board, involving new expenses. The past year (1875), instead of giving to a specially appointed and paid commission the duty of examining into the sources and remedies for the pollutions of the various rivers of the Commonwealth, that duty was submitted to the State Board of Health. In order to enable it to employ the best scientific engineering and professional skill of the country, in the elucidation of the important questions involved, an extra appropriation of ten thousand dollars was freely granted by the State authorities. The result was that a most valuable report was made by James P. Kirkwood, C.E., of Brooklyn, New York, Dr. F. Winsor, of Massachusetts, and the Secretary of the Board, Dr. C. F. Folsom. This report is important, not only now, but will be in the future of value, not only to Massachusetts, but to the whole country.

State Board directed to report on the pollution of Massachusetts rivers, &c.

c. Are any Occasional and Extra Grants made for Special Investigations?

The following answers were received to this question, viz.: —

   Forty-three (43) . . . . . No.
   One (1) . . . . Yes.
   One (1) . . . . Indefinite.
   One (1) . . . . No reply.

Forty-four of the governments say nay, or make no report as having no boards of health. One (Massachu-

setts) says yes. In other words, forty-six are either
<small>Small advances.</small> doubtful, or reply in the negative. This only again proves what small advances have been as yet made in State Preventive Medicine, and it fully confirms the statements in a former part of the address, of the very recent birth of the idea involved in the term. For further remarks upon the matter of special investigations, I refer to the statements under the previous question (*b*), p. 56.

d. Has such a Board any Organized Body of Correspondents or Inspectors throughout the State?

The following answers were received to this question, viz. : —

Twenty-three (23)	No.
Four (4)	Yes.
Twenty (20)	Indefinite.
One (1)	No reply.

Only four report affirmatively ; viz., Maryland, Massachusetts, Michigan, and Minnesota. In other words,
<small>No perfect State sanitary organization.</small> eight out of the twelve boards already established have no organized set of correspondents throughout their respective States. This fact, like so many previously stated, proves the imperfect ideas prevailing in regard to the responsibilities and duties devolving upon a State board of health. Part of this neglect of a most important means of carrying forward any health organization of the State is owing to the very recent establishment of the boards in any of the States, and in some to the fact that the necessity of it is not duly appreciated. In Massachusetts, we very early in our course became convinced of the value which intelligent medical and other corre-

spondents would be to our organization. They have more than surpassed the hopes of the Board. Their annual replies to our circulars in regard to the health of their respective towns; the eagerness which they have shown when requested to investigate any local epidemics, and the ability with which some of them have performed their tasks, have been most admirable. When first appointed, we requested the local boards of health, or the selectmen of the towns, to nominate good men. Of late, when a vacancy occurs, we fill the places with the best men we can find. It may seem strange, nevertheless it is true, that, instead of deeming the office an onerous one, the correspondents have usually considered it an honor to be thus selected to work for the well-being of the State.

Value of correspondents in Massachusetts.

The position considered an honor.

I cannot but heartily recommend the plan as worthy of being followed by every State. At present not a single State has yet *perfected* a system of correspondence, such as will be needed in the future.

c. What Executive Powers have been given to the Board with reference to Local Nuisances or Noxious Trades?

The following answers were received to this question, viz.: —

   Thirty-five (35) . . . . . No.
   Seven (7) . . . . Yes.
   Three (3) . . . . Indefinite.
   Three (3) . . . . No reply.

Thirty-five of my correspondents report no executive powers, because they have no boards of health. Seven give an affirmative reply, as follows: the District of Columbia has "am-

Imperfect executive powers.

ple" and "plenary for nuisance removal;" Louisiana, "plenary for New Orleans;" Massachusetts, "great, and with annually new powers given since the origin of the Board," especially over "noxious trades." Connecticut reports no State Board, but that partial powers are given to the cities; Michigan gives advisory power; Minnesota, "on all points relating to quarantine, the Board is supreme;" Wyoming, "no State Board, but city marshals have power."

Two or three important points are suggested by the returns given under these various headings.

First. Executive and plenary powers grow slowly, <small>Powers grow slowly.</small> and only under the influence of fear on the part of the people, not as yet from enlightened ideas on the subject of public health.

Second. These returns, though few, indicate what I believe really happens, judging from what my own experience and the correspondence teach; viz., that local boards spring up naturally under town laws and <small>Assumed without law.</small> the influence of special causes of fear of disease, but often without any definite State authority. A committee of health is chosen by the citizens to ward off danger. Gradually such a body becomes permanent. Out of these influences in various parts of the State is gradually developed the idea of a general board supervising a whole State.

Third. One of the most prominent causes, viz., the necessity of quarantining vessels coming from foreign <small>From quarantine necessities.</small> ports, is seen distinctly in two opposite States of the Union, Louisiana and Minnesota, both analogously situated, one on the Gulf of Mexico, the other on Lake Superior. See question 5.

Fourth Question.

Have any County Boards of Health been established by Law?

The following answers were received to this question, viz. : —

    Thirty-three (33) . . . . No.
    Four (4) . . . . Yes.
    Seven (7) . . . . Indefinite.
    Four (4) . . . . No reply.

Thirty-three report no county boards. Four — viz., Alabama, California, Colorado, and Georgia — make affirmative replies. In seven, the various correspondents answer undecidedly, except Texas, which says that, under Quarantine Law, such boards may be established. Four make no report. Evidently, the idea of a county board is not common; [Rare now, but eventually will be needed.] and yet, in a proper and thorough organization of a State, such boards might be of great value. The chairmen of such boards would be limited in number. Being acquainted with their own districts, they could meet and compare opinions occasionally with State boards and among themselves. These opinions would greatly aid a State board in its work for the Commonwealth. The functions, however, of the county board should be simply advisory as to the State at large, while supreme in the county, within certain well-defined limits.

Fifth Question.

Have any Town Boards of Health been established by Law?

The following answers were received to this question, viz. : —

<blockquote>
Eight (8) . . . . . No.
Fourteen (14) . . . Yes.
Twenty-two (22) . . Have them by local or municipal law.
One (1) . . . . . Indefinite.
Three (3) . . . . No reply.
</blockquote>

Natural growth. During the gradual growth of a new State, as each one of the United States has grown, the primary law of self-defence would give each town this right to take measures to preserve the health of the towns-people. By our returns, we see that they have exercised that right. Doubtless, in any modern, newly formed State, where territorial laws would be discussed, this right of self-defence against disease would be acknowledged. Evidently it has been assumed in at least one-half of the towns reporting to me ; and probably, for the reason above named, the same has been done in the majority of the towns of this Union.

Sixth Question.

Has the State passed any Law leading to a Thorough and Definite Improvement of the Public Health?

- *a.* By a Sanitary Survey of the State?
- *b.* By a Law for the Registration of Births, Deaths, and Marriages?
- *c.* If so, how long has it been in Operation?
- *d.* Has the Registrar been able to draw from such Records any Law governing the Public Health?
- *e.* Has any Law been passed relating to the Drainage of Land?
- *f.* Relating to the Irrigation of Land?
- *g.* Relating to the Checking of the Influence of Rivers by Levees, &c.?
- *h.* Relating to the Introduction of Water into Cities?
- *i.* Relating to the Prevention of Contagious Diseases; for example: —
    - α. Small Pox?
    - β. Cholera?
    - γ. Yellow Fever?
    - δ. Cattle Plague? &c., &c.
- *j.* Regulating Tenement Houses?
- *k.* Incorporating Building Companies for the Improvement of Dwellings for the Poor?

I prepared the above series of questions, in order to gain some general idea of what has been done throughout the Union in regard to laws having specific sanitary bearings. Compared with what might have been proposed, they will necessarily admit of criticism, according to the opinions of each one of my hearers. My sole object was to get a glance, as it

Object of the questions.

were, over some of the more important sanitary necessities of the Union as a whole, and of what had been done by each State to meet these necessities. I shall consider the general question under the specific heads given.

a. *By a Sanitary Survey of the State?*

One would suppose that this would be one of the first questions discussed by settlers in a new country. And yet it is commonly, or has hitherto been, one of the last thought of. Questions of trade, and of personal safety from obvious dangers, play a much more important part in the selection of sites of States and of their chief cities, than any sanitary reasons. A great mistake in the choice of a location has doubtless often arisen from these causes. Similar mistakes will hereafter be made from the insidious nature of endemic influences. A man may settle his homestead upon what is apparently a healthy spot, and find, to his sorrow, after months or perhaps years of ill-health, that he has been living and begetting children in a death-bearing region. The very breaking of the soil, in order to build homes for the families, may stir up the dormant malaria, which would have been hidden for centuries, if it had not been for the plough of the emigrant. But, after a State has been once formed, it would seem to be one of its first duties, as the sovereign guardian of the lives and health of the people, to look into all the influences, good and bad, bearing upon health.

Sanitary survey of a State.

Mistakes for want of such survey.

Such a survey seems appropriate.

In not one of the United States has a thorough sanitary survey of the State been even proposed, so far as I know or can gain such knowledge from my circulars.

SANITARY STATE SURVEY.

The tabular statement which may be made is as follows, viz.: —

Answers received to the question: —

  Forty (40) . . . . No.
  None (0) . . . . Yes.
  One (1) . . . . Indefinite.
  Seven (7) . . . . No reply.

Forty States report no sanitary surveys. One is reported "doubtful," viz., Minnesota, in which one correspondent says that it has been made by the State Board of Health. It is presumed, however, that by this term is not intended that a thorough and systematic survey has been made. That could not be undertaken and thoroughly carried out without a special appropriation from the State government. Seven make no returns, which is virtually a statement in the negative. *Minnesota claims to have made one.*

A few remarks only are necessary upon these reports.

If a State wishes to find out in a thorough manner any general question involving the interests of its inhabitants, the first step in the investigation which would seem to be proper, and which is usually taken, is to find out the precise status of the community, by a thorough survey of its actual condition in that particular. Can there be any thing more important than a precise knowledge of all the influences bearing upon the health of a people? And yet I presume that, however advantageous a sanitary survey of each State would be, it would be impossible to persuade a majority of the Legislature of any State in this Union to vote to have such a survey made at the present day. We vote thousands to gild the domes of our *Probably no Legislature would order one.*

State houses, and to make a show; but to dive into the mysteries of the industrial and social maladies of the State, we think too expensive. Jobbing of all kinds, under State and United States authority, we have; while a sanitary survey would be expensive to the State, and but slightly remunerative to those engaged in it. Hence it has no friends or defenders. Yet such a one should be made in every State, and doubtless will be made in every civilized community during the coming quarter or half century.

But eventually will be made by every State.

b. By a Law for Registration of Births, Deaths, and Marriages?

Registration of vital statistics. The following answers were received to this question, viz.: —

Sixteen (16) . . . . . . No.
Twenty (20) . . . . . . Yes.
Eight (8) . . . . . . Indefinite.
Four (4) . . . . . . No reply.

Less than a majority report definitely in the affirmative of this fundamental question, and even these have various exceptions to the thorough carrying out of the law, as is distinctly shown by the following qualifying clauses given by my various correspondents. Nebraska, Missouri, and New Hampshire (two correspondents) report the "law imperfect." California reports the law as "not carried out." In Kentucky, the "law is defective," and "there is no regular registration." Louisiana carries it out "only for New Orleans." Maine, Oregon, Colorado, and Idaho record "only marriages." In New Hampshire and New York (save in New York City), it "is a

None, or very imperfect, in all the States.

dead letter." Nebraska and Missouri report a law, but "not enforced." Pennsylvania has them for Philadelphia, &c., but not for the whole State. Nevada, "public health wholly neglected." New Jersey, a law, "but it is a farce." South Carolina had "registration before the war, but not since." Texas, "births and marriages," "but not yet in operation." Virginia, "not of births," and "imperfect" (two correspondents). Mississippi, "a law now before the Legislature." West Virginia, "imperfect," "not carried out" (two correspondents). Wisconsin, "eighteen years, neglected law," "imperfect" (two correspondents). Thus we find that, of the forty-eight governments, in only two is the registration of vital statistics claimed to be made with any approach to accuracy. Knowing what Massachusetts and Boston's [1] registration has been in the past, I think we should make very serious deductions from even this small number. This is but a sorry return in reference to what must be deemed by all an essential measure. Until accurate registration of vital statistics is thoroughly carried out by each State, it obviously will be impossible to have an efficient system of State Preventive Medicine. What we have said of the States may be applied to the United States. I cite the following fact as illustrative of these remarks. I was desirous of learning whether we had proof, from reliable statistics, that a man lives longer now than he did a century ago. This is believed to be true, if we may

State Preventive Medicine impossible without registration.

[1] In the 7th Report of Massachusetts State Board of Health, p. 495, under "Health of Boston," are the following suggestive comments on the registration of that city. "It was found that the records of the City Registrar did not contain information of sufficient exactness to make it advisable to publish a report based upon these returns." See also very important data, under "Registration," in 8th Report.

judge from past history, wherefrom it seems that the duration of life has been steadily augmenting with advancing civilization. To get accurate data, I consulted some noted experts in the community, but I have not been able to get satisfactory replies. Not one of them could refer me to printed vital statistics *proving the fact* for these United States. (Vide Appendix II. Correspondence with Drs. Jarvis of Massachusetts, and Baker of Michigan, and General Walker, in United States Census, for further illustration of this position.)

c. If so, how long has it (the Registration Law) been in Operation?

The following list is as nearly correct as I am able to make it: —

Name.	Years.	Remarks.
California	Many	
Connecticut	24	
District of Columbia	2	
Georgia	1	
Louisiana	Many	"For New Orleans only."
Maine	,,	"Marriages only."
Maryland	1	
Massachusetts	21	Imperfectly.
Michigan	9	
Minnesota	7	
Missouri	4	"Nominally, not enforced."
Nebraska	7	"Imperfectly."
New Hampshire	18	"A dead letter."
New York	20	Do, except for N. Y. City.
Ohio	8	
West Virginia	4	Imperfectly enforced.
Wisconsin	18	Neglected.

In connection with the above, it is singular to observe how different States, immediately contiguous, vary very much in their apparent interest in questions of vital statistics. As Massachusetts shows the influence of the

LAND DRAINAGE.

labors of certain men and of the Massachusetts Medical Society, a quarter of a century or more ago, so one can foresee how much advance will be made by Michigan, by the year 1900, over some of her sister States. Similar remarks might be made in reference to Louisiana, New York, and Pennsylvania, especially if the earnestness of work heretofore devoted to New Orleans, New York City, and Philadelphia, be directed to the States at large.

d. Has the Registrar been able to draw from such Records any Law governing the Public Health?

I watched the returns to this question with interest. The result is as follows, viz.: —

    Thirty-seven (37) . . . . No.
    Six (6) . . . . Yes.
    Five (5) . . . . No reply.

As it is similar to the general question proffered at the termination of this list, I refer the reader to my remarks upon the facts as given there, under question 20.

e. Has any Law been passed relating to the Drainage of Land?

Knowing what is now well established, — viz., the influence of the drainage of land upon the prevalence of malaria and consumption, — I proposed this question, and the returns of my correspondents are as follows: —

    Twenty-four (24) . . . . . No.
    Seven (7) . . . . Yes.
    Six (6) . . . . Indefinite.
    Eleven (11) . . . . . . No reply.

That is, exactly one-half admit that their States have done nothing in the premises. Only one-seventh reply affirmatively. Of the affirmative replies, we may make the following analysis, from which it will be observed that sanitary reasons have rarely, if ever, been the cause of the law. *Arkansas* says the "drainage was made for improving the land, but it really acted upon health." *California, Louisiana,* and *New York* say it was "for crops, not health." *Illinois,* through her correspondent, Dr. Breed, of Princeton, makes a most interesting statement of the results of drainage of at least one-half the land of three counties, — viz., 20,000 acres of "swamp land" (see Appendix II., Dr. Breed's letter), — with the most gratifying results upon the healthfulness of the country and the character of the settlers. Moreover, a great addition to the State School Fund resulted from the enhanced value of the lands when so improved. *New Jersey* and *Pennsylvania* have drained certain lands. It seems, therefore, that, though some of the States have drained certain parts of their domain, lucre, and not health, has been always the object aimed at. But the nobler and satisfactory results accruing in Illinois, I am sure, will have weight in localities where drainage is evidently needed.

f. Has any Law been passed relating to Irrigation of Land?

The following answers have been received to this question, viz. : —

        Thirty-one (31) . . . . . No.
        Five (5) . . . . Yes.
        Five (5) . . . . Indefinite.
        Seven (7) . . . . No reply.

Of the five affirmative replies, — viz., Arizona, Colorado, New Mexico, Utah, and Washington Territory, — New Mexico reports " for agriculture." Utah has "thousands of miles of ditches under a general law." Evidently, in the Mormon territory, irrigation was a necessity for two reasons: viz., first, that the people might have, for domestic uses, potable water; second, that the sterility and dryness of the soil might be modified. What the Moors did so effectually for Granada centuries ago, the monuments of whose beneficent action in this respect remain to the present day, the Mormons (and probably they are the only people that would have undertaken the task) have of late years been doing for the region of the Great Salt Lake. They have proved that parts, at least, of the "Great American Desert," are habitable by man. It is a singular coincidence that the domestic customs of Mormon and of Islam are the same. Both are aliens, by their religion and manners, to the soil they have cultivated; but both have been the greatest benefactors to the human race in this one respect, that they have proved what immense good to the life of man is obtained by a thorough system of irrigation of a territory, which otherwise would be sterile.

A necessity in Utah.

Mormonism and Islamism.

Among the States mentioned as doubtful, an Arkansas correspondent says "yes," " for land, and not for health." Similar remarks might be made on these returns as on those relative to drainage.

g. Has any Law been passed relating to Checking the Influence of Rivers by Levees, &c.?

The answers received to this question are as follows, viz.: —

Twenty-eight (28) . . . . No.
Four (4) . . . . Yes.
Five (5) . . . . Indefinite.
Eleven (11) . . . . . . No reply.

I felt little doubt that very few of the States would be called on to protect their cities or their borders by River levees. levees; and that, when such defence was called for, it would be from danger threatened to person or property rather than from sanitary reasons. I supposed, however, it possible that some of my correspondents on the banks of the great rivers of our country might allude to the sanitary view of the question. The problem of the entire safety of the noble city of New Orleans, save by a constant care of its levees, has always seemed to me important. I regret that I am able to present such slight returns. Two of my correspondents from Arkansas report that such levees have been made in their State "for agricultural reasons;" but one adds significantly, "but it has improved the health of the people residing near the place."

h. Has any Law been passed relating to the Introduction of Water into Cities?

The returns relative to this measure, so important for the health of the people of all the great cities of the Union, are as follows, viz.: —

Twenty-three (23) . . . . No.
Fourteen (14) . . . . . . Yes.
Four (4) . . . . Indefinite.
Seven (7) . . . . No reply.

The following specific statements are made, viz.: Indiana and Pennsylvania have a general law on the subject. Oregon and Illinois, and doubtless almost all

the other States, have permitted certain cities or towns to introduce water. But the question, although beginning to be mooted everywhere, has not perhaps anywhere received that attention which its importance demands, in a sanitary point of view; viz., that, while introducing water, every care possible should be taken to keep it absolutely pure. Boston and Charlestown in Massachusetts, Chicago in Illinois, Albany in New York, and Philadelphia in Pennsylvania, might be cited as cities which, while seeking an abundance of water, have not been equally cautious about its purity.

Water in cities, important question.

i. Has any Law been passed relating to the Prevention of Contagious Diseases?

a. Small-pox.

The following answers were received, viz.: —

    Sixteen (16) . . . . No.
    Twenty-one (21) . . . . . Yes.
    Seven (7) . . . . Indefinite.
    Four (4) . . . . No replies.

These returns I cannot but think erroneous. I cannot believe that sixteen of these States have not yet passed any law respecting vaccination. One of the former city physicians of Boston used to say that Boston could be kept free from small-pox, if it were not for Maine immigrants; alluding thus to the numbers of unvaccinated girls and others in domestic service, who formerly flocked from Maine into Boston, to get work. This assertion, though not strictly true, illustrates the utter inability of a State to defend itself, in case one adjacent to it fails of its

Unvaccinated immigrants pernicious.

duty in regard to vaccination. I see no remedy for this, save a national act for compulsory vaccination of every child in the United States within a very short period after its birth. Such an act will be passed eventually; but the people are not ready for it now, as may be inferred from the above returns.

<small>National vaccination act needed.</small>

Of the twenty-one that make an affirmative reply, the following items are given: They prove how indifferent we are as a nation to arrangements for warding off the plague of small-pox. Certain towns have local laws; viz., in Delaware, Louisiana, Nebraska, Oregon, Wisconsin, and Utah. General health laws exist in Indiana. General " quarantine laws " are found in South Carolina and Texas. In Louisiana, Nevada, and Oregon, the laws are "imperfect." "Vaccination, before the war," existed in Mississippi. "Compulsory vaccination" is the law in Iowa (law passed fifteen years ago). "Gratuitous vaccination" is ordered in Virginia. "No compulsory vaccination" in Pennsylvania. "Vaccination, and red flag of warning," are used in Connecticut. No person is allowed to go to school, in Massachusetts, unvaccinated. "Vaccination and quarantine" hold in Maryland. "Laws are very good, but a failure in execution," in Nevada. "The matter is under County Judges" in Tennessee. These replies require no comment from me. The shortcoming on the part of the country at large is patent.

<small>Laws everywhere imperfect, or poorly administered.</small>

β. *Has any Law been passed in relation to the Prevention of Cholera?*

The replies are as follows, viz.: —

    Twenty-one (21) . . . . . No.
    Sixteen (16) . . . . . . Yes.
    Four (4) . . . . Indefinite.
    Seven (7) . . . . No reply.

Additional specific replies came as follows, viz.: California, Connecticut, Nebraska, Texas, and Utah, say "only local laws." Quarantine laws are in Virginia. "Quarantine and removal to hospital saved us from cholera in Iowa during the last epidemic." "Left in United States hands" in North Carolina. "Laws insufficient" in Oregon. *[margin: Laws against cholera.]*

After the admirable and exhaustive report on cholera sent out by the United States Government,[1] it would be idle for me to attempt, in this place, to add any thing, save this; viz., that the necessity of an executive sanitary officer, a Secretary of Health for the nation, is proved by the terrible ravages of this disease. It is liable to affect the whole nation, and therefore appeals to every citizen of the United States. What we need is a sovereign power at the central seat of government, to give warning of the approach of cholera, or of any other similar plague; to give directions to check their spread; and to prevent, what is almost as bad, a panic among the people. *[margin: Admirable report on it by United States Government.]*

---

[1] The Cholera Epidemic of 1873 in the United States. House of Representatives, 43d Congress, 2d Session. Ex. Doc. No. 95. Washington, 1875.

A National Secretary of Health, the peer of the
Secretaries of the other departments of the
Government, — viz., of State, Law, War, Interior, &c., — and a Health Council, selected
from every State, will eventually be demanded, if we would efficiently meet and cope with these fatal and wide-spreading epidemics. In reference to this subject, I beg leave to refer to my address on Public Hygiene, delivered before the American Medical Association, at its meeting at Louisville, in 1875.

A National Health Secretary and Council needed.

γ. *Has any Law been passed in relation to the Prevention of Yellow Fever?*

My correspondents reply as follows, viz. : —

Twenty (20) . . . . . . No.
Twelve (12) . . . . . . Yes.
Ten (10) . . . . Indefinite.
Six (6) . . . . No reply.

It is evident that this disease has virtually left certain portions of the country ; viz., the more northern portions. Whether it has permanently done so, must remain an open question, until we know more than we now do of its essential character and cause. In Boston and New York, it was known by a brief personal experience by the late Dr. Jackson, Senior, and Dr. Hosack, and their compeers. I doubt whether any physicians now living in Boston ever saw a case existing as a menace to the public in that city. In New York, cases occur occasionally at the quarantine ground ; but no severe epidemic has prevailed the last half century. At Philadelphia, it was terrific in its effects, moral and physical, in the earlier years of the centennial period, as we learn from the graphic accounts left by Dr. Rush and

Less in the North than formerly.

Terrible formerly in Philadelphia.

his colleagues. I doubt whether it has appeared there, to seriously trouble the community, for very many years. Farther south, in Charleston, Savannah,[1] New Orleans, especially in the latter, it appears, according to some,[2] annually, with waves of rise and fall from time to time; sometimes scarcely known, save by sporadic cases, attended by a few physicians, and, at others, decimating the people. According to others (Herrick),[3] "it cannot be called wholly endemic in New Orleans;" and the same author asserts that "years have occurred during which the disease was not manifest," and "there is reason to believe that it might be extirpated, but from its introduction from tropical America." In other words, notwithstanding all the centenary of able men who have seen and investigated it during the whole period, we stand, in medical opinion, almost as divided as at the time of Rush. Upon these various points, I commend the remarks by my correspondents.[3] Among the replies, I find that Colorado, Dakota, and Michigan "never have the disease," that California "leaves its management to local boards," and Oregon "has very inefficient laws thereupon," — all proving the rarity of its occurrence in these States. Quarantine, more or less strictly and more or less judiciously enforced, is naturally the rule of most of the other States, though specifically stated only by Iowa, Louisiana, Maryland, Oregon, South Carolina, and Texas. Minnesota leaves the matter to the General Statutes of Health, and North Carolina in the hands of the United States. Rhode Island copes with the subject "indirectly."

Only in the South now.

Endemic?

Or imported?

---

[1] While these pages are passing through the press, a severe epidemic has been prevailing at Savannah.

[2] Dr. Chaillé's letter, Appendix II.   [3] See Appendix II.

δ. *Has any Law been passed in relation to the Prevention of the Cattle Disease?*

As this disease threatened so serious an injury to the comfort, and possibly to the health, of the people, I introduced this question with the thought that it was a legitimate object of inquiry on the present occasion. The returns are as follows, viz.: —

   Twenty (20) . . . . . . No.
   Eleven (11) . . . . . . Yes.
   Five (5) . . . . Indefinite.
   Twelve (12) . . . . . . No reply.

I received on this subject a very interesting letter from Illinois (Dr. S. P. Breed). The same writer gives a full account of what was done at a Convention of the Cattle-Dealers of the Northern States and Canada in 1868.[1] The Report of the Metropolitan Board of Health of New York and the doings of the Massachusetts Legislature upon the subject show the great interest felt in it.[2]

All of these doings, and the subsequent compara-
Advantage of co-operation of States and individuals in warding off pestilence. tive immunity from the disease, are proofs of what can be gained by co-operative scientific work, and by State law. On this point, the centennial period has not failed in its duty. Some States have spent thousands of dollars, and, by slaying the diseased cattle, have extirpated the affec-

---

[1] Appendix II. Dr. Breed's (Illinois) letters.

[2] Cattle Commissioners' Report, January, 1860, Senate Document, Mass. Also, law passed, April 11, 1876, on Texas Cattle Disease.

Report of the New York Cattle Commissioners in connection with the Report of the Metropolitan Board of Health, in relation to the Texas Cattle Disease, March 12, 1869, Senate Document, New York Legislature.

The Cattle Plague, with Official Reports of the International Congresses held at Hamburg, 1863, Vienna, 1865. By John Gamgee.

tion. Others have, by quarantine, inspection, and preventive laws, acted efficiently.

j. Has any Law been passed Regulating Tenement Houses?

The following answers were received to this question, viz. : —

Thirty-three (33)	No.
Four (4)	Yes.
Three (3)	Indefinite.
Eight (8)	No reply.

Upon this important subject, the centenary, save in two or three of the great cities, has failed of making much progress on this side of the Atlantic. England has made immense strides in this direction within five years. After years of discussion, the final enactment, in 1875, of the Artisans' and Laborers' Dwellings Improvement Act, has given almost unlimited power to scientific philanthropy, and enables it to act in behalf of the poorest of the citizens of England, — that class which epidemics of all kinds seize upon so readily. The Metropolitan Boards of Health of New York and Brooklyn; the admirable arrangements recently developed in Philadelphia, where thousands are enabled to own their own homesteads instead of being compelled to herd together, as heretofore; the co-operative building associations, public and private, of Boston and other cities, — have tended to elevate the degraded classes, and to prevent crime, disease, and death. But even these excellent influences have only recently come into full operation. There are millions of

Action in England.

New York.

Philadelphia.

Boston.

Millions still live filthily.

people living like swine, in their own filth, who have yet to be brought to a consciousness of the benefits to be derived from a cleanly homestead. In connection with this subject, we refer to the interesting letters by Dr. Ford and Mr. Blodget, of Pennsylvania; Drs. Harris and Thayer, of New York.[1] The Chinese, in their tendency to overcrowd, and thereby promote filth diseases, are presenting a very serious source of present and future trouble on our western coast, in California and Oregon.

<small>Overcrowding among Chinese in California.</small>

k. Has any Law been passed in relation to Incorporating Building Companies for the Improvement of Dwellings for the Poor?

This question is allied to the preceding, but is more comprehensive in its effects. The idea underlying it is this; viz., that capital and philanthropy should join hands, and endeavor to do an excellent service to the poor by providing comfortable homes for them, where their children may grow up in better health, and under less exposure to vice and crime, than can be procured in the uncared-for and filthy tenements now provided. In these latter abodes, the children are now really as well educated to crime as if they were in a primary school, expressly intended to inculcate it; or, if that does not happen, their lives are often cut short by disease before they have that baleful chance for the commission of crime. An immense field is open, in the future, for beneficent action in this direction.

<small>Combination of capital and philanthropy.</small>

<small>Tenement houses educators in crime.</small>

[1] See Appendix II.

BUILDING CORPORATIONS.

The replies of correspondents are as follows, viz.: —

    Twenty-nine (29) . . . . No.
    Three (3) . . . . Yes.
    Six (6) . . . . Indefinite.
    Ten (10) . . . . No reply.

A glance at the above shows the comparatively utter indifference with which the subject is regarded by most of the States of this Union. Only three out of forty-eight make an affirmative reply; viz., District of Columbia, Massachusetts, and Pennsylvania. In the District of Columbia, "speculation, rather than Public Hygiene," was the more evident object. *Nearly all the States indifferent.*

Philadelphia is undoubtedly the model city in this respect. Under the General Statutes for Building Associations, that city has built "thousands of small, comfortable houses, fitted up with all necessary conveniences, and owned by the occupants, through the beneficial provisions of these associations. They are a prominent feature of Philadelphia."[1] The experience of the Boston Co-operative Building Company has been peculiar; and, as it presents some points of great interest in this connection, and as I watched the course of proceeding from the beginning through four years and nine months, I shall enter into some few details. The State Board of Health early called attention to the fact of the necessity of doing something in regard to the vile tenements for the poor of Boston. In 1871 the Boston Co-operative Building Company was incorporated, with a capital of $200,000, subsequently increased to $300,000. The objects were: — *Philadelphia's admirable results.* *Boston.*

[1] Appendix II. Dr. Ford and Lorin Blodget, Esq., letters. Also, "The Industries of Philadelphia," by Lorin Blodget, 1877.

First. To co-operate, so far as possible, with the middle and lower classes of the people, in providing homes for them.

Second. To get a fair return for money expended. Seven per cent was the limit ordered by the Legislature. As the Act was obtained chiefly by the energy of women, and as it was believed that, in any object having benevolent ideas as one of its foundation elements, woman should be represented, it was decided that, in the list of the Directors, one-half should be women. Very soon a large block of brick houses, each Each family should have its own house. with a separate entrance, and four or five stories high, was erected. Each house could have only one, or, at the utmost, two tenements on a story. Every one room or two rooms were homes, with most of the family conveniences thereto attached. These houses, conducted by a committee of the Directors, have enabled the Corporation to pay six or seven per cent to the stockholders, and meet losses incurred by less favorable undertakings.[1] They are occupied by mechanics and laboring men and women, who, being thrifty, careful in their habits, fully appreciate their new abodes.

Third. We determined to hire old buildings, occupied Improvements of old tenements. by the vile and wretched, and, by adopting as far as possible Miss Octavia Hill's method,[2] try to raise the tenantry from their degraded state. This we hoped to accomplish, partially at least, by making the miserable abodes as cleanly and as healthy homes as the structures, originally faulty, would permit. Two places were selected. One was purchased, on

---

[1] Owing to depression of business, and these losses, the dividend of January, 1877, was passed over.

[2] McMillan's Magazine, July, 1869.

which there were six small wooden houses. The tenants were generally of a lower class than those occupying the new and larger block already named. As the sanitary arrangements in most particulars, though far from perfect, were tolerably fair, these tenements have remained in the state in which they were assumed, and have paid a good rent. A third undertaking was the renting of a very large, four-storied house, commonly styled, in contempt, "the Crystal Palace," containing tenements having two to four rooms each, and to which common corridors, front, and rear, and outside the building, lead. At the time of taking possession, both of these series of corridors had narrow and dark stairways, in which any persons, stealthily creeping at night, were perfectly concealed. The rear corridors themselves were screened from view. Four or five large privies, of the most filthy kind, were in the adjacent yard, quite near to the building. These were used in common by men, women, and children. When we took possession, these were in a state of most indecent filth. Slops and offal of all kinds were recklessly thrown down from the corridors into the yard or open public street, and upon the top of an adjacent building, used as a distillery. Doors and windows were everywhere in a dilapidated state. The plastering of the rooms was broken in many places. Not a sleeping chamber, save in a very few of the tenements, had any light or air, except what could be got through the front door and window, opening into the only other room, used for every purpose except sleeping. A grog-shop of the lowest kind was in one corner, dealing out its miserable influences upon every tenant. The lessee lived on the premises,

The Crystal Palace of Boston.

Its infamous condition.

Common privies and universal filth.

Little light or air in the chambers.

and one may judge of his character and of his tenants by the fact that the Superintendent of the State Prison told me that the "Crystal Palace" was known as the primary school of his institution. Thieves and drunkards occupied it. Oaths and obscenity were heard as common speech. The dark corridors were used as assignation spots for the lowest vice. All the scoundrels and lewd men and women in the community had free access to them day and night, as to their head-quarters. Drunken men and women were daily found, and allowed to remain, in the corridors, provided they were so drunk that they could not move to disturb the neighborhood; and there they slept away their beastly condition of mind and body. Occasionally, infuriated drunkards, male or female, would appear on the corridors, and, smashing in doors, or any thing else that resisted them, would excite a crowd of angry men and women into a pitched battle. This fight would be watched, enjoyed, and stimulated by shouts from the people in the street below. Often loud cries of murder would awaken at midnight the sleepers in a respectable hotel not far off. The landlord told one of the Committee, when he visited him, to tell him the Corporation had taken charge of the building, that he would willingly give "a thousand dollars for its removal." At the first official visit made by the Committee, a drunken woman lay across one of the main avenues. She was one of the old residents. The tenants were Irish, save one family of Scotch descent, which, from long association, was very much like its neighbors, except that it had a certain degree of Scotch thrift. On September 1, 1871, the Company took the building on a lease of five years,

The primary school for the State Prison.

Drunkenness everywhere.

Fighting and murder.

A nuisance to the neighborhood.

at a rent of $2,300, and with the privilege of renewing the lease for another five years. At the expiration of the lease, it was not renewed. Pecuniary reasons forbade it. When taking possession of the house, we had to make repairs, rearrange the building, which expenses, with our rent-roll as it then stood, we felt sure we could repay, with interest. We moreover were obliged, for sanitary reasons, to shut up the cellars, which had previously been used as tenements, and where the death-rate was double that of the remainder of the building. These places were soon used for junk-shops, storage, &c. Another item of expense was the sinking of two shafts from roof to base, in order to let light and air into the sleeping-chambers; and these cuttings lessened the number of tenements. Notwithstanding these expenses, we more than met all dues, and repaid, during the first two years, a part of the original outlay. In the autumn of 1873, "the panic" occurred, with the well-known prostration in business of all kinds, from which the community has not yet recovered (June, 1876). But, from that date until the building was resigned, there was a slow but steady decrease in the amount of receipts: owing, first, to the fact that many persons left the city to find work elsewhere; second, that those remaining became less and less able to pay their rent, owing to want of work. In vain the Committee decided that rent should be paid in advance. It was impossible to get it; and from some cause, either interest in the parents or children, or from a trust too confident that arrearages of small amounts would be eventually paid, these sums gradually amounted from two to fifteen or twenty dollars. Then finally came the expulsion of the delinquent, and

Varied expenses.

The panic of 1873 ruined the plan.

Decrease of receipts.

entire loss of that tenant's rent. No tenant of that class ever thought of paying money after leaving the building. Third, another very decided influence towards reducing the rent-roll was an effort, during the last year of our occupancy, to improve the character of the tenants by sending away the incorrigible drunkards, even if they disturbed no one but themselves.

Previously, we believed in retaining every one who was not notoriously and offensively brutal in drunkenness, or whose premises were not used for brothel purposes. This change was undertaken by our third and last agent, with the full permission of the Committee. This agent was a woman of energy and of excellent character. Her influence upon some of the tenants was good, — excellent, at times. But, with all her prudence, she was too often deceived, and tenants obtained rooms who proved after admission to be either of bad character or bad paymasters. Many applicants were refused if they could not bring good references.

The result was disastrous financially. We wished to improve our tenants, and give a new character to the building. But we found that it was impossible to give a new character to a building constructed as that was, or to get a better tenantry in a building whose previous reputation weighed like a monstrous incubus upon it. Our rents continued steadily to decrease; and the giving up of the building was finally decided upon, in order to save a greater loss. It will be seen that the main cause of this result was "the panic," aided, perhaps, by the new *régime* entered upon in the last third of our term of occupancy.

But the experience gained by members of the Committee, who had been connected with it from the earliest days of the lease, was such that they would have declined

EVIL OF DARK CORRIDORS.

to renew it, on sanitary and moral grounds. *They were compelled by that experience to feel that any large tenement house, occupied by the lowest classes, who are accustomed to filth, and are regardless of making filth on the common territory, is in itself bad for the health and morality of the community. The long, dark, common corridors, in which vice can lurk wholly hidden at night, are of themselves provocative of the worst crimes. If to these errors of construction are added four or five privies in the adjacent yard, for two hundred and fifty or three hundred people, men, women, and children, all* liable to meet at or about the same time for purposes of personal convenience, the result becomes shocking to think of. *Such a place must necessarily lead to filth, vice, and crime; and, with filth, will come disease and death.* Therefore, even if our rent-roll had been far more than necessary to meet expenses, those of us who saw, week after week, the evil necessarily connected with such a building, were of the opinion that it was a grievous nuisance to the community. We felt that no such building ought to be allowed; or, if built, it should be summarily removed. Corridors facing on the street, with open means of access, may be allowable; but even they cannot be so good as several entrances, each leading only to a very few tenements. *Dark or tortuous rear corridors, away from sight, are essentially faulty, and tend to crime.* These alone would have been a sufficient reason for our non-renewal of the lease.

Having thus given our experience of the evil that we met in the "Crystal Palace," it is but just to make the following statements, viz.: The death-rate of the building, after our occupancy, was less than that of the tenement

<small>Results of the experiment.</small>

<small>No such building should be allowed.</small>

<small>The Company's lease of it reduced death-rate.</small>

houses adjacent. Crime, vice, and drunkenness have been more or less constant there. But although the corridors have been at times the scenes of debauchery, and it has been impossible to prevent drunkenness and other evils, the building has not been a *public* nuisance, as it was before we took it. The neighbors confess that the Corporation has done a good work in making it no longer a curse to all near it, as well as to its inhabitants. In regard to the influence of the Committee on the tenantry, we have but little to say; but we cannot forbear stating that never was there any thing stolen from us, although we knew that we had thieves always there. In one or two instances, also, we found a few of the most obdurate of the adults and children were finally led to lives of more self-respect; and from all our tenants we met with a certain amount of kindness, manifested even by those least tending to the courtesies of life.

<small>Made the building less a public nuisance.</small>

<small>And a few of the amenities of life also appeared.</small>

An industrial school was established, which taught a few boys how to cane-bottom chairs; and, for a time, a sewing school for girls was in operation.

During the time we held the building, one or more of the Committee met the children, generally once in two weeks, for deposits in the savings bank. Nearly three hundred dollars were deposited by them, and it is hoped that some few were led to more thrifty ideas than they would otherwise have had. Nevertheless, I regret to say that we saw some boys grow up into thieves, and girls fall into unchaste lives, in spite of any influence we, as a committee, could exert. In fact, I deem it impossible for any *committee* to give that personal attention to the tenants which Miss Hill did.

<small>No committee can have the personal supervision exercised by Miss Hill.</small>

The teaching of the whole experience is: — *Teachings of our experience.*

First. It is the duty of public law to provide proper homes for the people, — homes that will enable each family to have at least some of the amenities of life. The "Crystal Palace," or "Lincoln Building," as we called it, and all like it, fail, from their very structure, in gaining this end. *Public law should see that proper homes are provided.*

Second. We believe that this can be done, even for the poorest persons, and that it will pay pecuniarily, as well as morally, to erect more appropriate buildings.

Third. Such buildings, under the influence of State Preventive Medicine, will, I doubt not, be built during the coming century, so that we shall look back with disgust and horror upon the purlieus of filth now existing in this country, in England, and on the continent, which are similar to those that, in former times, were the nuclei of the Black Death and of other similar pestilences of the Middle Ages. *State Preventive Medicine will require this.*

Seventh Question.

Are there any Well-attested Facts proving that any Disease, formerly prevalent in your State, has

a. Ceased to appear?

The following answers were received to this question, viz.: —

Twenty-five (25).	No.
Nine (9)	Yes.
Eight (8)	Indefinite.
Six (6)	No reply.

Of the nine affirmative and eight indefinite replies, I glean the following suggestions, though no proofs are

offered. The District of Columbia, according to Dr. William D. Stewart, has less malarial disease, less zymotics, cholera infantum, and cholera morbus. In Connecticut, Dr. Ashbel Woodward, of Franklin, thinks small-pox and croup much more manageable, while his five colleagues answer in the negative to the same question.

District of Columbia.

Connecticut.

From Delaware, Dr. Lewis P. Bush, of Wilmington, reports that large sections of Delaware are now comparatively free from malarious diseases, formerly so prevalent.[1] From Kentucky, Dr. L. P. Yandell, of Louisville, states that bilious remittent was almost annual formerly, but prevails much less now. Dr. J. L. Cook, of Henderson, in the same State, remarks that "milk sickness" was a common disease in the south-western part of the State many years ago, and "malarial disease had been usually less prevalent since the Board of Health had filled up about a dozen ponds" existing in the city. Dr. J. W. Bright, of Lexington, and Dr. G. Cowan, of Danville, reply definitely that they are not aware of any disease having ceased to appear. In Louisiana, Dr. U. R. Milner, of New Orleans, reports that the "Black Tongue" among animals, and thence extending to man, arose about twenty-five years since, and became endemic for a time, but it has now disappeared. (See Appendix.) Dr. Stanford E. Chaillé, of New Orleans, writes that typhoid fever is much less prevalent since 1855. Dr. J. D. Bruns, of New Orleans, and Dr. David M. Clay, of Shreveport, reply in the negative. In reference to Massachusetts, I will report that there is no evidence of any

Delaware.

Kentucky.

Louisiana.

Massachusetts.

[1] Report on the Climatology and Epidemic Diseases of Delaware. Am. Med. Assoc. Trans., 1872, p. 371.

disease, generally distributed over the State, having ceased to exist. I never heard that such was the fact from my masters in medicine, nor from my seniors of the profession, save, perhaps, in regard to intermittent fever. It is admitted, however, that that fever formerly prevailed in certain localities where now it is not known. This is due, undoubtedly, to the cultivation and drainage of the soil, and not to any efforts to overcome it.

From Michigan, Dr. Robert C. Kedzie, of Lansing, reports malarial disease lessened by drainage.[1]   Michigan.
Dr. J. H. Beech contends, in a very decided manner, for the influence of drainage at Coldwater in lessening the frequency of pernicious zymotics. Dr. G. E. Corbin, of St. John's, makes similar statements. On the contrary, Dr. Edward Cox, of Battle Creek, and Dr. Henry B. Baker, of Lansing, who, from the position he holds of Secretary of the State Board of Health, and from his intelligent zeal in behalf of preventive medicine, is an admirable witness, make negative replies to the main question.

From Mississippi, Dr. J. D. Burch, of Yazoo City, says, with Dr. Cook, of Kentucky, "that   Mississippi.
malarial fevers have lessened since the clearing of the swamps from timber, and the more rapid drying of the soil after overflows." Dr. P. F. Whitehead, of Vicksburg, replies negatively; and Dr. F. W. Dancy, of Holly Springs, makes no answer.   New York.
From New York, Dr. Elisha Harris, that veteran and most able sanitarian, replies that malignant congestive fevers have lessened.

Dr. W. H. Thayer, of Brooklyn, states that "peri-

---

[1] Trans. Am. Med. Assn. Vol. 25, 1874, pages 402 to 424.

odic fever has diminished materially in some localities which have been well drained."[1] Dr. Austin Flint, Senior, "facile princeps" of the medical profession of the United States, says that yellow fever was formerly prevalent, and every year now is at Staten Island, but not at New York. In this connection, I beg leave to draw attention to the clear, concise account of the method of quarantine as at present administered by Dr. S. Oakley Vanderpoel.[2]

Finally, Dr. Janes says that, if urged, "he should say that pernicious intermittent, formerly somewhat prevalent in certain parts of the State of New York, has nearly, if not quite, disappeared."

Dr. E. A. Anderson, of Wilmington, N.C., replies that "bilious remittent and pernicious fever have almost entirely gone." Dr. William A. B. Norcom, of Edenton, N.C., replies in the negative.

North Carolina.

From Ohio, Dr. Frank Wells, of Cleveland, reports that intermittent fevers have greatly lessened under drainage of marshes and redeeming of the land. Drs. O. M. Langdon, W. H. Mussey, and William Carson, all of Cincinnati, have negative replies.

Ohio.

From Pennsylvania, the large central State of our Union, I receive either negative or doubtful replies.

Pennsylvania.

In Rhode Island, the admirable statistician and sanitarian, Dr. E. M. Snow, of Providence, reports only three-tenths of one per cent of all deaths are from small-pox. Finally, Dr. L. C. Butler, of Essex, Vermont, replies that he knows

Rhode Island.

Vermont.

---

[1] Trans. Med. Soc. State N. Y. 1875. Report of the Committee on Hygiene.
[2] Appendix II.

of no disease having disappeared, though his experience goes back forty years. But Dr. A. T. Woodward, of Brandon, says that intermittents have ceased in certain districts.

The summary of the whole return seems to be that intermittent and pernicious malarial fevers have apparently ceased in some Northern States, and materially lessened in the Middle and Southern States, under drainage and tillage; that yellow fever, which formerly existed in most of the great cities of the Union, now seems driven to the extreme South, where we cannot but hope, under preventive measures and disinfectants, and cleaning, before and during the prevalence of the disease, it may, during the coming century, become still more mitigated. *Summary. Pernicious fevers lessened in North. Yellow Fever gone South.*

Of small-pox, which, in the commencement of the centennial period, spread like wild-fire, carrying panic intolerable with it, we may say that only the folly of individual men, and utter neglect on the part of the State, or, as in Canada at the present hour, the frenzy of bigotry and of base ignorance, alone prevent us from extirpating the disgusting disease from the face of our portion of the earth. *Small-pox.*

These replies, though quite imperfect, from the absence of reliable statistical data, give us brighter hopes for the future most blessed influence which will be exerted by State Preventive Medicine, when all the States and the National Government shall have thoroughly organized State Departments of Health. *Hopes for the future.*

b. Are there any Well-attested Facts proving that any Disease, formerly prevalent in the State, has been crushed by the State or by Individual Action?

The replies are as follows, viz. : —

    Thirty-seven (37) . . . . No.
    None (0) . . . . Yes.
    Four (4) . . . . Indefinite.
    Seven (7) . . . . No reply.

No disease has been crushed out. The above result very distinctly intimates that the idea of any disease having been crushed out, either by State or individual action, is unknown in this country. Not a single person replies affirmatively. No one points to any fact even suggesting the affirmative of the question. Of the five correspondents from Louisiana, four reply in the negative, and the fifth makes no reply, though he writes that the "Black Tongue" has disappeared, how or why he apparently does not know. In other words, I can get no evidence from my correspondents that any disease, formerly prevalent, has been crushed by any special, well-defined means, inaugurated by State or individual action.

Black tongue gone from Louisiana.

Eighth Question.

Are there any Similar Facts proving that any Special Disease has arisen, or been generated, or been introduced into the State during the Past Century, which did not exist in Colonial Times, and which now remains endemic?

EIGHTH QUESTION.

The replies are as follows, viz.: —

    Twenty-seven (27) . . . . No.
    Six (6) . . . . Yes.
    Two (2) . . . . Indefinite.
    Thirteen (13) . . . . . . No reply.

In addition to the monosyllabic replies, I obtained the following particular data: Dr. W. H. Johnson, of Selma, Alabama, says, " Malarial hæmorrhagic fever has occurred since the war," also " typhoid fever." From Colorado, Dr. Charles Dennison, of Denver, writes that " perhaps phthisis has been introduced." Colorado has been inhabited only recently (as Territory, Feb. 28, 1861, as State, 1875). Denver is among the highest (5,267 feet above sea level) of places for man to dwell in; and from the experience of Switzerland, Mexico, and Peru, we know that lofty plains do not engender or have phthisis as a common disease, or it is practically unknown. Finally, as Denver is the spot sought now by very many pulmonary invalids, it is probable that phthisis is now prevalent to a much greater degree than formerly. And it may be presumed that before many years have elapsed phthisis will be found among the native inhabitants, born of immigrating phthisical parents. Moreover, if contagion has any influence, it may be well questioned whether that element of causation may not be even now playing strongly its part towards an increase of, and the permanent existence of, the disease in these lofty regions.

Malarial hæmorrhagic fever.

Phthisis in Colorado.

From Connecticut, we have three who report their belief in the introduction of new diseases, viz.: Dr. J. S. Butler, of Hartford, thinks diphtheria and cerebro-spinal meningitis are such. Dr.

Connecticut.

B. H. Catlin, of West Meriden, inclines also to have the same opinion of cerebro-spinal meningitis; while Dr. S. G. Hubbard, of New Haven, Dr. L. C. Butler, of Essex, Vt., Dr. E. A. Anderson, of Wilmington, N.C., Dr. E. B. Turnipseed, of Columbia, S.C., and Dr. J. S. D. Cullen, of Richmond, Va., incline to the probability of diphtheria being a new disease. Dr. J. E. Reeves, of Wheeling, W. Va., definitely asserts that no diphtheria was seen before 1844. Of both these opinions I presume there may be some doubt; and a belief may be readily entertained that a disease similar to diphtheria was described as occurring in England in the last century, although it has doubtless been more extensive, and, as an epidemic, more fatal in this country, during the last half of this centennial period.

 Dr. William Duncan, of Savannah, Georgia, replies affirmatively, and says, in partial proof, that Dr. R. D. Arnold, of Savannah, Georgia, claims that cholera and yellow fever have become endemic; but Dr. Duncan significantly adds, the profession generally doubt the validity of the assertion.

 Dr. N. Field, of Jeffersonville, Indiana, and Dr. R. C. Kedzie, of Lansing, Michigan, suggest that cerebro-spinal meningitis has been newly introduced into these States. Dr. George W. Mears, of Indianapolis, Indiana, claims that trichiniasis is a new disease. I would suggest the same doubt about trichiniasis being a new disease as about cerebro-spinal meningitis; because there is no doubt, from morbid specimens existing in European cabinets, that trichiniasis existed many years ago, without being recognized in the complete manner which it is at the present day.

 Dr. J. W. Bright, of Lexington, Kentucky,

EIGHTH QUESTION.

writes that scarlatina, cholera, typhoid fever, and diphtheria, have all been introduced into the State. Doubtless they all have been so introduced, for the State itself has been settled chiefly during the centennial period.

Dr. U. R. Milner, of New Orleans, writes that cholera, having been introduced into Louisiana in 1832, prevailed again much in 1849 and 1850; and that since that time it has occurred sporadically and virtually is endemic. <small>Louisiana.</small>

Dr. S. S. Herrick, of New Orleans, thinks yellow fever was introduced into Louisiana during the last century, and that it might be crushed out, if new importations of it were prevented.

Dr. W. H. Thayer, of Brooklyn, New York, regards diphtheria as a new disease. (See Report Metropolitan Board of Health, and Appendix II. for correspondence.) Dr. Elisha Harris, of New York City, does not believe in the introduction of a new disease, but that scarlatina and diphtheria were more fatal formerly than now. <small>New York.</small>

Dr. E. H. James, of New York, an authority of weight, in a letter to Dr. Austin Flint, states what I am inclined to believe is a truth; viz., that the nomenclature of diseases has changed, but that no new diseases have been introduced. He, however, adds that typhoid fever may have taken the place of the malarial fevers prevalent in colonial times. But what is this but a change of name, perhaps, rather than of disease?

Dr. A. R. Kilpatrick, of Navasota, Texas, thinks black jaundice, and perhaps neuralgia, are more common than thirty years ago. Dr. T. J. Heard, of Galveston, Texas, says the same of typhoid fever, diphtheria, cerebro-spinal meningitis, and malarial disease. <small>Texas.</small>

Virginia. Dr. F. Horner, Jr., of Salem, Virginia, contends that typhoid fever appeared in 1814–15, and since has been endemic.

NINTH QUESTION.

If there be any such New Disease, has it been investigated by the State or by Individuals?

When?   By whom?

The replies are as follows, viz. : —

Twenty-seven (27) . . . . No.
Six (6) . . . . Yes.
Two (2) . . . . Indefinite.
Thirteen (13) . . . . . . No reply.

Louisiana. Among those who reply affirmatively is Dr. Stanford E. Chaillé, of New Orleans, who cites typhoid fever as having been investigated by a commission of the City Council of New Orleans, in 1853. Dr. H. B. Baker, of Lansing, Michigan, as reported by R. C. Kedzie, made investigations on cerebro-spinal meningitis in 1875.

Michigan.

New York. Dr. W. H. Thayer, of Brooklyn, New York, writes that diphtheria was reported on by the Metropolitan Board of Health of New York. This meagre statement does not contain any evidence in regard to the many investigations into local diseases in the various States, which are so numerous in journals and volumes that it would be impossible to name them. It simply intimates the small number of really new affections, or thought to be new affections, upon which some investigations have been made. In answering for Massachusetts, I say nothing, because I

think we have no proof that all the diseases named by my correspondents may not have existed in colonial times, although we know them more definitely now than they were known formerly.

Tenth Question.

Has the Town or City, in which you reside, taken any Measures for the Improvement of the Public Health?

a. By Health Laws?

The replies are as follows, viz. : —

Nine (9) . . . . No.
Twenty-five (25) . . . . . Yes.
Nine (9) . . . . Indefinite.
Five (5) . . . . No reply.

Dr. D. A. Linthicum, of Helena, Arkansas, reports none but police rules, when in fear of danger. Arkansas.
Dr. J. H. Reed, of Black Hawk, Colorado, says laws "passed not specially for the object of health." Colorado.
Dr. J. M. Carn, of Centreville, Florida, "for street cleaning." Florida.
Dr. William A. B. Norcom, of Edenton, North Carolina, "none important, and insufficient at times." Dr. E. A. Anderson, of Wilmington, in the same State, reports "laws for drainage around the city." N. Carolina.
Dr. Frank Wells, of Cleveland, Ohio, reports $24,000 appropriated by the city. Ohio.
Dr. O. P. S. Plummer, of Albany, Oregon, laws "against special nuisances." Oregon.
Dr. C. C. Strong, Portland, Oregon, laws "against small-pox."

Dr. E. B. Turnipseed, of Columbia, South Carolina,
replies that "political trials interfere with
proper action."

S. Carolina.

Dr. A. R. Kilpatrick, of Navasota, Texas, reports
"a board of health formerly, but none now;"
and Dr. T. J. Heard, of Galveston, Texas,
that "the city has spent much for drainage." Dr. J.
H. Finfrock, of Laramie City, in Wyoming
Territory, records the existence of laws, but
thinks they are inefficient. The same remark may be
made of Massachusetts, and generally in the
country. The cities and towns of Massachusetts have more or less efficiently constructed plans of
health laws, some very primitive, others more
elaborate. But I know of no town in that
State, which can be said to have a thorough
regard for the health of the people.

Texas.

Wyoming.

Massachusetts.

Results all imperfect, probably.

b. By Special Action in Specific Cases?

The replies are as follows, viz.: —

Three (3) . . . . No.
Twenty-five (25) . . . . . Yes.
Eleven (11) . . . . . . Indefinite.
Nine (9) . . . . No reply.

Dr. W. O. Baldwin, of Montgomery, Alabama, reports the "general powers given the Board
of Health" as meeting the question of special work.

Alabama.

Dr. Stanford E. Chaillé and others report New Orleans as "making efforts to check small-pox,"
&c. Dr. E. A. Anderson, of Wilmington,
writes of "special efforts for drainage of the
suburbs." From Albany and Portland, in

Louisiana.

North Carolina.

Oregon.

Oregon, we learn from Dr. O. P. S. Plummer and C. C. Strong that laws to "oppose special nuisances, smallpox, &c., have been enacted."

Dr. J. F. Rothrock, of Wilkesbarre, Pennsylvania, Dr. W. C. Dabney, of Charlottesville, Virginia, Dr. L. C. Butler, of Essex, Vermont, and Dr. J. H. Van Deman, of Chattanooga, Tennessee, write of "laws for compulsory vaccination." Pennsylvania. Virginia. Vermont. Tennessee.

Dr. W. F. Anderson, of Salt Lake City, Utah Territory, and Dr. G. H. Russell of Cheyenne, Wyoming Territory, write that they have "quarantine laws against small-pox." Utah. Wyoming.

ELEVENTH QUESTION.

Does your Town or City use Well-water for Culinary Purposes?

TWELFTH QUESTION.

Is Care taken to prevent Pollution?

THIRTEENTH QUESTION.

Do you have a Water Supply from a Distant Lake or River?

FOURTEENTH QUESTION.

Is Care taken to prevent Pollution?

I think it best to include these four questions in one category; and, in order to do so, I present returns from one hundred and forty-three (143) towns and cities of

the Union, distributed through the various States composing it. Of these, eighty-two (82) use wells, and sixty-one (61) avail themselves of rivers. Of the eighty-two (82) using wells, only twenty-one (21) claim that there is an attempt to get the water pure before using it; while forty-six (46) admit a total inattention to this important matter; fifteen (15) either do not report at all, or indefinitely. Of the sixty-one (61) availing themselves of rivers, twenty-eight (28) are said to be careful of the purity of the water, while twenty-three (23) take no care, and ten (10) make no reply, or are doubtful. Combining these two sets of figures, we get the following table, representing, with at least tolerable accuracy, the towns and cities of the United States. I am quite sure that it is applicable to Massachusetts; and, from what I have observed and learned from other States, I think it applies equally well to towns and cities in all the other States.

Drinking water for towns.

49 or 34.26 per cent . . Try to make the water pure.
69 or 48.25 ,, ,, . . Make little attempt to get it pure.
25 or 17.48 ,, ,, . . Make no reply, or are indefinite.

In other words, only one-third (34.26) of the towns and cities of this nation make any claims, even the most trivial, of endeavoring to procure pure potable water for their inhabitants.

Very few try to keep it pure.

The remainder, 65.73 per cent, either confess carelessness or ignorance of the subject. In other words, over one-half of the people of these United States are openly and avowedly living in a senseless disregard as to

whether they are drinking pure water, or water contaminated by every kind of filth.

We may be quite sure that such recklessness in regard to human life will not exist a half century hence.

Fifteenth Question.

Have you Sewers to carry off such Water Supply?

The replies are as follows, viz.: —

    Eleven (11) . . . . . . No.
    Thirteen (13) . . . . . . Yes.
    Twenty (20) . . . . . . Indefinite.
    Four (4) . . . . No reply.

These replies coincide fully with all that precede, and point to the very primitive ideas still existing in regard to the introduction of water into our towns, without at the same time making ample provision for the speedy removal of it, after being made impure by use. *A priori*, one would suppose that none but the most foolish community would ever introduce water in large quantities into a district without making some such provision.

Very primitive ideas of our people on the subject.

If this should not be done in any case, the land would be constantly soaked, not only with water, but water containing decomposing animal matter, and at times the contagia of diseases of various kinds, which the earth, under such circumstances, could not entirely purify.

But other evil consequences would be likely to follow; viz., that, with a damp soil, certainly consumption, possibly other diseases, would be more likely to arise than in a drier soil. Especially are sewers needed

when water-closets are to be flushed. Yet, of only thirteen (13) out of the forty-seven (47) governments, is it definitely stated that sewers were to be found in all the places reported from. Among affirmative replies, we found the following additional items: —

Alabama, California, District of Columbia, and Louisiana report their cities and towns as using the surface street drains as well as sewers, thus making imperfect the whole sewerage of these places, even where some sewers are said to be properly laid down.

Alabama. California. District of Columbia. Louisiana.

Florida and North Carolina report sewers for certain individual houses.

Florida. North Carolina.

Indiana, Minnesota, and Washington Territory speak of them as imperfect.

Indiana. Minnesota. Washington Territory.

Massachusetts and New York have them generally in cities, but mixed, even in crowded thoroughfares, with vile privies.

Massachusetts. New York.

Rhode Island reports a perfect system of sewerage in progress for Providence. Of the State generally, we have no returns. In Newport, there is a miserable arrangement, totally imperfect for such a place of resort for thousands during the time that enteric diseases and all zymoties prevail.[1]

Rhode Island. Newport.

Finally, Kansas reports "one-half mile of sewers" for Leavenworth.

Kansas.

Even from those giving an affirmative reply, we see that sewerage is everywhere in this country lamentably neglected. I am well aware that, in many cities, large sums of money are annually expended for sewerage. Moreover, I know that some cities claim especial praise

---

[1] This statement was true at the time the Address was delivered. At present, however, it is believed that ample arrangements for sewerage are in preparation at Newport.

for their excellent arrangements for this purpose. Even Boston claimed as much as that, until compelled, by its own recent commissions on the subject, to give up its unfounded pretensions. *[Boston one vast cesspool.]* In that city, among other faults, the following disgusting fact was found; viz., that a huge *cloaca maxima*, intended to drain the whole of the old historic portion of the city, but now occupied by an immense number of our poorest people, is really nothing but a vast cesspool, while, *theoretically*, it is supposed to be swept by the tide twice daily. Its six feet depth of passage is nearly filled with filthy decomposing sewage and mud, which has been collecting for years. Into this already filled-up sewer, thousands of the poor people of the North End of the city are throwing daily new collections of dirty water, slops, and the contents of their water-closets. No wonder the drains of houses in that part of the city have had a frightful odor under such circumstances. And what makes this especially galling is the fact that there is reason to believe that this state of things was evident and known years since, but nothing for our relief has as yet been done. I summon thus this the chief city of my native State to the bar of public sanitary judgment, not because I think her more guilty than others, but simply because I know her merits and demerits; and, when she claims to be well drained by sewers, I think she ought to be used as a warning to others. During the last year, an able Commission has recommended a system worthy of such a metropolis; but, as it is an expensive *[Proposed changes this year.]* undertaking, and other less expensive plans have been suggested, the authorities are undecided as to undertaking it. In fact, the chief civil engineer of the city violently opposes the plan. Under a due appreciation

of the power of sanitary law, such folly could not exist. The fact is that, by the public and by private citizens, little or no attention has been paid to this matter. So strangely has it been ignored, that two out of the three chief hospitals in the city are built on land taken from the sea, filled up in many places with the most stinking refuse from the purlieus and streets of the city. And, in proof of the same inattention to sanitary laws, I might cite the fact that two magnificently warmed, ventilated, and sun-bathed wards, recently erected in the chief hospital, rest directly over a large wooden drain, which carries not only the contents of their own water-closets and drains, but all that which comes from those of the main original building. And what makes them still worse is the fact that a great part of the solid contents of these drains and water-closets, instead of being washed out into the open sea, as it had been foolishly thought they would be by each returning tide, are really driven up into an immense cesspool, situated between the two new wards and the old main building. It has thence to be carted away twice a year. This work is usually done much to the detriment of the health of the workman while so employed. He suffers at least twenty-four hours afterwards with painful diarrhœa and general malaise. What can we think of that Public Hygiene which, within five years, has permitted such terrible mistakes in the construction of places, destined specially for the cure of disease?

Sidenotes: Hospitals built on improper land. Wooden drains and cesspools under the building. Unfortunate results.

Sixteenth Question.

How far are the Sewer Outlets from the Source of Water Supply?

The returns are as follows, viz.: —

Boston has hers all around the city, with openings in every direction, within the sight and smell of the inhabitants. Black Hawk, Colorado, sends her refuse "into a flume," distance not stated. Philadelphia, Penn., Charleston, S.C., Chattanooga, Tenn., and Wilmington, N.C., have sewer outlets at times "very near." Boston. Colorado. Philadelphia. Charleston. Chattanooga. Wilmington, N.C.

The following have them at the distances marked, viz.: —

One mile or under. — Montgomery, Ala.; Chattanooga, Tenn.; St. Louis, Mo.

Two miles or under. — Norwich, Conn.; Indianapolis, Ind.; Bangor, Me.; Portland, Me.; Minneapolis, Minn.; Portsmouth, N.H.; Richmond, Va.; Prince George, Va.; Wheeling, W. Va.

Three miles or under. — New Haven, Conn.; Chicago, Ill.; Louisville, Ky.; St. Paul, Minn.; Philadelphia, Penn.; Richmond, Va.

Four miles or under. — New York City.

Five miles or under. — Boise City, Idaho; Wilkesbarre, Penn.

Six miles or under. — Hartford, Conn.; Providence, R. I.

Ten miles or under. — Brooklyn, N.Y.; New Orleans, La.

Eleven and a half or under. — Savannah, Ga.

Fifteen or under. — Hot Springs, Ark.

Sixteen or under. — Washington, D.C.

Twenty to thirty. — San Francisco, Cal.

It will be seen by the above that, of all the cities re-
<small>Boston among the worst.</small> ported, no one is so pre-eminent in its filthy arrangements for sewers as Boston. Fortunately, the city's supply of water comes from a distant lake, and the imperfect sewerage does not harm it.

It may be questioned whether Philadelphia, in its
<small>Albany, Chicago, Philadelphia, not blameless.</small> growth, has paid sufficient attention to keeping its waters and air perfectly pure from contamination.

Chicago, too, seems not altogether blameless. Albany, as I know by personal examination, is careless in this matter. I do not quote these cities as especially worse
<small>Wide-spread inattention.</small> than others, but simply as examples of the wide-spread inattention to the necessity for carrying our sewage far from the possibility of its contaminating ourselves or others.

SEVENTEENTH QUESTION.

What is your Method of disposing of Sewage?
House Offal?
Slops or Filth liable to accumulate about Homesteads?

Of the sewage, we have the following reports from eighty-four (84) towns, viz.:—

It is passed into sewers in 22
    Of which it is said that six (6) are either "partial," "imperfect," or "obstructed." Two (2) simply report no sewers, and give no indication of how the sewage is disposed of.
It is thrown into the "bay," or "river," or "flume," in 19
Surface drainage or "ditches" is deemed enough in . 13
                                                                                    ———
            Carry over 54

SEVENTEENTH QUESTION.

Brought forward	54

And the following various methods are pursued by the remainder, viz. : —

Removed from the city, three times weekly	2
Removed from the city, in epidemic times	1
Removed from the city by river	1
In barnyards, or covered with dry earth	5
Exposed in open field	5
By scavengers	2
By scavengers, or not at all	1
Thrown into streets or vacant lots	2
Into "rear of houses"	1
Into "covered ravine"	1
Thrown to hogs	1
Ordinary methods of N.E. towns	1
Wretched	2
Partial	2
No regulation	2
Individual acts	1
	84

Can any thing be more chaotic than the arrangements for the removal of sewage from the dwellings of most of the inhabitants of this country? *Chaos, generally.*

That the removal of *house offal* is similarly imperfect is shown by the following reports from eighty-nine (89) towns, viz. : — *House offal, similarly neglected.*

It is carted off in	25
One of which admits that sometimes even this is not done.	
It is thrown into the streets and vacant lots in	4
Is taken away by scavengers in	3
Thrown into river or bay in	5
Carry over	37

Brought forward	37
Thrown into cesspools in	4
Used as fertilizer, or covered with dry earth in	8
Thrown into privies in	2
"No regulation," or "imperfect," in	3
"Hogs, the only scavengers" in	4
Open drainage	5
Removed three times a week	2
Removed regularly	3
	68

And of the following, at times, very grotesque and primitive arrangements, we have one report each, viz. : —

"Covered with lime," "thrown into the rear of the houses," "alleys," "open field," "covered ravine," "taken by vagabond Indians," "carted away during epidemics," "usually left for swill," "in gutters," "barnyards," "dumped in valley to fill up," "in gutters and courts," "in back yards to produce enteric disease," "wretched," "primitive," "New England town method," "pig-sty and manure heap," "air of climate dry, so dry that no decomposition occurs wherever left," "carried away by private speculations,"................. 19

Finally, in two (2), it is "do as you please," "public opinion only law"............. 2

89

If one did not have these positive statements as above given, we could not imagine such wide-spread folly to prevail in these United States.

The removal of *slops* is in a like state of great imperfection throughout the Union, if we may judge from the following data from seventy-three (73) localities, viz. : —

By carts	25
By sewers	7
By sewers and privies	2
Thrown into river	5
Thrown to hogs and fowls	5
Used as a fertilizer	4
Thrown into "vacant lots," "open drains," on "compost heaps," "back yards," or "where each one wishes"	10
"No regulations"	3
"Liable to accumulate"	2
Under following headings one return for each: It is "put in wells," "wells and privies," "pernicious cesspools," "natural drainage," "buried," "dumped in valley to fill up," "primitive" and "shameful," "means to remove if persons would avail themselves of the privilege," and, finally, "air is so dry that it can be exposed without decomposition"	10
	73

Do we wonder now at the vast number of preventable diseases that occur everywhere in this country? <small>Preventable diseases arising therefrom.</small>

Eighteenth Question.

Have any State, County, or City Reports of Health or Deaths, &c., been published?

Of the States it is reported: —

    Thirty (30) . . . . . . No.
    Nine (9) . . . . Yes.
    Two (2) . . . . Indefinite replies.
    Seven (7) . . . . . . No reply.

More than half of the States (62.50 per cent) have no registration. 18.75 per cent have had registration in most of them only for a few years past. And the same percentages make doubtful or no replies. Adding the first and last percentages together, we have the very probable fact that 81.25 per cent of the States have wholly neglected vital statistics during the entire centennial period. Add to this statement the following items from my correspondents, viz.: that in California the law is virtually "a dead letter" for the State at large; that in the District of Columbia, Pennsylvania, and Louisiana, only the great cities of Washington, Philadelphia, and New Orleans, are registered; that in South Carolina registration "has been neglected since the late civil war;" that in Colorado, Idaho, and Maine, " only marriages" are recorded; and in Texas and Virginia "only marriages and deaths," — we must deduct very much from even the small percentage of States apparently not faithless in their duties of registration. In this connection I refer to what I have already stated of the statistics of Boston and Massachusetts.[1]

Interest in vital statistics very small.

Only nine States claim to have registration.

And the law is imperfect or a dead letter in most.

Nineteenth Question.

How many years (approximatively or definitely) have they been published?

It is unfortunate that, in arranging the previous question, I did not separate the States from the towns.

The following however, it is believed, is nearly accurate. Approximatively, I doubt not that it gives us an

[1] Page 67.

NINETEENTH QUESTION.

idea of the length of time vital statistics have been attended to in the places named; and, as I believe, they also give nearly, if not quite, a correct view of the state of the country generally.

LIST OF THE STATES AND SOME OF THE CITIES AND TOWNS HAVING REGISTRATION OF VITAL STATISTICS, WITH THE NUMBER OF YEARS PUBLISHED.[1]

States, Cities, and Towns.	Years published.	
	By State.	By City or Town.
ALABAMA		
Mobile		1840 to 1856
Montgomery		10 years
ARKANSAS		
Little Rock		5 years
CALIFORNIA		
Santa Barbara		2 years
COLORADO		
Denver		Several years in daily newspapers.
CONNECTICUT	27 years	
Hartford		27 years
Franklin		? ,,
Norwich		? ,,
New Haven		20 years
DELAWARE		
Wilmington		30 years
GEORGIA	1 year	
ILLINOIS		
Chicago		Several years, 5 or 7
INDIANA		
Indianapolis		1 year
IOWA		
Keokuk		15 years
KENTUCKY		
Louisville		8 or 9 years
Henderson		Formerly
LOUISIANA		
New Orleans		22 years
MASSACHUSETTS	33 years	
Boston		Many years
Worcester		,,
Several Towns		,,
MICHIGAN	3 years	

[1] It must be obvious to the reader that this list is very imperfect. It only shows how irregularly the whole subject of registration has been attended to in the various States.

States, Cities, and Towns.	Years published.	
	By State.	By City or Town.
MINNESOTA		
Minneapolis		3 years
Winona		6 ,,
St. Paul		6 ,,
MISSISSIPPI		
Vicksburg		Daily newspapers
MISSOURI		
St. Louis		9 years
NEW HAMPSHIRE		
Hampton Falls		Newspapers sometimes, 25 years
NEW JERSEY		
Metuchen		20 years. No use
Bridgeton		5 or 10 years
NEW YORK	Deaths, 10 years	
Brooklyn		10 years
New York		? ,,
Newburg		? ,,
Troy		? ,,
Rochester		? ,,
OHIO	Deaths, 10 years	
Cincinnati		10 years
PENNSYLVANIA		
Philadelphia		70 years
RHODE ISLAND	22 years	
Providence		20 years
SOUTH CAROLINA		
Columbia		8 years before war.
Charleston		50 years, more or less
TENNESSEE		
Knoxville		2 years
Chattanooga		4 ,,
TEXAS		
Navasota		Since the war
San Antonio		4 years
Galveston		A few years
UTAH		
Salt Lake City		Deaths, 20 years
VERMONT	17 years	
Burlington		3 years
Brandon		3 years
VIRGINIA		
Richmond		6 years
Prince George		Several years
WISCONSIN	1853	
Milwaukee		5 years

NINETEENTH QUESTION. 115

The United States commenced its censuses in 1790, and they have been made every ten years since. However important these may be in some of their details, I have felt, after consulting experts in regard to them, that I could not draw therefrom any sufficiently certain data to warrant any further use of them. In proof of the justice of this remark, I quote the following in reference to the last census: "The gross incompleteness of the returns of deaths in the census of the United States is shown by Mr. Elliot's Approximate Life Tables." "What, it may be asked, is the value of statistics confessedly so imperfect?"[1] Mr. Walker elsewhere admits that the number of deaths falls short 40 per cent of what must actually be the fact. *United States censuses.* *Inaccuracy admitted by the government officials.*

Mr. Elliot, who calculates the "Approximate Life Table" from these returns, admits that he is obliged "to resort to this somewhat arbitrary assumption, viz., 40 per cent discount; limited, however, by an investigation of the rates of mortality relative to population, which obtain in other communities, so far as accessible, and in portions of our own country."[2]

Still further, being desirous of learning whether life lasts longer now than it did at the first part of this centennial period, as is confidently believed to be the fact, I consulted one of the wisest statisticians and accomplished experts in life insurance as to whether I could find, in the census returns, sufficiently accurate data to prove any thing on the subject, or where I could find any documents that would tell me; and he replied in the negative on *Opinions of experts on this question.*

---

[1] Statistical Atlas of the United States, by F. A. Walker.
[2] Ibid. Approximate Life Table for the United States, by E. B. Elliot.

both points. Dr. Edward Jarvis, of Boston, writes to me thus on the same subject: "I wish I could help you, but I do not see the way clearly to do the work. But it may be done, so I think. It will require great labor to find the facts of the beginning and end of the century. Bills of mortality, grave-yard records, family Bibles, traditions of the former and the latter time, will show whether we have gained or lost in longevity." With all due deference to my learned correspondent, this seems to me a lame and impotent conclusion, compared with what might have been the result, if vital statistics had been carried out carefully during this centennial period. The life insurance expert and Dr. Jarvis, by their replies, virtually sustain my position.[1]

It is very unpleasant to me, as it would be to any American, to be compelled to take, before such an assembly as this, any position so derogatory to the honor of my country. But from my knowledge of registration in Massachusetts, and from what I have learned from my correspondents relative to other States, which I have thus briefly laid before you, I affirm, without fear of contradiction, that not a single State in this Union, nor the United States as a nation, has, at the present time, any proper system for the registration of vital statistics; or, if any system exists, it is, with very few exceptions per-

Not a single State in United States has made any but imperfect registration.

---

[1] While these pages are printing, the last report of the Massachusetts State Board of Health has been presented to the Legislature. The reader will find in that document ample proof of the truth of the general facts stated in the text. Moreover, he will find there a proof that, notwithstanding the registration law has been in operation nearly thirty years in Massachusetts, the carelessness of the various persons, empowered and directed to get the original returns, is so great that, in some most important particulars, the registration reports are very defective. As to the causes of death, for example, they are comparatively worthless.

haps, but of whose existence I know nothing, carried out so imperfectly that it will be considered almost valueless, when State Preventive Medicine has been firmly and intelligently established. To my young countrymen everywhere, I would fervently appeal, and ask them to consider well the task that lies before them. Let them see to it that, in their private conversation and in their public speech, they never let pass a proper opportunity for urging upon their different States, and upon the United States Government, the duty of assuming a broad and generous mode of action upon these topics, so vital to the well-being, health, and happiness of generations yet unborn.

Appeal to the youth of the country.

Twentieth Question.

Has any Law of Development, or of Partial Development, of any Disease, been discovered by Individual or State Action, by Attention to which, in Coming Centuries, we may hope to greatly lessen or destroy such Disease?

I proposed this question of fact as my last and most important one. It was to be the culmination, so to speak, of all the rest, the test of the real work of the centennial period. The first of this series of questions was one admitting of and calling for the expression of opinion only. This last allows of no opinion, but asks for a positive statement.

Test question of the century.

The answers are: —

  Thirty-nine (39) . . . . . No.
  Six (6) . . . . Yes.
  None (0) . . . . Indefinite reply.
  Three (3) . . . . No reply.

The returns indicate that my correspondents have a more decided opinion upon this question than upon any other of the series. There are only three who fail to make any answer, and not a single State has replied indefinitely. Again, 39 out of 48 States, or 81.25 per cent, reply in the negative: 9 of the 48, or 12.50 per cent, reply affirmatively.

But let us look carefully at the affirmative answers, and interpret more closely their exact meaning. The replies, I think, may be justly arranged in two categories.

First. Those in which it appears that, by close attention to sanitary arrangements and their rigid enforcement, certain diseases are checked. One correspondent remarks, " All the acquired knowledge concerning all and each of the typho-contagia and the factors of their propagation is equivalent to discovery" (Dr. Harris, of New York). From other States we are informed that "the laws of development of typhoid fever are all known better" (Drs. Plummer, of Oregon, Butler, of Vermont). Drs. Stewart and Toner, of Washington, D.C., say they are "able to control and prevent zymotics by sanitary enforcement." Dr. Baker, of Lansing, the self-sacrificing, efficient Secretary of the State Board of Health of Michigan, writes as follows: " It seems proper to modify very much the 'yes' which I have placed opposite the question. If we substitute for 'law of development, or partial development of,' the words *general truth respecting*, I think the answer will be truthfully 'yes.'" He then cites " scarlet fever, which will be lessened in the near future, because of the accumulated evidence of the great mortality caused by it." He also thinks " croup

[1] Appendix II.

and pneumonia will be eventually greatly lessened, from the fact that a cold and dry atmosphere causes the greatest mortality from both. And by securing such favorable conditions in our houses, and particularly in our sleeping-rooms, it is reasonable, he thinks, to hope that many deaths from pneumonia and croup may in the future be prevented." These statements may be placed in one category.

Second. Let us grant that they are all true. Nevertheless, I do not see that any "law" of development of disease similar in degree, at least, if in character, to that of "soil moisture," as a very prominent cause of phthisis, has been presented by any one of my excellent correspondents. Massachusetts, through the agency of the Massachusetts Medical Society,[1] proved, many years ago, by data received from her three hundred and twenty-five towns, and where consumption had been previously considered everywhere equally endemic, that there were dry spots where it was very rare, and wet where it was very rife. By accurate statistical data, laboriously gathered, it was further proved that, of two families growing up, one on a wet soil and the other on a dry soil; the one resident on the wet, by that fact, became twice, if not three times, as liable to phthisis as the other, resident on a dry spot. That law was first discovered and announced in New England. Subsequently, by ample statistical data, it was proved to exist in Old England. I think it may now be said to be a cosmic law; and as such it seems to me I am justified in placing it alone in the second category under this final question.

[1] Appendix VI.

In order to meet the numerous similar questions which will inevitably arise in the future, we need, as Mr. Elliot suggests, a national system for the registration of all the births, marriages, and deaths, taking place in the country. Moreover, the Registrar should, for the whole country, learn the exact character of the localities in which the deaths take place, if we would learn precisely and broadly the endemic influences of any place.

SUMMARY.

GENTLEMEN, — My work is done. I have endeavored to place before you the exact truth in these matters, so far as I could obtain it. No one can feel more keenly than I do that it has, at times, been most unpalatable, and that it seems to be but little creditable to the country. Nevertheless, looking at the very recent growth of a regard for Public Hygiene, and at the certain, though small, advances made in various parts of the country in State Preventive Medicine, I have the brightest hopes for the future of this country and the world in this regard. We could not, with the influences hitherto surrounding us, have advanced further. System-making, the outgrowth of many previous centuries, prevented all progress in this direction during our first epoch. The overthrow of these theories and theory-makers, and the bringing of medical inquiries into line with the methods pursued by modern science, are the great points gained during the second. Although these have been followed by a sweeping and wide-spread scepticism in our own art, we must remember that this same scepti-

cism is found everywhere within the domains of modern thought. Good will ultimately result from it. But these facts have not allowed of the growth of Preventive Medicine, until within a very recent period of time.

We stand now at the very dawn of the grandest epoch, yet seen in the progress of medicine. While philosophically, accurately, and with the most minute skill studying, by means of physiology, pathological anatomy, chemistry, the microscope, and, above all, by careful clinical observation, the natural history of disease and the effects of remedies, our art at the present time looks still higher; viz., to the *prevention of* as well as to the *cure of* disease. And this is to be done by sanitary organizations throughout each State; the nation, the laity, and the profession, heartily joining hands in this most noble cause.

Our Present Duty.

Our PRESENT DUTY is organization, National, State, Municipal, and Village. From the highest place in the National Council, down to the smallest village board of health, we need organization: with these organizations, we can study and often prevent disease.

This great and beneficent object, the prevention of disease, appeals to all. The aged may give counsel. To the young of this and of future generations belongs the solid work, which is to bless the coming centuries. I appeal, therefore, with all the earnestness at my command, to the young men of the present hour. Can there be any thing more inspiring to a generous-hearted, intelligent youth, than the thought that, by laborious research into the causes of disease, by the discovery of

means for its prevention, and by the teaching of these various causes and means to the people, he may help to save even a few of the more than two hundred thousand human beings, now annually slaughtered in this country by preventable disease?

Our Hopes for the Future.

I trust that this discussion will have given rise in your minds to some of the bright hopes for the future, which have arisen in my own. Although Public Hygiene has made but few advances hitherto, it is nevertheless founded upon natural law. It has been legitimately and healthfully growing during a portion of the last quarter of this century. Modern science greets it, and brings it within its domain, as one of its most precious objects for thorough investigation. I hope therefore that, standing as we now are, near the close of this fair centennial birth-year of our nation, up to whose festival all nations of the earth have been invited, I may be allowed to appeal to all, whether young or old, American or collaborating friends from other lands, to join with me in a *cordial all-hail to coming centuries*, not only in America, but in every civilized spot of God's earth, because everywhere, and to all coming time, human life will be lengthened, made more healthy, and consequently more truly happy, by the potent influence of

State Preventive Medicine.

APPENDIX.

APPENDIX.

I.

The following circular was addressed to correspondents. Appended to it is a list of those from whom answers were received. To one and all of them I tender my sincere thanks.

BOSTON, January 1, 1876,
113 Boylston Street.

Dr.   of   State of

MY DEAR SIR, — I have been asked to deliver the Address on Public Hygiene and Preventive or State Medicine, before the International Medical Congress, which is to be held in Philadelphia, in September next.

To do this thoroughly, and as nearly as possible with historic accuracy, even on a few points, I need the assistance of my professional associates throughout the United States. I therefore frankly appeal to you in the hope that you will feel able to answer, at least monosyllabically, one or more, and perhaps all, of the following questions. An answer to even one of them would be gratefully received.

By their tenor, you will see that I want facts rather than opinions. I will add, moreover, that the shorter and more compact (consistently with exactness) the answers are given, the easier will be the subsequent analysis of them. I hope to get some from every State.

In submitting these questions to the friendly courtesies of my professional associates throughout our Union, I feel the great favor that I ask. But the object I have at heart will, I trust, be my sufficient excuse. It will be, moreover, my greatest pleasure to give public credit to every one who consents to aid me.

I shall be ready to meet all expenses for expressing documents to my care, and likewise to pay for the documents themselves, if such payment be necessary or proper.

As it is important for me to get my data as soon as possible, I hope that I shall hear from you (provided you think you can answer at all) on or before March 1, 1876. Let me still further say, that negative answers to many questions may be as important as positive ones.

Respectfully yours,

HENRY I. BOWDITCH.

	Yes.	No.
1. Does your State, by its legislation, show a due appreciation of the duty, devolving upon a State, to be careful of the health of its people?		
2. Is it willing to expend money: —		
a. To support State or local Boards of Health?		
b. To carry out scientific investigations as to the causes of disease?		
c. To repress noxious or offensive trades?		
d. To prevent adulteration of food?		
e. „ „ cattle disease?		
f. Or to carry on any other investigations tending to public health, or to prevent ill-health?		
3. Has your State established a State Board of Health?		
a. If so, when was it established?		
b. What amount of annual appropriation is made for its support?		
c. Are any occasional and extra grants made for special investigations?		
d. Has such a board any organized body of correspondents or inspectors throughout the State?		
e. What executive powers have been given to the board with reference to local nuisances or noxious trades?		

QUESTIONS.

Yes. No.

4. Have any *county* boards of health been established by law?

5. Have any *town* boards of health been established by law?

6. Has the State passed any law leading to a thorough and definite improvement of the public health: —
    a. By a sanitary survey of the State?
    b. By a law for registration of births, deaths, and marriages?
    c. If so, how long has it been in operation?
    d. Has the Registrar been able to draw from such records any law governing the public health?
    e. Has any law been passed relating to the drainage of land?
    f. Relating to irrigation of land?
    g. Relating to checking of the influence of rivers by levees, &c.?
    h. Relating to the introduction of water into cities?
    i. Relating to the prevention of contagious diseases, for example: —
        α. Small-pox?
        β. Cholera?
        γ. Yellow Fever?
        δ. Cattle Plague? &c., &c.
    j. Regulating tenement houses?
    k. Incorporating building companies, for the improvement of dwellings for the poor?

7. Are there any well-attested facts proving that any disease formerly prevalent in your State has
    a. Ceased to appear?
    b. Or that any has been crushed by the State or by individual action?

8. Are there any similar facts proving that any special disease has arisen or been generated, or introduced into the State, during the past century, which did not exist in colonial times, and which now remains as an endemic?

	Yes.	No.

9. If there be any such new disease, has it been investigated by the State or by individuals?
  When? By whom?

10. Has the *town or city* in which you reside taken any measures for the improvement of the public health?
  a. By health laws?
  b. By special action in specific cases?

11. Does your town or city use well water for culinary purposes?

12. Is care taken to prevent pollution?

13. Do you have a water supply from a distant lake or river?

14. Is care taken to prevent pollution?

15. Have you sewers to carry off such water supply?

16. How far are the sewer outlets from the source of water supply?

17. What is your method of disposing of
  Sewage?
  House offal?
  Slops, or other filth liable to accumulate about homesteads?

18. Have any State, county, or city reports of health or death, &c., been published?

19. How many years (approximatively or definitely) have they been published?

20. Has any law of development, or partial development, of any disease been discovered by individual or State action, by attention to which, in coming centuries, we may hope to greatly lessen or destroy such disease?

NOTE. — In regard to any one or all of the above questions, Dr. Bowditch would, of course, be gratified to have as fully detailed facts as his correspondent can give. The above tabular and compact statement is made for two reasons: 1st, To relieve the correspondent of labor; and, 2d, in order to get answers about a few points from the entire country.

CORRESPONDENTS' NAMES.

List of correspondents from whom either monosyllabic or more detailed replies have been received:—

Baldwin, William O., M.D.	Montgomery	Alabama.
Cochran, Jerome, M.D.	Mobile	,,
Hill, S. H., M.D.	Carrollton	,,
Johnston, William H., M.D.	Selma	,,
Scales, T. S., M.D.	Mobile	,,
McCandless, James Newton, M.D.	Prescott	Arizona Terr.
Lawrence, George W., M.D.	Hot Springs	Arkansas.
Linthicum, D. A., M.D.	Helena	,,
Welch, William Blackwell, M.D.	Boonsboro'	,,
Bates, Charles B., M.D.	Santa Barbara,	California.
Gibbons, Henry, Sr., M.D.	San Francisco	,,
McKee, J. H., M.D.	Los Angelos	,,
Denison, Charles, M.D.	Denver	Colorado.
Mack, David, Jr., M.D.	Los Pinos Indian Agency	,,
Marsh, Libbæus Eaton, M.D.	Central City	,,
Ried, James H., M.D.	Black Hawk	,,
Butler, John S., M.D.	Hartford	Connecticut.
Carleton, Charles M., M.D.	Norwich	,,
Catlin, Benjamin Hopkins, M.D.	West Meriden	,,
Hubbard, Stephen G., M.D.	New Haven	,,
Ives, C. L., M.D.	,,	,,
Kent, John Bryden, M.D.	Putnam	,,
Woodward, Ashbel, M.D.	Franklin	,,
Brecht, Frederick Adolph, M.D.	Yankton	Dakota Terr.

130   APPENDIX.

Askew, Henry F., M.D. . . . Wilmington . Delaware.
  by Grimke, A. R.

Billings, John S., Ass. Sur. U.S.A. Washington . Dis. of Col.
Stewart, William D., M.D. . .   „   „
Toner, Joseph Meridith, M.D. .   „   „
Woodward, J. J., Ass. Sur. U.S.A.   „   „

Belton, George W., M.D. . . . Tallahassee . Florida.
Carn, Julius Marcellus, M.D. . Centreville .   „

Duncan, William, M.D. . . . . Savannah . Georgia.
Nottingham, Custis B., M.D. . . Macon . . .   „
Pettigru, William, M.D. . . . Augusta . .   „
Thomas, J. G., M.D. . . . . Athens . .   „

Smith, Ephraim, M.D. . . . . Boise City . Idaho Terr.

Breed, S. P., M.D. . . . . . Princeton . . Illinois.
Davis, Nathan Smith, M.D. . . Chicago . .   „
Johnson, Hosney A., M.D. . .   „   „

Field, Nathaniel, M.D. . . . . Jeffersonville, Indiana.
Mears, George W., M.D. . . . Indianapolis   „

Angear, John J. M., M.D. . . . Fort Madison, Iowa.
Carpenter, Ab. Miller, M.D. . . Keokuk . .   „

Sinks, Tiffin, M.D. . . . . . Leavenworth, Kansas.
Stormont, David W., M.D. . . Topeka . .   „

Bell, T. S., M.D. . . . . . Louisville . . Kentucky.
Bright, J. W., M.D. . . . . Lexington .   „
Cook, John L., M.D. . . . . Henderson .   „
Cowan, George, M.D. . . . . Danville . .   „
Yandell, Lunsford P., M.D. . . Louisville . .   „

Bruns, J. Dickson, M.D. . . . New Orleans . Louisiana.
Chaillé, Standford E., M.D. . .   „   „

CORRESPONDENTS' NAMES.

Clay, David Milton . . . . . Shreveport . Louisiana.
Herrick, S. S., M.D. . . . . New Orleans ,,
Langworthy, O. P., M.D. . . . Clinton . . ,,
Milner, U. R., M.D. . . . . . New Orleans ,,
White, Charles B., M.D. . . . ,, ,,

Brooks, John G., M.D. . . . . Belfast . . Maine
French, George F., M.D. . . . Portland . . ,,
Hamlin, Augustus C., M.D. . . Bangor . . ,,
Jones, Ralph K., M.D. . . . . ,, ,,

Donaldson, Frank, M.D. . . . Baltimore . . Maryland.
Forward, W. Stump, M.D. . . Darlington . ,,
Hill, Charles G., M.D. . . . . Arlington . . ,,

Allen, Nathan, M.D. . . . . Lowell . . . Massachusetts.
Appolonio, N. A., City Registrar . Boston . . . ,,
Jarvis, Edward, M.D. . . . . Dorchester . ,,
Pickering, Henry G., Esq., . . Boston . . . ,,

Baker, Henry B., M.D. . . . Lansing . . Michigan.
Beach, J. H., M.D. . . . . . Coldwater . ,,
Corbin, Gilbert E., M.D. . . . St. John's . ,,
Cox, Edward, M.D. . . . . . Battle Creek . ,,
Ford, Corydon L., M.D. . . . Ann Arbor . ,,
Kedzie, Robert C., M.D. . . . Lansing . . ,,
Palmer, Alonzo B., M.D. . . . Ann Arbor . ,,

Goodrich, C. G., M.D. . . . . Minneapolis . Minnesota.
Hand, D. W., M.D. . . . . . St. Paul . . ,,
Simpson, Charles, M.D. . . . Minneapolis . ,,
Staples, Franklin, M.D. . . . Winona . . ,,

Burch, James Drummond, M.D. . Yazoo City . Mississippi.
Dancy, F. W., M.D. . . . . Holly Springs ,,
Johnston, Wirt, M.D. . . . . Jackson . . ,,
Whitehead, P. F., M.D. . . . Vicksburg . ,,

Green, John . . . . St. Louis . . Missouri.

APPENDIX.

Johnson, James B.	St. Louis	Missouri.
Oliphant, Robert W.	,,	,,
Holmes, L. E., M.D.	Deer Lodge	Montana Terr.
Henshey, David W., M.D.	Nebraska City,	Nebraska.
Livingston, R. R., M.D.	Plattsmouth	,,
Peabody, James Henry, M.D.	Omaha	,,
Van Buren, E., M.D.	Fremont	,,
Grindley, T. R., Esq., Librarian State Library	Carson City	Nevada
Meigs, John J., M.D.	Elko	,,
Conn, Granville P., M.D.	Concord	N. Hampshire.
Downes, Charles S.	Nottingham	,,
Ham, John Randolph	Dover	,,
Parsons, John William	Portsmouth	,,
Sanborn, Charles Henry	Hampton Falls	,,
Twitchell, George B.	Keene	,,
Elmer, William, M.D.	Bridgeton	New Jersey.
Holden, Edgar, M.D.	Newark	,,
Hunt, Ezra M., M.D.	Metuchen	,,
Varick, Theodore R., M.D.	Jersey City	,,
Warman, David, M.D.	Trenton	,,
Woodworth, O. H., M.D.	La Mesilla	New Mexico.
Bell, A. N., M.D.	Brooklyn	New York.
Flint, Austin, Sen., M.D.	New York	,,
Harris, Elisha, M.D.	,,	,,
James, E., M.D.	,,	,,
Peaslee, Edmund R., M.D.	,,	,,
Thayer, William Henry, M.D.	Brooklyn	,,
Vanderpoel, S. Oakley, M.D.	New York	,,
Wey, W. C., M.D.	Elmira	,,
Anderson, Edwin Alexander, M.D.	Wilmington	N. Carolina.

CORRESPONDENTS' NAMES.

Norcom, William A. B., M.D. . Edenton . . N. Carolina.

Carson, William, M.D. . . . . Cincinnati . . Ohio.
Langdon, O. M., M.D. . . . .   „   „
Mussey, William H., M.D. . .   „   „
Wells, Franklin, M.D. . . . . Cleveland . . „

Glisan, Rodney, M.D. . . . . Portland . . Oregon.
Plummer, Orlando P. S., M.D. . Albany . . „
Strong, Curtis Clark, M.D. . . Portland . . „

Atlee, Washington L., M.D. . . Philadelphia . Pennsylvania.
Blodget, Lorin, Esq. . . . .   „   „
Ford, William H., M.D. . . .   „   „
Kirkbride, Thomas K., M.D. . .   „   „
Le Conte, J. L., M.D. . . . .   „   „
Pollock, A. M. M.D. . . . . Pittsburg . . „
Rothrock, J. T., M.D. . . . . Wilkesbarre . „
Ruschenberger, W. S. W., M.D. . Philadelphia . „
Smyth, Francis G., M.D. . . .   „   „
Stillé, Alfred, M.D. . . . . .   „   „

Arnold, Edmund S. F., M.D. . . Newport . . Rhode Island.
Collins, George L., M.D. . . . Providence . „
Jenckes, George Washington, M.D. Woonsocket . „
Snow, Edwin Miller, M.D. . . Providence . „

Baruch, Simon, M.D. . . . . Camden . . S. Carolina.
Huger, William Harleston, M.D. . Charleston . „
Kinlock, Robert Alexander, M.D.   „   „
Turnipseed, Edward Berrian, M.D. Columbia . . „

Bailey, Frederick K., M.D. . . Knoxville . . Tennessee.
Bowling, W. K., M.D. . . . . Nashville . . „
Eve, Paul F., M.D. . . . . .   „   „
Van Deman, Joseph H., M.D. . Chattanooga . „

Heard, T. J., M.D. . . . . . Galveston . . Texas.
Irion, John Lewis, M.D. . . . Montgomery . „

Kilpatrick, Andrew Robert, M.D. Navasota . . Texas.
McKinney, R. A., M.D. . . . La Grange . „
Petterson, Frederick V., M.D. . San Antonio . „
Wallace, David Richard, M.D. . Waco. . . . „

Anderson, Washington F., M.D. Salt Lake City, Utah Terr.
Crockwell, J. D., M.D. . . . . „ „

Butler, Lucius C., M.D. . . . Essex . . . Vermont.
Fassett, Oscar F., M.D. . . . St. Albans . „
Putnam, Sumner, M.D. . . . . Montpelier . „
Woodward, Adrian Theodore, M.D. Brandon . . „

Brown, Bedford, M.D. . . . . Alexandria . Virginia.
Cabell, James L., M.D. . . . . University of Va. „
„ John Grattan, M.D. . . Richmond . . „
Clairborne, John H., M.D. . . Petersburg . „
Cullen, J. S. Dorsey, M.D. . . Richmond . . „
Dabney, William C., M.D. . . . Charlottesville „
Hall, Theophilus Agricola, M.D. . Prince George „
Horner, Frederick, Jr., M.D. . . Salem . . . „
Joynes, Levin S., M.D. . . . . Richmond . . „
Nash, Herbert M., M.D. . . . Norfolk . . „
Powell, R. C., M.D. . . . . . Alexandria . „

Goodwin, L. H., M.D. . . . . Walla-Walla . Wash. Terr.

Lazzell, James M., M.D. . . . Fairmount . W. Virginia.
Moore, Eli H., M.D. . . . . Wellsburgh . „
Reeves, James E., M.D. . . . Wheeling . . „

Davis, James Cardell, M.D. . . Fort Atkinson, Wisconsin.
Gott, William A., M.D. . . . Viroqua . . „
Reeve, James T., M.D. . . . . Appleton . . „
Strong, Henry Partridge, M.D. . Beloit . . . „

Finfrock, John Henry, M.D. . . Laramie City, Wyoming Terr.
Russell, George H., M.D. . . . Cheyenne . . „

APPENDIX II.

EXTRACTS FROM CORRESPONDENTS' LETTERS.

II.

This part contains the more detailed replies of correspondents from thirty-three States and Territories; viz., Alabama, Arkansas, California, Colorado, Connecticut, District of Columbia, Florida, Illinois, Iowa, Kansas, Kentucky, Louisiana, Maine, Massachusetts, Michigan, Mississippi, Missouri, Nebraska, Nevada, New Hampshire, New Jersey, New York, North Carolina, Pennsylvania, Rhode Island, South Carolina, Tennessee, Texas, Utah, Vermont, Virginia, Wisconsin, Wyoming.

The States, &c., are arranged alphabetically. The letters, also, from each are placed alphabetically, according to the names of the correspondents.

ALABAMA.

(From DR. JEROME COCHRAN, Mobile, Ala.)

MOBILE, Jan. 20, 1876.

. . . Our State has just commenced the work of legislation in behalf of the public health. I think there is every disposition on the part of the Legislature to do all that the financial condition of the State, and the circumstances of the people, will admit. Our organization is a peculiar one, and has been established on plans, proposed by myself, and by the influence of the physicians of the State. The Medical Association of the State is the State Board of Health; and the counties' medical societies are county boards of health. You will find our whole scheme in the Report of the Board, in the Transactions of the State Association for 1876. . . .

(From DR. WILLIAM HENRY JOHNSTON, Selma, Ala.)

. . . This city is situated on a sand bed. Sanitary regulation is enforced from May till December. Water can be had here by driving down a pump from twenty-five to thirty-five feet, and pumping out the sand, and then the water comes. . . .

(From Dr. T. S. Scales, Mobile, Ala.)

Our State Board of Health was established in 1875, and simply exists, and nothing more. No executive authority as yet exercised. Our City Board of Health acts as a county board of health, and exercises such authority in the county, as is delegated by the Board of County Commissioners. Our City Board of Health exercises such authority as is invested by our municipal enactments; a copy of which I will send you, if desired, with our annual report for 1875, when printed, — *now nearly ready.*

The water, principally used here, is from a clear creek, some eight miles from the city, and is conducted through the pipes in ordinary use for that purpose.

ARKANSAS.

(From Dr. George W. Lawrence, Hot Springs, Ark.)

Hot Springs, Ark., Jan. 1, 1876.

. . . It is to be regretted that our profession has not been able to procure legislative action in our State, necessary to give satisfactory statistical information for the public welfare.

(From Dr. D. A. Linthicum, Helena, Ark.)

Helena, Ark., Jan. 22, 1876.

. . . It gives me genuine pleasure to add my mite; although, in answering many of the questions, I am compelled to reflect discredit upon the intelligence and philanthropy of our previous legislators. My answers have been necessarily monosyllabic, by reason of so little space in the blank; therefore, so unsatisfactory to myself, that I have deemed it my duty to write you, and endeavor to give more general answers, and the reasons for our very unsanitary condition. I hope thereby to take a good deal of the odium, resulting therefrom, from off the shoulders of my profession, and place it where it very properly belongs; viz., at the feet of our law-makers. Through committees, we have asked for a State board of health, and for the passage of a law for the registration of births, deaths, and marriages. We have asked for an appropriation for a sanitary survey of the State; but without avail. We have labored hard

to obtain at their hands a medical bill, regulating the practice of medicine, to prevent charlatanism, with which our State abounds; but with no satisfactory results as yet. We have asked for a law for compulsory vaccination; also, for surface and under-draining of our low lands, both with regard to health and profit. We have no State or county reports of health or deaths. Therefore, not having had the necessary statistics, the diseases of our State, in very many localities, have not received their proper names. In this, the eastern part of Arkansas, lies the richest and most alluvial portion of our State. It is admirably adapted to the growth of cotton, grain, and grasses, and for the generation of those poisonous gases, said to be so active in the development of swamp or paludal fever, during the summer and autumn months. It lies, for three hundred miles, fronting upon that great artery of commerce, the Mississippi River. Our water supply is very poor. We have to rely upon cisterns. Consequently, only the affluent have a full supply of pure water, thoroughly protected from pollution. The poorer classes of whites and colored people, which largely predominate in this portion of the State, have to depend upon stagnant water from neighboring lakes and bayous, or upon the water obtained under the surface by means of "driven wells"; *i.e.*, long iron pipes thrust down into the earth until water can be drawn by means of a pump. Nearly all of this water is impure, and contaminated with unhealthy material. Consequently, we are peculiarly cursed with malarial fevers, and all diseases, partaking more or less of that character, both in winter and summer. Dr. R. G. Jennings, of Little Rock, the capital of this State, made a sanitary survey of that city in 1870. He prepared an able document, which was published in the Proceedings of the State Medical Society of that year. I made a sanitary report to the mayor and aldermen of our town, in the spring of 1875, upon the sanitary condition of this city, Helena, with statistics of diseases for the past year, as accurate as I could obtain them. In it I threw out several suggestions for the improvement of the public health and the organization of a sanitary board. These investigations were purely labors of love upon our part, and have, as yet, brought forth no fruit. We are a comparatively new State, and situated upon the frontier; and have been for

the past ten years groaning and suffering through the ordeal of reconstruction, and have been taxed beyond measure, both in pocket and endurance. This is something in extenuation of our want of statutory enactments tending to the public weal, and our failure to bring ourselves up to that standing of excellence, that characterizes many of our sister States. But the genuine men of our profession have made up their minds to persevere in their labors in the Legislature upon these great questions of sanitary reforms, and they hope finally to succeed. This success being once gained, we shall be led to other and greater reforms, until our State will occupy that position, in a sanitary point of view in the sisterhood of States, that she is so well deserving of in agriculture.

CALIFORNIA.

(From Dr. Charles B. Bates, Santa Barbara, Cal.)

Santa Barbara, March 1, 1876.

Our town is but a very small and a very new one. Owing to its favorable situation — on a slope, gently inclined to the ocean, the daily breezes from the ocean reaching it, — and, until very recently, containing a small number of inhabitants, drainage was not the necessity it is in other places. Now, however, that it is becoming a place of more importance, and a favorite resort of invalids, a thorough system of drainage is in contemplation, and will be carried out before long. During the past six years, I have been a resident of this place; and, with the exception of a few cases of typhoid fever, I have seen no diseases, that I could fairly ascribe to lack of sanitary measures.

(From Dr. J. H. McKee, Los Angelos, Cal.)

Los Angelos, Cal., Feb. 29, 1876.

Having made this place my permanent home, I send some responses pertaining to this State, &c.; but for the State I cannot answer fully, as I have not full data at hand. I have been health officer here for over a year; but our City Council give little support to efforts for sanitary improvement. I am now out of the office. No successor has been appointed, as the Council choose to save the petty salary to the treasury during the winter months.

COLORADO.

(From Dr. Charles Denison, Denver, Col.)

Denver, April 24, 1876.

When I received your letter of inquiry, our Legislature was just coming together. I therefore delayed answering, in order to get at something of use to write you.

The Legislature established a Territorial Board of Health; giving it much to do, and but little pay. The Board consists of nine physicians, appointed by the Governor.

The Board of Health of the city of Denver has important duties to perform, due to the peculiar necessities of the climate, in establishing a system of sewerage; procuring a water supply, so that it will be perfectly pure when the city has been long in existence and largely increased in size; and in promoting good ventilation, for the health of invalids sojourning in this peculiar climate. The new Board of Health is composed of the Mayor, Dr. Buckingham, and four physicians, including the city physician. We have our first important meeting this week.[1]

(From Dr. David Mack, Jr., Los Pinos Indian Agency.)

Los Pinos Indian Agency, Col., 30th May, 1875.

Dr. Henry I. Bowditch, Boston, Mass.

Dear Sir:

. . . .

I was fortunate in making the journey out here, although late in December, without drawback of any kind; having finished my journey before the great snow blockade of the railroads, and the cold, that came on just after the first of the year.

Although the cold weather prevented me from enjoying the journey through the mountains to this place, I still believe that it would always seem less beautiful and attractive than I had expected of a trip in the midst of, and crossing, the Rocky Mountains. They are very *rocky*, bleak, bare, but not grand. There

---

[1] In answer to 2d question (viz., whether any law of development of any disease had been discovered, attention to which in the future will tend to lessen disease), he says, "Approximatively only." "There is a great saving of years and of comfort to asthmatics and consumptives, coming from the rest of the United States to this elevated country."

are no forests worthy of the name; the varieties of timber being few, — chiefly, smallest pines, firs, some spruces and aspens.

On the road from Cañon City, at the end of the railroad, to here, there were some three or four picturesque scenes. Mr. S. W. Bowles, of the "Springfield Republican," in his "Switzerland of America," speaks similarly of the trips he took in these mountains. . . . While last winter was unusually severe throughout the greater part of the country, and even at Cañon City, Pueblo, and Denver; in this part of the mountains, it was unusually mild. There was less extreme cold; 20° below zero being our lowest here, while last year it was 40° below. The snow, too, was quite scarce in January and February; so that, quite unexpectedly to myself, it was frequently pleasant to take horseback rides in those months; and in March, when most snow fell, there was at no time more than two feet on the ground at once, while the year before they had over three feet. But, the snow is very dry here; and we often have high winds, which make travelling difficult, and dangerous also. I enclose a copy of the temperatures, taken during last January and February, which may be of interest to you; and am sorry that the others were burned, or I should have sent more.[1] Our elevation here is 9,250 feet, according to Hayden's surveying party; and this place is on the Pacific slope, about seventeen miles southwest from the Coochetopa Pass, in the Sierra Madre range of the Rocky Mountains. Frost occurs every month in the year, and nearly every night; so that no crops can be raised, and the Indians are about here only some five months in the year. They are thus very little brought under civilizing influences. And, as the Bureau found out from Mr. Bond that this place is not on the reservation, it has ordered the agency to be removed; and Mr. Bond is now looking at a new site in the Uncompahgre Valley, a branch of the Gunnison and that of the Colorado, where, at about 5,000 feet elevation, there is a beautiful valley, with rich land, and a climate so much milder, that corn, melons, &c., can be grown there. Life there would be far more agreeable than here, and the Indians might be induced to learn herding and farming; which as yet, though very friendly and good-natured, they are quite indisposed to do. At this alti-

[1] See end of letter.

tude, our barometer averages 21.5 inches, and water boils at so low a temperature (though I don't know at what) that cooking is very different from what it is at sea level. Eggs require some fifteen minutes to be well and hard done, and some vegetables and meats have to be partly cooked the day before they are eaten. The air is so dry that the snow would rapidly disappear into it, leaving very little mud behind: quite different from what it is at the East. The absence of moisture is, I presume, the cause of the great brilliancy of the sun, moon, and stars, which I have never seen equalled elsewhere. In winter time, snow blindness is quite common in consequence, but partly owing to the great carelessness of the travelling miners, who usually have no protection for their eyes. Some smear charcoal around their eyes, and insist that their eyes feel the glare less thus. Not only men, but horses, mules, asses, and dogs, are made snow-blind, and I have seen instances of each during the winter. The moonlight is often so bright that the outlines of the surrounding mountains are as distinct at night as by day, and the stars are wonderfully bright. During all the winter, I did not once see the Northern Lights; but, instead, something I never saw elsewhere, the Zodiacal Light, which was very clear and distinct an hour or so after sundown, — more so, considerably, than the Milky Way. The dryness of the air is so irritating to the mucous membranes, that chronic catarrhs are rather common, and quite troublesome, in the mountains. Another consequence of the dryness is the rapid radiation of heat, which is very noticeable in the rapid changes of temperature after sundown, which I never noticed so sudden elsewhere. So far as I have experienced, the most common difficulty, in coming to this height, is a disturbance of the heart and lungs; making one very easily out of breath, and bringing on palpitation, even on slight exertion. Severe exercise, even after a residence of some years, is not as well borne as lower down. For myself, I have noticed no trouble of the kind for some time, unless when taking violent exercise. I have heard that those having weak lungs cannot safely come rapidly into the high mountains. One person here, with weak lungs, had discomfort, almost pain, about the chest for a good deal of the time in winter, which was not felt at a place some 1,500 feet lower down. I have

been told that menstruation is apt to be more profuse at this height than lower. Another person, subject to sick-headaches, has them more frequently here than at the East; but I do not know that this is usual. Although our air is usually so very dry, there has been, during the present month, an unusual amount of rain; and something of a thunder-storm almost every day, as well as rain or hail. These come and are gone quite rapidly, so that our weather is very changeable. These sudden changes are not well suited to rheumatics, and most people think the mountains a bad place for such persons. I have slight trouble from rheumatic twinges; but as I am not overworked, and have good opportunity of taking care of myself, I get along very well. Still, I have seen some who have had their rheumatism come upon them while making short trips in the mountains. The Indians are troubled with this disease a good deal. The sky here, at this season of the year, is very beautiful indeed; and the sunsets gorgeous, and of very great variety. Very often rain, or mist, falls very gently, and hangs down like long curtains from the sky, adding an unusual appearance. Similar veils of snow, ceasing abruptly, and coming in front of mountains on which the sun is shining, pass slowly across the valley at times, and are very beautiful, — like great lace veils sailing across some immense stage. So you see that there are features of interest in this region, although the forests, and vegetation generally, are not striking. Sage brush and grease wood are very common on the foot-hills; pine, fir, spruce, and aspen, higher up; and in the meadows, a coarse grass, generally looking like hay, though now considerably mingled with green. Game, which most people would expect to be plenty here, is very hard to find, and pretty scarce. . . . These Ute Indians are very good-natured, but very little disposed to be civilized. They have never liked to have a school, and recently the Bureau ordered the one here to be discontinued. Hardly any of them dress in their original manner, having clothes served out to them by government. All the men have one gun, or more, — many, revolvers; and their chief wealth, which they value, is in ponies, many of which are quite handsome, and which they will not sell, except at high rates. They are great gamblers, — women as well as men, — and their goods change hands soon after being

COLORADO.

served out. The crack of their rifles is heard almost any half hour in the day; for they are always shooting for prizes. Chronic conjunctivitis, catarrhs, muscular rheumatism, constipation, and indigestion seem, so far as I have experienced, to be their chief troubles. I have a few cases of bronchitis and lung fever. Acute rheumatism and venereal diseases are pretty common, I hear. I was called to a midwifery case, which was tedious; but, as I was not allowed to examine at all to learn what to do, I refused to give any medicine, which was all they wanted. The difficulty of making one's self fully understood makes treating them quite unsatisfactory. . . .

TEMPERATURES TAKEN AT LOS PINOS INDIAN AGENCY, COLORADO, IN JANUARY AND FEBRUARY, 1875.

1875.	7 A.M.	12 M.	9 P.M.	1875.	7 A.M.	12 M.	9 P.M.
January 1	− 8	+ 8	—	February 1	−12	+22	0
,, 2	0	+32	+12	,, 2	+10	+10	− 4
,, 3	+ 8	+36	+12	,, 3	+ 6	+30	0
,, 4	+ 6	+28	+20	,, 4	− 5	+28	+ 2
,, 5	+20	+25	+13	,, 5	− 9	+18	+ 8
,, 6	−13	+30	− 1	,, 6	+12	+32	+ 2
,, 7	−10	—	+23	,, 7	+10	+36	+20
,, 8	—	—	+20	,, 8	+ 3	+30	+18
,, 9	+14	—	—	,, 9	+15	+30	+20
,, 10	+10	—	—	,, 10	+12	+20	+10
,, 11	+10	+24	+19	,, 11	− 6	+29	+ 6
,, 12	+17	+19	+ 9	,, 12	+ 3	+32	+12
,, 13	+10	+24	+23	,, 13	0	+32	+11
,, 14	+23	+34	+29	,, 14	+ 8	+32	+ 7
,, 15	+29	+32	+30	,, 15	− 2	+24	+10
,, 16	+22	+30	+32	,, 16	+ 5	+27	+12
,, 17	+26	+32	+30	,, 17	+ 8	+34	+22
,, 18	+26	+32	+33	,, 18	+20	+24	+ 7
,, 19	+13	+40	+20	,, 19	+ 8	+20	+17
,, 20	+28	+31	+26	,, 20	+18	+26	+14
,, 21	+ 7	+20	− 8	,, 21	+ 2	+30	+22
,, 22	−20	+12	− 6	,, 22	+10	+30	+13
,, 23	−16	+18	− 8	,, 23	+ 8	+28	+11
,, 24	−20	+16	+ 6	,, 24	+13	+17	0
,, 25	0	+19	+14	,, 25	0	+28	0
,, 26	+10	+37	+26	,, 26	− 2	—	—
,, 27	+ 8	+31	+ 6	,, 27	− 4	—	—
,, 28	+ 6	+26	+16	,, 28	+ 8	—	—
,, 29	+12	+26	+20				
,, 30	+ 9	+26	+ 4				
,, 31	+ 8	+30	0				

CONNECTICUT.

(From Dr. Benjamin H. Catlin, W. Meriden, Conn.)

W. Meriden, April 8, 1876.

One of the questions, and perhaps the most important one, related to a State board of health. That I cannot answer.[1]

I find, by examining the statutes of Connecticut, that as early as 1750 the Legislature enacted laws respecting the diseases then prevalent, particularly small-pox and yellow fever.

They also provided for the care of the sick. Officers were directed to see that the sick had nurses, and they were authorized to impress men, if none were willing to engage in such capacity. About 1821 (it might have been earlier), laws were enacted constituting the civil authority (justice of the peace), and selectmen of the several towns a board of health. These laws remain substantially the same to the present time. "It shall be lawful for such board, or such health officer, or health officers, or health committee, to examine into all nuisances, with power to remove them."

These laws have been practically a dead letter, except during the prevalence of some contagious or infectious diseases, as small-pox or cholera. The cities of the State have health officers, which are more efficient than those in the towns.

An act was passed, May session, 1848, making provision for the registration of births, marriages, and deaths, and the first report was presented May session, 1849; since which, reports have been made regularly, with the exception of 1853.

The State Librarian, who makes up the reports, writes me: "I have no means of knowing just how complete the records of births and deaths are, but am certain that the duty of their office is very ill performed by some registrars." We have no board of health, in the modern acceptation of the term; the old law being mostly a dead letter.

Considerable effort has been made by some of the physicians of the State to have new laws passed, constituting a board of health, which shall also have charge of the registration of births and deaths. The Legislature of 1874 authorized the Governor

[1] Connecticut has no State Board of Health. — H. I. B.

to appoint a number of gentlemen, physicians and laymen, to consider the subject, and report to the Legislature of 1875.

The committee had several meetings, and proposed a law for the appointment of a board of health, which was presented to the Legislature. I cannot learn that any action was taken on the report by the Legislature. Dr. Lindsley, of New Haven, informed me that the proposition was opposed, he thought, on political grounds. The registrars in some of the towns have considerable income from their office; and they, as well as others, are opposed to any change in the law.

We intend to continue pressing the subject upon the attention of legislators; and hope, after a time, longer or shorter, we shall succeed. If, next November, we elect a Republican Legislature, we shall have greater hopes of succeeding.

The disease variously called spotted fever, typhus syncopalis, or cerebro-spinal meningitis, has prevailed during the last century, and was not known to have prevailed during the Colonial times. It first appeared in Medfield, Mass., in 1806, and in Connecticut, in 1807. I would refer you to a Report on Climatology and Epidemic Diseases of Connecticut, in the 16th volume (1865) of the "Transactions of the American Medical Association," p. 469. I endeavored, in that article, to refer to every publication.

(From Dr. C. M. CARLETON, Norwich, Conn.)

Our State has passed laws giving cities and towns ample powers in relation to matters of health; but no action is taken unless diseases of a contagious nature break out, such as smallpox, &c. In this section of the State, phthisis and pneumonia are the most frequent causes of death.

(From Dr. STEPHEN G. HUBBARD, New Haven.)

NEW HAVEN, April 3, 1876.

The State of Connecticut has as yet done nothing for the public health, in the direction indicated by your queries. Twenty years ago, I began the agitation of the subject anew (it had before been fruitlessly talked about), and prepared a bill for a public act, which I fought through two legislatures,

and which was enacted by the session of 1856 (?), after having been emasculated of many of its most important provisions. By statute, as of old, every town has a "board of health:" but it has had a vital existence only in exceptional cases, and that only for brief periods; such as the prevalence of some epidemic, — small-pox, and once or twice of yellow fever.

More recently an attempt has been made, and not yet abandoned, by . . . . to procure the creation by the Legislature of a State Board of Health, with considerable salaries provided.

The movement, begun in good faith by persons competent to serve the State with honesty and fidelity, ... has thus far failed of securing the co-operation of the few men of the State, who really have *any* knowledge of the science of Public Hygiene.

. . . .

At present, therefore, the status and interests of this exceedingly important subject have not received, in Connecticut, such attention as they deserve. . . .

(From Ashbel Woodward, Franklin, Conn.)

7. In answer to question No. 7, I would state that Connecticut was scourged with a peculiar form of typhus gravior, or spotted fever, from the year 1807 to the winter of 1812 and 1813, causing great mortality. This form of fever has not prevailed since.

The cholera asphyxia, so fatal in 1832, prevailed only for a brief season.

Some other diseases which still prevail, as the small-pox, croup, &c., are much more manageable than formerly.

8. Of the diseases which have appeared of late, I will mention intermittent fever, albuminuria, cerebro-spinal meningitis, diphtheritis, &c. If these last are not new diseases, they are forms of trouble better understood than formerly.

DISTRICT OF COLUMBIA.

I wrote to J. S. Billings, Assistant Surgeon U. S. A., requesting his opinion as to the influence the late civil war, and the Army Museum and Library, had had on Public Hygiene. His reply is as follows:—

Surgeon-General's Office,
Washington, D.C., Jan. 4, 1876.

Your note of January 1st just received.

The influence of the Medical Department of the Government upon the progress of Public Hygiene, being almost entirely indirect, is very difficult to estimate. In what I may say on this subject, I shall only speak of the army.

Every one knows that the most effective sanitary teachers are pestilence and war and the cholera; and our recent military experiences have done more for the cause of Public Hygiene in this country than any other agencies.

There are now scattered, all over the country, physicians who have had more or less army experience, and whose ideas about remediable causes of disease, and the best mode of dealing with them, have been, to a considerable extent, derived from that source. The causes and prevention of disease have but a small place in our schemes of medical education. The army medical officer has not only a direct and personal interest in the preservation of the health of his command, but his attention is daily called to it by the bigness of his morning's sick-report; and he has the great advantage, over his brother in civil life, of having the means of estimating the effect of his work. He is stimulated and guided by daily statistics of disease, and not by mortality statistics, issued a year or two too late to be much more than a source of regret. His faith, therefore, in the efficacy and necessity of pure air and water, and of cleanliness, is a living one, derived from repeated experiences, and not a mere formula derived from text-books.

Were it possible to present to the households of a city, in each morning paper, the statistics of the cases of disease occurring the day before, with streets and numbers, the interest, taken in Public Hygiene by that community, would increase amazingly.

Another lesson, that is better learned in the army than elsewhere, is the necessity of occasional sacrifices for the general good. And this is a lesson that must be learned, before the position and work of a public sanitarian can be made satisfactory.

Just how far, and in what way, it is proper to curtail individual liberty, and give certain men power over the property of others, is an old and grave question. *The real trouble is to get the right men.*

I enclose a list of the publications of this office relating more or less directly to Hygiene.

With regard to hospitals, I think that the book recently published by the Trustees of the Johns Hopkins Hospital, at Baltimore, is a summary of the present knowledge on that subject; and military hospitals have done much to shape the opinions there expressed.

In forming the National Medical Library, which is at present under the charge of the Medical Department of the Army, special attention has been given to the section on Hygiene; for it is recognized as probable that the day is not far distant, when legislation on this subject will be undertaken by the general government, in which case all the data obtainable will be required. To obtain a good collection of this class of literature requires rather vigilance and labor than money, since most of the statistical documents, upon which the foundations of the science rest, are official publications, and are not obtained through the ordinary channels of trade.

P. S. — I am very much afraid that, in the present rage for economy, the small appropriation for our library will be cut off or down. I hope that you will be here in a month or so, to raise the voice of the medical profession in Boston against such a step, if it is taken.

LIST OF ARMY PUBLICATIONS REFERRED TO IN THIS LETTER.

Statistical Report on the Sickness and Mortality in the Army of the United States. Compiled from the records of the Surgeon and Adjutant General's Offices; embracing a period of twenty years, from January, 1819, to January, 1839. Pre-

pared under the direction of Thomas Lawson, Surgeon-General. Washington, 1840.

Statistical Report on the Sickness and Mortality in the Army of the United States. Compiled from the records of the Surgeon-General's Office, by R. H. Coolidge; embracing a period of sixteen years, from 1839 to January, 1855. 4to. Washington, 1856.

[The same.] Embracing a period of five years, from 1855 to 1860. 515 pp. Washington, 1860.

Circular No. 1.   June 10, 1868.

Report on Epidemic Cholera and Yellow Fever in the Army of the United States during the Year 1867. By J. J. Woodward, Assistant Surgeon U. S. A. Washington, Government Printing Office, 1868.

Circular No. 4.   1870.

Report on Barracks and Hospitals, with Descriptions of Military Posts. [John S. Billings.] Washington, &c., 1870.

Circular No. 5.   May 4, 1867.

Report on Epidemic Cholera in the Army of the United States during the Year 1866. [By J. J. Woodward.] Washington, &c., 1867.

Circular No. 8.   May 1, 1875.

Report on the Hygiene of the United States Army, with Descriptions of Military Posts. Washington, &c., 1875.

Circular No 15.

Sickness and Mortality in the Army during the First Year of the War. Surgeon-General's Office, Washington, Sept. 8, 1863. 8 pp. 8vo.

A Medical Report upon the Uniform and Clothing of the Soldiers of the United States Army. By A. A. Woodhull, Assistant Surgeon U. S. A., Washington, 1868.

Letter from the Secretary of War; communicating, in obedience to law, information in regard to quarantine on the South-

ern and Gulf coasts. [Report of Assistant Surgeon Harvey E. Brown, U. S. A., with communication from the Surgeon-General U. S. A. in regard to same.] Senate 42d Congress, 3d Session, Ex. Doc. 9, parts 1 and 2, 117. 2 pp. 8vo. [1872.]

The Cholera Epidemic of 1873 in the United States. Reports prepared under the direction of the Surgeon of the Army. 1875.

(From J. M. Toner. M.D., Washington, D.C.)

Washington, D.C., April 1, 1876.

I have filled the inquiries to the best of my ability.

As our government rests on the will of the people, it is fair to presume that laws will be passed, as early as they can be appreciated and efficiently executed.

As sanitarians, we are at sixes and sevens, as to the extent of powers that ought to be given to boards of health. We have not agreed upon this among ourselves. Should its officers remove nuisances through the ordinary channels of courts, so as to insure the rights of all citizens; or should they have legislative and executive powers in the same body? If so, this will be an anomaly in our government. Is such a course and condition of laws necessary? We have much to do to educate the public mind, as well as to accumulate, in the profession, a stock of exact information on sanitary science. That we are progressing in this direction, I think, is manifest to all unprejudiced minds.

I wrote to J. J. Woodward, Assistant Surgeon U. S. A., asking his opinion as to the influence of the Army Medical Museum and Library on Public Hygiene; and his reply is as follows: —

Washington, D.C., Jan. 19, 1876.

In reply to your inquiry of January 17th, I unhesitatingly express the opinion, that a great collection of pathological anatomy, like the Army Medical Museum, if it continues to receive such pecuniary support from Congress, that its development and growth may be continuous, must certainly exercise a beneficial influence upon the public health, and especially by aiding medical investigators, in their study of the causes of dis-

eases, a knowledge of which underlies all wise preventive measures.

Undoubtedly, the chief reason, why our best preventive measures fall so far short of our need, is because we have so little exact knowledge of the causes of disease. I know it is fashionable for certain sanitarians to talk flippantly, in public addresses, as if we knew all about these causes; and I am often moved by scorn and pity at the complacency, with which they utter their platitudes. But those, who know most of disease, know best how inadequate are the general causes, which figure in the sanitary jargon of the day, to produce the specific morbid processes, which are causing so much sickness and death around us; and we recognize humbly how much we have got to learn with regard to etiology.

The causes of disease must, of course, be investigated otherwise than by the road of pathological anatomy alone. Especially is the path of experimental pathology full of promise: but the knowledge of the morbid processes, which can only be attained by the help of anatomical investigation, is an indispensable collateral study; and so much remains to be done in this direction that, for a long time to come, the activity of many industrious workers will be required.

So long as this is the case, museums such as ours is becoming, and ought to be, must have a vast sphere of usefulness. It is vain to hope such institutions will grow up without government patronage; for they require what is to individuals considerable pecuniary outlay, and bring in no pecuniary recompense. Recognizing this fact, every civilized government in the world, except our own, has long granted liberal pecuniary aid to institutions of this class. The Army Medical Museum is the first step of our own government in the right direction.

In conclusion, I may add that the Library of the Surgeon-General's Office cannot fail to exercise a beneficial influence in the same direction. It is already the largest medical library in America.

The same pecuniary reasons, which must prevent the establishment of a great pathological museum except by government aid, will prevent the creation of a great medical library, except with the same assistance. I cannot but hope that our

legislators will have the intelligence to sustain these promising nurslings, to whose future growth all medical investigators and scholars in the United States look forward with so much hope.

FLORIDA.

(From GEORGE W. BELTON, Tallahassee, Fla.)

TALLAHASSEE, Feb. 16, 1876.

I regret to say that our State has as yet made but little progress in Public Hygiene, or in any "scientific investigations" as to the cause of disease. We have just organized a State Medical Society; within the last two years. At the next meeting of the Legislature, a committee, appointed for the purpose, will apply for a charter to organize a State Board of Health; and probably two years more will see it in operation. Our town is situated on a high hill, 250 feet above the level of the Gulf. No permanent sanitary laws or ordinances have been established. The rains wash the streets, and the city carts carry off the offal. We have no sewers. Intermittent fever is the prevailing disease in the autumn, though sometimes we are exempt from that. We have no epidemic diseases to ravage the country. Scarlatina is very rare, and apt to appear sporadically, when it does break out. No diphtheria, small-pox, and very rarely the measles. Dr. A. S. Baldwin will send, or probably has sent, you a copy of his address on "Climate in its Relation to Medicine, Preventive and Remedial."

GEORGIA.

The following appears in the "Daily Constitution," published in Atlanta, Georgia, Feb. 10, 1877. It fully illustrates what is stated in the Address, that only under the influence of terror from an epidemic do individuals or States act efficiently in endeavoring to ward off deadly epidemics. The late epidemic of yellow fever in Savannah will do immense good, if it so stimulate the people of Georgia that they will, by State and municipal action, thoroughly inaugurate State Preventive Medicine.

THE HEALTH OF OUR SEABOARD.

"Our sister city of Savannah, which was so terribly scourged last summer, is, we are glad to observe, taking measures to prevent a recurrence of the plague. A health ordinance has been introduced in the City Council, which, in our opinion, will go far towards achieving that much-desired result. The ordinance in question provides for the creation of a Sanitary Board, composed of the mayor and the health officers as *ex officio* members, two aldermen, and three citizens, whose duty it shall be to supervise the administration of all the health laws of the city. Among other things, it is made the duty of every practising physician in the city to report to the Board every case of contagious, infectious, or pestilential disease, that he may be called upon to treat; and the report must be made within twenty-four hours, after the character of the disease has been ascertained; and every citizen, upon whose premises such diseases occur, is required in like manner to report, provided such cases are not under treatment by a physician. The Board is to have the aid, whenever it is deemed necessary, of the city attorney, city surveyor, city marshal, and the police force. Quarantine regulations are also provided for; but, in the very nature of things, these provisions are inadequate. In the harbor of New York, every vessel at the quarantine station, from an infected port or elsewhere, is placed under a guard furnished by the health officer. This system is expensive; but it is perfect."

"Savannah, however, has been so impoverished by the recent epidemic, that it is almost too much to expect that such a system will be inaugurated in her harbor; and it is out of the question to suppose that it can be adopted at either Brunswick or Doboy. Without this special guard, no quarantine system is perfect. The captain of a vessel may be in collusion with his crew, or the crew may elude the supervision of their superior officers, — a supervision that is by no means rigid in port; and yet it is absolutely necessary that a perfect system of quarantine be established at our seaports during the coming summer. It seems to us that this is a subject that might better engage the attention of our legislators than some of the questions, with which they have lately been wrestling. They could do no bet-

ter service for Georgia than by establishing a system of quarantine, to be upheld and maintained by the State in co-operation with the quarantine officers of our sea-coast cities. Such a system might be made to apply particularly to Brunswick and Doboy. It is utterly impossible for these points, in their present condition, to maintain a perfect quarantine, — such a quarantine as the welfare of their inhabitants demands. The health officers of our ports are efficient and tireless; but all their efforts will be in vain, if vessels from ports supposed to be infected are not placed under the personal surveillance of trustworthy men. The report of our State Board of Health, which we took occasion to review in these columns recently, shows, almost beyond a doubt, that the yellow fever plague was brought by foreign vessels to every point on the Georgia sea-coast where it made its appearance, and this, in spite of the quarantine regulations that now exist."

While these sheets are printing, I receive the report made by Drs. J. P. Logan and George Little, in behalf of the State Board of Health, upon the recent epidemic of yellow fever at Savannah. The following are some of the conclusions of the committee : —

" We find that the course of the fever in this epidemic was, to a great extent, the duplicate of its history in other localities, in following the lines of trade and travel, as illustrated on the Gulf coast, in Louisiana and Texas." The committee further say that " the direct argument is equally conclusive as to the efficacy of quarantine, with disinfection, as strikingly exhibited in connection with the practical working of these measures in the ports of New York, New Orleans, Philadelphia, Baltimore, Natchez, on the coast of Texas, and elsewhere." But " it is admitted that in Savannah, and probably to a greater or less extent at other points where the fever prevailed, local influences operated largely in extending the disease," and making it more malignant. Hence, the argument must be drawn in favor of a reasonable quarantine and thorough cleansing of vessels, disinfection of persons and places, and, as far as possible, perfect sanitary arrangements in the locality on which the pest falls.

ILLINOIS.

(From Dr. S. P. BREED, Princeton, Ill.)

PRINCETON, ILL., Feb. 6, 1876.

I herewith return your circular, with such replies as I am able to make. In regard to the first and second questions, it seems proper that I should make this explanation: We have no State Board of Health in our State. The State, as such, has not attempted any scientific investigations, or authorized any survey for sanitary purposes. But the Legislature has, from time to time, granted charters to towns and cities, with liberal provisions for carrying out such sanitary measures, as they seem to require. Under such charters, all these matters are left entirely to these municipal authorities. Every considerable town, I believe, has its board of health; and some of them are thoroughly organized and equipped, with a sanitary superintendent, boards for inspection of food, and proper officers to look after the question of sewage, house offal, and street drainage. Perhaps few cities are better provided and equipped, in these particulars, than Chicago.

In case of imminent danger to our cities from threatened small-pox, cholera, or any other contagious or infectious diseases, ample powers are given to boards of health to take such preventive measures, as they deem necessary to secure the safety of the inhabitants, as far as practicable. Such timely measures have, there can be no reasonable doubt, in several instances, saved many of the people from falling victims to these diseases. You will, no doubt, get full information from these boards themselves.

2–e. In answer to this question, as to whether our State has instituted any measures to prevent cattle disease, I may say, that, immediately, when that immense stream of Texas cattle was passing through our State on its way to Eastern cities, it was soon found that, when these cattle came in contact with our native herds, they communicated to them, or left in their trail, the germs of a fatal distemper, which swept off vast numbers of our own cattle. Many of our largest cattle-dealers in this State were themselves extensively engaged in bringing for-

ward these Texas cattle. By mixing them up with their native herds, they soon found themselves suffering greatly by the loss of many of their most valuable stock by this "Texas Fever." The infection spread far and wide; but the excitement and feeling of apprehension among our people extended much further. Much obscurity at first necessarily prevailed in regard to the nature and cause of the disease; and our farmers along the line of transit, who suffered most, fearing that this disease might become epidemic, and thereby permanently injure their business of cattle-trading, threatened, in their blind rage, to tear up the railroad track, and otherwise oppose by force the passage of the Texas cattle through our State. Vast numbers of diseased cattle might be seen at almost any of the stockyards of the cities from Chicago to New York City. Added to the feeling of apprehension here among our home dealers, the fear in the Eastern cities was quite as great lest their supply of wholesome meats should be cut off. Moreover, it was feared that some of these diseased animals might be slaughtered and sold in their markets, and thereby communicate disease to the human subject. In this state of excitement and alarm, all parties were put on the *qui vive* to find out the true state of affairs, to know the extent of the danger, and, if possible, to provide for it. The Boards of Health in Chicago, Cincinnati, Buffalo, and New York, immediately put into operation the most effective measures at their command to investigate the whole subject, and reduce the phenomena, if possible, to something like order, by discovering the true nature of the affection and its laws of development. Owners of these herds freely gave up their diseased cattle to be slaughtered for *post mortem* inspection. The chemist, the pathologist, the microscopist, with the latest researches of their sciences, were put to work. Money was not spared to obtain the ablest adepts in these branches to unveil the mysteries. All the facts within reach were sought. An extensive correspondence was opened with various parties, whose opportunities had enabled them to observe the peculiarities of this distemper, from all parts of the country, — from East to West. Months were thus spent in this investigation. Rarely, if ever before, perhaps, were so many and so varied appliances, so much money, employed in so short a time, for the investiga-

tion of any disease. Human health and human life, and more potent than these, perhaps, vast sums of money, great pecuniary interests, were at stake. During this investigation, important facts were discovered; but it was seen that nothing effectual could be done by local efforts. These facts, while they remained in the possession of these few experts, could avail nothing in formulating and executing preventive measures. In the midst of this perplexing state of affairs, some one (I do not know who it was) had the good sense to recommend a general convention of cattle-dealers from all the States interested, in order to collect and publish to the world all the information, that had been and could be obtained, bearing upon the subject; and, moreover, to prepare the draft of a law, which should be uniform in all the States interested in the raising, purchase, and sale of cattle, with the view of regulating the trade on a safe and equal basis, and securing the most perfect protection possible to all parties. In compliance with this recommendation, commissioners having been duly appointed from, I believe, all the Northern States, from Massachusetts to Kansas, together with the Dominion of Canada, the then Governor of Illinois, Richard J. Oglesby, invited said commissioners to hold their convention at Springfield, Illinois, on the first day of December, 1868. The Convention met pursuant to said call; and it was a very interesting sight to see so many men, coming from so many States, each bearing his budget of news, facts, and figures; practical, observing, business men, scientific men, patient investigators in the minutest details of the pathology of the disease, together with philanthropists, intent on doing all in their power to protect the lives and health of the people, — all joining hands in one common effort to meet and obviate a threatened evil.

You will find a full report of the proceedings in the Transactions of the Agricultural Society for 1868.[1]

[1] Transactions Illinois Agricultural Society for 1868: Cattle Commissioners' Report, p. 134. Also, Texas Cattle, p. 426.
Report of the Department of Agriculture of United States, 1868–69, pp. 4, 5, 38.
Report of New York State Cattle Commissioners, 1868. Sen. Doc. Rinderpest, very full and valuable report, with plates.
Massachusetts Commissioners' Report. E. T. Thayer, January, 1869. Sen. Doc.

Nothing could be more satisfactory or trustworthy than some of the reports from these experts from the Metropolitan Board of Health of New York. I will not stop to give the details of the discoveries, made with the microscope in this disease; for it is a part of the history of the triumph of science during the nineteenth century. And I doubt not you have the excellent Report of the New York Board on that subject; but I will close this note by saying that our State Legislature soon after passed the law recommended by the Cattle Commissioners' Convention, and I think other States did the same. Some seven years elapsed since that Convention met, and during this time, so effectually was its work performed, that no occasion of anxiety or alarm has ever occurred in our State since the adoption of the measures recommended by that Convention.[1]

I do not know whether there is any thing in all this that will be of any use to you in your forthcoming Centennial Address; but it seems to be a direct answer to one of your questions, and it strikes me that the facts here briefly presented are of great importance.

To promptly meet this new phase of danger to a great people, with the varied appliances of scientific skill now at our command, — to satisfactorily demonstrate its nature, causes, and cure, and to put in operation the various forces, necessarily diversified and complex, to bring about the ultimate result, — was an Herculean task.

6–e. I am not able to state what laws our Legislature has passed for the drainage of lands; though there must be some enactments for this purpose, for there are several places along the rivers where considerable money has been expended for that purpose. But it is probable that the object has been chiefly to redeem the lands, and not improve the health of the people. A corps of men are now cutting a ditch through an embankment below Alton, for the purpose of draining Long Lake. It is interesting to note, in this connection, that this ditch has opened an ancient burying-ground, revealing skeletons supposed to be those of the mound-builders, together with such relics as are commonly found interred with their dead.

[1] Account of Convention of Dealers at Springfield, Ill. Twelve States, and Ontario County, Canada, being represented by thirty-six commissioners, with rules and resolutions adopted by them.

In regard to our own country, I will say that, some ten years ago, one-half of the lands in three of the townships in Bureau County were, during a great portion of the year, quite covered with water, varying from a few inches to several feet deep.

They were called swamp lands, and were, by act of Congress, donated to the State, and by the State to the county. The county authorities, on coming into possession of them, had them surveyed, by which the practicability of draining them was demonstrated. Commissioners were appointed by the County Court, and the work of draining, under contract, immediately commenced. This work has been continued for several years, until it is now completed. Over one hundred miles of linear ditching have been done. Through some twenty miles of this, called the "heavy work," the ditch ranges from two to five feet in depth, and twenty feet in width on the bottom. This is the main ditch. Side ditches, narrower and shallower, are made to bring the water into the main passage. Dykes have also been thrown up in several places where they were thought necessary. In this work some one hundred and seventy-five thousand dollars ($175,000) have been expended by the county. The result is, that about thirty-six thousand acres of these inundated or swamp lands have been either greatly improved or quite redeemed. Twenty thousand acres, hitherto of little or no value, have been converted into excellent pasture and meadow lands, while no inconsiderable portion has been rendered good tillage land. Thus, by these means, thousands of acres, once nearly covered with water, swampy, and grown up and covered with reeds, brakes, and coarse grass, interspersed with knolls covered with small trees and tanglewood, the favorite haunts of water fowls, reptiles, and musk-rats, sending forth over the adjacent country a noisome and pestilential miasm, have been converted into dry land, rich pastures, and meadows, where vast herds of cattle may be seen cropping the rich and luxuriant grasses. As a natural sequence, although it does not appear to have had any influence in inducing the powers that be to do the work, the health of the people in these townships has been incidentally improved; and, moreover, as the county has been rendered more inviting, a new and better class of citizens has gone there to live. All the lands have greatly increased in

value, so that this part of the country is destined to be one of the richest and best settlements in the county.

The proceeds of the sales of these lands have already reimbursed the county, with a surplus of several thousand dollars, added to the school fund.

While we are clearly within the limits of the catarrhal zone (41° 30′ north latitude), we still feel, to some extent, the influence of the great malarial zone south of us. This imaginary line, separating these two zones, is not distinctly drawn. There appears to be a tendency to vibrate occasionally sometimes further north, and at others to recede further southward, with a gradual mitigation of the severity of the affections. Several seasons will sometimes pass during which we have little or none of the malarial fevers, when, perhaps, under exceptional circumstances, a season will, now and then, occur in which this element will be a decided characteristic of a large number of our diseases. While these malarial affections are by no means as common or as severe as formerly, the catarrhal and pulmonary diseases are correspondingly increased. Whether the time will ever come when this particular region will enjoy an entire immunity from the former affections or not, we are quite unable to predict. But, should we feel justified in promising ourselves such a result, it may reasonably be questioned, in view of the apparent alternative, viz., a substitution of a corresponding increase of the less manageable diseases, such as tuberculosis, scarlatina, diphtheria, &c., whether the outlook would be particularly inviting, or the result more desirable.

As the county becomes improved, settled, and generally cultivated, the diseases prevalent have undergone a change, and some of them, that were a terror to the early settlers, are now but seldom heard of or seen. Of this class may be mentioned the malignant, congestive types of fever, milk-sickness, and the Illinois mange.

There was a temporary recurrence of the last disease during the war, under the title of "army itch," or prurigo; but I think we have had nothing like it for several years. I do not believe that any sanitary measures, directed especially to the removal of these affections, have had any influence in bringing about this result.

I think our diseases are less violent in their attack, and more chronic in character; and, moreover, less amenable to treatment.

Probably, over one-half of the deaths are from catarrhal and pulmonary affections.

When I read your circular, I thought I would answer some of your questions more fully; but indisposition of body has rendered me unable to do so.

These few thoughts, crudely thrown together, must suffice.

(From Dr. Nathan S. Davis, Chicago, Ill.)

"The supervisors, assessors, and town-clerk of every township shall constitute a board of health; and, on the breaking out of any contagious disease in their township or immediate vicinity, they shall have power to make and enforce any rules and regulations tending to check the spreading of such disease within the limits of their townships, as they may deem proper; and for this purpose they shall have power to shut up any house where any infected person may be, or remove such person to any pest-house within the limits of such township," &c.

The City of Chicago has a Board of Health, composed of three physicians and three non-medical men, with full powers for regulating all matters pertaining to the health of the city, under State law; but it is dependent on the City Council for appropriations of money. The members are appointed by the Judges of the Superior Court.

(From Dr. Hosmer A. Johnson, Chicago.)

Chicago, March 6, 1876.

First. The supply of water from the Lake during north-east storms contains sand and a fine clay, with a few diatoms, such as gomphonema, pleurosigma, &c. These probably come from the Lake shore north of the city, as there is a continuous current, from north to south, along the west shore of the Lake. The water supply is taken from a shaft two (2) miles from the shore, and about one and one-half miles north of the outlets of the river. The depth of the cup or shaft in the creek is about thirty feet.

Second. I do not think the water is contaminated with sewage, for two reasons:—

1. The current in the Lake bears the sewage or water, from the Lake shore, south instead of north.

2. The larger part of the sewage is discharged into the Chicago River, through which, a current of pure Lake water is, during the most of the year, continuously flowing into the canal, and from it into the Illinois River. The largest part of the sewage is, therefore, taken towards the Mississippi River. Since the establishment of this current from the Lake inward, I do not think our water supply has ever been contaminated with sewage. Before that, with a strong south-west wind, such pollution was possible, and I think did, sometimes, obtain.

IOWA.

(From Dr. A. M. CARPENTER, Keokuk, Iowa.)

. . . .

I have just returned from a meeting of the Iowa State Medical Society. And, as of old, we had a discussion on State Medicine, and prepared matter for State legislation. Heretofore it has been like casting pearls before swine; and we fear a like fate under the present *régime*.

Our great endeavor hitherto has been to have enacted some provisions, protective to the regular profession. . . .

KANSAS.

(From Dr. TIFFIN SINKS, Leavenworth, Kan.)

LEAVENWORTH, KAN., Feb. 7, 1876.

Your circular letter of January 1 is received. I regret that I am compelled to say that no legislation has been had in this State, in reference to health. Several efforts have been made by the profession; but, as yet, we have not succeeded in getting even a registration law.

The State, as you are aware, is very large; and, excepting in the Eastern portion, is sparsely populated. By the terms of the constitution of the State, all legislation must be general; and, therefore, the large municipalities have no chartered powers for enforcing health ordinances, whatever may be their disposition

to do so. Several years ago, our City Council passed appropriate health ordinances, in anticipation of an advent of cholera; but the members of the Health Board soon found that they had no legal right to enforce their mandates.[1]

The State is young, the people are poor, and as yet not educated to the importance of sanitary laws. I very much doubt if any general law could be framed, that would not be onerous in the main, by virtue of the expense, which would attach to its faithful execution.

KENTUCKY.

(From Dr. GEORGE COWAN, Danville, Ky.)

DANVILLE, KY., Feb. 22, 1876.

To my surprise and mortification, the response from my friend, our representative, is "so busy," "forgot me," &c., and no opinion offered as to the temper or disposition of our Legislature, as regards your inquiries Nos. 1, 2, 3. I infer that our Legislature, of the present winter, is as indifferent to such matters as their predecessors. They believe in little or no prevention of disease, except by the use of amulets, charms, and incantations, or our Old Bourbon, mixed with all sorts of abominations, to "keep off" any and every thing. Dr. L. P. Blackburn, of Louisville, has been endeavoring to create an interest in the public mind in behalf of State Medicine, by going before the present Legislature, and making a public address, a copy of which I hope to be able to send you.

(From Dr. JOHN L. COOK, Henderson, Ky.)

HENDERSON, KY., Jan. 21, 1876.

From my answers, you will observe that sanitary laws for Kentucky have been neglected by the State.

[1] Kansas, in its endeavors to avoid special legislation, certainly goes to an unwise extent, when its laws would prevent a city from taking measures to ward off pestilence. It is to be hoped and believed that such a course renders Kansas a unique State. It is a young commonwealth,— and perhaps inexperienced, on that account, in sanitary requirements; although, in some other ways, its early experience was severe.

It is generally believed that the Legislature, during this winter, will pass a law creating a State Board of Health. I alluded to milk-sickness as a common disease in this, the southwestern part of the State, many years ago. I will also state that this is a great tobacco-growing section. Our section is quite the opposite of the blue-grass-grazing region. Grass don't grow well. The lands are flat.

Typhoid fever is making its appearance here. Some physicians have doubted if it ever existed in the county until four or five years ago. In the middle or upper part of the State, it has been met for years.

Cholera prevailed in our city in 1873. It hugged close to filthy alleys, low, flat, and wet places, and shunned the elevated grounds. Our City Board of Health had about a dozen ponds filled in the city; and malarial diseases, except last fall, have been less than usual.

LOUISIANA.

(From Dr. U. R. Milner, New Orleans.)

New Orleans, Feb. 21, 1876.

. . . I have no medical statistics of the State, nor legislative acts referring to those questions. Therefore my answers, at best, could only be approximative. I will, however, venture a few brief and general remarks, and I hope that you may find something in them to interest and serve you. To questions 1 to 6, inclusive: The State certainly does naught but counter to them. Our State, for the last eleven years, has been the arena for political wrangling, and scrambling for the spoils of office; and our legislators have given their time to the interests of monopolies of various kinds. . . .

Our State Board of Health owes whatever of usefulness it has to the necessity of the case, rather than to wise legislation.

To question 7th: The disease called "black tongue," which first made its appearance, some twenty-five or thirty years ago, among the wild deer of the Mississippi Valley, and is said to have infected and reached an endemic form among the inhabitants, seems to have disappeared. As to the cause or real nature, nothing has ever been known with certainty. It is said that it behaved very much like malignant erysipelas.

To question 8th: Cholera seems to be such a disease. The first epidemic in this country, I think, was about the year 1832. In 1849 and 1850, this disease prevailed on the Mississippi, especially on steamboats and in towns on the river, to a very alarming extent. It has since become quite a common sporadic disease. In the year 1866, there appeared, in the mortuary report of this city, nearly seven hundred deaths from cholera.

To question 20th: My observation and study of yellow fever have convinced me that it is only a high grade of paludal fever; its intensity and mortal nature, being the result of an intermingling of animal effluvia with the paludal poison, aided by certain meteorological conditions; and, as such, I think proper drainage and other sanitary regulations would soon entirely prevent it. In the year 1843, in the "New Orleans Times" of September 21st, October 5th, October 19th, and November 9th, will be found four letters of mine, entitled "Yellow Fever, Intrinsically the same as Intermittent Fever: Quarantine Wholly Useless." I will quote the concluding remarks of my last letter, "What of small-pox during that period? [The period of military occupation under General Butler.] Dr. Harris [then medical director or inspector of this port] says: 'We have seen that small-pox appeared as a wide-spread epidemic; and it was checked by a house-to-house visitation of a medical police, armed with vaccine virus.'

"How shall we account for this epidemic of small-pox, while yellow fever was wholly confined to local quarters? The fact proves that small-pox is a contagious disease, while yellow fever is not. Contagious diseases will spread, independent of local conditions; but non-contagious diseases must be fed by bad air, or else they will not spread. And such is yellow fever. Remove all local causes, — especially animal effluvia arising from garbage, cess-pools, and filthy privies, — and New Orleans shall enjoy a perpetual immunity from her dreadful scourge, with unrestricted commercial intercourse with all the world's infected ports."

(From Dr. S. S. Herrick, New Orleans.)

New Orleans, Feb. 19, 1876.

There are some questions to which I am not prepared to give categorical answers. To questions 1 and 2, I answer "No." This ought not to be done without some explanation. For a number of years our Legislature has not fairly represented the property and intelligence of the people; and, though appropriations have been made to carry out the purposes of the Board of Health, this has been effected by the personal influence and efforts of its members, and especially of the President of the Board. This body has made some investigations into the causes of infection and miasmatic diseases, and has been empowered to abate nuisances in the city of New Orleans, besides being charged with the execution of the quarantine laws.

8. Yellow fever appeared in the last decade of the last century. It cannot strictly be called endemic here, as years have occurred during which the disease was not manifested. There is reason to believe that it has completely died out, and that it might be extirpated but for its introduction from tropical America.[1]

10. Most of the efforts here have been made by the Board of Health. It is proper to say that this body is composed of nine (9) members, six of whom are appointed by the Governor, and three elected by the City Council. All are commissioned by the Governor, for one year. In 1853, the city authorities made some rude efforts to stay the progress of the epidemic of yellow fever, and, after its subsidence, had the matter investigated by a sanitary commission, who published a long report.

There is a system of water-works here, drawing the supply from the river. The water is not filtered, and contains so much sediment as to be perfectly opaque, unless time is allowed for it to settle, or something is added to hasten precipitation. Most dwellings are provided with wooden cisterns above ground, in the open air.

15 and 16. Our location is too level to admit of subterranean

[1] My friend Dr. Chaillé, just quoted, holds a totally different view, and says it is always more or less present. — The Yellow Fever. Sanitary Condition and Vital Statistics of New Orleans during its Military Occupation the Four Years 1862–65.

drainage. The plan is by open-street gutters, which discharge into canals in the rear. From these the water is lifted over protection levees between the inhabited portion of the city and the lake, and thus it flows to the lake in the rear. In high water, the surface of the river is several feet above the level of the city; and drainage, at all times, is in the opposite direction.

17. Sewage flows back to the lake. House offal, &c., is carried off in carts to dumping grounds, which are mostly in the rear of the city.

18. By Board of Health, having reference to the city alone.

19. Since 1855.

20. As the best answer to this question, I shall see that you receive copies of the Board of Health reports for several years, wherein you will find detailed the results of its labors in this direction.

MARCH 5, 1876.

With regard to the powers conferred on our Board of Health by the Legislature, and the measures adopted by the Board in accordance therewith, I refer you to the Code of Ordinances, of which a copy is herewith transmitted. In reference to questions 7 and 22, I would indicate references to the annual report of the Board of Health, as follows: 1870, pp. 40 and following; 1871, pp. 17 and following;[1] 1873, pp. 66 and following; 1874, pp. 19 and 23.

[1] On page 66 report for 1873 is an account of disinfecting adopted; viz., as follows: "The usual plan adopted was, by means of cart tank and sprinkler, to distribute so-called crude carbolic acid in the roadway of the streets in the vicinity of a case of fever, but at a distance, considered to be beyond the point, actually infected by the fever contagium. Similar distributions were then made in the roadway crossing the space thus marked out, and the premises in the vicinity of the case; the yards, walls, &c., were disinfected with colorless carbolic acid dissolved in water, by means of hand-sprinkling pots.

"When the case terminated with death, removal, or recovery, the premises were disinfected."

"When time and appliances were sufficient, these places were sprinkled with dilute carbolic acid. Clothing and bedding were sprinkled in the same way, or put in boiling water."

"Walls, ceilings, and furniture were disinfected by a steam atomizer, throwing a spray of white carbolic acid."

"Chlorine gas and sulphurous acid were used as disinfectants of rooms in a few cases."

The result was apparent success in limiting the spread of the disease.

It is proper to observe that the "germ theory," as applied to yellow fever, is adopted only provisionally, as is also our idea of its mode and rate of progress. In the present state of our knowledge, such mode of reasoning serves to account for existing phenomena more satisfactorily than any other theory. At the same time, the results of efforts at checking the spread of yellow fever, based on the above theory, are not claimed to be perfect. The doctrine is not traced to a divine source, and the agencies employed are not supposed to be infallible. The strongest evidence in favor of the plan, used here for several years, is found in comparison between the ravages of the disease at other cities in the south-west, and at New Orleans, since 1869. You are not to presume that any one here regards carbolic acid disinfection a specific for yellow fever infection, even theoretically; while, practically, the difficulties in administration of the plan are manifold. We are fighting an enemy in the dark, which has never been seen, and can only be judged by its effects. We are unable to control the movements of people in the city, so as to prevent them from entering infected localities. It is practically impossible to carry out the plan thoroughly, so as to destroy all germs *in situ*. Besides, opposition is sometimes made, even by medical men, to the plan of disinfection; and it is believed that cases are sometimes concealed, with their connivance, to prevent the practice of disinfection. On this subject quite a controversy took place in 1875, which has led to some public discussions, and publication by medical men. I send you some of these, on both sides, which may be of some interest. The principal papers in opposition will be found in the November number of the "New Orleans Medical and Surgical Journal," which is one of the exchanges of the "Boston Medical and Surgical Journal." Dr. White's reply to the same will be found in the March number of our Journal, of which I shall be able to send you an extra copy. Within the last two years, a new and very effectual apparatus has been devised by Dr. A. W. Perry, of this city, for the fumigation of ships. It consists of a furnace for burning brimstone, and, in connection, a blower, similar to those used in blast furnaces, for forcing a current of sulphurous-acid gas from the furnace into the ship's hold. This plan has been used, with complete satis-

faction, at the Mississippi Quarantine during the years 1874 and 1875; and our Legislature has just empowered the Board of Health, at their discretion, to substitute it for the usual specific detention at quarantine. We are satisfied that it is more efficacious than detention; and, at the same time, it relieves commerce of a heavy burden. In what is written, I am sensible that your request has not been strictly complied with, inasmuch as it is not claimed that the theory and practice indicated have been "proved true" in a truly scientific sense. I think, however, that there is a decided leaning in the direction of truth; and, if what is written should be of any service to you, my purpose will be fully answered.

(From DR. STANFORD E. CHAILLÉ, M.D., New Orleans.)

"*From Ray's Revised Statutes of Louisiana,*" 1870.

Marriages are recorded, but no registration is required of all marriages, in one central office, to subserve statistical purposes.

Births and Deaths. — The law [1855] directs the registration of births and deaths, but provides, Section 344, that "no person out of the parish of Orleans [*i.e.*, city of New Orleans] shall be under any legal obligations to have any birth or death recorded."

In Orleans Parish, $5 to $10 fine for not recording a birth or death, and 50 cents charge for doing so.

N. B. — Through Board of Health, deaths in city of New Orleans *only* are correctly reported. But the record of births, by the Recorder of Births and Deaths, is worthless for statistical and sanitary purposes, from non-execution of the law.

Quarantine, and State Board of Health. — The law [1856] established the quarantine of New Orleans and the State Board of Health *especially*, to enforce said quarantine. In addition to powers requisite to enforce said quarantine, the Board of Health is authorized to remove, or cause to be removed, any substance which they may deem detrimental to the health of New Orleans; and the Street Commissioner shall execute the orders of the Board of Health, *whenever not in conflict with the ordinances of the city*, or the laws of the State, — to pass sanitary ordinances for the city; provided such are approved by

the Council, and published as city ordinances. See Document No. 3.

N. B. — Law of 1870 extended power of Board of Health, rendering it more independent of City Council. See Document No. 4, p. 1.

Section 3062 (1855). The authorities of incorporated towns and cities are authorized " to enact ordinances to protect them from the introduction of contagious and epidemical diseases."

Section 3063 (1835). " The police juries shall have power to enact ordinances and regulations, not inconsistent with the laws and Constitution of the United States, or of this State, to protect their respective parishes against the introduction of all and every kind of contagious or epidemical disease."

Sections 2263–65 (1869) make it the duty of the Board of Metropolitan Police for New Orleans, if in their judgment advisable, to set apart a Metropolitan Sanitary Police Committee, appointing a captain, &c.; assigning to said Committee such special powers and duties as may be publicly advantageous.

It is made the duty of any such Committee to report to the Metropolitan Board — which is empowered in some cases, and instructed in others — how to correct any abuses, endangering the safety, health, or life, by ferry-boats, manufactories, slaughter-houses, *tenement*-houses, hotels, boarding-houses, or any edifices, and by any premises in a filthy condition, or in a condition dangerous to health."

N. B. — Such are all the laws I can find in " Ray's Revised Statutes," 1870, bearing on health in any way. These, with Document No. 4, will give you, I believe, thorough legal information on the subject.

I may add, however, that " Voorhies's Revised Statutes of Louisiana " are more recent. They have been long promised, but not yet published. We *have* " Voorhies's Civil Code," and " Revised *Civil Code*," and " Revised Civil Code of Practice." ($10 each.)

I should add that I have failed to obtain the law of March 16, 1870, referred to in Document No. 4, p. 1.

MAINE.

(From Dr. GEORGE F. FRENCH, Maine.)

PORTLAND, March 19, 1876.

As chairman of a committee, appointed by the Maine Medical Association, to effect the establishment of a State Board of Health, I brought this matter earnestly before the Legislature at its last session, and met with sufficient encouragement to make me confident of success, another year.

The Judiciary Committee, before whom we advocated the bill, were evenly divided on the vote to recommend the bill; and, on canvassing the House, with a view to obtaining a minority report, I found it inadvisable to have the bill reported. The people and their representatives need further enlightenment.

MASSACHUSETTS.

(From Dr. NATHAN ALLEN, Massachusetts.)

LOWELL, April 24, 1876.

In your remarks on "Preventive Medicine," and mode of treating the same, at the Centennial, I was much interested. It is not so much what has been done, but that the starting of great principles, true grounds of prevention of disease, is commenced.

The *first lessons*, founded in the laws of nature, foreshadow a glorious future. The next one hundred years will witness wonderful changes in this respect.

The medical profession has been grossly delinquent. Only one, here and there, is posted or interested in the matter of Public Hygiene. It is the profession, too, who won't do this work. It stands right in the way.

I wish to call your attention to an article in the April number, just out, of the "American Journal of Obstetrics," on the Normal Standard of Women, Physiologically Considered, for Propagation. . . . Prevention of pain and of disease is a prominent object in the discussion.

I present the following brief summary of the registration reports, State and National, from the veteran sanitarian,

Dr. Edward Jarvis, Massachusetts.

Dorchester, Mass., Nov. 20, 1876.

But few of our States and cities have kept and printed the records of their births, marriages, and deaths. Massachusetts began in 1843, and has published thirty-two reports; Vermont began in 1857, and has published sixteen reports; Rhode Island, from 1853, twenty-one reports; Connecticut, from 1845. New York published, in 1847 and 1848, two very small reports. Virginia published, for 1856, 1857, and 1858, three meagre reports. South Carolina, in the years 1857, 1858, and 1859, and in 1860, 1861, printed five reports. In 1861 the editor wrote me that the Legislature had repealed the law, appropriating the money, in order, he said, to expend the same "in the war." He had only $600 for doing the whole work of collecting the facts, and digesting and publishing them. His wife assisted him, without remuneration. Kentucky, in the year 1852–58, under the editorship of the excellent Dr. Sutton, published six valuable reports; one, afterwards, by Dr. Bemis. These reports, like Minerva, seemed to be born mature, and to spring, all at once, into fulness of power. Michigan, under the energy and intelligence of Dr. Baker, has published six reports; the last including the parts of 1871. New Hampshire passed a law, ordering a system of registration; but it never went into operation. The New York law, after the second year, was suffered to be neglected. I think it was not repealed; but, as it was entirely unsatisfactory even to the friends of the system, it was thought best to let it die, in hope of resuscitating it in better form. The two reports were of very little value. I do not know whether the Virginia law was repealed or not. The three reports were very meagre, and worth but little. The South Carolina reports were very valuable. So, also, those of Kentucky.

The registration of cities is older, and more permanent. The Boston reports are in sheets, 1813 to 1849, and in pamphlet form from that time; but they were not printed in the years 1860 and 1861. The Providence reports were in sheets from

1841 to 1852; and in good, valuable, excellent pamphlets, from the hand of the most faithful, intelligent Dr. Snow, from 1852 to the present. The New York City reports were in one condensed sheet for 1804 to 1821; then pamphlets; and, at last, books, very valuable. The Brooklyn reports have been published. Generally, they are in pamphlet form. Buffalo has published reports. Troy has published reports, apparently irregularly. Philadelphia published in large sheets from 1825 to 1859, and perhaps earlier. I have only these. Since 1859, the city has published pamphlet reports; which, since then, have grown to books, very valuable. Baltimore printed several sheet reports, from 1836 to 1856; subsequently, in pamphlet form. Washington printed pamphlet reports, from 1849 to 1859, and suspended, but has lately revived them. I think I have all; certainly, from 1849 to 1859, and the late reports of Dr. Coxe. Charleston printed, in condensed form, the reports from 1834 to 1846; and thenceforward, annual reports, in sheets and semi-pamphlets, until the war, when they seemed to cease. My last is 1860. New Orleans has printed many occasional reports as to the mortality; but not of births and marriages. I think no regular series of any. Memphis, also, printed occasional reports.

Some of these documents are of very great value. The best are the late reports of New York City. The next are those of Massachusetts and Rhode Island, or rather Providence. The Michigan reports are worthy of all confidence, and very instructive. The late reports of Washington, by Dr. Coxe, are excellent.

Unfortunately, many state merely the few facts of numbers dying, their age; and, in part, their diseases. The New Jersey reports tell but little; and some of them give no clew to the time. . . . Nevertheless, all of these contain some parts that are worth preserving.

Now, my dear doctor, this is all I can tell you of the published record of mortality of the United States.

But I have all of them complete, or nearly complete, from their beginning to their end, or to a few; and they are all at your service. They will aid you much in your summary of the history of recorded mortality of our country. Besides these, probably there are other reports. St. Louis, Chicago, Cincin-

nati print on sheets. Certainly, it is worth while to inquire of some friends in these or other places.

You have, doubtless, the National Reports of 1850, 1860, and 1870; also, the Canadian and Nova Scotian reports.

(From DR. EDWARD JARVIS, Dorchester, Mass.)

DORCHESTER, March 6, 1876.

I wish I could help you;[1] but I do not see the way clearly to do the work. But it may be done; so I think. It will require great labor to find the facts of the beginning and end of the century. Bills of mortality, graveyard records, family Bibles, traditions of the former and the latter time, will show whether we have gained or lost in longevity. So I wrought out my article in the "Atlantic Monthly," showing the increase of life within one hundred, and one thousand years and more.

You will need to work, in a similar manner, for the century character of diseases. Were those of childhood more prevalent formerly than now? Did they shorten life more than those of maturity and age? Compare the life tables of former and present time; that in "Leybert's Statistical Annual" (p. 55) with that now in use. You will not find much to show positively the decrease or increase; but much, very much, that indicates the comparative value of life now and then. I am certain that, in two hundred years, life has increased. I think it has in the last one hundred, even in the last fifty, years. You have a great and pleasant work before you in this inquiry. May you be prospered in it! Have you a copy of my pamphlet on "Increase of Human Life"?

MICHIGAN.

(From DR. HENRY B. BAKER, Secretary State Board of Health, Mich.)

LANSING, MICH.

In reply to your question 6–*a:* no law has been passed with the distinctly avowed object of a sanitary survey of the State; but, under the law for its organization, the State Board of

---

[1] My question was simply this: "Are there any printed, reliable, American statistics, whereby I can find out exactly whether man lives longer now, than at the commencement of the Centennial period?"

Health has, in a measure, entered upon such a work, as you will see by a blank form which I send you herewith; viz., for annual reports of clerks of local boards of health.

The information, sought to be thus obtained, is such as would render it possible to construct sanitary maps or charts, which would exhibit many of the conditions, which it is desirable to study in connection with the records of diseases and deaths from certain diseases, reported by the same officers; and also with the records of deaths returned to the State Department.

As a sanitarian, and a member of the State Board of Health, Professor Kedzie has also made a sanitary inspection of most of the State institutions, the reports of which inspection have been published in the second annual report of the Board, and, it is believed, have already led to some real sanitary improvements.

In reply to question 6–d: perhaps it is hardly proper to claim that any law "governing the public health" has been drawn from the vital statistics of the State. I think it certain, however, that many general truths, respecting deaths in Michigan, have been ascertained; and that our knowledge of the death-rate from several diseases, with respect to the co-existing conditions, has been very materially advanced by the evidence thus collected. One very important truth, learned through this means, has been the comparative mortality from different diseases. This is important, because it leads directly to practical results. People seldom take vigorous measures, and still less frequently intelligent action, for avoiding a danger that is not very manifest; but, when once a real danger is made plain to them, they generally act accordingly. As an instance, the vital statistics of Michigan have convinced many in this State that scarlatina is, at present, a much greater danger to the public health than small-pox; and this fact is beginning to have its influence in promoting measures for its prevention. The vital statistics give the warnings which prompt the people to ask, How can these dangers be avoided? The State Board of Health aims to disseminate among the people alike the warnings and the best means for avoiding danger.

In reply to your question 6, it is proper to say that there is a chapter in our compiled laws, relating to the introduction of water into cities and villages; but in it there appears to be no

mention whatever of any condition or influence connected with the public health.

In reply to your question 7–*b*: it seems to be the general opinion among our physicians that malarial diseases are very much less prevalent in this State than formerly; and this is, in part, attributed to the extensive drainage of swamps, marshes, and other low lands, which has been encouraged by State action.

In reply to your question 20, it seems proper to modify the "yes" which I have placed opposite the question, very much as I have the answer to the question 6–*d*. If we substitute for "law of development, or partial development of," the words "general truth respecting," I think the answer will be truthfully "Yes." I would instance the disease before mentioned, scarlet fever, which I have no doubt will be lessened in the near future, because of the accumulated evidence of the great mortality caused by it. It seems to me that, in coming centuries, we may hope to greatly lessen the mortality from croup, and also from pneumonia, through a knowledge of the fact that both of these diseases prove fatal to the greatest number, when the atmosphere is cold and dry. This fact appears to be established by the vital statistics of Michigan, so far as can well be done by statistics for so short a period, as has been studied. It is well known that, for a short period, men can endure great extremes of heat, cold, dryness, and moisture, without serious danger, if they can afterwards be placed under favorable conditions. Under such circumstances, alternations of exposure may not be much more dangerous than alternations of labor and repose. By securing such favorable conditions in our houses, and particularly in our sleeping-rooms, it is reasonable to hope that many deaths from pneumonia and croup may, in the future, be prevented. If this is brought about, it will be largely due to statistics of mortality, united with those of meteorology.

(From DR. J. H. BEECH, Coldwater Mich.)
COLDWATER, Jan. 19, 1876.

. . . .

The southern portion of the State of Michigan, in its unimproved condition, was proverbially unhealthy. The land, level, or but slightly undulating, abounding in lakelets and marshes;

streams in no portion rapid, and often sluggish; vegetation everywhere prolific, and often redundant; humidity unusually equal throughout the year, and somewhat excessive, with temperature (doubtless modified by the large bodies of water on either side and the numerous smaller bodies of still and deep water interspersed) disproportionally less subject to extremes than the central portion of the peninsula, was tempting, in all of its natural characteristics, to emigrating agriculturists. But it is doubtful if any portion of the Northern temperate regions furnished early adventurers with more universal, or more pertinacious, zymoses. The drainage laws of Michigan — passed, by county law, in 1867; township law, in 1871 — were hailed by the people with more than ordinary appreciation, and the clearing of streams of fallen timber, of ill-advised dams and unprofitable windings, was embraced with avidity. Marshes became cornfields; lakelets became meadows; the crossing trunks of the black ash, and the hawk-perches upon the dead limbs of the sycamore, gave place to the orchard and garden. . . .

And I doubt if a more prosperous, healthy, and happy people can be found than the agriculturists of Southern Michigan. I do not say they are wealthy, or æsthetic, or prosperous because of the drainage law; but that they could have no greater boon, unless it be that of wisdom to avail themselves of all its advantages.

. . . .

In the first years of the settlement of this city (Coldwater), *dysentery annually slaughtered the infants, and decimated the adults*, until May, 1842, when a *Village Board of Health* condemned and destroyed a mill-dam within its limits; and from that day banished the epidemic fever, and the former unparalleled malignancy of the disease.

(From Dr. G. E. Corbin, St. Johns, Mich.)

St. Johns, Mich.

. . . .

Malarial diseases, near swamps and stagnant water, are much more severe on *east* than on *west* banks; because west winds prevail. Drainage, and the removal of obstructions to free cir-

culation of air, mitigate and eradicate malarial diseases in many localities in this State. . . .

(From Dr. R. C. Kedzie, Lansing, Mich.)

Lansing, Mich.

By our system of correspondents, and by reports of local boards of health, also by meteorological observers, we are making a partial sanitary survey of the State. A complete survey has not yet been attempted.

But sanitary inspection by State law can hardly be said to exist with us. We attempt something in this direction, by correspondents, &c.

A volunteer sanitary inspection of school-houses was undertaken by myself, for the State Medical Society, in 1873. This inspection was made entirely at my own expense. In 1874, I made an inspection of the sanitary condition of our penal, pauper, and reformatory institutions. The State Board of Health paid my travelling expenses.

A partial sanitary inspection of illuminating oils was also made by myself, in 1873, without cost to the State. These subjects you will find treated, more in detail, in the Reports of the State Board of Health for Michigan, for 1873 and 1874.

MISSISSIPPI.

(From Dr. James Drummond Burch, Yazoo City, Miss.)

Yazoo City, Miss.

I regret very much that I am able to send you but a poor report from this State. I might come before you at greater length in reference to the resignation of the Board of Health of this city, and the probable causes of the *seeming* indifference or ignorance on such matters of other towns and cities; but we might misapprehend each other, — you being in Boston, I in Mississippi. May the day speedily come, when men in distant parts of our common country may talk and write freely, without being suspected of entertaining sectional prejudices and hatred! [I heartily say "Amen" to the last remark of my correspondent; and have only to regret that he has not, in the present instance,

exhibited greater confidence in his own warm aspirations for a cordial co-operation between the different sections of the country. He may be assured that they would meet with a cordial response.]

(From Dr. WIRT JOHNSON, Jackson, Miss.)

JACKSON, March 22, 1876.

I regret very much that a protracted absence from home has been the cause of your communication having remained unanswered, until this late day. I hasten to reply, hoping it will not be too late for your purposes. I will answer most of the questions asked, by telling you that we have no State Board of Health, and there is not, that I am aware of, a County Board of Health in the State. During the prevalence of epidemics, or when they are anticipated, some of our towns create, for temporary purposes, boards of health. There is only one incorporated town in the State (Vicksburg), that I am aware of, which has a permanent organization of this kind. When epidemics threaten from abroad, the executive of our State, in accordance with law, establishes a quarantine along our coast.

Outside of the establishment of quarantine, I am not aware that our Legislature has ever done any thing, towards protecting the health of the people of our State. We have no law for the registration of births, deaths, or marriages. I know of no new disease that has made its appearance in the State, unless a new type of malarial disease could be so regarded. I mean "hæmaturic malarial fever."

Our town uses cistern water. It is provided with sewers. We have a health officer, the City Physician, who supplies the place of a regularly organized health board.

I regret exceedingly the unavoidable delay in answering your communication; but, when you see how little of interest we can furnish you, I do not think you will conclude that you have been the loser by it.

(From Dr. P. F. WHITEHEAD, Vicksburg, Miss.)

VICKSBURG, MISS., March 20, 1876.

As you will perceive, by the answers to the enclosed interrogations, we lack every thing, we ought to have, in the way of

sanitary law. Appreciating this, I, at the last meeting of the State Association, called attention to the matter; and a committee was appointed to memorialize the Legislature on the subject. So far, no action has been taken. I trust, however, that we will improve in these matters.

(From DR. F. W. DANCY, Holly Springs, Miss.)

HOLLY SPRINGS, MISS., Feb. 23, 1876.

I regret to say that I have to answer all your questions in the negative. The State of Mississippi has been, for the past eight years, under *carpet-bag* and *negro rule*, and the people so taxed and robbed that they have had no means or spirit to engage in State Hygiene. The rule is now changed; and I trust, in the course of another decade, that I will be able to answer your inquiries affirmatively.

MISSOURI.

(From DR. JOHN B. JOHNSON, St. Louis, Mo.)

ST. LOUIS, Mo., March 7, 1876.

I am sorry that I can give you no better report from our State, than such as I send you. The people do not seem to appreciate the importance or necessity of attention "to Public Hygiene and Preventive or State Medicine." I hope the time will soon come when, by proper information given to the people through our State, and by the influence of local medical societies, our Commonwealth, through its Legislature and State Councils, will enact such laws, as shall insure the increased health and happiness of its now large, and fast-increasing, population.

(From DR. JOHN GREEN, St. Louis, Mo.)

ST. LOUIS, Mo.

Our State has no Board of Health, or other health commission, of any kind. It has practically abandoned its geological survey; and, in the cause of science, supports only an entomologist, who has done good service. St. Louis has a so-called Board of Health; which is, in part, a police board, with authority to abate nuisances, and, in part, a dispenser of patronage. The mem-

bership of the Board changes every two years, with the change in the office of mayor; he having the appointment of them, out of his four colleagues. What the Board has to do, it does spasmodically, and without much method, — certainly without any persistency. Its "patronage" kills it, and its appointments are mainly political. I hope, under our new city constitution, now in the progress of evolution, we may have something better.

(From Dr. Robert W. Oliphant, St. Louis, Mo.)
St. Louis, Feb. 24, 1876.

The enclosed is an unsatisfactory showing for so great a State as Missouri; the only facts of any importance, belonging to St. Louis. We have, at least, a population of 500,000, with abundant sewerage, a high and rolling ground for buildings, a full supply of water, which flows with rapid current down the Missouri and Yellowstone Rivers, for thousands of miles; consequently, our health statistics are among the best.

NEBRASKA.

(From Dr. David W. Henshey, Nebraska City, Neb.)

. . . .

The State of Nebraska is too new to afford any statistics or information, I think, that would contribute any thing to you, which would be of value.

Our State Medical Society was organized in 1868; and the influence of its organized effort, on the part of the medical profession, has not yet made itself felt. . . .

(From Dr. James H. Peabody, Omaha, Neb.)
Omaha, Neb., Feb. 22, 1876.

Our State is so young, and as yet so sparsely settled, that it is next to impossible to get its Legislature to see the importance of State Medicine. The matter has been brought before the Senate and House at every meeting for five years past; and, although I have been ably seconded by our State Medical Society, no law has yet been enacted. Our State is exceedingly well drained by nature; being mostly rolling prairie, with

a natural slope, of about nine feet to the mile, from Laramie Plains to the Missouri River, and scarcely an acre of marsh land in the State. We have had no epidemic or endemic diseases, since its settlement by the whites; and, in fact, with the exception of a very light grade of remittent and intermittent fever, we have scarcely any disease, except that caught by careless exposure, and, during July and August, cholera infantum.

Typhoid fever seldom occurs, only seven cases being observed out of over a thousand, classed under miasmatic diseases. I presume that, as the larger cities, such as Omaha, begin to experience the effects of the pernicious habit of burying sewage matter, typhoid, or typhoid malarial, will be more common. I regret that I have no matter of interest to you in framing your address, and only mention the above facts, incidentally.

NEVADA.

(From T. R. GRINDLEY, ESQ., Librarian of the State Library at Carson City, Nevada.)

The State has been settled only sixteen years. Prevailing diseases are malarial and typhoid fever, pneumonia, and so-called "mountain fever," which is undoubtedly typho-malarial.

Well water is used to some extent; but the principal supply is brought from the foot of the mountains in pipes. No precaution is taken to prevent pollution.

We have no sewers; nor is there any mode of disposing of house offal or slops, prescribed by law.

NEW HAMPSHIRE.

(From DR. GRANVILLE P. CONN, Concord, N.H.)

CONCORD, Jan. 19, 1876.

. . . .

It is with shame that I am obliged to report that the old Granite State, and one of the original thirteen, is so far behind her sister States, in the advancement of medical science, and especially that of Preventive or State Medicine.

Years ago, the New Hampshire Medical Society succeeded in

NEW HAMPSHIRE. 183

securing the passage of a registration act, similar to those of other States; but the Secretary of State was to be the registrar, and the returns have simply remained on file.

We made an effort to secure a State Board of Health last year; and I hope we shall succeed this year.

(From Dr. George B. Twitchell, Keene, N.H.)
KEENE, N.H., Feb. 27, 1876.

It would have been no use to you to have had our earlier reply, as our city and State are far behind the times; but, as you only want facts, I can only give you negative facts.

(From Dr. Charles L. Downes, Nottingham, N.H.)
NOTTINGHAM, N.H., Jan. 20, 1876.

I send you a few replies to questions in your circulars, reserving answers to others till I know more certainly.

Ques. 1. Yes, to a small extent.

Ques. 2–*a*. No, except incidentally to town-health officers.

Ques. 2–*b*. No.

Ques. 2–*c*. Power conferred on town-health officers. General Statutes, ch. 101.

Ques. 2–*d*. General Statutes, ch. 253, act of 1862, provides for imprisonment for six months, or fine of $200, for knowingly selling diseased or unwholesome provisions.

Ques. 2–*d*. Act of 1860, imprisonment for a year, or fine of $300, for adulterating bread.

Imprisonment a year, or a fine of $1,000, and forfeiture of liquor, for adulteration of liquor.

Act of 1860 and 1866, a forfeiture of $50 for each offence of selling adulterated, or unwholesome, milk.

Imprisonment a year, or fine not exceeding $400, and forfeiture of drugs and medicines, for adulterating or knowingly selling the same.

Act of 1848 and 1850 require a record of all sales of poison, specifying the kind and quantity, and name of the purchaser. Record to be open to inspection. Fine for neglect, $100. Physician's prescriptions and recipes for patients excluded.

Ques. 2–*e*. Act of 1871. Pamphlet Laws creates a board of

commissioners, with power to prohibit the introduction and transportation of domestic animals by railroad or otherwise, and constitutes the selectmen of towns agents to execute all measures, prescribed to arrest, or exclude infecticus or troublesome diseases.

Ques. 3–*a, b, c, d, e.* No, or none.

Ques. 4. No.

Ques. 5. General Statutes, 37, § 4, provides for the election of town-health officers; and, if they are not elected, that the selectmen shall discharge the duties, and have the power, of health officers. General Statutes, ch. 101, 102 103, confer power to make regulations for the prevention and removal of nuisances, and such other regulations, as in their judgment the health and safety of the people may require; which regulations, when recorded by the town-clerk, with the approval of the selectmen, and published, give the health officers ample power to remove nuisances, to prevent the spread of pestilent diseases, to compel vessels to perform quarantine, to suppress slaughter-houses and some noxious trades; and authorize them to call for assistance, and give them the same protection, in the exercise of their duties, that sheriffs have.

Ques. 5. Notwithstanding this, a very small percentage of the towns in the State ever elect health officers; and, as a rule, selectmen ignore and neglect the duties of health officers. People seem to fear no disease except small-pox, — an epidemic of which may stir them to appoint some person to vaccinate the inhabitants, by either inserting lymph, *accidentally* pure, or more or less mixed with *purulent* matter, inducing erysipelatous inflammation, and paying no farther attention to the matter; while scarlet fever, and more fatal diseases, are suffered to prevail, without any attempt to check them.

Ques. 6–*a.* No.

Ques. 6–*b.* Yes. Act passed 1858: Revised Statutes, ch. 162; amended 1866.

Ques. 6–*c.* Seventeen years.

Ques. 6–*d.* I have not met with a statement of such a law.

Ques. 6–*e.* Pamphlet Laws: An act was passed in 1870, by adopting which any town or city may make and maintain all main drains or common sewers adjudged necessary for public

convenience or public health, in force in any town or city, from the time of its adoption of it.

Ques. 6–*h*. Several cities and towns are named as having been authorized to introduce water; the earliest date being 1869, into Manchester.

Ques. 6–*i*. Four health boards have powers, under the General Statutes, to ward off these diseases.

Ques. 6–*j*. No special law in regard to tenement houses, more than for all dwellings. Pamphlet Laws, 1869, make regulations in regard to sink water and privy vaults.

Ques. 6–*k*. Revised Statutes, ch. 137, 1866, authorize any five or more persons to form a voluntary corporation for agricultural education, or charitable purposes; or for carrying on any lawful business, except banking; and constructing and maintaining a railroad, having its capital stock limited, — minimum being $1,000, its maximum, $1,000,000. I am not aware that any company has been formed for the purpose named.

Ques. 12. In many cases, they are polluted by sink water, drainage of cattle yards, and sometimes by privies. In one case of a dry well, water was hauled from a pond, and poured into it. The result was typhoid fever in the family, and some deaths.

Ques. 14. No. I will state a case: One of the prominent men of the town persists, against remonstrance, in ventilating his privy and stable cellar into a closet opening into his kitchen; and, still, one third of his family are yet alive![1]

Ques. 17. The few, who make sewers, make the outlets as far from their dwellings as they can. My individual method is to conduct the sink water in an open pipe, hung on a pivot at the sink end, on to the kitchen garden when needed; the distal end being often moved so as to promote absorption and prevent accumulation and all odors. House slops, offal, &c., are mixed with dry earth, and composted.

Surface water is excluded from the privy, and a box of dry earth is kept therein; and it is the law of the house that, whoever makes a deposit therein, is required to cover it immediately with a large scoop-full of dry earth; and by these means

[1] See letter, page 186.

it is kept free from unpleasant odors, even in the hottest summer weather.

I wrote to Dr. Downes to give me more details in regard to the family above alluded to, as living in a house, permeated with odors from the privy and stable yard, and I received from him the following reply: —

JANUARY 22, 1876.

Yours of the 20th inst. received. In relation to the privy referred to, I will reply that it is in the second story of a ten-foot-posted building, and the lower story of which is used as a country store. A tube, 8 × 8 inches inside diameter, lined by zinc, and 12 feet long, extends from the closet, into which it opens, perpendicularly through the stairway and stair, into an excavation communicating with the cellar of the stable, attached to the store. The only external opening into the cellar is by means of a door, usually shut. This door faces the East, from which the prevailing winds blow. The owner thinks this a great improvement on the previous state of the premises.

The family consisted of the owner, wife and child. The child died in 1872, before eighteen months old; the wife died in the spring of 1875, of tubercular disease; the man has been sick some ten weeks; is now able to go out and take the air occasionally. His respiration is impeded, and his appearance is unhealthy. I have, however, made no examination in his case.

A townsman, a strong, active, healthy man, of about sixty-five years, a carpenter by trade, who spends most of his time from home, has, for many years, suffered his sink water to pollute his well, so that in hot weather, in summer, the family cannot drink the water. He has already buried three wives. And report says one of them died of consumption; the other two, of typhoid fever. He is now living with his fourth wife, who exhibits symptoms of declining health, although a young woman and previously healthy. He has two surviving children, — one of them by a former wife, who spent much time from home; the other, not yet four years old, who appears strong and healthy, by his present wife. He has abundant means, and could procure a supply of pure water, at an expense not exceeding

twenty-five dollars; yet, against the advice of his doctor and clergyman, this state of things continues.

Some years since I was desired, by the authorities of a town in Vermont, to investigate the condition of their poor farm (town almshouse), to ascertain the cause of the mortality then prevailing among its inmates. I found several paupers, and the wife and daughter of the superintendent, sick with typhoid fever. Several deaths had occurred, and evidently more would soon occur. The sick were and had been under the care of a Thompsonian doctor. The house, on the east side, was elevated about four feet above the surface of the ground. Six feet from the door on that side there was a privy elevated on posts to a level with the house. Underneath it was more than one year's accumulation, the odor of which was present in the cellar of the dwelling. On directing the attention of the superintendent to its condition, he said, "That is for the paupers: I have made a better one for the family since I came." And thereupon took me through the kitchen (used also for an eating-room), into a closed passage, at the end of which was a privy, whose vault was only a pen of boards made tight to the surface of the ground, but exposed to surface water, and the only ventilation of which was into the passage, opening into the kitchen!

I suggested that, although he had things very convenient, he might make some improvement by constructing a privy upon trucks, to be kept under his table, which would prevent the necessity of any travel in connection with its use.

I directed the authorities to remove the privies, and cart off the contaminated soil about them; to erect suitable structures for the purpose; to ventilate the house, and cleanse it, as far as possible; and to employ a neighboring physician, whom I knew to be competent, and to follow his directions implicitly. With this advice they complied; and subsequently the doctor informed me that only two more deaths occurred, and that no new cases proved fatal.

That the disease was caused by the filth, I have no doubt; and that the mortality might, in some degree, be occasioned by mismanagement, may be possible.

The foregoing are extreme cases; yet I find more or less careless, if not criminal, neglect of sanitary measures through-

out the country, wherever I go, — and notably in some parts of cities, not excepting the capital of the United States.

It seems unaccountable to me that man, with all his boasted progress, has not yet generally acquired that degree of sanitary knowledge, *somehow* obtained by the cat, and acted upon by it, within the first three months of its existence. There is an article in my own personal creed, that no one has the right to pollute the atmosphere, or the water, which a bountiful Creator has provided for the common use of his creatures.

I state, in Question 6, letter *d*, in your circular, that certificates of marriages, births, and deaths, are finally returned to the Secretary of State, in whose department they yet continue to lie. The Secretary informed me, yesterday, that no report of them had ever been published. No law can be drawn from the reports.

(From' CHARLES S. DOWNES, Nottingham, N.H.)

NOTTINGHAM, March 3, 1876.

As a further reply to your circular in relation to drainage, the Pamphlet Laws of New Hampshire of 1875, No. 640, provide that, on the petition of any person, the selectmen of a town may authorize the construction of any drain, by them deemed necessary for the preservation of health; and they are allowed to take land for the same, and assess the damages, as in the case of highways. In relation to Question 8, I state from memory, and not from record. In the autumn of 1842, phlegmonous erysipelas prevailed as an epidemic; and continued the following winter in Grafton County, N.H., and in Corinth, Topsham, and Orange, and neighboring towns in Orange County, Vt. Some physicians thought it a new disease. Under the direction of my instructor, Israel Hinckley, M.D., I saw seventy cases of it, — only two of which proved fatal. In the towns of Bath and Lyman, the reported mortality was nearly fifty per cent. The disease was particularly fatal to pregnant women; some sixty of whom, giving birth to children, died of the disease in those two towns within the year, and these deaths occurring in the practice of certain physicians. From this great mortality, confined to them, there is a possibility that the patients might have been infected by the hand of

the accoucheur. From subsequent observation, I do not think this was a new disease. In 1863 a disease appeared, called by some spotted fever, or cerebro-spinal meningitis. I have seen, in my own practice and in consultation, but seven well-marked cases of this disease. The last one occurred in 1865. Three cases proved fatal. All of these patients had been exposed to cold and dampness immediately before the attack; and two of them in the same manner, yet not in the same year. Both were laborers, — young, robust men, — and had been husking wet corn for several days, in a cold barn. Another, of the same class, had been exposed for some time, after violent exercise, to a temperature of 24° below zero Fahrenheit. The fourth was a United States soldier stationed at the South, but home at the North on a short furlough. He took a long drive, in an open sleigh, on a very cold day, very imperfectly protected, and got thoroughly chilled, and was attacked during that night. Two others were children residing on the borders of a large swamp, and the adjacent land sparsely occupied. They had been playing on the ground in the early spring, immediately previous to the attack. I am not aware that the foregoing, or similar cases, have been particularly investigated by any person since their occurrence.

(From Dr. John W. Parsons, Portsmouth, N.H.)

Portsmouth, N.H., Feb. 21, 1876.

Our State sanitary laws are such as necessity has created from time to time, and relate to vaccination in public schools, removal of nuisances, prevention of contagious and pestilential diseases, and quarantine law. As the within report shows, we have no State Board of Health, nor county boards: but all towns have the appointment of health officers; and, in case none are appointed, the selectmen act as health officers.

We have tried to get a State Board of Health; but the Legislature did not see fit to grant it. Our registration law is a good one; but, through the neglect of physicians and authorities, returns are only incompletely made.

APPENDIX.

NEW JERSEY.

(From Dr. David Warman, Trenton, N.J.)

Trenton, N.J., Feb. 28, 1876.

Most, if not all, the important questions you propounded could have been answered truthfully by an emphatic negative.

Our State seems to exhibit the most profound apathy and indifference in regard to the great question of "Public Hygiene and Preventive Medicine." Three years ago, a Health Commission was appointed. They made a lengthy report, and drafted a bill for the purpose of establishing a State Board of Health, similar to the one in your own State. This was presented to the Legislature; but was buried in committee by the influence of homœopathists and other irregular practitioners, who wished to be recognized as "a part of the State Board of Health."

Since then, no effort has been put forth to secure a board of health for the State; but we hope the day is not far distant, when we shall have such an organization in New Jersey. I herewith transmit you a copy of the Report of the Health Commission of the State of New Jersey; also, a copy of the transactions of our State Society from 1776 to 1800; to both of which I refer you for information, as they will answer most, if not all, the questions you ask.

NEW YORK.

(From Dr. A. N. Bell, Editor of the "Sanitarian," New York, N.Y.)

New York, Feb. 9, 1876.

"How many journals are devoted to sanitary work in this country" is beyond my ability to tell. Vol. 3, Army Catalogue, under Periodicals, gives a full list of all of the, so-called, health journals there have been, and of those which are now, published. But few of them have been devoted to sanitary work. They are, indeed, almost without exception devoted to other purposes. Fowler & Wells's "Science of Health," New York; Woods & Holbrook's "Herald of Health, New York; the "Health Reformer," Battle Creek, Michigan, — these I

receive in exchange. They occasionally contain articles of some sense; but they are devoted exclusively to hydropathy: and those three, I believe, have the largest circulation of any "health" journals in the country.

Of others I sometimes receive copies; but they are decidedly unsanitary in all their works, — devoted to quackery. In Canada there are two, — the "Sanitary Journal," Toronto, and "Public Health Magazine," Montreal, devoted to sanitary work. The former is one year old; the latter, eight months. For the rest, I must refer you to the catalogues, for names and ages.

You will find there have been several attempts to publish journals devoted to sanitarian work in this country; but, so far as I know, the "Sanitarian" is the only one at present sustained.

I present, with pleasure, the following letters, giving a brief *résumé* of the gradual growth of sanitary enactments in this country. It was kindly prepared for me by Dr. Elisha Harris: —

(From DR. ELISHA HARRIS, New York, N.Y.)

NEW YORK, May 1, 1876.

The first *great* step in the sanitary work of our own times seems to me to have been taken in the faithful report made to the Massachusetts General Court by Lemuel Shattuck and his associates, in 1849–50. It remains the monument to Mr. Shattuck's large and fervent mind, and his plans of usefulness. Then came your own report, in 1863. Both of the reports chance, at this moment, to be before me, as models for a temporary outline I am preparing for use in the *preliminary reconnoissance* of the Survey Commissioners in our own State of New York, who are about to devise the general scheme for a survey; which we hope will be as perfect a piece of contour and geodetic mapping as has ever been made.

The State of New York has been growing rich, and its people are becoming educated and enlightened; but our legislators are more or less of speculators in the games of party politics, and gain in the spoils of office, and in law making.

We may not have a State Board of Health this year, though a good bill is now on its final passage. If it becomes a law, I will forward you a revised copy of it.

In answer to questions, Dr. Harris writes thus: —

1. The State laws to promote vaccination have been absolute and mandatory; but never executed, because there is no central or other specific authority. This is in the hands of common-school officers.

2. The State has expended over three millions of dollars to guard the port of New York against the yellow fever; all in providing for *structures* and extra expenditures at the Quarantine Station. The Legislature never refuses the money, asked for the Quarantine Commissioners, not one of whom is a physician. The State has given all power and right necessary for controlling all the affluents of the Croton for the City of New York. For four years past, the Adirondacks Commission has, by State order, surveyed and reported for the preservation of the sources of the Hudson River, which will ultimately supply half the population of the State with pure water. New York City will eventually take half its supply from the Hudson, above Poughkeepsie.

3. The law of 1867 for New York and Brooklyn has greatly reformed the system of tenement construction; but has not and cannot remodel the old tenements, except as regards ventilation and lighting. We need the powers of the Glasgow authorities to recast bad quarters.

Though no single discovery has been made, the *tout ensemble* of acquired knowledge concerning all and each of the *typh. contagia*, and the factors of their propagation, is equivalent to discovery; and the deduction from such knowledge gives the elements of absolute prevention and protective skill. This is equivalent to special discovery.

In regard to several of the special fever-poisons, viz., scarlatina, diphtheria, relapsing fever, and the paludal fevers, the recently acquired knowledge may be regarded as equivalent to discovery of the means of prevention.

Physicians in the State of New York are cultivating such knowledge; and they accept the contributions of observers like Drs. Bowditch, Kline, John Simon, M. Crocq, on the propaga-

tion of tubercles, as lights on the pathway of true discovery. Thus the direct outcome of recent observations and physiological studies results in logical deductions, which can be expressed as sanitary truths in the field of Preventive Medicine. Such practical uses of accumulated facts we deem to be equal to discovery.

The State of New York has encouraged the cultivation of all of the physical sciences; and has, for sixty years, regularly published and given very wide circulation to the Annual Reports of the State Medical Society. Those reports frequently embody special and elaborate records of epidemics, and reports on drainage, and the sources of malaria. Drainage laws have been put into operation, and the State is about to organize the most elaborate topographical and economical survey of its entire domain.

The City of New York has, for ten (10) years, had the services of upwards of thirty (30) well-educated medical men, and a certain number of engineers, chemists, and other experts in physical knowledge, steadily devoted to the public health problems. Even amidst the adversities of political strife, the Metropolitan Sanitary Code has maintained its sway, and the sanitary service has not been interrupted. Hundreds of cellar habitations and thousands of insalubrious tenements have been vacated, and the latter have been radically reformed. Forty thousand ventilating windows and shafts were constructed by owners and lessees of tenements, in half as many habitations in the city, during the last twelve months of my service as Sanitary Superintendent; and, during the same period, a thorough sanitary survey and registry of every tenement house in the city was made. The incursions of various contagious fevers were arrested; and, from the 1st of March, 1869, to January, 1876, nearly six hundred thousand persons were gratuitously and well vaccinated by medical officers of the Board of Health; thereby not only giving security to more than one-half the people of the city, but securing great benefits to the entire country, and the commercial world.

The people generally sustain the public health measures. The courts of appeal have, in every case, sustained the Sanitary Code. The merchants of the city, in 1864–65, when

fevers and small-pox threatened the welfare of commerce and of human life, and even jeopardized the national cause, provided for a voluntary sanitary inspection survey and report, by a volunteer Council of Hygiene. When there was no board of health, that work, by the Citizen's Council of Hygiene, was organized and conducted by fifty (50) expert medical men; and the two editions of the volume of reports, with the charts, maps, and special labors, cost $18,000, and became the *raison d'être* of the Metropolitan Sanitary Code. Thus, wealth and intellect gave origin to the present sanitary system.

The death-rate has fallen from 34 in the 1,000 inhabitants, occasionally to 27, 28, or 28.9, &c., per 1,000. The value of health and life is more generally appreciated, or there has been a marked increase in the security and chance or expectation of life, between fifteen and forty-five years of age.

The influence and example of the Sanitary Code itself, and of the method and proceedings under the Code, have extended far over our continent, and have especially prepared the State soon to take action upon sanitary duties, throughout the Commonwealth.

(From Dr. ELISHA HARRIS, New York, N.Y.)

NEW YORK, May 7, 1876.

Legislation in regard to the public health began early in Massachusetts; principally, at first, for the prevention of small-pox. Quarantine was partially established in 1784. Acts for the prevention of the spread of small-pox were passed in 1701, 1730, 1731, 1742, 1757, 1776, 1777, 1792, 1793. In 1809 it was made compulsory, by law, that a committee be chosen in each town to superintend vaccination. The first Board of Health was established in 1799, in Boston and in Salem; a few years later, in Marblehead, Plymouth, Charlestown, Lynn, and Cambridge. Most of these boards were, however, twenty years later, merged into the common councils. The most important sanitary act passed in the United States, prior to the passage of the Massachusetts Registration Laws, was to prevent the spreading of contagious sickness, and to establish better regulations for quarantine. In 1835, the whole matter was again looked into, and Revised Statutes passed. None of the

early legislative acts comprehended Preventive Medicine, except in the narrow sense of preventing the extremely contagious diseases.

That local causes would promote the development of diseases was early believed by some. Dr. John Warren, in 1796, in regard to typhus or (typhoid) fever, which was very prevalent one or two years, wrote, " The filthy state of the streets and alleys, as the population becomes more dense, will expose us to the danger of such diseases." In the first year of the century, there was a lawsuit before the courts on the destruction of a dam by certain parties, who believed that, by promoting on its borders, at every increase of water, the decomposition of vegetable matter, an epidemic of malarial fever was caused. The testimony of various physicians and others was taken to prove the connection of the dam with the spread of the disease. The court, however, decided in favor of the owner of the dam.

In 1839 and 1841, Dr. John D. Fisher, of Boston, issued circulars to obtain information as to the causes and fatality of consumption. He received only three answers. In 1835, a circular was extensively distributed, inquiring into the history of intermittent fevers, and only two answers were received. In 1845, the Massachusetts Medical Society sent other circulars to the several towns, but received only one answer.[1]

The laws passed in New York, preceding and following the year 1800, were properly quarantine laws, like those in Massachusetts, to shut out contagious diseases. Later, important laws were passed; but they were not comprehensive enough to be of any great value.

Dr. John Griscom, of New York, was one of the first in this country to bring into prominence the idea of State Preventive Medicine, being incited by the work of Mr. Chadwick and others, of England. In 1845, Dr. Griscom presented a letter

---

[1] It is but just to the profession of Massachusetts to state that, during my investigations on the prevalence of consumption in that State, I obtained replies to my circular from every one of the three hundred and twenty-five towns, — all then existing. It is true, however, that they were obtained only after issuing three circulars, between January, 1854, and February, 1858. By them I was able, in 1855–56, to state the law of soil moisture, although I only fully declared it before the Society, at its annual meeting in 1862.

to the Mayor of New York, appealing to the City Government for legislative acts towards sanitary reform. His letter begins as follows : " No duty can engage the attention of the magistracy of a city or State more dignified in itself, more beneficial to the present generation, or more likely to prove useful to their descendants, than the procuring and maintaining a sound state of public health." This appeal (published afterwards under the title of " The Sanitary Condition of the Laboring Population of New York ") was transmitted by the Mayor to the Common Council ; but was returned by that body, with the report that they " did not think it proper, at this time, to go into such a measure." The paper contained few practical suggestions, being rather an *exposé* of the bad condition of the poor.

In 1847, the American Statistical Association appointed a committee to prepare a petition to the General Court of Massachusetts, for a sanitary survey of the State. In this paper (House Document 16, 1848), written by Dr. Edward Jarvis, of Dorchester, it is urged upon the Legislature that the promotion of the public health is as much the duty of a State Legislature, as the encouragement of agriculture, or the fostering of fine breeds of cattle. " It is not expected that any act or power of government can directly cause a man to be healthy ; but it can work as effectually for this, as it can make wheat grain, or an ox become fat."

The sanitary condition of the largest cities in the country was a subject, which attracted the attention of the American Medical Association in 1848–49. A committee was appointed, and several valuable papers were brought out.

A committee (Mr. Lemuel Shattuck, and others) appointed by the Massachusetts Legislature presented, in 1850, a thorough report of a general plan for the promotion of Public and personal health.[1] The belief is expressed that thousands of cases of sickness yearly occur that might have been prevented,

[1] Report of a General Plan for the Promotion of the Public and Personal Health, derived, prepared, and recommended by the Commissioners appointed under a Resolve of the Legislature of Massachusetts relating to a Sanitary Survey of the State, passed May 2, 1849. Boston : Dutton & Wentworth, State Printers, 1860.

and that the means of prevention are in the hands of the community.

This committee recommended that the laws of the State relating to public health be revised, and that a general board of health be established, that local boards be appointed, and that the formation of sanitary associations throughout the State be encouraged.

Several unsuccessful attempts were made by physicians in New York to obtain better legislation on sanitary matters, and to establish a board of health, with full powers. Finally, in 1864, the Citizen's Association began a sanitary inspection of New York. Medical men were appointed as inspectors, and their work was well done; leading, in 1866, to the passage of an act "to create a Metropolitan Sanitary District and Board of Health therein, for the preservation of life and health, and to prevent the spreading of disease."

(From Dr. ELISHA HARRIS, New York City, N.Y.)
NEW YORK, June 21, 1876.

. . . The best mode I can think of for contributing a summary of recent accurate information is this: —

In the general report of information concerning the paludal fevers and malarial areas in the United States, which I am preparing for the permanent uses of the American Public Health Association, and a part of which may be offered in the International Congress, I find it possible to glean out some completely demonstrated records, — 1st, of the *extinction* of malaria; 2d, the occasional return of brief periods of its prevalence, in certain localities; 3d, the permanent relapse into it, when a period of general culture has been followed by neglect of culture (suburban districts *in transitu* to city lots, &c.); 4th, the *prevalence* as well as the *removal* of certain *equivalents* of paludal malaria, in regions not subject to the paludal fevers, but wherein the drainage and drying of the ground is proved to be the most essential sanitary problem. These equivalents are such, as you have described in connection with consumption, and such as physicians recognize as arthritic, neuralgic, anæmic, and some of the diathetic diseases of localities. . . .

(From Dr. E. H. JANES to Dr. AUSTIN FLINT, Sen., New York, N.Y.)

NEW YORK, April 15, 1876.

I return to you the accompanying document, handed me by Dr. Janeway, with such answers as I have been able to make.

You will see that some of the questions I have left unanswered. I might say, in regard to the 1st, and the 2d with most of its subdivisions, the questions have never been sufficiently agitated to test the willingness of the State to expend money. The 7th, 8th, and 9th, I think you are far more competent to answer than I am.

If I were strongly pressed for an answer, I would say, in regard to the 7th, that pernicious intermittent, and yellow fever, formerly somewhat prevalent in portions of the State, have nearly or quite ceased to appear. This might not quite meet your views; therefore, I leave the question to be answered by aid of your more extended observation. As to 8th and 9th, though there may be changes in nomenclature, I do not think any new diseases have been introduced; except, perhaps, that typhoid may be said to have, in some degree taken the place of the malarial fevers, which were prevalent in colonial times.

(Dr. JANEWAY'S Statement, made by request of Dr. AUSTIN FLINT, Sen., New York, N.Y.)

NEW YORK.

Ques. 2–*a*. A bill is now before the Legislature for the establishment of a State Board of Health, with fair prospects of becoming a law.

2–*e*. Since the appearance of pleuro-pneumonia in this country, the State has supported a Cattle Commission; which, from time to time, has done good work in the investigation and suppression of the Texas cattle disease. In 1867, the State authorized an expenditure of $5,000 in the investigation of the cause of abortion among cows, which led to some good results in the improvement of our dairies.

4. In the winter of 1871, at the request of the medical profession, a County Board of Health was established for Richmond County. It operated well for two years, when it was abolished through the influence of persons, who felt themselves aggrieved by its requirements.

5. In the year 1850 the Legislature passed "An Act for the preservation of public health," by virtue of which the supervisors and justices of each town were constituted a Town Board of Health, and invested with powers of abating nuisances, of dealing with contagious diseases by quarantine measures, the establishment of hospitals in times of pestilence, and of other measures necessary for the preservation of public health. Municipal boards of health are established by special laws.

6–*b*. In 1847, an act was passed providing for the registry of births, marriages, and deaths; whereby it was made the duty of the clerks of the several school-districts to obtain the necessary statistics, and report the same, annually, to the several town clerks. This law has never been in successful operation. There is at present before the Legislature a bill, providing for general registration.

6–*e*. Title 16, ch. 8, of Revised Statutes, amended in 1869, authorizes the appointment of commissioners to decide in regard to the drainage of lands, upon the establishment of sufficient proofs of its necessity. In 1871, an act was passed requiring the Board of Health of the City of New York to direct the Department of Public Works to cause certain lands, within the corporate limits of said city, to be drained by other means than by sewers, whenever the City Sanitary Inspectors and Sanitary Superintendent shall "certify that such action is necessary for the protection of public health."

6–*i*. In 1860, an act was passed directing school boards to exclude from public schools all unvaccinated children; and authorizing trustees to appoint physicians to vaccinate children, the expense to be included in the annual tax.

In 1874, an act was passed authorizing the Board of Health of the City of New York to organize a corps of vaccinators, subject to the Sanitary Bureau, for the purpose of affording gratuitous vaccination.

6–*j*. In 1867, "An Act for the regulation of tenement and lodging houses in New York and Brooklyn" was passed. This law has had the effect to improve the condition of tenement-houses in regard to ventilation, drainage, cleanliness, cellar habitation, &c.

(From Dr. WILLIAM HENRY THAYER, Brooklyn, N.Y.)

BROOKLYN, N.Y., March 1, 1876.

I have taken great pains to be accurate and thorough, and have confined myself to facts; looking through the acts of Legislature (*Assembly* I should say, to speak exactly) for all the sanitary enactments. The other questions are answered from my personal knowledge, or the sanitary and other reports which I have quoted.

Replies to Questions on Sanitary Condition of the State of New York.

Ques. 1. The State of New York cannot be said to show, by its legislation, a true appreciation of the duty devolving upon a State to be careful of the health of its people; since it has not yet established a State Board of Health, nor a Registrar of Vital Statistics.

Ques. 2. No expenditure of money has thus far been necessary; as all the sanitary operations, carried on within the State, have been local, under laws authorizing or requiring towns and cities to organize health departments.

Ques. 5. By act of Legislature, every town and city in the State was ordered to establish a board of health (1850).

Ques. 6–*b*, *c*. A law for the registration of marriages, births, and deaths, was enacted in 1847, which required an annual report from every town and city to be made to the State government. Only a few, imperfect reports were made, which were never published; and, since 1852, the law has been absolutely a dead letter. There has never been a legislative report, nor have any steps been taken to secure the enforcement of the law. There is no penalty attached to its violation; and it is probable that few towns have ever taken steps to secure its observance.

In New York and Brooklyn and some other cities, registration of births, deaths, and marriages, is attempted.[1] The record of deaths is reliable, since no interment is permitted without a certificate from a physician or coroner; but the record of mar-

[1] Deaths have been registered in New York City since 1803; in Brooklyn, since 1848.

riages and births is incomplete, on account of the difficulty of enforcing returns.

The State census is still less reliable. That of 1855 gave 11,022 as the number of deaths in that year in New York City; whereas the City Inspector had reported 23,042, *i.e.* more than twice as many, during the same period.

6–*d*. There is no State Registrar, and no person appointed under the law to secure the enforcement of the Registration Law. The creation of such an office would seem to be the only way of enforcing its observance.

6–*e*. The only law, providing for drainage for sanitary reasons, is one passed in 1852 to drain the swamp lands on Indian River.

6–*h*. In 1834, an act for introducing lake water into New York City. Between 1853 and 1865, acts for the introduction of water into Brooklyn, Troy, Binghampton, Auburn, Rochester, Buffalo, Oswego, and Syracuse.

6–*i*. In 1832, all towns, situated on the Canada line, and on the canals, were ordered to appoint boards of health, with special reference to the danger of the introduction of cholera from Canada.

In 1784, 1794, 1796, 1797, 1798, 1801, 1804, 1811, 1820, and 1823, quarantine acts were passed for maritime cities, directed against the importation of yellow fever.

In 1866, an act was passed creating a Board of Commissioners to prevent the introduction of diseased cattle and sheep into the State. This act continued in force five years.

6–*j*. In 1867, an act was passed, regulating the construction and management of tenement-houses in New York City and Brooklyn; all the provisions of which law were very faithfully carried out under the Metropolitan Board of Health.[1]

---

[1] The following list contains all the sanitary laws passed by the Legislature of New York: —

1784. Quarantine act.
1794. Quarantine act, and general health law.
1796. More comprehensive act for New York City.
1797. Same, amended.
1798. Act to provide for yellow fever, and repealing all previous acts, having all the powers granted in them all.
1800. New quarantine acts.

Ques. 7. Periodic fever has diminished materially in some localities, which have been well drained. (See Report of the Committee on Hygiene of the Medical Society of the State of New York. Transactions of the State Society, 1875.)

Ques. 8. Diphtheria appeared in Albany, and other parts of New York, in 1859; and prevailed in one locality, with severity, till about 1865. From that time until 1870 it was rare and mild. Since 1870, it has been constantly present in New York City, Brooklyn, and in the neighboring counties, with much increased severity; *i.e.*, of graver type, and more infectious character. There is no evidence that it is influenced by local conditions, except in such degree and manner as all zymotic diseases are affected by them. In fact, it does not seem to be produced by any of the causes, which develop typhoid or periodic fevers; but appears to be of as grave and infectious a character in families of more than average physical vigor, and living under the best sanitary influences.

1801. Act repeating, in its provisions for internal health, the law of 1798.

1804. Two quarantine acts,— one relating to Albany and Hudson City.

1811. A new health law, with some additional powers.

1820. Health law for New York City, Albany, and Hudson City.

1823. Additional powers granted.

1827. Health laws revised, and all previous laws abrogated.

1832. Act requiring immediate establishment of a board of health in every town on the Canada line, and along the canals, and giving the same authority to all other towns in the State; expiring by limitation in February, 1833.

1847. Universal registration act.

1850. Act requiring every town and city to establish boards of health.

1852. Act to drain swamp lands on Indian River.

1859–65. Acts empowering certain cities to introduce water.

1866. Act creating Metropolitan Board of Health.

1866. Act for preserving health, during transportation, of animals used for food.

1866. Act appointing commissioners to prevent the introduction of diseased cattle and sheep in the State, to be in force three years; and, in 1869, extended two years.

1867. Act requiring quarantine ordinances to be passed in all cities and towns, outside of the Metropolitan Sanitary District.

1870. Act forbidding unwholesome substances to be deposited on, or near any highway.

Ques. 9. Diphtheria has occupied a portion of the health reports of the Metropolitan Board of Health. No annual reports have been published in Brooklyn.

Ques. 10. The Brooklyn Health Department was established by city ordinances in 1856; superseded, in 1866, by the Metropolitan Board of Health; and this followed, in 1870, by the Brooklyn Board of Health, established (like the Metropolitan Board of Health) by act of Legislature.

Ques. 11, 12. Ridgewood water is in general use. But many pumps, in old wells, still stand in the streets in the older part of Brooklyn, and are in constant use, — resorted to from an ignorant belief in the superior quality of well water; or, during the summer months, for its coldness. There is no reason to doubt that this water is polluted with matter, which the neighboring soil has derived from privies, cesspools, and drains; but the Board of Health has never taken steps to prevent the use of it.

Ques. 13. "Brooklyn enjoys an exhaustless and excellent source of water supply, though its population should increase to a million, or more." [Dr. Harris, in the Report of the Metropolitan Board of Health, New York, 1867.] The Ridgewood water, so called, is derived from a series of ponds and rivulets on the southerly slope of the ridge of land, which traverses Long Island from West to East. The water is intercepted near tide level, and conducted twelve miles, with a slight descending grade, to a great pump-well, five miles from City Hall, where it is pumped into a reservoir, 170 feet above tide level. "The water is nearly, if not quite, equal to the Croton water in purity; but the liability to contamination is much greater. Consequently, the importance of constant watchfulness against sewage defilement of the rivulet-sources of supply is correspondingly greater." [Harris, 1867.] Professor C. F. Chandler, of Columbia College, at that time chemist to the Metropolitan Board of Health, now President of the Board, undertook, in 1867, to make a weekly analysis of the Croton and Ridgewood waters at the reservoirs; but the examination of the Ridgewood water was not continued. In 1874, on complaint of the Water Board that a brook in the town of Hempstead, Long Island, an affluent of the Ridgewood reservoir, was defiled by

drainage from numerous privies and barn-yards, the Supreme Court granted an injunction, restraining the defendants from all such defilements. This is understood to have been effectual; but it is a matter for grave consideration, and presents a difficulty that is likely to be of frequent recurrence, as the population increases.

Ques. 16. The common sewers discharge into East River.

Ques. 17. The Board of City Works annually makes contracts with a number of persons, one for each ward of the city, for the removal of house offal twice a week. The contractors sublet the contracts to numerous irresponsible persons, who keep pigs in the suburbs. The work is done irregularly and imperfectly. Much organic material is put into the ash barrels; which are emptied by the contractors once a week, and the contents used to fill up sunken lots within the city limits.

Ques. 18. No State reports.

The Metropolitan Board of Health published four annual reports (1867–70), which were full and valuable. The New York City Board has published annual reports since 1870. The Brooklyn Health Board publishes a weekly report in one of the newspapers, but nothing more elaborate. It is required by law to publish an annual report.

Ques. 19. Mortality records have been kept in New York City since 1803; in Brooklyn, since 1848. No health reports were published prior to 1867.

Ques. 20. The Medical Society of the State of New York has manifested a lively interest in sanitary matters, from its foundation; and an interest that has taken more practical form with advancing years, keeping pace with the general development of sanitary science in Europe and the United States. At its first annual meeting (1807), it passed resolutions, directing each member to prepare an account of the medical topography of his own county, and a sketch of its diseases. In 1830, a committee was appointed to take steps for a medical, topographical survey of the State. In 1861, a committee, of which Dr. Elisha Harris was chairman, made a report on the necessity of a topographical and hydrographical survey of the State, with reference to systematic drainage, as a hygienic measure; based

on information derived from physicians of the State, to one thousand of whom a circular had been addressed.[1]

(Dr. S. Oakley Vanderpoel on Quarantine in New York.)

New York, through the agency of its always extended commerce, was devastated, even during the last century, with epidemics of yellow fever. One is recorded as early as 1719, and several during succeeding years. During the thirty-four years prior to 1809, there were seventeen of these terrible visitations, some of which were exceedingly extensive and fatal.

[1] The necessity of a system of permanent drainage of the towns, composing the Metropolitan Sanitary District, *i.e.*, the counties of New York, Richmond [Staten Island], King's and Queen's [Long Island], and West Chester, was advocated in the annual reports of the Metropolitan Board of Health (especially that for 1869), accompanied with detailed reports of sanitary inspectors on the prevalence of zymotic diseases, traceable to the neglect of drainage.

In 1875 the Committee on Hygiene of the Medical Society of the State of New York made an interesting and valuable report on drainage [see Transactions, 1875], showing, on the testimony of many members of the Society, the intimate dependence of malarial diseases, especially, on excessive moisture in the soil, with a few instances of the disappearance or sensible reduction of that class of diseases in districts which had been properly drained, — notably in New York City, in Brooklyn, and New Utrecht, in King's County; in the counties of Saratoga, Erie, and St. Lawrence. The report contained a very telling statement of the condition of Cayuga and Genesee Counties, with reference to the want of drainage, with a proposition for a radical cure of the difficulty.

In many parts of the State, where similar conditions exist, medical men are examining, and reporting the necessity of thorough drainage; and the State Medical Society is endeavoring to secure suitable legislation for this end. A bill for the drainage of swamp lands throughout the State, and one for the creation of a State Board of Health, were introduced to the Legislature of 1874, but were not enacted; and efforts are continued to secure their passage. These measures will be furthered by the publication of a topographical map of the State, now in preparation by General Vielé. But the supposed antagonism of sanitary to pecuniary interests, in different localities, will render it extremely difficult to secure legislation on this subject. A special act was passed, twenty years ago, for the drainage of parts of Genesee, Ontario, and Niagara Counties, for sanitary ends, on petition of citizens of those counties; but it was repealed by the next Legislature, by the influence of mill-owners, who claimed that their interests and rights were invaded.

In 1784, in order, as much as possible, to prevent the same, a law was enacted which forbade the approach "nearer the city of New York than Bedloe's Island, or into any of the harbors of the State, of any vessels having on board any person infected with yellow fever, or any other infectious distemper." The vessel was required to perform such quarantine as the Governor, or, in his absence, the Mayor of the city, should see proper and direct; "and, until released from such detention, . . . "no person . . . or goods or merchandise could be brought ashore or unloaded, or put on board any other vessel within the State, or the neighboring States of New Jersey or Connecticut." Heavy penalties were established for violation of this law, and pilots were made responsible for the proper location, and report of such vessels. A physician was appointed by the Governor to go on board, and make due examinations, with full powers to enforce the provisions of the law.

This act remained without extensive amendment until 1790, when a new act was passed; and this was replaced by another, in 1796, which was variously amended, until, in 1811, it was repealed by a general law, reorganizing the quarantine service. In like manner, new organic acts, repealing all laws inconsistent with them, have been passed, in 1820, 1823, 1832, 1839, 1846, and 1863. Many acts of amendment, standing on the statute books between these dates, were harmonized, and sometimes embodied, in the laws then passed. In all this legislation, valuable restrictions, which had resulted from experience, in administering quarantine restraint upon commerce, became permanent laws; and much more of undigested and crude experiment crept into the system, to make confusion and to work harm for a brief time, and then disappear.

The sanitary theories were aggressive, and full of experimental crudities; and commerce, yielding only under the pressure of public clamor, pricked on by epidemic devastation and traditional fear, would sometimes rally in times of health, and hold a short-lived triumph, only until another visitation of disease.

Thus, at one time, a distance of one mile above, and the same distance below, the cities and towns along the Hudson was a quarantine limit for the water-fronts of the places, and

NEW YORK.

the sanitary questions involved were to be decided by the parties of the place.

Under the action of that law, Alexander Hamilton, then Secretary of the United States, was placed on quarantine opposite Albany, in 1793, because he, with Mrs. Hamilton, was on his way from Philadelphia, where there was yellow fever. This law was soon after repealed.

In 1794, a lazaretto was established on Governor's Island, and, two years later, a health officer and health board for the city of New York. At this time, some discrimination was made in the law, based upon the circumstances of the vessel arriving, as to passengers, and the port from which she came; and pilots were to be suspended for breach of quarantine law.

In 1806, further discrimination was made in the quarantine restrictions, based upon the season of the year; and, five years later, vessels from parts infected with yellow fever or other pestilential disease were, besides these restrictions, previously enforced, required to discharge their cargoes before receiving *pratique*, and detained thirty (30) days before, and twenty (20) after, their cargoes were out. A marine hospital was erected on Staten Island, over five miles from the city, and the quarantine station removed to that place.

These hospitals remained until the growth of New York rendered them dangerous to population; and they ceased in 1867, to be re-established, a few years later, on artificial islands in the harbor.

With this change, the location of the boarding station is, at this time, on Staten Island, near where it was then established. Under this law was adopted the distinctive flag of quarantine for the State, and regulations made for its use.

In 1823, vessels, navigated by steam, were made subject to the decision of the health officer, and released from the legal restrictions prescribed for other vessels; and the laws made applicable to "all diseases which might, in the opinion of the Board of Health, be deemed pestilential, contagious, or infectious, or otherwise dangerous to the health of the city." These diseases were specified, in 1863, as yellow fever, cholera, typhus or ship fever, and small-pox, and any new disease, not now known, of a contagious, infectious, or pestilential nature;

and these are the diseases whose care on shipboard now occupies the attention of the quarantine authorities.

A commission of appeal from the decisions of the health officers was organized in 1839; but, under the judicious system now enforced, an appeal is unknown.

In such manner, has the quarantine supervision of New York grown; under the combined experience of the wants of its port, both sanitary and commercial, and in the full light of the scientific advance made in sanitary matters. Originating in the fears of the multitude, it started with the traditional superstitions, which have attached to sanitary precaution from the tenth to the present century. Its advance has been contested at each step by the ignorant and interested, each on their own part; and it is only as disease has been deprived of its relation to sorcery, and subjected to the tests of known natural laws, that judicious care could be maintained; which satisfied [by protecting] the ignorant and timid, and removed the prejudices of commerce, by imposing only rational and legitimate restraint. Each advance has been the removal of some inherited absurdity. The very name remains, shorn of the meaning in which it originated; and the justice to all that is meted out includes, in its measure, the traveller and the merchant.

Quarantine to-day means, in New York, simply sanitary inspection for infectious disease on ships, and sanitary care for those so unfortunate as to be affected by it, with only such detention from business, in each case, as the particular case requires.

At my request, Dr. Vanderpoel has kindly given the following description of the manner in which quarantine is enforced in New York:—

The quarantine department of the port of New York consists of a boarding station, at Clifton, on Staten Island; a summer boarding station, on a station-ship anchored in the lower bay, four miles below the Narrows; two artificial islands, viz., Hoffman Island, of about three and a half acres, and Dix Island, of about three acres. The burying-ground is at Seguin's Point, on the south-eastern part of Staten Island, about a mile north of the Prince's Bay light-house.

Beside these, the hospitals on Ward's and Blackwell's Islands are used for the reception of certain patients, which are cared for, under the law, by the quarantine department.

This quarantine was originally established to guard against the importation, by shipping, of "yellow fever or any other infectious distemper." (1784.) The diseases against which it now applies are "yellow fever, cholera, typhus, or ship fever, and any new disease not now known of a contagious, infectious, or pestilential nature." In the management of these diseases, of which the four named are subject to treatment, small-pox patients are sent to the small-pox hospital on Blackwell's Island; typhus fever, to the emigrant's hospital for that disease, on Ward's Island; and cholera and yellow fever, to the quarantine hospital, on Dix Island. If both the latter diseases are in the harbor at the same time, the station-ship is used as a hospital for the treatment of one of them.

The two artificial islands of the department are wonders of artificial construction. They are built on West Bank, — a shoal which forms the western limit of the ship channel (East Bank being on the other side of it); and, at the time of their construction, stood in water about seven feet deep at low water. Dix Island, the most southerly, is covered by a hospital structure of wood, containing eight hospital wards, one story high, one hundred feet long, and with room for beds on each side. Two additional buildings, of the same size, are used for attendants and store-rooms and kitchen, and the engine-house, and disinfection chamber, where disinfection is practised with super-heated steam, hot water, chlorine, or other gases, and liquid disinfectants, as required.

The laundry and work-shop occupy another building, of about 180 feet long. The construction of the hospital is that known as the "American Pavilion," of which style this is an improved and favorable specimen; the general plan being a long corridor, with doors along the side, opening into the wards, which are arranged parallel to each other, and at right angles with it; and at its end is the two-story residence of the superintendent: thus giving, by windows and other means, the most unobstructed ventilation to a hospital, built in a location where the surrounding conditions of hygiene are unexcelled. The record

of this hospital shows the effect of these conditions, in the unexampled recoveries from disease among those under treatment. Hoffman Island has three large brick buildings, of two full stories each, for the reception of healthy persons; including passengers and crews of vessels so infected with epidemic disease that their disembarkation is required before it can be stayed. The buildings are of brick, and the two larger ones not divided into rooms; each story being a large ward, in which berths can be placed, with accommodation for several thousand steerage, the third building being divided into rooms for the other, passengers. These islands were first recommended as possible by General Benham, United States Engineer Corps, in the New York Assembly, Dec. 19, 1859. He furnished working estimates and plans; and their construction was commenced in 1867, and completed 1874, at an expense somewhat above one million dollars.

All vessels arriving from a foreign port during the entire year, and all vessels from any place in America, in the ordinary passage from which they pass south of Cape Henlopen, arriving between the first day of April and the first day of November, and all vessels on board of which any person shall have been sick of severe or doubtful disease, are subject to the visitation, inspection, and decisions of the health officer of the port. After inspection by him, they are permitted to proceed, without detention, if free from conditions dangerous to the public health. In case of infectious disease being on board, the measures taken are based upon the circumstances surrounding each particular case. The sick are removed to one of the quarantine hospitals; and, if there is no further danger apprehended, the vessel allowed to pass. If, however, there exists further danger, such precautions are taken, as the nature of the case demands.

In summer, with yellow fever on board, and from a port where yellow fever prevails, the vessel discharges its cargo in lighters, in the stream, before going to dock; is cleansed carefully, has its bilges washed, besides being thoroughly disinfected and ventilated. The importance of deciding the detention and measures necessary in each case, upon an investigation of the circumstances surrounding it, is evident in the case of yellow fever and cholera. Under the process of "quarantine," prac-

tised formerly (and in the East still in use), of which only the name remains in the New York system, the detention for a case of either of these diseases would be either for a month, or perhaps an entire season. As it is at present, a single case of cholera having occurred before arrival, and a period elapsed equal to the time of incubation, and followed by no others, would secure a detention long enough only to furnish an accurate and thorough inspection of the vessel, her condition, and that of the passengers, and she would then proceed. In case of an extensive and fatal epidemic of cholera, occurring on a vessel arriving in warm weather, every person would be removed to Hoffman Island, and the vessel, after purification, permitted to go to the city. The people from her could be detained until no more disease appeared; those who became sick being at once removed to Dix Island in the steamboat, which is kept for this purpose, and being under circumstances favorable for the suppression of the disease, and those attacked being treated for it in a place suitable for its cure, there would result the least detention and fatality probable under the circumstances.

All of the advances, made in the New York quarantine, have had for their motive the reduction of the detention and annoyance of delay in case of disease, which the fears and traditions of the populace would not permit ashore, and which were included in the meaning of the popular word "pest;" while, at the same time, commerce should be as little embarrassed as possible. Naturally, some evils crept into the management of affairs, so delicate and so full of temptation, as the adjustment between business interests and sanitary requirement; but the progressive march of improvement has, at last, placed this department in a position, where the health officer is sustained in all his official acts by the commercial interest of New York, which finds in his pass a protection from the further obstacle to trade, which would invariably follow a commerce, in which there was no sanitary restriction. Thus the apparent incongruous interests of quarantine and commerce are united at this port, upon a system, which is satisfactory to and is adequate for both.

(From Dr. W. C. Wey, Elmira, N.Y.)

Elmira, N.Y., Jan. 10, 1876.

Ques. 1. The Legislature has, on several occasions, partially responded to the urgent wishes and arguments of physicians and others informed on such subjects, by passing laws in the interest of public health; but it has never shown "a due appreciation of the duty, devolving upon a State to be careful of the health of its people."

Ques. 2–b. For local measures only.

Ques. 5. Town boards of health are provided for by statute, to consist of a justice of the peace, the supervisor of the town, and a competent physician, named by the foregoing officers; and such boards have control over small-pox and other contagious diseases.

Ques. 6–e. Yes; but with reference to agricultural uses, and inoperative as regards the public health.

6–h. Yes; but the laws are local in operation.

6–i. Yes; by rigid quarantine laws; and, as regards *small-pox*, by a general law, which forbids boards of education to permit unvaccinated children to enter the public schools.

6–j. Applicable to New York City.

Ques. 7–a. In many regions, — the Chemung Valley, for instance, — the early settlers were greatly disturbed by intermittent fever, which has "ceased to appear."

7–b. I can only recall the crushing out of cholera by Professor Frank H. Hamilton, on Blackwell's Island, New York, a few years since. I have no data at hand to refresh my mind on this subject.

Ques. 8. Cerebro-spinal meningitis and diphtheria, I think, fall under this question. I am not aware that reference is made to these diseases, in the colony of New York, by early writers. Dr. Samuel Bard, of the city of New York, in 1789, described an epidemic, which is believed to have been diphtheria. Trichiniasis, a recent outbreak of which occurred in the adjoining county of Steuben, may, and doubtless did, exist in a former century.

Ques. 9. I am not aware that the State has authorized investigations to be made, concerning the affections mentioned opposite question 8. Many individuals, however, have written

on the subjects indicated; among whom may be noted Dr. T. H. Squire, of Elmira, who contributed a paper on cerebro-spinal meningitis to the "Transactions of the Medical Society of the State of New York," in 1858; Dr. John C. Dalton, of New York, who furnished a very elaborate paper on Trichina Spiralis to the Academy of Medicine, in that city, vol. iii. 1864; Dr. Edward A. Hun, of Albany, who describes a fatal case, and reviews the history of Trichina Spiralis, in the "Transactions of the Medical Society of the State of New York" for 1869; and a list of writers on diphtheria, too numerous to cite.

Ques. 10–a. Yes, through the efforts of successive boards of health.

Ques. 10–b. Yes, in small-pox and typhoid fever.

Ques. 13. From small streams in the hills, three miles from the city, which are collected by means of a dam, and conveyed to a distributing reservoir.

Ques. 15. The city is partially and imperfectly supplied with sewers.

Ques. 17. Sewage is conveyed to the Chemung River,—a shallow stream, which passes directly through the city,—and, under the influence of the sun, it is permitted to poison the atmosphere over a large extent of surface.

House offal is conveyed to the sewers, to a very limited extent. It is commonly disposed of on the premises, in vaults dug in porous ground.

Slops, &c. In well-ordered houses, pipes communicate with cesspools. Ordinarily, slops are thrown directly on the surface; thus poisoning the water supply where wells are used, and otherwise involving the health of residents.

Ques. 19. City reports for nine years.

Ques. 22. Generally, I would answer, No. In all directions of inquiry, however, and especially in respect to the laws of heredity, I feel as if such progress had been made as to warrant the conviction, that a marked influence will be exerted upon the sum total of disease, in time to come.

214 APPENDIX.

RECORD OF TEMPERATURE AND RAINFALL AT ASHEVILLE, BUNCOME COUNTY, NORTH CAROLINA.

	JANUARY.				FEBRUARY.				MARCH.				APRIL.				MAY.				JUNE.				JULY.			
	Highest.	Lowest.	Mean.	Rainfall.	Highest.	Lowest.	Mean.	Rainfall.	Highest.	Lowest.	Mean.	Rainfall.	Highest.	Lowest.	Mean.	Rainfall.	Highest.	Lowest.	Mean.	Rainfall.	Highest.	Lowest.	Mean.	Rainfall.	Highest.	Lowest.	Mean.	Rainfall.
1867	.	.	.	.	.	.	.	.	.	.	.	.	.	.	.	.	.	.	.	.	.	.	.	.	88	60	73.11	.
1868	61	3	33.03	.	62	4	35.46	.	75	17	48.90	.	78	31	53.12	3.6	82	38	61.77	.	85	59	70.41	.	86	66	71.19	.
1869	60	20	42.30	.	62	16	40.77	2.	70	12	43.52	3.7	76	30	53.51	.	82	42	60.00	.	86	57	68.36	6.4	84	60	70.40	1.5
1870	65	12	41.29	3.7	64	7	38.54	2.3	68	14	41.68	4.5	81	36	53.75	3.5	85	43	59.44	3.8	85	57	67.37	4.7	87	61	73.15	6.4
1871	60	19	39.13	2.2	65	27	43.00	5.0	60	30	50.85	5.	80	41	57.66	1.3	86	45	61.81	5.7	87	54	67.87	4.1	90	53	70.43	3.2
1872	61	10	32.43	.2	68	9	38.16	1.6	69	18	40.11	1.7	81	38	55.71	1.8	83	41	62.06	3.6	85	56	71.09	3.7	88	65	72.99	4.2
1873	63	7	34.76	4.7	66	4	39.96	9.6	67	3	41.92	3.3	83	36	53.90	3.7	83	46	62.52	2.	87	55	68.37	2.	89	63	71.52	1.1
1874	67	9	39.29	1.	69	22	40.51	3.	70	22	46.97	4.4	76	30	51.03	3.7	83	45	62.11	6.3	85	56	68.83	6.3	88	62	72.87	11.2
1875	63	.5	36.48	2.6	60	6	34.52	6.2	.	.	.	.	.	.	.	.	86	44	62.54	2.7	86	60	72.17	3.7	.	.	.	.
Extremes & Averages.	67	3	37.34	2.4	69	4	38.94	4.4	75	3	44.85	3.8	83	30	54.10	2.3	86	38	61.53	4.	87	54	69.31	4.1	90	53	71.96	4.6

NORTH CAROLINA.

	AUGUST.				SEPTEMBER.				OCTOBER.				NOVEMBER.				DECEMBER.				YEAR.			
	Highest.	Lowest.	Mean.	Rainfall.	Highest.	Lowest.	Mean.	Rainfall.	Highest.	Lowest.	Mean.	Rainfall.	Highest.	Lowest.	Mean.	Rainfall.	Highest.	Lowest.	Mean.	Rainfall.	Highest.	Lowest.	Mean.	Rainfall.
1867	87	60	67.59	.	86	53	67.98	.	81	31	51.94	.	72	19	47.59	.	67	13	43.01	.	88		53.18	
1868	83	58	70.56	.	83	42	66.08	.	75	31	55.27	.	70	21	43.06	.	60	−1	33.18	.	86	−1	52.99	33.5
1869	86	51	73.78	2.2	76	36	58.61	1.5	68	24	48.55	1.8	64	24	40.43	1.4	60	15	37.23	5.6	86	15	53.89	43.5
1870	85	63	71.81	5.6	77	48	64.04	2.5	74	35	54.60	2.	69	19	44.31	3.6	64	−1	33.82	2.5	87	−1	53.89	42.7
1871	88	57	71.91	7.4	77	34	60.97	2.4	75	36	56.86	2.8	69	23	44.64	2.2	65	4	36.95	.4	90	4	55.51	30.3
1872	86	56	71.02	5.5	86	44	63.70	2.2	78	32	52.57	2.7	69	7	39.50	1.2	60	8	33.57	4.	88	8	52.55	43.
1873	88	60	70.57	4.7	85	43	64.80	2.5	76	24	50.40	9	64	15	41.51	4.5	68	8	40.31	1.6	89	4	53.38	43.
1874	83	56	69.93	3.4	80	52	65.71	2.8	76	32	54.59	2.	72	21	45.87	3.6	72	17	40.80	1.9	88	9	55.19	43.4
1875	.	.	.	.	.	.	.	.	.	.	.	.	.	.	.	.	.	.	.	.	.	5		
Extremes and Averages	88	51	70.90	4.8	86	34	63.99	2.3	81	24	53.10	2.	72	7	43.36	2.8	72	−1	37.36	2.7	90	−1	53.89	40.2

Mean temperature of Spring, 53.49; Summer, 70.72; Autumn, 53.48; Winter, 37.87. During the above period of eight years, the thermometer but twice reached above 88°, and but three times below 3°. (11 months.)

The above report is based upon observations of thermometer made at 7 A.M., 2 P.M., and 9 P.M.

The means of temperature are obtained as directed by the Chief Signal Officer, "by adding together the morning and afternoon observations, and twice the evening observation, and dividing the sum by 4."

Presented by E. J. ASTON.

NORTH CAROLINA.

(From Dr. Edwin A. Anderson, Wilmington, N.C.)

. . . .
I am very sorry to have to reply to all your questions in the negative; such is the poverty of our people, caused by the severity of the late war.

Peculations, enormous and excessive, ruinous taxation, and negro rule, have existed to so great extent that, struggling for the means of existence, our people are utterly unable to adopt such improvements or sanitary regulations, as are common in more favored communities.

(From Dr. William A. B. Norcom, Edenton, N.C.)

Edenton, N.C., Jan. 21, 1876.

. . . .
Our State is so sparsely settled that we do not so much need a State Board of Health as you do; but we must have one. I have been, for several years, on the Committee of "American Medical Association on State Medicine and Public Hygiene;" but we have not yet been able to do any thing in this State. I shall bring the matter before our State Medical Society in May next, and make a strong effort in so good a cause. I should like to know something about your State Board of Health, to guide me. Our largest city (Wilmington) contains only about fifteen hundred, and Raleigh, now, about nine thousand inhabitants.

PENNSYLVANIA.

(From Lorin Blodgett, Esq., Philadelphia, Penn.)

Philadelphia, Penn., June 21, 1876.

. . . . I intended, some days ago, to prepare and forward to you a sketch of the actual operations in house-building in this city, as illustrated in the groups and streets I had the pleasure to show to yourself and Dr. Harris, on the occasion of your recent visit here. The work was begun in September, 1875, some twenty houses being finished before the winter compelled the temporary

stoppage of work; the remainder being finished this spring and summer. Of the one hundred and thirty-one houses erected on the square, or portion of the actual area enclosed by the principal streets, all are now sold; and the interest in the property is wholly in the resident owners, or in the hands of sub-contractors, the principals being released from risk or responsibility. And the results have generally been so satisfactory to both these principals, that the square adjoining this, on the south, is now being built up rapidly, in precisely the same manner; over forty cellars being walled up, and the brick walls half erected. The owners of the real estate, in both cases, are a firm of most active and intelligent capitalists; and the most important feature of the case is the advantage the plan offers to capitalists everywhere. The area built upon is exactly 400 by 400 feet, or nearly $3\frac{2}{3}$ acres. Adding half the street width on each side (three sides), it is 425 feet by 450 feet, to include all the land represented $4\frac{4}{10}$ acres. The value assumed for the land was $100,000, or $22,750 per acre; the owners of the estate advancing $100,000 in cash in addition, and placing in first mortgages on the one hundred and thirty-one houses an aggregate of $200,000, on which interest began April 25, 1876. And all these being first mortgages on houses, worth two and one-half times the amount of each mortgage, they are considered here among the best of securities, perfectly good for the amount represented in each case. The conditions under which the advances to the builder were made were as follows; namely:—

One-fourth on laying the posts of the first floor.
One-eighth on laying the posts of the second floor.
One-eighth on putting on roof.
One-fourth when rough cast.
One-eighth when white plastered.
One-eighth when fully finished.

The largest houses are three stories high, and valued at $5,000, on which is a mortgage of 2,250.

The second-sized are two-stories; value, $3,500 to $4,000; on mortgage, $2,000.

Third size, value, $3,500; mortgage, $1,500.

Fourth, and smallest, 2 storied; value, $1,600.

The condition of advancement of the buildings was, in all cases, security for the advance.

The same property was, at one time, proposed to be built upon differently; the builder in that case was to advance the money, and to take alternate first mortgages, giving the estate an equal and alternate part, or half the houses of each class, that might be built. The principle is the same; the land, in each case, taking half the first mortgages, and the money advanced to build with taking the other half. Above the amount of these mortgages, in every case, there is an estimated value equal to the mortgage; as, for example, in the smaller houses, 14×48 feet, the proportions are: —

Land	$400
Cash advanced	400
Mortgage	$800
Net cash value of house	1,600
Trade or negotiable value	1,700 to 1,800

The builder informs me that he can sell these houses at $800 cash above the mortgage, and make money: he can, in fact, sell at $700, and make some money; the purchaser having the option to pay interest at six per cent on the $800 ($48 per year), or to pay that off also. This, for the smallest houses. On the others, the mortgage rises to $2,250, on the three-story, ten-roomed houses, fronting on 13th Street; the selling value being $5,000. The rental is fixed at $14 per month on the smallest, which is ten per cent on their cost; to $25 and $30 per month on the three-story houses, which is also ten per cent on their cost, but not ten per cent on their selling value, the margin of profit being greater in these. All these houses are taken as fast as they are built. There are no finished ones vacant; and many are occupied before the builders can entirely complete them.

The second square, upon which one hundred and thirty-one more are to be erected, by the same estate, would not be put in rapid progress by such owners, if there was reason to anticipate an excess.

I have been impressed for years with the power that this building system has to advance the social condition of the

people, and have actively participated in its extension, by showing and enforcing its advantages. There can be no loss to either the land-owner or the party (whoever he may be) that advances the money. I drew the contracts of the second plan named, in several cases; or the plan by which the builder, or any third party, makes the money advances. In that case, the $100,000 represented by the land value would take half the one hundred and thirty-one mortgages; and whoever advanced the $100,000 ready money would take the other half; and the principle is the same if applied to any smaller area, or smaller sum, — even to $1,000 on land, and $1,000 in money. Next in importance is the fact that all this building is co-operative: the party who supplied the bricks took his pay in houses, the painter, the plumber, and hard-ware furnisher, the stone-mason and stone furnisher. On the original builder's plan of this property, as built, the names of the chief suppliers of material appear as owners of assigned houses, — two or three each.

I think I need not say to you that these houses are built of the best materials, and in the best manner. You saw how they were built, finished, and furnished. There can be no neater or more tasteful dwelling than a two-story brick, with pressed brick front, marble window-sills and doorsteps, deep cornice, and heavy tin-roof. Yet these are to be bought for $800, or to be rented for $14 per month, in any number, on the most cleanly and best-paved streets, with street-cars passing the door; and they are built with the aid of the most intelligent of capitalists, who own the land.

. . . . I repeat that I have been profoundly impressed with the change that this building system, with its associate building associations, has effected in the condition of the working-people of this city, during my residence here of twenty years. I have watched it, with intense interest, during this entire period, have written much upon it, and am now more than ever assured that it is entirely practicable in both Boston and New York.

. . . . I believe that many tracts, within easy reach of Boston and New York, would be well paid for at this price per acre ($22,750, the price of the land built upon in this illustration at Philadelphia), which includes the street surface, as will be seen. And, as these rents and prices are very low, twenty-five per

cent might easily be added to the value of the land, without obstructing the enterprise, or embarrassing the sale or rental when built. Perhaps I should say, that I have at no time been pecuniarily interested, as owner, builder, agent, or otherwise, in any of these building enterprises. Their influence, in withdrawing the body of the people from the social hot-beds of great cities, and their elevating power in giving them attractive homes of their own, constitute my only inducement to urge their adoption elsewhere.

I beg leave to call the attention of the reader to the following excellent letter from

Dr. William Ford, Philadelphia, Pa.

PENNSYLVANIA AND PHILADELPHIA.

"Ques. 1. Does your State, by its legislation, show a due appreciation of the duty devolving upon a State to be careful of the health of its people?"

The answer to this question involves a matter of opinion. If I were to answer it according to a rigid interpretation of the standard of the requirements of State Medicine of the present day, and with the knowledge of what has been done by State and Governmental authorities, both in this country and abroad, I should unhesitatingly say, No. But, while it appears that some measures, deemed highly essential for the better protection of the health of the people, have not been authorized and made obligatory by legislative enactments, the State should receive due credit for a very considerate interest in the sanitary welfare of her subjects, as evinced by the numerous laws on her statute-books, framed for the protection of life and health, extracts of which I shall append, under proper headings.

Many of the laws are of comparatively recent date, indicating that a spirit of progress in health matters exists in the Commonwealth, which it is to be hoped, and confidently expected, from present indications,[1] will lead to the supplying of the more manifest deficiencies in our State laws.

---

[1] A thorough scientific survey of the entire State has been in progress for several years, and is being pushed forward with zeal.

The Legislature has now under consideration the establishment of a

"Ques. 2. Is it willing to expend money, —

"2-*a*. To support State or Local Boards of Health?"

There has never been a State Board of Health in Pennsylvania; but, at the present time, there is before the Legislature "An Act to create a State Board of Health," &c., which has the support of many influential citizens of the Commonwealth, — principally of the medical profession; and it is thought that it will become a law. The act, which was defeated at the last session of the Legislature, contained many objectionable provisions, which have been omitted in the present draft.

Boards of health have been established in Philadelphia, Allegheny City, Reading, Harrisburg, and in some other places. That of Philadelphia dates back to the year 1794, though health laws were in operation at a much earlier period.

They are supported by local funds.

"2-*b*. To carry out scientific investigations as to the causes of disease?"

No regularly organized body, acting under State authority, has ever been created, so far as I can learn, which included among its objects "scientific investigations as to the causes of disease;" but the act under consideration, above alluded to, provides for such investigations to be made annually, at the expense of the State.

"2-*c*. To repress noxious or offensive trades?

"2-*d*. To prevent adulteration of food?

"2-*e*. To prevent cattle disease?"

I know of no laws under the provisions of which the State assumes, directly, the pecuniary responsibilities of repressing noxious or offensive trades, of preventing adulteration of food, or of preventing cattle disease; but there are special acts upon these subjects, which depend, for their efficient enforcement, entirely upon the local administrations.

The expense of carrying out these laws is defrayed by the local authorities.

The proposed act establishing a State Board of Health, provides, in a general way, for the investigation of such subjects

State Board of Health, and a Bureau of Vital Statistics, for the whole State. A new and carefully-drawn bill, regulating the practice of medicine, is also before the Legislature at the present time.

at the State's cost; and the duty is imposed upon the Board of recommending, from time to time, such additional legislation as may be suggested by these investigations and examinations.

"2–f. To carry on any other investigations tending to public health, or to prevent ill-health?"

Yes. Under this head may be mentioned two important works now being conducted by the State. The one is a thorough and extended geological survey of the State, including a full chemical examination of clays, soils, and water; the other, the appointment of fishery commissioners, and the making of liberal appropriations for the purpose of hatching and propagating useful tribes of edible fishes, with which all the streams, lakes, and fresh waters of the Commonwealth are being stocked and supplied.

"Ques. 3. Has your State established a State Board of Health?"

There is, at the present time, before the Legislature a bill to create a State Board of Health, which will probably become a law.

In the event of its failure to pass that body at its present session, the delay can be but temporary; for a well-organized, central board is deemed very essential to the proper supervision and systematic management of health matters throughout the State, by a large number of citizens, who will continue their efforts to have such a board created, until attended with success.

"3–a. If so, when was it established?"

Answered above.

"3–b. What amount of annual appropriations is made for its support?"

Eight thousand dollars, proposed.

"3–c. Are any occasional and extra grants made for special investigation?"

The expenses for special sanitary service are to be paid out of the above appropriation.

"3–a. Has such a board any organized body of correspondents or inspectors throughout the State?"

The health officers and boards of health in the State are to act as correspondents; and the *act* also provides for the receiv-

ing of reports and information relating to the safety of life, and promotion of health, from all public dispensaries, hospitals, asylums, infirmaries, prisons, and schools; and from the managers, principals, and officers thereof; and from proprietors, managers, lessees, of places of public resort in the State, &c.

"3-e. What executive powers have been given to the Board with reference to local nuisances or noxious trades?"

The proposed act confers authority upon the Board to enter, examine, and survey, at any time, all grounds, erections, vehicles, structures, apartments, buildings, and places, with the object of carrying out the design of the act; to co-operate with local authorities in suppressing nuisances, threatening the public health; and, when deemed necessary, to suggest further legislative action: but the executive powers are almost entirely confined to the local authorities.

"Ques. 4. Have any County Boards of Health been established by law?"

"Ques. 5. Have any Town Boards of Health been established by law?"

No County Boards of Health have been established by law except in Philadelphia; the city and county limits being the same. Boards of health have been established by law in the boroughs of Carlisle and Lebanon, and in the cities of Philadelphia, Pittsburg, Harrisburg, Reading, and Allegheny City. Some towns have health officers, acting under the chief burgess and Town Council: York and Allentown, for example.

In 1874, an act was passed by the Legislature providing that the City Councils of any city of the third class (having more than ten thousand, and less than one hundred thousand, inhabitants), in which there does not now exist a board of health organized according to law, shall have the power to create a board of health, in accordance with the provisions of the act, which furnishes an excellent sanitary code for its government.

Among the cities of this class are Altoona, Lancaster, Allentown, Scranton, Wilkesbarre, and Williamsport. The boroughs of Norristown, Easton, Pottsville, Cornplanter, and York, have each over ten thousand inhabitants (the requisite number for incorporation); but I am not informed if they have been incorporated; nor have I been able to find out how many of the cities

mentioned have organized a board of health, under the provisions of this Act.

" Ques. 6. Has the State passed any law leading to a thorough and definite improvement of the public health ?

" 6–a. By a sanitary survey of the State?"

Under an act of Assembly, a thorough scientific survey of the State has been conducted for several years past, and is now progressing rapidly.

This survey will include the chemical examinations of the various soils, and of the waters of rivers; will point out the natural drainage; and furnish data by which waste and marshy land may be recovered, and water-courses improved.

The results of these investigations will be of great value to the State, considered from a sanitary point of view. A strictly sanitary survey of the State has never been made.

" 6–b. By a law for the registration of births, deaths, and marriages ? "

There is no such law applying to the whole State; but many cities and boroughs have such a law. In the act creating a State Board of Health, provision has been made for the establishment of a Bureau of Vital Statistics.

" 6–c. If so, how long has it been in operation ? "

No general State law. An act requiring the registration of births in Philadelphia dates back to the year 1819. The death returns were registered as early as 1794; but the register is not complete earlier than 1807.

The registration law prior to 1818, I have not been able to find. In 1860, a new act for the registration of births, deaths, and marriages, was passed; since which time the statistics have been carefully recorded, and published annually by the Board of Health. An act for the registration of births, deaths, and marriages, in the city of Pittsburg, was passed in 1870; and in Allentown, in 1873. Reading, Allegheny City, and some other cities and boroughs, keep such records; but the registration of these statistics in Pennsylvania has been greatly neglected.

An act of 1874 authorizes all cities having a population over ten thousand, and less than one hundred thousand, " to create a complete and accurate system of registration of marriages, births, deaths, and interments, occurring in or near such city,

for purposes of legal and genealogical investigation; and to furnish facts for statistical, scientific, and particularly for sanitary, inquiries." I have no knowledge of the extent to which the power thus conferred has been made use of.

" 6–d. Has the registrar been able to draw from such records any law governing the public health?"

No central bureau of registration in this State. For conclusions from such records for Philadelphia, see Health Reports.

" 6–e. Has any law been passed relating to the drainage of land?"

By Acts of Assembly, provision has been made for the drainage of wet and spouty lands; also, for the drainage and ventilation of coal and other mines. If the land be a public nuisance, a portion of the expense shall be borne by the township; otherwise, the expense shall be assessed on landholders, &c.

" 6–f. Relating to the irrigation of land?"

I know of no such laws.

" 6–g. Relating to checking of the influence of rivers by levees, &c?"

Levees have been constructed in this State to check the influence of rivers, and to reclaim submerged lands; but I have been unable to find any law relating to this subject, except that of 1874, which authorizes certain cities "to provide for the construction and maintenance of levees."

" 6–h. Relating to the introduction of water into cities?"

There is a general law relating to the organization, corporate powers, and duties of water companies; but there is no act making it incumbent upon towns and cities to furnish a constant and abundant supply of fresh and pure water. It seems to have been the policy of the Legislature to leave the subject of the introduction of water into cities to the local authorities, with the conviction that self-interest would impel them to seek proper legislation, when required.

A large number of special acts, relating to the introduction of water into different towns and cities, have been passed. Few places of any size are without works for supplying water.

There are laws against the pollution of the sources of water-supplies.

" 6–i. Relating to the prevention of contagious disease; for

example, small-pox, cholera, yellow fever, cattle plague, &c. ?"

There is no law applying to the whole State, except in relation to the cattle plague; but there are laws relating to the prevention of these diseases in certain boroughs, towns, and cities, most of which have been adopted within late years.

Over nearly all the State are good laws on this subject. The laws of the city and port of Philadelphia, covering these diseases, are full, explicit, and efficient, except in regard to vaccination. While gratuitous vaccination is provided for, no coercive means are permitted; and the only disability imposed is upon children frequenting public schools. No child is admitted, or continued as a pupil, in such schools, who has not been vaccinated. The city of Chester has a law making vaccination compulsory; and, I believe, in some other parts of the State a similar law is in force.

The general law of 1874, applying to cities having more than ten thousand, and less than one hundred thousand, inhabitants, confers upon such cities full authority to make ordinances and regulations for the prevention and suppressing of infectious and contagious diseases (defined in the act), which shall be operative, so soon as such cities adopt the provisions of the act.

The Act of Assembly, April 12, 1866, declares (section 1) that "it shall not be lawful for any person who may own any cattle or sheep, affected by the disease known as the pleuro-pneumonia, or other contagious or infectious disease, to sell or otherwise dispose of any cattle, either alive or slaughtered, from the premises where such disease is known to exist, nor for a period of two months after such disease shall have disappeared from said premises."

Sec. 2. "No cattle or sheep shall be allowed to run at large in any township or borough, where any contagious disease prevails; and the constables of such townships are hereby authorized and required to take up and confine any so found running at large, until called for, and until all costs are paid; and, in townships where there are no constables, it shall be the duty of the township clerk to perform this service; and the said officers shall be entitled to receive one dollar for each head of cattle

so taken up; and any officer who shall refuse to perform the duties of this act shall be liable to a fine of ten dollars.

Sec. 3. "Any person offending against the provisions of the first section of this act shall be guilty of a misdemeanor; and, upon conviction, be sentenced to pay a fine not exceeding five hundred dollars, or undergo an imprisonment not exceeding six months."

"6–*j*. Regulating tenement-houses?"

I have not been able to find any specific law upon this subject.

Tenement-houses are regulated under the authority and general provisions of the health laws, in cities which have boards of health.

"6–*k*. Incorporating building companies for the improvement of dwellings for the poor?"

There is no such law, that I am aware of. There is a society in Philadelphia having this as one of its objects. There are doubtless others incorporated, which have the same object in view. The building association acts, which are very numerous, have their influence on the public health, by affording means of providing independent and comfortable homes for people of the poorer classes of the community, who would otherwise be the occupants of tenement-houses.

Thousands of small, comfortable houses, fitted up with all necessary conveniences and owned by the occupants, through the beneficial provisions of building associations, are a prominent feature of Philadelphia. [See Mr. Blodget's letter, immediately preceding this, for a fuller account of these associations.]

"Ques. 7. Are there any well-attested facts proving that any disease, formerly prevalent in your State, has

"7–*a*. Ceased to appear?"

"Ques. 10. Has the *town* or *city* in which you reside taken any measures for the improvement of the public health?"

Yes.

"10–*a*. By health laws?"

Yes. April 22, 1794, an act was passed "to establish a health office for securing the city and port of Philadelphia from the introduction of pestilential and contagious diseases,

and for regulating the importation of German and other passengers." This law repealed a number of former acts, as follows: "An act to prevent sickly vessels coming into this government," passed in 1700: "An act for vesting Province Island, and buildings thereon erected, in trustees, for providing hospitals for such passengers as should be imported into this province, and to prevent the spreading of infectious distempers," passed 1749, 1750; "An act to prohibit the importation of German or other passengers, in too great numbers, in any one vessel," 1765; and "An act to prevent infectious diseases being brought into this province," 1774.

A supplement to the Act of April, 1794, was passed Sept. 23, 1794, which made provision for the appointment of *twenty-four* "Inspectors of the Health Office," who shall form a board of inspectors, and be empowered to make rules and regulations, governing their own body and the Health Office, and officers thereof. They were also empowered to make quarantine regulations, and to carry into effect all provisions of the health laws.

This was the first organization of the Board of Health of Philadelphia. At the close of the century, the lazaretto was established at its present location [ten or twelve miles below the city, on the Delaware River]. Some of the health laws, now in force, date back as far as 1802, in which year a law was enacted "for the preservation of the people of the city and port of Philadelphia from pestilential and contagious diseases." The foundation of the present health laws, particularly those relating to quarantine, now in force, were passed in that year. Since then, modifications and additions have been made, from period to period; so that, at the present time, Philadelphia may be said to have a good sanitary code.

"10–*b*. By special action in specific cases?"

Yes. Information on this point may be found in the annual reports of the Board of Health. Two or three instances, of recent date, may be mentioned, in which the action of the Board must tend to improve the public health.

1. Encouragement given to the movement to establish an abattoir (for completeness and capacity probably not surpassed by any in the United States), which, in time, will lead to the

abolishment of the numerous small slaughter-houses so frequently indicted as nuisances to the neighborhood in which they are located, and dangerous to the public health, on account of the facilities that exist for placing unsound meat upon the market, owing to the difficulty of proper sanitary inspection.

2. The abolishment of the old-fashioned and offensive " bucket and cart systems " for removing the contents of privy wells and vaults, and the substitution of a method by suction-hose and air-tight tanks.

3. The providing of a new and capacious hospital for the treatment of infectious diseases. This building has a capacity of about two hundred beds, which may be greatly increased by extemporizing wards from the corridors. All persons suffering from contagious or infectious diseases, who cannot be properly attended to at home, are removed to this hospital; and the public are thus protected from many sources of dangerous infection. Other instances might be mentioned; but these will probably suffice.

" Ques. 11. Does your town or city use well water for culinary purposes ? "

No.

" Ques. 12. Is care taken to prevent pollution ? "

See answer to preceding question.

" Ques. 13. Do you have a water-supply from a distant lake or river ? "

The water-supply of Philadelphia is chiefly drawn from the Schuylkill River. A small portion of the city receives its supply from the Delaware River.

" Ques. 14. Is care taken to prevent pollution ? "

The waters of the Schuylkill and Delaware Rivers, naturally excellent water for domestic purposes, have not escaped pollution from the vicious system of drainage of towns and cities upon their banks. An attempt has been made to prevent contamination of the Schuylkill (the chief source of the city's supply), by acquiring possession of lands, on both banks, for several miles above the city, which have been set apart for park purposes. A number of sources of contamination have thus been discontinued. There still exist sources of pollution. The Board of Health have frequently brought this fact to the notice

of the civil authorities, and have urged the great importance of keeping all impurities out of the river, as will be seen by recent reports of the Board. During the past year, the subject of the water-supply of Philadelphia was referred to a board of experts; who have made a comprehensive report, which has been published. And, already, measures are under consideration for carrying out their recommendation.

"Ques. 15. Have you sewers to carry off such water-supply?"

Yes.

"Ques. 16. How far are the sewer outlets from the source of water-supply?"

The sewers in the western part of the city empty into the Schuylkill, below Fairmount Dam, and therefore cannot possibly affect the water-supply.

Sewage flows into the Schuylkill River from a village and a small town, five and seven and one-half miles above the point whence the chief supply is drawn. A single sewer empties into the river at a nearer point, which is a source of danger; but a means of diverting its contents into a channel emptying into the river, below the dam, is now under consideration.

Mantua Creek, spoken of in Dr. Gresson's report as one of the chief sources of defilement of the water, has recently been turned into the stream below Fairmount Dam, by the building of a sewer six feet in diameter; and, therefore, now it does not pollute the water-supply.

Sewers empty into the Delaware River along the city front, principally at its middle section. The Kensington works draw their supply from the upper part of the river front, but from a point several hundred feet from the wharf. The volume of water is very great, the river being a mile or more in width, and of a good depth. These works supply only a limited portion of the city; and the reservoirs are connected with the Schuylkill basins, from which they can be supplied in case of necessity.

The use of the Kensington works will no doubt be discontinued when new structures, already commenced, at a point miles above the city, recommended by experts, shall have been completed.

PENNSYLVANIA.

"Ques. 17. What is your method of disposing of *sewage, house-offal, slops*, and *other filth* liable to accumulate about homesteads?"

Sewage is discharged from the sewer outlets into the rivers Delaware and Schuylkill. No attempt is made to utilize it. The contents of sinks and wells are removed by suction-pumps and air-tight receivers, and used as a fertilizer, either after being manufactured into a *poudrette*, or after rude manipulation. House offal is removed by contract, under the direction of the Board of Health, daily, from 1st of June to 1st of November, and not less than three times a week in the remaining months of the year.

"Ques. 18. Have any State, county, or city reports, health and death, &c., been published?"

I know of no State or county reports of this character having been published.

Several cities and towns publish such reports; *e.g.*, Philadelphia, Pittsburg, Allegheny, Reading, and Harrisburg.

"Ques. 19. How many years (approximatively or definitely) have they been published?"

I have information in regard to Philadelphia only. From 1807[1] to 1859, inclusive, brief reports of deaths were published, which include statistics of births, marriages, and deaths. Great care has been taken to secure as full and accurate returns as possible; and they have been presented in the forms usually adopted in this country and in Great Britain.

No slight effort has been made in setting forth, as fully as possible, all matters connected with the administration of the Health Board, by showing what has been done, and by pointing out the sanitary defects and wants of the city. Weekly bulletins of deaths, containing meteorological observations and other particulars, have been published for three years.

These, in a limited number, are distributed in the city, and exchanged for similar reports from other places in this and other countries.

---

[1] Deaths were recorded before 1807; but it is not clear that they were annually published before this year. The published records of deaths from 1807 to 1859, inclusive, are accessible; but I am not able to say how complete these returns are. Those from 1860 I consider reliable.

STATEMENT OF THE LAWS OF PENNSYLVANIA RELATING TO THE PUBLIC HEALTH, AS PREPARED BY DOCTOR WILLIAM H. FORD.

By an Act of Assembly (April 12, 1872), a commissioner of labor statistics and agriculture has been appointed, whose duties "shall be to collect, compile, and systemize statistics with reference to the subject of labor, in its relations to the social, educational, industrial, and general condition wages and treatment, of all classes of our working-people, and how the same affect the permanent prosperity and productive industry of the Commonwealth." Expense borne by the State.

Apothecaries' Act.

The Apothecaries' Act was passed in 1872. It requires that apothecaries shall have a certificate of competency, to be granted by the Pharmaceutical Examining Board, upon examination of applicants. Apothecaries are to be registered. A penalty is imposed for practising without a certificate. Those who may compound prescriptions designated; qualified assistants provided for; penalty attached for adulterating drugs. This act applies only to Philadelphia.

Among the powers granted to every borough within the Commonwealth, under the act of April 3, 1851, are the following:—

"To make all needful regulations respecting the foundations and party-walls of buildings, and respecting vaults, cess-pools, sinks, drains, and partition fences."

"To authorize and direct the killing of dogs running at large, contrary to the regulations of the borough."

"To prohibit and remove any obstacles in the highways of the borough, and any nuisance or offensive matter, whether in the highways or in public or private grounds, and to require the removal of the same by the owner or occupier of such grounds; in default of which, the corporation may cause the same to be done, and collect the cost thereof, with 20 per cent advance thereon, in the manner provided herein for the costs of pavements made by the corporation."

"To prohibit within the borough the carrying on of any manufactures, art, trade, or business, which may be noxious or offensive to the inhabitants; the manufacture, sale, or exposure of fire-works, or other inflammable or dangerous articles; and to limit and prescribe the quantities that may be kept, in one place, of gunpowder, fire-works, turpentine, and other inflammable articles; and to prescribe such other safeguards as may be necessary."

"To make such regulations relative to the accumulation of manure, compost, and the like, in barns, stable-yards, and other places; and to prohibit the keeping of hogs within the borough, or within such limits within the same as they may prescribe."

"To prohibit within the borough the burial or interment of deceased persons, or within such partial limits within the same as they may from time to time prescribe; and to regulate the depth of graves."

"To make such other regulations as may be necessary for the health and cleanliness of the borough."

Removal of Burial-Grounds

in Philadelphia, to be subject to the approbation of the Board of Health. Act of April 10, 1852.

There are charitable and correctional institutions, prisons, almshouses, asylums, homes, and hospitals, established throughout the State, under State and local administration.

The Care of Cattle during Transportation, and while in Stock and Cattle Yards.

The Act of Assembly, Dec. 16, 1863, provides for the feeding, taking care of, and the supply of suitable bedding for cattle, sheep, hogs, and other animals, during transportation on the several railroads of the Commonwealth, or while in the stock or cattle yards, waiting for transportation, by drovers, owners, or shippers of such cattle, &c.

Nostrums for Secret Diseases, and for the Prevention of Conception or procuring Abortion, prohibited.

The law of March 16, 1870, prohibits the publication of nostrums, apparatus, &c., for secret diseases; and also the pub-

lication of nostrums, &c., for preventing conception or procuring abortion, and the sale thereof.

Act on the Adulteration of Food, Liquors, &c.

The act of March 31, 1860, declares that, "If any person shall sell or expose the flesh of any diseased animal, or any other unwholesome flesh, or sell or expose for sale unwholesome bread, drink, or liquor, knowing the same to be unwholesome; or shall adulterate for the purpose of sale, or sell, any flour, meal, or any article of food, any wine, beer, spirits of any kind, or other liquor intended for drinking, knowing the same to be adulterated; or shall adulterate for sale, or shall sell, knowing them to be so adulterated, any drugs or medicines, — such person so offending shall be deemed guilty of a misdemeanor, and, upon conviction, be sentenced to pay a fine not exceeding one hundred dollars, or undergo an imprisonment not exceeding six months, or both or either, at the discretion of the court." The same act regulates the sale of poisons; its object being "to prevent mistakes in the sale of noxious drugs, to throw impediments in the way of malicious and wicked persons obtaining them for murderous purposes, and to facilitate the detection of such persons, when their malignant purpose has been accomplished."

The sale of any *tainted* or *unwholesome meat* or *fish*, or *any veal* less than three weeks old when killed, is forbidden, under a penalty of ten dollars for each offence. Act of April 17, 1861.

Inspection of Milk.

The councils of cities and boroughs in this Commonwealth are authorized and empowered to provide for the inspection of milks, under such rules and regulations, as will protect the people from adulteration and dilution of the same. April 20, 1869.

Adulteration of Liquors.

The act of April 14, 1863, prohibits the use of deleterious drugs in the manufacture of liquors. The act directs that any suspected liquor shall be analyzed by a competent person, under the direction of the court before whom the case is pending.

PENNSYLVANIA.

Regulation of Labor, &c.

The day's labor in factories is regulated by law. It is not lawful to employ a minor under thirteen years of age; and, between thirteen and sixteen years, only for nine calendar months, and then only provided that he or she shall have attended school for at least three consecutive months within the same year.

There are laws for *inspection of flour and meal*, for determining the grade and quality; also, *regulating the sale of intoxicating liquors, prohibiting the adulteration of liquors*, and *the furnishing intoxicating drinks to persons of intemperate habits, to minors, or to insane persons, and prohibiting the sale of liquors on Sundays.* Some of these laws are generally applicable; others apply to particular districts only. In some parts of the State, what is called the *Local-Option Law* is in force. This law provides for an election every three years; at which time the people may decide whether or not it shall be lawful to sell any kind of liquors in the county for the succeeding three years.

Laws regulating Mining, Ventilation, Use of Precautionary Measures, &c.

There are extensive laws on the statute-books of the State of Pennsylvania regulating the mining interests; certain laws regulating the construction of mines, their ventilation, the use of safety-lamps, the division of mines containing explosive gases; the use of signal bells, safety catches, &c. Boys under twelve are not to be employed. To see that the provisions of the law are carried out, inspectors are appointed, who may enter the mines at all times, and who are directed to make reports of their examination. These laws tend materially to prevent sickness, injury, and loss of life.

Patent Medicines.

The sale of *patent medicines* is not prohibited by law, except in special cases, above referred to; but the venders thereof are required to be licensed.

Petroleum and Explosive Compounds.

The storage of petroleum and other inflammable or explosive compounds is regulated by law. There is a law against the sale of explosive compounds, to be used for illuminating purposes.

Practice of Medicine.

There is a law regulating the practice of medicine; guards against imposture, &c.

Laws governing Public Halls, &c., requiring Easy Ingress and Egress, during the Time they are used by the Public, &c.

In certain cities in the Commonwealth, it is not lawful to obstruct, or allow to be obstructed by others, any aisles or passage-ways in the auditorium of any public halls or place of amusement, in any manner so as to prevent free ingress or egress during the hours said places may be open to the public. And the doors of such places are to be constructed, and to be managed, during the time such halls or places of amusement are open to the public, so as in no way to prevent instant and easy egress.

In Philadelphia, in the principal theatres, sufficient fire-hose to reach the furthest limits of the building must be kept attached to a plug or water attachment, during the time they are open to the public.

These are not all the laws bearing on the subject of public health, but will probably be sufficient for the purpose of the circular.

(From Dr. J. L. Le Conte, Philadelphia, Pa.)

Philadelphia, Pa., March 21, 1876.

I fear that my answers to your questions on sanitary precautions, as enforced in this State and municipality, will be of the nature of what we were taught to call, in our early days of logical instruction, a universal negative.

Nevertheless, in the hope that I am perhaps prejudiced in my judgment, or that there may be promise of better times to come, I send you, by to-day's mail, a copy of the last report

printed by our Board of Health. Several of the queries will be answered by rapidly glancing over this volume, in a more satisfactory manner, than by the imperfect indications I have placed upon your blank. I shall be very glad to answer any other inquiries you may have occasion to make; and generally to aid you, to the extent of my power, in exposing the usual inattention to sanitary science which prevails in large towns.

Hearing that Dr. Rothrok had established a summer school at Wilkesbarre, in which the principal instruction would be, by able teachers, in the field and in the woods, I wrote, making inquiries, and enclosing one of my circulars. His reply is as follows: —

(From DR. J. T. ROTHROK, Wilkesbarre, Luzerne County, Pa.)
WILKESBARRE, PA., March 30, 1876.

I have just received yours, asking for information in regard to my *proposed* School of Physical Culture, and hasten to reply.

The idea at the bottom is not *mental* culture, but, as stated, *physical culture*, — first, last, *and all the time*, — combined with as much instruction and object-teaching as the lads can receive by constant association with older, well-informed gentlemen, who are still young enough to thoroughly adapt themselves to boys, and be in sympathy with them. The course of instruction is mainly to allure the pupil out of doors, and with healthful exercise. Yet it keeps them constantly supplied with mental occupation, and stimulates observation, and must enable the boys (almost, may I say, by absorption?) to gather much information. The lectures will be on the discoveries of the day; and will be at the camp-fire at night, or rather evening. I have a fine body of assistants, and among them a rising artist, who will give instructions in sketching from nature.

The location is about two thousand five hundred feet above the sea, and in the heart of a large pine and hemlock forest. I offer no luxuries at the table; but will have *good* plain fare, and plenty of it. To what extent I may modify my plans, of course I cannot say, as that has to be decided by actual trial.

You have doubtless received, from more authoritative sources, information upon our State laws, and their relation to disease.

But I will state that our chief diseases are malarial; and fevers, pneumonias, diarrhœa, &c., all are stamped by this character.

I should have added that the privies are sunk to the gravel, and but few of them connect with any sewer. Our city has a population of twenty-five thousand; and, within a radius of three miles from the public square, we have a population not far from one hundred thousand.

(From Dr W. S. W. Rushenberger, Philadelphia, Pa.)

Philadelphia, Pa., Feb. 20, 1876.

Pennsylvania has not established a State Board of Health, although the Legislature has been requested to enact a proper law for the purpose. The request was made at both the sessions of 1874 and 1875.

A Board of Health for Philadelphia, by Act of Assembly passed March, 1799, was created. The organization was modified by "an act establishing a health officer, and to secure the city and port of Philadelphia from the introduction of pestilential and contagious diseases, and for other purposes," approved Jan. 29, 1818.

An act approved March 27, 1819, directs the "registration of the births of children in the city of Philadelphia and vicinity."

An act approved April 2, 1821, supplementary to the act establishing a health office.

An act, April 7, 1859, changed the organization of the Board of Health, and places the appointment of its members in the hands of the Judges of the District Court, and of the Court of Common Pleas.

An act, March 8, 1860, directs the registration of marriages, births, and deaths, in the city and county of Philadelphia.

The Board of Health of Philadelphia issued weekly or monthly a printed report of interments, in sheets (foolscap size), from 1807 till June, 1834; and since then a weekly report of the mortality has been published in the newspapers.

For the last six months of 1860, and since, for each entire year, the Board of Health reports to the Mayor of the city the marriages, births, and deaths; submitting, also, statements rela-

tive to nuisances, condition of highways, vaccination, pestilential disease, such as occasion suggests.

An act, March 22, 1872, established a Board of Health in the city of Harrisburg, Pa.

An act April 4, 1872, authorizes the City Council of Williamsport, Pa., to establish a Board of Health.

An act, April 12, 1872, amends the health laws of Pittsburg, Pa.

An act of May 19, 1873, establishes a board of health in Allegheny, Pa.

An act approved May 23, 1874, "divides the cities of this State into three classes, and authorizes councils of cities of the third class to appoint boards of health, with power. Section 8, to make general regulations to secure the general health of the city, and to remove and prevent nuisances."

RHODE ISLAND.

(From Dr. Edmund S. F. Arnold, Newport, R.I.)

Newport, R.I., April 3, 1876.

Having, I think, obtained the most reliable information as to local questions, I answer as far as circumstances permit. All questions relating to State Hygiene, as I stated before, could best be answered by Dr. Snow, of Providence. I have never practised in this State myself: my answers, therefore, must be limited to a few questions. I say nothing of private dwellings of the higher class, with sufficient ground about them to provide for their own drainage, by tight and distant cesspools, of which the contents can be emptied and utilized from time to time.

1. As a general rule, houses in the more densely populated portions of the city (Newport) have open (uncemented) stone basement walls, open stone cesspools, and open stone walls to the wells, which become more or less contaminated by surface drainage, rendered worse by the hardpan of clay, with streaks of gravel intervening, which underlies the surface at a few feet depth. Many houses use cistern water; but they are not in the majority.

2. No: though abundant facilities for it, in the opinion of many.

3. I have a full list of the sewers before me. Certainly not more than a quarter of the sparsely inhabited part of the town is sewered. The sewers are partly of pipe, partly of brick, partly of open stone, connected only partially with the houses on their line; and there are no means of properly flushing them. The streets (or a few main ones) and avenues are watered in the summer with salt water, taken up from the bay.

4. Considering that the drainage is for the most part surface drainage, the sewage and water-supply are in too close contact for health.

5. My method — being on a place with nine acres of ground, with slope on all sides — is to carry all the sewage, through tight cesspools and pipes, to two cesspools — one seventy feet, the other two hundred feet, from the house. These may be disinfected from time to time; and, when there is any accumulation, the contents can be baled out, and used as manure on the grounds.

I should recommend all who have sufficient ground, and who cannot communicate with good sewers, to have tight cesspools at a point most distant from the house: to which, together with the overflow from equally tight privies, all the sewage and drainage might be carried; these, especially during the warm months, disinfected from time to time, and carried off as often as necessary.

The hygienic arrangements of Newport City are simply nil. The drainage and sewerage are deficient; and the water, as far as drawn from wells, differing only in degrees of impurity. If there is any State legislation on the subject, it is here a dead letter; and there is, as far as I can see, no sign of improvement, until public opinion, through the efforts of the medical profession, shall be educated up to a perception of the requirements of a need, not only existing in cities and towns, but too often in more thinly populated localities, where thousands are apt to seek health and recreation in the summer season.[1]

[1] Recent plans have been proposed, of a most thorough character, wherefrom it is hoped that Newport will, ere long, have a complete system of sewerage. — H. I. B.

(From Dr. G. W. Jenckes, Woonsocket, R.I.)

. . . .
Our system of registration does not, of course, give us absolutely correct returns, but approximately so.

It is the duty of physicians, clergymen, and undertakers to make monthly reports of births, marriages, and deaths (by them attended), to the town or city clerk; and, besides, an officer is appointed annually, in each town, to canvass the towns with reference to these statistics.

SOUTH CAROLINA.

(From Dr. Simon Baruch, Camden, S.C.)

It would afford me pleasure to be able to give you a more encouraging report of sanitary science and practice in the State. But, unfortunately, our Legislature has hitherto paid no attention to this most important of all subjects. We hope, however, to awaken some activity, through our State Medical Society, which is now upon a more solid basis than it ever was, even prior to the late unhappy struggle. . . .

It is singular that typhoid fever is rare. There have not been a half-dozen cases in ten years.

(From Dr. William H. Huger, Charleston, S.C.)

Charleston, S.C., March 25, 1876.

I have endeavored to answer the questions as concisely as possible. I will add, further, a few remarks as regards the quarantine regulations, which are under the control of the State. These regulations are defective in many particulars, and apply only to vessels coming into our ports. There are no restrictions on persons coming into our town or State by land; as per railroads, &c. The quarantine station in this port is so near the city that it is doubtful if any advantage is derived from it. We have no water-supply here, beyond the wells and cisterns. Wells certainly furnish the larger supply; and the water is used for culinary purposes. No attempt is made to purify it. House offal is received in dry wells and privy vaults. The filth which accumulates about homesteads is placed in the

streets, and removed by scavenger carts, in many instances. The wells, which supply the water for cooking and drinking, are only a few feet removed from the privy vaults and dry wells. The Board of Health of this place (and, in fact, wherever such boards are in other towns), is organized by appointments by the Town Council, and has no authority whatever: consequently, their efficiency amounts to very little. The City Registrar makes an annual report to the Council.

The drainage of the city is by means of sewers or drains, which run through the streets, and empty themselves into one of the rivers on either side of the town. The only legislation of the State for the protection of public health is the quarantine law.

(From ROBERT A. KINLOCH, Charleston, S.C.)

There is a strong disposition on the part of the medical men of the State to have health laws enacted; but, at present, our impoverished condition and political status render such enactments impossible. Formerly, we had a registration of births, deaths, &c.; but this law has not been enforced for many years. The city of Charleston has been doing something, every year, towards improving its local condition, and adding to the quarantine regulations; but, beyond the controlling of *malarial diseases* in the city proper, I can't say that much has been accomplished. Yellow fever has visited us periodically within my experience; and I do not think that it has been kept out by quarantine. I think the present system a farce. It is impossible to say, on the other hand, whether our local hygienic laws have done any more to protect us. We spend money, and hope and imagine that we are spending it to some purpose. I despair of the State, in its present Africanized condition, spending money to improve health. Two-thirds of our Legislature would think such money thrown away.

BATTLE-FIELD SUCCOR, NORTH AND SOUTH.

We all remember with pride the great sanitary work accomplished by the various "commissions" in the North during the late civil war. This was done by wise preventive measures, as

well as by active battle-field and hospital service to the sick and wounded. It has seemed to me appropriate, in connection with this address, that some allusion should be made to the doings of these Northern Associations. But I wished also to learn whether similar institutions had not arisen in connection with the Southern armies. From the publications of the Northern associations, I glean certain facts, which are given below. Through the kindness of my correspondent, Dr. Turnipseed, of Columbia, S.C., I am enabled to show that similar institutions existed in the South; so, not only in the North, but all through the country, there was, during the civil war, a great and beautiful uprising of human sympathy and wise forethought, which inaugurated and accomplished many excellent measures, and caused an unstinted outpouring of wealth to save life and to prevent extra suffering, on both sides of the line of battle. The following items, taken from the Northern and Southern public and private reports and letters, will enable one to get at least a glimpse of what was done during the war by both parties.

For the details of what was accomplished at the North, I refer to the various documents published by the three chief associations; viz., the United States Sanitary Commission,[1] the United States Christian Commission,[2] and the Western Sanitary Commission.[3]

I shall give, in this place, only the amounts of money received and expended by the three associations. These sums indicate the amount of real sanitary work carried on by them.

Stillé says (p. 487) "that the aggregate amount of money

---

[1] "History of the United States Sanitary Commission; being the General Report of its Work during the War of the Rebellion." By Charles J. Stillé. Philadelphia: Lippincott & Co. 1866. Also, the various reports published by the Commission, at various times, during the War.

[2] "The United States Christian Commission for the Army and Navy." Annual Reports, Philadelphia, 1863–66.

[3] "The Western Sanitary Commission. A Sketch of its Origin, History, and Labors for the Sick and Wounded of the Western Army, and Aid given to the Freedman and Union Refugees, with Incidents of Hospital Life." St. Louis: published by the Mississippi Valley Sanitary Fair. R. P. Shedley & Co., 1864.

expended" by the Sanitary Commission, and the money value of the supplies sent to the field, hospital, &c., and used for other legitimate purposes connected with the troops, "cannot be stated with precision."

The value of the *supplies* is estimated at about fifteen millions	$15,000,000.00
Cash receipts, at the Central Treasury (those received and expended at the branches being never returned) were, up to May, 1866 . . .	4,962,014.26
The branches must have been, at least	2,000,000.00
"Besides the above (p. 288), there were hundreds and thousands of sewing-circles in the various loyal towns, villages, and country places. What they expended cannot be ascertained, but it must have been enormous." From the few replies received to a circular asking for information, it is estimated that the sum must have exceeded the cash receipts of the Central Treasury and branches together (p. 489); say at least	6,000,000.00
	$27,962,014.26

The Western Sanitary Commission (p. 130) gives the following items: —

From Sept. 10, 1861, to date, value of articles used for or sent to the troops	$1,250,000
Cash expenditures during the same period . . .	275,000
	$1,525,000

The Christian Commission (Exhibit G, Third Annual Report, Philadelphia, 1865) gives the following accounts of expenses during the years 1862–65: —

Cash receipts at central and branch offices . . .	$2,524,512.56
Value of stores donated to do	2,839,445.17
	$5,363,957.73
Value of various publications given to the soldiers, salaries of delegates, rents, &c.	927,149.95
	$6,291,107.68

Combining the three, we have the following as the estimated results of expenditures at the North, all derived from private munificence, in addition to the usual military provisions for the same purpose: —

United States Sanitary Commission	$27,962,014.26
United States Christian Commission	6,291,107.68
Western Sanitary Commission	1,525,000.00
	$35,778,121.94

Certainly a very grand result; eminently suggestive not only of the resources of the people of the North, but also of the willingness of that people to spend freely of their wealth in support of a cause, which they deemed that of liberty and of country.

I regret that I cannot give even an approximation to the amount expended, for similar purposes, in the Southern States. I have seen no printed public documents relative thereto, save brief notices in the journals of the day. My correspondent at Columbia enables me to present some details of what was done for the wounded and sick in the Southern army; individuals and associations working with the public and military authorities. The same correspondent forwarded, for my inspection, files of South Carolina papers published between 1862 and 1865. From these documents, I learned that identically similar means were used in the South as in the Northern armies and hospitals.

The following letters speak for themselves in reference to public acts. I wish to draw especial attention to the private letter from a Southern lady to a Northern mother, whose son died in a Southern home, within the American lines, while the youth was serving in the Union army. I would fain hope that not a few similar acts of mercy may have been performed by individuals within the lines of both armies. Wherever they have occurred, they must have tended to alleviate, very greatly, the horrors and distresses incident to battle.

(From Dr. E. P. Turnipseed, Columbia, S.C.)

Columbia, S.C., July 20, 1876.

Doubtless you have been enabled, from information gathered from the files of the "Charleston Courier," 1862–64, sent you, to collate a sufficient number of facts in regard to the workings, in that city and vicinity, of the various charitable associations, under different names and organizations, for the relief of sick and wounded soldiers during the late civil war. I now, however, propose to give you some idea of the operations of the societies in other parts of this State, as well as in Richmond, Va., and along the different railroads used for the transportation of troops.

Sometime in September, 1861, F. W. Pickens, then Governor of South Carolina, sent for Colonel R. G. M. Dunovant and myself, then at the camp of instruction for South Carolina, called Tightwood Knot Springs, distant from Columbia six or eight miles. Colonel Dunovant had been a Brigadier-General of the State troops, and former Adjutant-General; and, at the time sent for, he was acting in the capacity of Brigadier-General, C. S. A., and I as Brigade Surgeon. The soldiers, in great numbers, were prostrated with measles; and Governor Pickens, learning that we had only hospital tents, left it with us whether or not to accede to a proposition, coming from the ladies, to establish a hospital at the State Fair Grounds in this city. This proposition was accepted; and we at once forwarded by railroad all the sick, and had physicians appointed, from civil practice, to administer to their medical wants. The officers of this association of ladies were Mrs. Dr. George Howe, President; Mrs. John Bryce; Mrs. Colonel William Wallace, Secretary and Treasurer. This was, as far as I can ascertain, the first charitable organization of the kind in this State, and was called the "Ladies' Hospital Association." This hospital was supported entirely by private contributions, and both governed by, and the wants of the sick supplied by, lady attendants; the physicians only prescribing and advising. The "Wayside Home" was an outgrowth of this institution, in this way: Some young ladies realizing, as did numbers of others, the necessity of caring for the sick and wounded soldiers in transit from their regiments, hospitals, or battle-fields, for their

homes or remote hospitals, proposed that they would organize themselves, with others who would join them, to supply this much-needed comfort. The parents of these young women advised them to associate themselves with the older and married ladies in this laudable work, and the organization was effected by accepting the supervision of the same officers elected under the first organization, except that an executive committee was appointed or elected; viz., Mrs. John Bryce, Chairman; Mrs. John Fisher, Secretary and Treasurer; and the other members were Miss Mary Stark and Miss C. R. Bryce; and, after the resignation of the latter, Mrs. M. A. McFie. These ladies tell me that the name, "Wayside Home," was first suggested to them by General John S. Preston. I have thus given minutely the origin of this institution, because, so far as we know, this was the first organization of the kind under the name of "Wayside Home;" and, therefore, we desire to claim the distinction for the ladies of Columbia, S.C. Notwithstanding this seemingly legitimate claim, under a fixed organization, with the name "Wayside Home" as the adopted designation, I am fully aware that soldiers passing from the west through Augusta, Ga., to Virginia, were fed at the railroad depots in that city by the ladies, during the months of April and May, 1861. In fact, the response to all the wants of those in the service of the Confederacy was almost spontaneous, throughout the country; and associations developed themselves, under different names and organizations, but all with a common purpose.

Early in February, 1862, a single room was provided, to be used as a "Wayside Home," near the Charlotte and Columbia Railroad depot. A concert was given to obtain funds to support it. The regular "Wayside Hospital," however, was established near the South Carolina Railroad depot, at Columbia, on the 10th of March, 1862; and continued in operation until the 15th of Feb., 1865. It was supported entirely by private contributions. It furnished a place of rest and refreshments for all sick and wounded furloughed soldiers, passing to and from the armies. Visiting committees were formed for each day in the week. These committees were responsible for their particular day, and were always at the "Home" on the arrival of the trains,

with physicians and other gentlemen to aid them. This building, as necessity required, was enlarged; and the comforts of water and gas were added. Matrons, stewards, and other assistants lived in the hospital, and were, consequently, always on hand. The number of soldiers entertained per day was not uniform. Over one hundred were often supplied with a cot for the night; and from two to three hundred were fed per day. During the existence of the ",Home" (nearly three years), about seventy-five thousand (75,000) soldiers were accommodated; and the amount of money received and expended, one hundred and thirty-nine thousand two hundred and sixty (139,260) dollars. Double this amount is supposed to have been received in provisions, and dispensed; also, a large amount of clothing.

Besides these "Wayside Homes" in Columbia, there was a sort of bureau, of mixed character, upon the officers of which devolved the duties of expending properly all funds contributed, either by the State or individuals, for the benefit of the State troops, or those in Confederate service; also, forwarding the same to the different regiments, and forwarding and distributing to the soldiers, in the various regiments, any clothes, hats, provisions, or money intended for them.

In July, 1861, an association was formed, called the "South Carolina Hospital Association," to establish hospitals along the line of defences in Virginia, for the benefit of South Carolina soldiers; also, to receive and forward supplies contributed by their families or friends. Temporary hospitals and depots were arranged; but the only permanent establishments were at Charlottesville, Petersburg, and Richmond Here, also, were fed soldiers, in transit to and from their regiments; the former without charge, and the latter with a very moderate charge. Mr. George W. McMaster, who was in charge of the hospital organized for this purpose at Richmond, writes me that " this ' Home ' was one of the greatest blessings that was ever devised for the good of the soldiers, as will be testified to by every soldier or officer who received shelter there.' The books and papers of these hospitals being either captured or destroyed, I cannot give you any statistical account of their management.

Louisiana, Georgia, North Carolina, and perhaps other States, had similar hospital organizations, conducted upon about the

same plan. In very many cities, towns, and villages, along the great railroad thoroughfares, there were organizations formed to furnish food, and also to have wounds of soldiers dressed in the trains, while remaining over for the short time allowed for dinner.

In whatever details I have given you, they have been, for the most part, confined to the origin and management of the charitable institutions by the people of South Carolina. This is explained by my greater familiarity with them; but similar institutions for the relief of suffering humanity, conducted by persons in civil life, and furnished almost entirely by private contributions, existed throughout the so-called Confederate States. Where so many in private life bore the brunt and burden in relieving suffering humanity, and smoothing the pillows of the dying, who, in the midst of strangers, gave up that which is priceless, it would be invidious to make distinctions.

In addition to what is given in the above letter, my correspondent sends documents, showing that a similar "home" was established by the people of Charleston, at the suggestion of Major E. Willis, in 1863. The chief inhabitants, gentlemen and ladies, joined with him. Major Willis agreed to be responsible for fifty per cent of all the expenses necessary to "inaugurate and keep it in operation." This he was to obtain from a "liberal public." Officers and soldiers from all the Confederate States were admitted. Ladies gave not only pecuniary aid to it, but their personal attendance. Pecuniary assistance came from Georgia, North and South Carolina, Liverpool, &c. Many individuals dispensed of their bounty "more like States than as individuals," so freely was it given. New buildings were added to the original hospital. Some gentlemen issued money in $1 and $2 bills for the Wayside Home. It was loaned to soldiers, and "spent for them," and "passed as freely as Confederate money." The institution, assisted as it was by the community and by the Commanding-General Beauregard, endeavored to alleviate the necessities of all those wounded in any fight near the city, "as the participants of Sumter, Wagner, Morris's Island, Fort Johnson, James Island, and the Fleet,

can testify." Dec. 25, 1863, no less than one thousand and nine men received a Christmas dinner. It is estimated that from May 1, 1863, till January 1, 1864, twenty-five thousand men were cared for; receiving from a single meal, when passing, to having not only food, but at times "a full suit of clothing" and, if required, medical attendance.

No salaried officers were employed. " The Home fully and certainly carried out all it was organized to do, and the benefits received were gratefully acknowledged by their recipients."

A hospital was kept in operation at Augusta, Ga., during the war. " Its successful establishment was in a large measure due to the zeal and energy of the ladies, who devoted a great part of what they realized from a fair, established for the relief of sick and wounded soldiers." Many ladies gave personal attention to the patients. Soldiers were fed on their way, at the different depots, from whatever Southern State they might come. In the account given by Dr. Pettigru, it appears that over three thousand per month passed through the Home, were fed, and, if need be, clothed.

Dr. Campbell, of Georgia,[1] gives details, most interesting, of the establishment of Georgia State Hospitals sustained at Richmond during the war. From it, it would seem that Georgia supported three buildings. The one specially described contained two hundred beds. They were virtually Confederate Government hospitals, supplemented by the gifts from individuals of the State. In each ward was at least one Georgia lady nurse. Every thing appears to have been done to soothe the sick and wounded; and a similar devotion of private labor and money seems to have prevailed in them as in those of the North. The writer says that the several States of the South established similar hospitals at Richmond, each for its own people; and although bearing the names of the various States, and under their patronage and management, they were, in reality, Confederate Governmental military hospitals, subject

[1] " Report on the Condition of the Georgia Hospitals at Richmond, Va., by Henry F. Campbell, M.D., Secretary of the Medical Directors of the Georgia Hospitals in Virginia, to the Georgia Relief and Hospital Association, Augusta, Ga., 1862." Printed at the office of the " Constitutionalist."

to the Confederate authorities at Richmond. The surgeons made weekly and monthly returns to the Government, as was done by other hospitals, directly sustained by the Government.

The "offer of States to establish hospitals in Virginia was without precedent." But Dr. S. P. Moore, Surgeon-General, C.S.A., says that "they added much to the welfare of the army, when embarrassments of every kind pressed upon it."

Government rations were chiefly issued to them. "The Georgia Association laid up immense stores," — "all that might be needed, at a moment's warning, for the relief and comfort of the sick." The nurses, after a time, were not detailed soldiers; but the hospital authorities were allowed to choose others, paying what a soldier would receive. The authorities at times employed more, at their own expense. "Among them were noble women, to stand at the bedsides like mothers and sisters."

From the above even few details, it would seem that the same fine spirit of self-sacrifice and of generosity to the wounded and sick, the same desire for the inauguration of preventive measures, were as widely shown throughout the South as in the Northern States.

But our civil war brought out not only great public acts of benevolence and self-sacrifice, but also not a few beautiful examples of thoughtfulness, and of tender care of the wounded or sick, even when in the hands of the so-called "enemy." Among them, I know of none more touching than that displayed by the wife and mother of Confederate soldiers to a young captain of the Union army, who fell ill at their house. The tale is told with such simple pathos by the Confederate lady herself, that I asked the recipient of the letter to allow me to publish part of it in this connection. It seems wholly germane to my object, which is to prove that always, during all the horrors of our civil war, a beautiful tide of humane feeling was everywhere not only present, but swaying human souls to acts of kindness, quite inconsistent with the annals of war, as it has hitherto been carried on, in all previous contests. The letter referred to is given below. For obvious reasons, I shall not print the names of any of the parties. Suffice to say that the young Northern officer was one of the most cherished sons of Massachusetts,

and from one of her best families; and that the Confederate lady, that sweet minister of a divine charity even to an "enemy," was living in one of the most Southern States, over a portion of which the Union forces had gained control. Consequently the two ladies, the writer and recipient of the letter, were diametrically opposed to one another in sentiment, and thousands of miles asunder in their places of residence.

DEC. 13, 1863.

DEAR MADAM, — I am a stranger to you, divided not only by many miles, but by sentiments and opinions, created by this cruel war; yet, notwithstanding all this, I feel that the sad decree of fate has cast a cord of sympathy between us, and that a letter from one who knew and mourns with you the death of your son will not be unwelcome. It may, in a measure, soothe your sorrow-stricken heart to know that, although your son died far from home, among strangers, yet he had true friends around his bedside. He was watched and nursed with a mother's love. All that human aid could do, or affection suggest, was done; but it could not save him. . . . Need I tell you how many prayers I offered for the preservation of that precious young life? No; but you can feel it, when I tell you that I too have a noble boy far from home, engaged in this terrible war, and I know not how soon a stranger may do for him what I have done for your child. I know that a mother's heart yearns for every particular, concerning the last days of a beloved child. I feel that it has been my privilege to know your son, and minister to him in his illness.

The first time I met Captain ——— was in the evening of October 3. I live very near where his regiment was encamped, and he called, with Lieutenant ———, to request me to take them as boarders. The following morning he took his place at the head of my table, and, as he said, "installed himself as the head of the family" (for my family, as almost every one in our unfortunate South, is severed; I at my home in the Federal lines, my husband and son in the Confederacy). He never seemed a stranger, but interested himself in the welfare of my family, as though he were one of us. He endeared himself to all by his many attentions. To my two little daughters he was perfectly

devoted, and told them he was to be their brother until the war was over and their other brother came home. . . . They, in return, loved him most tenderly, and mourn for him as a dear lost brother. He was indisposed for a week before he was confined to his bed, his ambitious spirit keeping him at his duties. On Sunday, November 15, he scarcely left the fireside, and slept at his tent that night; but came to the house on Monday morning, feeling so badly that he asked for a room. Tuesday, the 17th, found him with a high fever, and he never left his room again. On the 21st, he received your letter, expressing so much anxiety at his long silence. He told me he had not written home for two months, and thought it most prudent not to write until he recovered, as it would only add to your anxiety to know that he was sick. He, however, on the 26th, requested me to write for him, as he feared his mother would hear some exaggerated report of his illness. He wished, also, a convalescent wardrobe. I wrote as he requested, sitting by his bedside; little thinking that, in another short week, a letter would be written, bidding you to expect the worst. On that day, he appeared much better, and wished me to read to him all his late papers, all the marriages and deaths from home, and asked how long it would be before he could go out to the table. I told him that I hoped, in another week, to see him in his place. But his apparent improvement was only the treacherous deception of typhoid fever. His fever again rose, and his mind wandered; although, at all times, he knew every one. I seldom left his bedside, day or night: when I did so, he would call for me. From me alone he received his medicine, his nourishment and his drinks. He thought all I did for him was well done. He trusted me in every thing concerning his welfare. Even in his delirium I could soothe, when others only irritated. He seemed to look upon me as another mother, and confided in me as such. And God, who is the judge of all hearts, knows how faithfully, how willingly, and as a sacred privilege, I fulfilled the trust. He alone can know my anguish of heart when I knew that the object of my care, my prayers, and my tears, was to be taken from this world, from friends who loved him, from you, *devoted, sorely tried mother.* Oh! if sympathy could soothe your heart, you would

not mourn; for those, who know what you have lost, have hearts full of sympathy. You were proud of your son, so *noble*, so *brave*, so *good;* and now he is gone, but not for ever. There is comfort in the thought that it is not for ever. " He is not dead, the child of your affection." May it comfort you to know that he felt, during his whole illness, that nothing was left undone. He told me that he was becoming a spoiled child. I am thankful that I was permitted to minister to his wants to the last, and that his dying blessing was whispered in my ear; that from my hands he received his last drop of water.

What more can I say? I know a mother's heart cannot be comforted. It is a cruel fate that ordains our destinies at times; that sends our dear ones away to die among strangers, as in your case. But many — oh, how many! — are without any friend to soothe their last moments. How many die even from neglect! die, and are forgotten.

" The air is full of farewells, and mourning for the dead."

I know not how soon your case may be mine. I thought, as I watched the fading countenance of your lovéd one, some mother may watch my darling boy.

" There is no fireside, howsoe'er defended, but has one vacant chair."

How many vacant chairs has this war made, and how many more will it make! I also must look on his vacant chair; and it may be that another will be added before this unholy war is ended. O God! help me to say, " Thy will be done." To-day, my thoughts are far away, following the remains of my lost friend to his home. They are with you, bereaved mother, — with your anguish when you receive all that is left of your noble " Willie." I felt your presence near as I imprinted a kiss on his cold brow, and saw the coffin close over him for ever.

SUNDAY, 20th.

One short week has passed since the above was written. O merciful Father! the misery enveloped in that one week! Even while I was endeavoring to offer words of comfort, the *cruel, cruel* messenger of death came to me. My darling boy was dead: my *noble, beautiful, brave* boy, — my worshipped idol, that I loved

as my own soul, — wounded far from home, the very evening the body of your son left my house. He died in twenty-four hours, and with none but his soldier companions around him. Ten days after his death, I received the box containing all that was left of my beautiful boy. O God! still the murmurings of my rebellious heart. I feel almost how like a mockery are words of sympathy and comfort. How deeply now can I sympathize with you! To-day, perhaps, you have the last of your once proud soldier boy. I have just seen the grave close over mine. God of mercy, grant that the souls of these two victims of a cruel war may be resting in eternal bliss, freed from the troubles of this unhappy world! Farewell, dear madam. I can write no more. Enclosed is a lock of your son's hair. If it is agreeable, I shall be pleased to hear from you.

[Appended to the letter is the following brief inscription, giving the age of the young Southern soldier.]

" Died on Sunday night, 5th instant,
——, eldest son of —— and ——.
Aged 16 years."

Can we not now, in conclusion, most fitly apply to the *whole* country the eloquent peroration of Mr. Stillé, when closing his " History of the United States Sanitary Commission "? —

" However opinions may differ in regard to the policy of the Government, or the strategy of the generals, during the late war, the organized sympathy and care of the American people for those who suffered in their cause stands out all alone, in its ever-fresh beauty, from the dark background of civil strife, and must always and everywhere call forth the homage and admiration of mankind. It is the true glory of our age and country, — one of the most shining monuments of its civilization. May it ever prove a beacon to warn, to guide, and to encourage those who, in future ages or other countries, may be afflicted with the dire calamity of war!"

TENNESSEE.

(From Dr. Joseph H. Van Deman, Tennessee.)

CHATTANOOGA, TENN., Jan. 19, 1876.

. . . .

Our State has been very backward and careless in relation to health matters. Most of her legislators are mountaineers, who never need or care for any laws being made in relation to health or sanitary matters. A measure (introduced by the Medical Faculty of our State Medical Society) looking to the establishment of a State Board of Health, with sundry sanitary matters, was soon reported upon adversely [1] by the committee on health and hospitals, as a measure not now needed by the people; and of course our measure fell to the ground.

We intend, hereafter, to keep the matter before the people, in the hope that, in some future day, we will accomplish what we have undertaken.

The first part of this year, commencing Aug. 1, 1873, was marked with few cholera deaths; but, owing to the disinfecting of the city and the extreme sanitary rules laid down by the City Board of Health, it was soon wiped out. So as to the yellow fever in Memphis, Tenn. When it was raging there, our Board of Physicians, under the advice of the Board of Health, went to Stevenson, Ala., thirty-eight miles (over the road from here to Memphis), and there every train, that was coming this way, was examined by them. Every person who was sick was taken off and cared for there. The consequence was simply this; viz., that we never had a case of yellow fever here, though directly in daily connection with Memphis, Tenn.; thus showing the apparent advantages of street-quarantine laws.

. . . .

The mortality of this year is much lessened from that of the two preceding years, and our place is peculiarly free from all disease of an epidemic character. Indeed, during the past year, when small-pox made its appearance amongst us, by the assistance of our Medical Faculty I secured an ordinance passed

---

[1] This year, 1877, a Board has been legally established. — H. I. B.

in our City Council for compulsory vaccination, and making it obligatory upon all persons to see that the law was enforced in their families, and fining them if they did not attend to it. In two weeks, the disease weakened, and in a very short time had disappeared. While our neighboring cities are scourged with it, we have been entirely free from its ravages for now more than eighteen months. . . .

(From Dr. Frederick K. Bailey, Knoxville, Tenn.)

Knoxville, Tenn., April 14, 1876.

. . . This State, as you must know, is behind in every thing which involves expense, and the labor necessary to develop any public sanitary measures. I have appended answers to your queries in the circulars, which are fearfully negative.

There are general State laws regarding the suppression of contagious diseases, and the city of Memphis may have some municipal regulations to suppress yellow-fever; but I do not know what they are. I hope you have received all requisite information from her resident physicians. In this city of less than ten thousand within corporate limits, some energetic measures were adopted, in 1873, to stop the spread of cholera. A Board of Health was organized in June; and in August I was appointed health officer, with almost unlimited power to act.

The most important fact, which I desire to present to you, is that cholera was to almost a certainty stamped out by energetic measures adopted and carried out strictly. I made it my duty and practice to visit any house, in which a case of cholera or cholerine was reported, and to see that all dejections were buried, or otherwise effectually disposed of. Privy vaults were not allowed to be disturbed, except in the free use of lime and fresh earth, so as to cover up or bury the old contents. Sulphate of iron was freely used about the premises, and carbolic acid put in all chamber vaults, or other utensils used by the sick. Clothing was at once put into boiling water with carbolic acid, or burned. The people soon learned what was requisite; and those able and sufficiently intelligent provided themselves with disinfectants, in advance. Sanitary policemen were constantly employed in inspecting premises, and much good was done. To my knowledge, but few cases occurred in any houses when proper precau-

tions were observed. So thorough was the inspection of premises, and precautions used against a spread of the disease in a family, that it may be said that no two cases occurred in the same house.

When one followed the other, the disease was principally confined to the lowest and most filthy localities; and from even such spots the disease was driven out, or prevented by prompt management. There were not more than one hundred and twenty-five cases in all, and less than forty (40) deaths. I am very confident myself, and that is the general belief of the citizens, that cholera did not decimate our population, because the above measures were adopted. I published an account of our epidemic in the "Nashville Journal of Medicine," and also furnished a paper to Dr. Ely McClellan, who embodied it in his report. The above I will transmit to you, not to be used at all *verbatim* in your report; but that you may, if it should be an item, make mention of the fact that the *stamping-out system* is feasible under some circumstances.

It must be adopted at once, upon the appearance of the first case, and followed up without any neglect, in a single instance. After the disease becomes general in a community, it will, for obvious reasons, be too late.

TEXAS.

(From Dr. Andrew R. Kilpatrick, Navasota, Texas.)

Navasota, Texas, Jan. 26, 1876.

. . . .

Texas is behind many other States in the matter of Public Hygiene; but many of the members of the medical profession are actively engaged in an effort to establish rules, or laws and regulations, for its promotion. In the last Legislature, a move was made by some of its members (some of whom were physicians) to create and organize a Public Board of Health, or State Board; but they failed. In the new Constitution, a copy of which I enclose you, there is a clause providing for the establishment of such a Board.

Several large towns have organized Boards of Health by municipal law; but their action, as yet, seems to be irregular and inefficient. No general reports have been made; but reports are printed weekly, or monthly, in the newspapers. Irrigation is provided for by law; and, in many places in the western part of Texas, it is practised quite effectually; but all east of the Colorado River has little need of irrigation, and it is unknown there. . . .

Ditching and draining are very little employed here, and underground drainage is unknown. I know of no disease ceasing, or being "stamped out." Diseases vary in their recurrence or visitation; sometimes long periods elapsing between their visits. Neuralgia has come to be a very prevalent disease in Texas. I have practised medicine for forty years, beginning in Georgia, in 1836, and have practised in Mississippi and Louisiana, in the great alluvial region of Mississippi swamp: yet I find more neuralgia here than anywhere else; and old people who have lived here forty years say it is far more prevalent here in the last fifteen or twenty years than before that time. Sometimes, I think it may arise from the excessive use of tobacco or coffee or quinine, as these are more generally used than before the late war. Some physicians contend that hæmaturia miasmatica, or black jaundice, is a new disease, sprung up since 1845. I never saw it till since my advent here, in 1866: though I cannot say how long it has prevailed in Texas. It is more fatal than any other disease, — a greater percentage of deaths from it. Our State employs an oculist for the different asylums of Austin. . . .

Dr. Pettersén sends me the following: —

260   APPENDIX.

TABLE OF MEAN TEMPERATURE, RELATIVE HUMIDITY OF THE AIR AND RAINFALL, &c., AT SAN ANTONIO, TEXAS, FOR THE YEAR 1873, AS OBSERVED BY DR. FRED PETTERSÉN.

	Mean standard thermometer.	Mean Hygrometer.	Mean relative humidity of the air.	Maximum temperature.	Minimum temperature.	Extreme range.	Mean range of temperature from day to day.	Rainfall in inches.	Number of rain days.	Number of days cloudy.	Number of days clear.	Remarks.		
													Maximum 14th.	Minimum 29th.
January	49.59	43.61	62.4	75	16	59	3.8	0.50	3	21	10		18. and 20.	2.
February	58.72	52.63	65.8	82	34	48	2.2	0.61	7	22	6	,,	30.	26.
March	64.50	59.27	72.6	92	31	61	3.0	2.43	9	28	3	,,	28.	9. and 16.
April	67.67	59.08	63.4	97	36	61	1.5	0.58	2	23	7	,,	15.	2.
May	75.79	69.06	71.7	98	48	50	1.6	4.34	10	29	2	,,	29.	2.
June	78.56	75.24	86.9	96	65	31	0.9	9.37	18	29	4	,,	11. and 13.	20.
July	81.16	74.37	76.1	97.5	69	27.5	0.5	2.56	7	26	4	,,	5. and 21.	20. and 27.
August	80.16	75.00	78.1	96	71	25	0.8	1.89	8	27	3	,,	22.	17.
September	76.27	71.52	79.3	94.5	60	34.5	0.4	5.94	5	28	8	,,	5.	29.
October	65.66	61.49	74.1	93.5	57	36.5	0.7	3.96	7	22	9	,,	16.	19.
November	58.73	54.21	75.6	87	31.5	55.5	1.6	1.66	7	18	12	,,	3.	27. and 28.
December	55.76	52.65	77.9	86	31	55	1.0	0.37	5	20	5			
Means.	67.62	62.29	73.6	91.2	44.1	47	1.5	34.21	88	292	73			

Mean temperature for the seasons and year (means obtained from six years' observation). Spring, 69.94. Summer, 83.56. Autumn, 68.95. Winter, 52.94. Year, 68.85. Mean annual rainfall (six years), 36.90.

TEXAS.

TABLE.

Table showing the number of times in each month during which the wind blew from each direction at the several observation hours (6 h. 8 m. A.M., 3 h. 8 m. P.M, and 9 h. 33 m. P.M.).

	N.	N.E.	E.	S.E.	S.	S.W.	W.	N.W.	Calms.	Mean velocity of each wind, in miles, per hour.							
										N.	N.E.	E.	S.E.	S.	S.W.	W.	N.W.
January	14	6	3	15	10	1	1	8	35	11.2	4	5	4.5	4.5	2	3	10
February	5	19	0	15	3	4	3	0	35	8	3.9	0	6.2	4.3	3.2	18.6	0
March	8	8	3	32	5	3	0	1	33	22.6	3.8	0	6.5	2	3.6	0	16
April	10	7	0	32	2	2	0	5	32	11	4.2	0	5.9	4.5	5	0	27
May	2	19	15	21	1	1	1	6	27	11.5	3.5	4.2	8	3	4	28	5.8
June	1	9	7	36	0	6	0	3	28	7	4.7	2	4.4	0	3	0	2.3
July	3	7	7	40	5	3	0	0	28	6.3	2.4	3.1	5.1	3.2	1.6	0	0
August	4	17	11	18	2	1	0	1	39	2.4	3.8	3.6	3.3	2	3	0	4
September	1	19	5	21	13	6	0	0	25	10	4.5	3.6	4.9	2.9	1.6	0	0
October	6	22	5	9	21	2	0	0	28	7	5.1	1.8	4.5	3.1	1.5	0	0
November	10	12	4	7	7	9	1	3	37	9.8	6	2.5	3.4	2.7	4.1	6	18.3
December	12	14	3	14	18	1	1	1	29	9.4	6	2.6	4.8	5.8	1	3	1
Sums.	76	79	63	260	87	39	7	28	376	9.7	4.3	2.3	5.1	3.1	2.8	4.8	7.1

UTAH TERRITORY.

(From Dr. W. F. Anderson, Salt Lake City, Utah.)

Salt Lake City, February, 1876.

Our territorial Solons have passed no law relating to Public Hygiene. Utah is in a primitive condition in this respect, unless something should be done by the present Legislature, now in session, which I think improbable. The irrigation of land in the summer months is practised generally by the farming community; but the atmosphere is so very dry that no malarial influence is observed therefrom. In the southern portion of the Territory, where the rivers and creeks are not under so thorough control as here, there are immense overflows in the spring and summer months, and fever and ague prevail.

(From Dr. J. D. Crockwell, Salt Lake City, Utah.)

. . . .

The usages of the President of the Church of Jesus Christ of Latterday Saints, through the various officers of the church, have regulated the hygiene of the Territory so far; and, from that fact, the Legislature has not passed any general laws. For the poor outlook by the church aforesaid, and what the church has not attended to, the various city corporations have ordinances on the subject of the public health.

VERMONT.

(From Dr. Oscar F. Fassett, St. Albans, Vt.)

St. Albans, Vt., Feb. 28, 1876.

In reply to your circular letter, I regret to say that the answers are nearly all negative ones. In 1873, a strong effort was made, by individual action and through the State Medical Society, to establish a State Board of Health: also, to incorporate a pharmaceutical association, providing for the education of apothecaries and druggists, and to regulate the sale of certain drugs; but the effort failed, because it required an appropriation.

We have one city, Burlington, with a local Health Board.

We have a State law providing for the registration of births and deaths, — enacted in 1846, I think, and carefully kept by the labors of an efficient Secretary of State, aided by a committee, elected by the State Medical Society.

No new disease has appeared, except perhaps diphtheria, during the past century. This has been much investigated by medical societies (so has typhoid fever) with special reference to its causes; by individuals, to a small extent, — by Dr. L. G. Butler, Dr. Middleton Goldsmith, and others. Cerebro-spinal meningitis, too, has received some investigation as a disease, which, though prevalent in 1812–14, had disappeared until 1857–58; since which it has prevailed up to the present time, to a greater or less extent.

St. Albans, through the efforts of its physicians, has done much, by way of drainage and water supply, to protect the health of its citizens.

Our State is sadly behind in sanitary matters; but we hope to do something soon. I have thus imperfectly answered your inquiries: I wish they were of more value to you.

(From Dr. Sumner Putnam, Montpelier, Vt.)

Montpelier, Vt., Jan. 19, 1876.

Registration Reports, from 1857 to 1872, show that consumption has annually destroyed in Vermont about 820 persons, or 1 to every 487 living; and pneumonia, about 258, or 1 to 785 living. These diseases have varied little from year to year; and, except on occasional years during which epidemic diseases have prevailed largely, they have invariably caused more than one-fourth of all the deaths occurring in the *Green Mountain State*.

During the years from 1860 up to 1867, an epidemic of diphtheria destroyed 4,100 people, mostly children and young persons; in 1863, reaching a mortality of 1,225 persons.

In 1862–65, there was an unusual prevalence of typhoid fever and scarlatina. Fevers, mostly typhoid, have, in Vermont, during sixteen years, on an average destroyed annually 1 person to every 1,000 living; during the first eight years of registration, 1 person to every 1,046 living; and, during the last eight years of registration, 1 person to every 992 living;

thus showing an increase of prevalence for the period commencing in 1856 and ending in 1872. Scarlatina, during the same period, destroyed 2,718 persons; an average, annually, of 1 to every 1,740 living: during the eight years from 1856 to 1865, 1 in 1,056; during the eight years from 1864 to 1872, 1 to 2,424 living. This shows a decided diminution of mortality in the last eight years of registration, — doubtless owing to the fact that many children had just been removed beyond its further ravages, by a recent epidemic of diphtheria and scarlatina.

I wish I could do more to help you to more valuable facts in relation to a subject really the most important, and beneficent, which could engage the attention of the true physician, at the present day.

A practice of thirty years, mostly in isolated country farmhouses, to which every visitant could be readily traced, has convinced me that typhoid fever, scarlatina, &c., originate *de novo*, as well as from contagion or miasm, proceeding from the sick. I know I once saw a case of typhoid fever, and a case of typhus fever, originate within a week of each other, in a house with bad hygiene, situated alone in the woods, with only a few new acres cleared about it, and with no possibility of importation or previous deposition of buds, germs, &c.

VIRGINIA.

My thanks are due, in an especial manner, to Professor Cabell, of the University of Virginia, through whose very active co-operation, I was able to get the following documents from various cities of that State: —

(From Dr. BEDFORD BROWN, Alexandria, Va.)

ALEXANDRIA, VA., Jan. 19, 1876.

. . . . During our recent war, a brigade, of which I was senior surgeon, was, for months, stationed in a flat country, without the ability of removing or changing its location. For some time after the encampment was formed, the command was infested with an alarming amount of sickness. The plan was finally adopted of taking down the tents every third day, and placing them on the ground occupied as streets, and thoroughly

cleansing the old locations. Again, on the third day afterwards, the order of things was reversed; so that perfect cleansing and purification were accomplished, without changing our position. After this, universal health prevailed.

. . . According to those best informed, this region has undergone a remarkable change during the past forty years, both in relation to the physical condition of the superficies of the localities, and also in regard to the health of the inhabitants. About the period referred to, all of this portion of the Potomac region was subject to annual visitations of malarial fevers of malignant character. At the same time, a considerable proportion of the land was covered with marshes, and with luxuriant vegetation. These marshes have almost disappeared, and their former sites are either cultivated or remain dry. During this period, the face of almost this entire section has been denuded of timber and forests. Hence, a vast surface being exposed to the action of the sun's rays, evaporation is so rapid and continuous as to cause a state of aridity, by which fountains, streams, and small lakes have vanished permanently. Vegetation has declined, and the area of marsh land, from this cause alone, has been reduced probably seventy per cent. Thus entire counties, when denuded of timber and vegetation, undergo not only marked changes in physical condition, but in point of health also, through the agency of evaporation. The city of Alexandria and vicinity. from having been noted for insalubrity, forty years ago, constitutes now one of the most healthy localities in the Union; where formerly malarial fever was frequent, and deadly in character; now it is by no means common, and is the mildest in type I have ever witnessed in any country.

But while malarial diseases have grown much less frequent, and undergone a marked amelioration in type, another affection is much more often met with than formerly. I allude to tubercular phthisis. Whether the increased prevalence of the latter disease is due to the more extensive and continuous evaporation going on during the winter and spring months, is a question of interest. I have been much impressed with the large number of cases of tubercular phthisis, coming under my observation during the past few years. I am also impressed with the fact that a large proportion of these cases, both hereditary and non-

hereditary, originate in primary attacks of catarrh, catarrhal pneumonia, and pneumonitis, of an acute character. The process of evaporation in this locality, from the large body of water in this vicinity, is very great, owing to rapid changes of temperature; and, consequently, the atmosphere is constantly saturated with exhaled moisture. This also finds its way into buildings, and produces, without care, permanent dampness. There can be no other cause for this state of things, as our population is otherwise healthy, and is abundantly supplied with the purest water, conducted into the city by extensive works, from large springs in the neighboring hills.

It is also plentifully supplied with wholesome food, and in great variety.

(From DR. JOHN H. CLAIBORNE, Health Officer of Petersburg, Va.)
Jan. 26, 1876.

The city of Petersburg has had for twenty years an admirable code of laws governing the public health. This code was framed by a most eminent jurist, the late Judge W. T. Joynes, of the Supreme Court of the State, who said, soon after they were published, "I intended to confer on the Board of Health of the city of Petersburg that which should be conferred upon the guardians of the public health everywhere; viz., powers as nearly despotic as possible under our institutions." With all of this, however, the law, until the 1st of August, 1875, was almost a dead letter, owing to the fact that the Board of Health was a *large body*, without *expert* knowledge. . . . At that date, on my recommendation, the number of the Board was reduced to *three persons;* two of whom should be physicians, and the third the Mayor of the city, *all salaried officers.* The first physician named by the Council takes the title of *Health Officer.* That dignity was conferred on me; and I am glad to be able to say that I have never asked any thing of the Council, *in my official capacity, which has not been granted, never made a recommendation in reference to the public health, which has not been adopted.* I have a police officer who constantly waits at the Health Office, for the purpose of sanitary inspection of designated localities, and who carries out, under authority of the Mayor, every order of the Health Office.

Private lots, streets, cellars, sinks, privies, public schools; also public buildings, and the sewerage attached to them, with their means of escape in case of fire, all are under my surveillance as Health Officer; also, questions of quarantine, and of the disposition of cases of contagious and infectious disease, and of city sewerage and scavenging, &c.

11. Our city is abundantly supplied with water from *springs*, outside of the suburbs, on the north, and from a running *stream*, situated beyond the suburbs, on the south. All of the sources of supply of this water are *beyond the water-shed which drains from the city;* and *therefore* the majority of the people are supplied with water, for culinary and drinking purposes, from the *city water*, as it is called, which is pumped into a reservoir above the city, on its southern suburbs; whence it is distributed by pipes, under the force of gravitation, all over it.

Great effort is made to preserve this water free from *organic* and *other impurities*, by fencing streams and reservoirs, and by a partial system of settling and percolation in the distributing reservoirs.

Still, *well water* is used by many for both *culinary* and *drinking* purposes, and *no effort* is made to prevent pollution.

This water is, beyond question, in the populous portions of the city, polluted; and, in some instances, very much so. As Health Officer, I have called the attention of citizens to the fact, and have known instances of the health of families being affected by it. I have seen a well used by a respectable family, the water of which was made so foul by a cesspool on an adjoining lot, that the fact could be detected, both by smell and sight, at the bottom of a vessel in which it was allowed to stand for some hours. As Health Officer, I, of course, had the cesspool cleaned and filled; and have invariably ordered all sinks and cesspools in the city to be filled, when I could reasonably do so. I have submitted an ordinance forbidding the digging of any such pit, in the future, unless it be carried ten feet into the earth, and be lined with brick and hydraulic cement. As soon as I can have our system of sewerage enlarged, I shall recommend the destruction of all such health traps, and their total prohibition.

12, 13, 14, see above.

15. We have an underground system of sewerage, very good as far as it extends, but not adequate in extent to supply the needs of the city. We are making efforts to enlarge it. Latterly, we have been using earthen piping for sewers, and so far have found it both *economical*, and *well adapted* to the purpose.

16. The *sewer outlets* are from a few hundred yards to one mile from the sources of the water supply, emptying into a creek running through the city, or into the river which skirts its northern boundary. It is so situated that it is impossible for the water supply to be affected by them.

Since the late war, *a new disease* has appeared in many sections of Tidewater and Piedmont, Virginia, which is called by the common people *yellow disease*, and, by some physicians, *interior yellow fever*. It is a malignant malarious fever, characterized by jaundice, yellow or bloody urine, vomiting sometimes simulating *il vomito*, hemorrhage from bowels, &c. It has been noted by many practitioners throughout the South, and it has almost invariably been attributed to *obstructed drainage*.

An account furnished by myself to Professor Cabell was published in the "Proceedings of the American Medical Association, for 1874."

(From Dr. J. H. Claiborne, Petersburg, Va.)

Petersburg, Va., Feb. 17, 1876.

In my report on "drainage and water supply" of this city, I omitted to state a fact which may have some pertinence to the subject; viz., we have no *typhoid fever here*. Omitting the period of the war, a good part of which time the city was one vast hospital or intrenched camp, where from five to ten thousand sick or wounded lay, and when typhus and *typho-malarial* fever was rife, I have never seen, in twenty-five (25) years *of most extensive practice* in city and vicinage, twenty-five cases of genuine *typhoid* or *enteric* fever. This I attribute to the fact that a portion of our people, especially the poor, get their drinking and cooking water from public fountains, whose sources render it impossible that they can be poisoned with animal matter.

VIRGINIA.

(From Dr. Frederick Horner, Jr., Salem, Va.)

. . . .

A Committee, appointed by the State Medical Society of Virginia, are, at present, urging the State Legislature to enact a law appointing a Board of Medical Examiners for the State, whose certificate will be required by parties before they will be allowed to practise medicine and surgery in Virginia. Said Committee have also been empowered to petition the Legislature to allow compensation to the members of the State Board of Health.

In connection with the subject of typhoid fever, I may mention, on the authority of a distinguished and old practitioner of Warrenton, Va., Dr. Samuel Chilton, that a late epidemic of this fever, which was fatal to a large number of the white and colored population of that town, was clearly traceable to impure drinking-water, obtained from wells and pumps, which had not been cleaned out for twenty years. Since our late war, another cause of this fever and of cerebro-spinal meningitis has been of a moral character, — depression, and loss of property.

Cattle plague has disappeared since 1871. The epizoötic was common among horses in 1872–75. Cattle plague was introduced by Texan or Spanish bullocks, which were crowded in the cars, and brought to Virginia in midsummer. These animals communicated a malignant form of zymotic disease or fever to the neat cattle, which died by hundreds. At the time, I dissected many of the latter, and from the results and symptoms proved the identity of the disease with the pleuropneumonia, so fatal in Germany, England, and New York. I also proved, by my dissections of hogs affected with so-called hog cholera, and from the symptoms and successful treatment, that the disease was a true typhoid fever. The same was proved of a fatal disease among sheep.

(From Dr. Levin S. Joynes, Richmond, Va.)

Note 1. The State of Virginia has shown no disposition to "spend money" to prevent adulteration of food; but has a *penal statute* against adulteration of articles of food or drink, as well as against the sale of diseased, corrupted, or unwholesome pro-

visions, whether meat or drink. There is also a law forbidding "distempered cattle," and horses affected with glanders or farcy, from being allowed to go, at large, off the grounds of the owner; and requiring them to be killed, and, without being skinned, to be buried by order of a justice of the peace, if this prohibition be disregarded. But the law, so far as known, does not deal farther with the subject.

Note 2. No formal arrangements have been consummated by the State Board of Health, though contemplated from the beginning, for the establishment of a system of correspondence, &c., throughout the State. The refusal of the Legislature to provide any means for the support of the Board has effectually checked the execution of its plans. It is, in fact, in a condition of only *nominal existence*. A copy of the Act establishing the Board is enclosed, from which it will be seen that it has *no powers* with respect to nuisances, &c., but is simply a *board of inquiry*, charged with the duty of collecting information, and reporting it in an available and useful form.

Note 3. If the word *town* be understood in the sense commonly accepted in New England, *i. e.*, as synonymous with *township*, it cannot be said that there are any " town boards of health" in Virginia. All the cities, however, and a number of the incorporated towns, have such boards.

Note 4. Our registration law, very defective in itself, has been very inefficiently executed; and it cannot be claimed to have afforded any results of practical value. The reports made by the Auditor of Public Accounts (who is the head of the registration system) have been based upon returns so partial and incomplete as to render it impossible to "draw from such records any law governing the public health," — at least, any which could be accepted with reasonable confidence.

Note 5. I know of no *general* law relating to the introduction of water into cities, except a provision authorizing the Circuit Courts to grant charters to water companies. But the charters of the cities give their municipal authorities all necessary power in the premises.

Note 6. The law provides for the annual appointment of a "vaccine agent," who is paid a fixed salary for his services, and is required to "furnish, by mail or otherwise, every citizen of

the State, who may apply therefor, with genuine vaccine matter, with directions how to use it, free of charge." The overseers of the poor, of every county, are also authorized to cause to be vaccinated, at the expense of the county, any person who may be unable to pay the expense thereof.

The following provision exists in relation to *inoculation:* "Any person who shall inoculate himself or another, or suffer himself to be inoculated, for the small-pox, unless at a hospital established by law, shall forfeit for every such offence a sum not exceeding three hundred dollars. And if any person shall bring into this State the small-pox, or any variolous disease, with the intent of propagating such disease, he shall forfeit one thousand dollars. When complaint is made to a justice of the peace, or he has reason to believe 'that there is, on any lot, tenement, or plantation, or on board any vessel in said county, any person infected with small-pox, or any other dangerous disease,' it is made his duty to require two physicians to examine the case or cases, and report as to their nature, and whether the public interest requires the establishment of a hospital for their reception. Full authority is given to the council of any town, or the court of any county, to establish and maintain hospitals, at the charge of such town or county.

"The council or health officer of a town, or any two justices of a county, may cause any person in said town or county, infected with any infectious disease dangerous to the public health, to be removed to a hospital, or other place of reception for the infected, unless *such person be sick in his own place of residence*, or cannot be removed without danger to his life." "If a person who has not had the small-pox or cow-pox go into a house in which any one is infected with the small-pox, and return thence, a justice may cause such person to be carried to the nearest hospital where the disease is, and to remain there until discharged on the certificate of the physician of the hospital that he may depart, without danger of spreading the contagion."

A penalty is imposed upon "any person" who knows himself to be infected with a dangerous, infectious disease, or who has recently had such disease, and has not had his person and clothes so cleansed as to be free from infection; "who shall

go into the company of any one who is liable to take the infection, or fail to retire from a public road or street on the approach of a passenger," &c.

"When the health officer of any town shall make complaint, under oath, that there is good cause of suspicion or belief that there is, on any lot or in any house in such town, or in any vessel arriving at the port thereof, any nuisance, source of filth, or cause of sickness, proper to be destroyed or removed, or one or more persons, not in his own place of residence, infected with contagious disease, and that he has been refused admittance into any such lot, building, or vessel, any justice of the corporation, or of the county in which such town is, may issue his warrant to the sheriff of the county, sergeant of the corporation, or any constable of either, requiring him to enter such lot, house, or vessel, and, under the direction of such health officer, to remove such infected person, or remove or destroy any such nuisance, source of filth, or cause of sickness." All expenses incurred for such removal, &c., to be paid by the infected person, or the owner of the house, lot, or vessel; but, if not so paid, to be chargeable to the town or county in which they were incurred.

Note 7. There are no *special* provisions in the law of this State, so far as I know, relating to cholera and yellow fever. These subjects are touched, to a certain extent, by some of the provisions cited in the preceding note. Any other legislation affecting them (among the "infectious diseases") is included in the general laws of quarantine. But in its provisions there is no specific mention of either disease.

Note 8. Every thing in the law relating to this subject has already been stated in note 1.

Note 9. The City of Richmond has adopted all needful sanitary ordinances, and has an efficient Board of Health charged with their enforcement. "Special action" has been taken with reference to actual or threatened epidemics of cholera and small-pox: in the former case, by extra provisions for cleansing, disinfecting, the prevention and abatement of nuisances, the exclusion of unwholesome food from the markets, &c.; in the latter case, by efficient measures for general vaccination, and the establishment of a hospital for the reception of patients

affected with the disease. To the timely adoption of these measures, and the thorough manner in which they have been carried out under the supervision of the Board of Health, Richmond is mainly indebted for its exemption from any serious visitation of the small-pox, which has prevailed, as an epidemic, in so many cities and towns, and with such fatal results, within the last five years. The following is a statement of the number of deaths by small-pox in each year, from 1871 to 1875, inclusive: 1871, 0; 1872, 3; 1873, 28; 1874, 1; 1875, 1.

The population of Richmond, according to the United States Census of 1870, was a little over 51,000. In January, 1874, according to an enumeration ordered by the city authorities, it was 60,700.

Note 10. There is no special need of care to prevent pollution, as the only town situated on the river above Richmond, exceeding a few hundreds in population, is Lynchburg (having a population of about 8,000), which is one hundred and twenty miles distant; and the only manufacturing establishment above the city, within many miles, is an iron furnace, five or six miles distant.[1]

Note 11. Some of these refuse matters are disposed of to the "soap-grease" men; others are removed by the city garbage carts, under the direction of the Board of Health; while the refuse water of the laundry and the kitchen flows into the sewers, after running (or stagnating), in some instances, a greater or less distance in open gutters.

Note 12. By a recent statute (1870–71), it is provided that any person desiring to drain lands, through the lands of others, may apply to the court of the county or corporation, for the appointment of commissioners to ascertain and report upon the propriety of granting the application, and the damages that may be sustained by the parties through whose lands the drainage is proposed to be made. They are also to inquire whether the mode of drainage proposed be proper, &c. If the report be favorable, the court may grant the application; and then

---

[1] If, in this establishment, there should be employed from one to two thousand men, with their families, and if their refuse and excreta were indiscriminately thrown into the river, I think this statement of there being "no special need of care" would be incorrect. — H. I. B.

the applicant, after paying or securing to be paid the damages, ascertained by the commissioners, may proceed to execute his proposed plans of drainage.

(From Dr. Herbert M. Nash, Norfclk, Va.)

Norfolk, Va., Feb. 5, 1876.

Below you will find such answers as I am able to give to the second series of questions in yours of the 18th.

4. The counties of Norfolk, Princess Anne, Nansemond, like most if not all the counties of the State, have no Boards of Health. Our opposite city of Portsmouth has a Board, which makes no attempt to collect vital statistics, but restricts its operations to the abatement of such nuisances, as are brought to its notice by the members, or the citizens generally.

5. I have not been able to find out the date of the legal establishment of the Board of Health of this city. It is, perhaps, as old as the State law upon the subject. It was certainly in existence in 1821. The Health Officer here was then appointed by the Governor; nor am I able to say when the State relinquished this right. The Health Officer is the executive officer, to a certain extent, of the Board; but is not selected by them, but by the Council; and hence *politics* often forces upon the Board an officer, no way fitted for the duty. The Board of Health, except in seasons of epidemics, has, prior to 1870, rarely exercised its power, except to abate such crying nuisances as were brought to its notice, and as a sort of court which settled all disputes as to sanitary matters. One or two physicians have always been among its members. For the last five years, it has been urgent in forcing the attention of the city government to the necessity of pursuing regular and definite plans for the improvement of the public health, and these efforts are beginning to tell.

7–*a*. This question ought, perhaps, to be answered in the negative. Diseases formerly prevalent still appear; but often in a greatly modified form, milder in type, and more amenable to treatment.

We have occasional deaths from pernicious intermittent fever; but such cases are rare, except in persons who have been exposed to malarial influences outside the city limits, or who are resi-

dents of the suburbs, unpaved and badly watered parts of the city. Cases of malignant dysentery are rarer than formerly, as are all bowel affections of adults, — particularly yellow fever, of which there have been several epidemics. It has always been imported; but we have had none since 1855. I may mention that the deaths from malarial fevers of all kinds, in 1873, numbered eighteen, of which fourteen were deaths of negroes; whole number of deaths being four hundred and sixty-five.

6. None formerly prevalent appear to have been crushed out entirely by the action of State or individual. In 1867, epidemic cholera made its appearance: and it was met by very active measures by the Board of Health; inspections and disinfectants, &c., following each case, with a result which no one doubts proved the wisdom of their course. The disease disappeared.

8. There are no established facts proving that any special disease has been generated or introduced into this section of the State during the past century, which did not exist in colonial times. Diphtheria has been thought by some to be a new disease here; but I have no doubt it existed heretofore as *putrid* and other forms of sore throat. So typhoid fever is believed to have been met with, and treated, under the names of nervous and typhus fever.

9. Must be answered in the negative.

10. Norfolk has taken active measures for the improvement of the public health, by extending its pavement, much of which has been recently done, as much for its sanitary effects as for public convenience. She has introduced a very fair water supply, independently of the action of individuals erecting cisterns. She has drained and filled unsightly and unwholesome ponds and marshes; and recently, at the suggestion of the Board of Health, has improved and rendered serviceable many natural drains, heretofore allowed to be obstructed, &c., and consequently, (a) by her ordinances concerning the public health, (Health Board and its duties), and (b) by special ordinances in specific cases, at the instance of the Board.

11. Well water is not used for cooking, except by a small number. City water and cistern water mostly used. In the outer section of the city, north of Queen and east of Brewer Streets, cisterns are rare, and city water is not extensively

used. This section is mostly inhabited by negroes, and a few whites of the poorer classes. Several families may here be found occupying one house; well water and rain water, collected in barrels, is principally used for domestic purposes. Here there is more sickness, and the death-rate is much higher.

12. Care is taken to prevent pollution, except in the section just referred to. The water of a leaky cistern has to be abandoned. It is brackish, disagreeable, and worthless.

13. Answered in the affirmative.

14. Due care is taken to prevent pollution, and much care is taken to keep them in order.

15. No public or general sewers. Some private residences and the hotels have them, discharging into the river.

16. Does not apply here, surrounded as we are by not potable salt-water.

17. We dispose of sewage (night soil) by removal from the city by the Odorless Excavating Company's apparatus (the pneumatic plan). As the sinks are frequently the receptacle for slops, all is removed, at once, by this method. This work is done by day, and entirely without odor. Other slops, as soapsuds, &c., are thrown into the gutters, to run, or to be swept off by the street gangs. House offal (garbage) is taken away, almost daily, by city carts, in barrels, and carried beyond city limits. During the past summer, by direction of the Board, these street gutters were regularly flushed by city water, and kept clean. But this is troublesome and difficult; and we hope ere long to introduce such improvements as are most practicable to this end.

18. The Health Officer has published a monthly report of deaths, in the city newspapers, for many years. Only within a very short time, has a regular annual report been made and published. That of 1874 was the first attempt at a report of the annual work of the Board. The report for the year 1875 is now in the hands of the printer. We are too poor to attempt any thing but the most modest form of report.

WISCONSIN.

(From Dr. WILLIAM A. GOTT, Viroqua, Wis.)

VIROQUA, WIS., Jan. 29, 1876.

In regard to Question No. 10, I have to remark, that, in the latter part of the summer and the fall of 1873, and part of the winter of 1874, an epidemic of the so-called typho-malarial fever made its appearance in this, usually healthy, village. The village is situated on high rolling prairie, in the midst of a rich agricultural section of the country of similar character, and, up to the time specified, had been remarkably exempt from the fevers of low type, that usually prevail in less-favored localities, due to malarial influences. The disease, in its ravages, confined itself almost exclusively to the northern section of the village, in which is located a burial-ground, which had been deserted on account of its being literally packed with human bodies. During the period above specified, a number of bodies were disinterred, for removal to a new cemetery, in the southern section of the village, and without its corporate limits; and, strange to say, the workmen engaged in the work of disinterment neglected to fill up the old graves. Thus, for weeks, the air in the vicinity was impregnated with poisonous emanations arising from those open graves; in some of which, on each side, could be seen other remains advanced in decomposition. I could attribute the prevalence of the disease, in the locality referred to, to no other evident cause.

(From Dr. EZRA L. GRIFFIN, Fond Du Lac, Wis.)

FOND DU LAC, WIS., March 24, 1876.

I regret we cannot do more for you, but will do better by and by. Through much effort, we have got a law passed and signed, but not yet published, creating a State Board of Health. The appointments have not yet been made, and will not be, until after the meeting of our State Society, in June. The Board will embrace seven members, to be appointed by the Governor.

Our appropriation is small, but will do until we get organized for work. As we are in our very *initiatory* steps in this work,

you will see I cannot answer many of your questions affirmatively.

As to the water supply of this city (16,000), we are supplied wholly by fountains or artesian wells. We bore or drill down from one hundred to three hundred and fifty feet, and get a running stream of moderately cool, but hard water (moderately so).

The fountains of one hundred feet deep draw water from a water-bearing sand, and the water flows just above the surface. Those from the strata three hundred or three hundred and fifty feet, will elevate the stream forty to sixty feet.

Our whole water supply is from these fountains: hence, we are not in danger of using water polluted by surface drainage.

Dr. Johnson, Health Officer of Milwaukee, will furnish you with all sanitary facts, pertaining to that city, which you may desire.

I see the Board of that city have just passed laws, by which all slaughtering shall be done at a public abattoir, &c.

WYOMING TERRITORY.

(From Dr. George H. Russell, Cheyenne, Wyoming Terr.)

Cheyenne, Wyoming Terr., Feb. 14, 1876.

Our Territory is still in its infancy, being only seven years old. We have had only three sessions of the Legislature; much has been done, and much is yet to be done.

Our last Legislature passed a very stringent law relating to the practice of medicine, surgery, and obstetrics. The law requires a physician to be a thorough scholar, and a graduate of some regularly chartered medical school. He must produce and file a copy of his diploma, and prove his identity by two competent persons.

APPENDIX III.

PUBLIC HYGIENE IN THE UNIVERSITIES AND COLLEGES.

III.

RETURNS FROM UNIVERSITIES AND COLLEGES, AND MEDICAL INSTITUTIONS, SHOWING THE AMOUNT OF INTEREST SHOWN BY THEM ON VARIOUS QUESTIONS, ALLIED TO THOSE PROPOUNDED IN THE ADDRESS.

I desired to learn how far the universities and colleges and medical colleges of the country attended to the subjects considered in the preceding address. Accordingly, I sent out the following circular to several of the more important institutions of learning in the country. I received replies from sixty-two universities or colleges, and from twenty-three medical colleges, the names of which appear below. They have enabled me to prepare two tables, showing the percentages of institutions which pay attention to these hygienic questions, by the side of similar percentages of those who neglect them. The general tenor of these returns sustains the various positions, taken in the address; viz., that the teaching of hygiene, as a part of a college curriculum, is rarely attended to. At the same time, they afford gratifying proof of the attention paid to athletic sports and various drills, which has been, of late, growing up among the youths attendant at these same institutions.

BOSTON, February, 1876.

To the President or Dean of the Faculty of
    College, in   State of

DEAR SIR, — In furtherance of a public duty which I have undertaken, I wish, as far as possible, to learn what amount of instruction is given on Private and Public Hygiene by the colleges of the United States; and also what opportunities are offered in them for physical exercises among the students.

I trust that you will not deem me intrusive, if I ask for, at least, monosyllabic replies to the following questions, so far as they apply to your institution.

APPENDIX.

Of course, I should be gratified to have more detailed answers, if you have the time and inclination to give me your opinion on the subjects touched upon.

I would like to have replies on or before April 1, 1876.

Yours respectfully,

HENRY I. BOWDITCH, M.D.

113 Boylston Street, Boston.

	Yes.	No.

1. Is any regular instruction given in your college upon —
     a. Public Hygiene?
     b. State Preventive Medicine?
     c. Private Hygiene?
 2. Have you any professor especially devoted to Hygiene, either private or public?
 3. Does he deliver a full course of instruction?
 or —
 4. Does he bring such lessons and instruction into any other course, and in a manner subsidiary to it?
 5. Has your college provided any means for encouraging or promoting physical culture among the students; as, for example, —
     a. By gymnasia?
     b. By ball playing?
     c. By boating?
     d. By any other methods?
 6. If you have had for a number of years any or all of these means for physical culture, has any perceptible effect been produced by them upon the "*physique*" of the students?
 7. If so, what effect?		

HYGIENE IN UNIVERSITIES.

I have received replies to the circular from the following sixty-two colleges or universities in the United States, exclusive of the medical colleges: —

Alabama	University of Alabama	Tuscaloosa.
,,	Southern University	Greenboro'.
Arkansas	Arkansas College	Fayetteville.
Colorado	Wolfe Hall	Denver.
Connecticut	Trinity College	Hartford.
,,	Yale College	New Haven.
Dist. of Col.	Georgetown College	Georgetown.
,,	Columbia College	Washington.
Georgia	University of Georgia	Athens.
Kentucky	University of Louisville	Louisville.
Illinois	University of Chicago	Chicago.
,,	Ewing University	Knoxville.
,,	Knox College	Galesburg.
,,	Monmouth College	Monmouth.
,,	North Western University	Evanston.
,,	Peoria University	Peoria.
,,	Shurtleff College	Upper Alton.
,,	Southern Illinois	Carbondale.
,,	State Normal University	Normal.
Indiana	Brookville College	Brookville.
,,	Franklin College	Franklin.
,,	Indiana State University	Bloomington.
,,	N. W. Christian University,	Indianapolis.
,,	Wabash College	Crawfordville.
Iowa	Iowa City University	Iowa City.

Maine	Bowdoin College	Brunswick.
Maryland	Washington College	Baltimore.
Massachusetts	Amherst College	Amherst.
”	Harvard College	Cambridge.
”	Holy Cross College	Worcester.
”	Phillips Academy	Andover.
”	Williamstown College	Williamstown.
Michigan	University of Michigan	Ann Arbor.
Mississippi	University of Mississippi	Oxford.
Missouri	St. Louis University	St. Louis.
N. Hampshire	Dartmouth College	Hanover.
New Jersey	Burlington College	Burlington.
”	Princeton College	Princeton.
”	Rutger's College	New Brunswick.
”	Seton Hall	Orange.
New York	Columbia College	New York.
”	Cornell University	Ithaca.
”	Syracuse College	Syracuse.
”	Union College	Schenectady.
North Carolina	University of North Carolina	Chapel Hill.
Ohio	Antioch College	Yellow Springs.
”	Marietta College	Marietta.
”	Oberlin College	Oberlin.
”	Wesleyan University	Delaware.
Pennsylvania	Lincoln University	Oxford.
Rhode Island	Brown University	Providence.

South Carolina, University of South Carolina, Columbia.

Tennessee . . Tennessee Agricul. College . Knoxville.
„ University of Nashville . . Nashville.

Vermont . . University of Vermont . . Burlington.
„ Middlebury College . . . Middlebury.

Virginia . . . University of Virginia . . Charlotteville.
„ Washington and Lee Univ. . Lexington.
„ William and Mary College . Williamsburg.

W. Virginia . Storer College . . . . . Harper's Ferry.

Wisconsin . . Ripon College . . . . . Ripon.
„ University of Wisconsin . . Madison.

TABLE I.

RESULTS OF CORRESPONDENCE ON PUBLIC OR PRIVATE HYGIENE WITH SIXTY-TWO UNIVERSITIES AND COLLEGES IN THE UNITED STATES, EXCLUSIVE OF MEDICAL COLLEGES.

No. of question.		Subject of question.	Attention paid.	No attention paid.	Doubtful, or no response.	Percentages of	
						Colleges which pay attention.	Colleges that pay no attention, or make no reply
1	a	Public Hygiene	11	35	16	17.74	82.26
	b	State Preventive Medicine	4	39	19	6 45	93 55
	c	Private Hygiene	23	25	14	37.09	62.90
2		Special instruction in Hygiene . .	5	34	23	8 06	91.94
3		Full course on Hygiene	3	13	46	4.84	95.16
4		Subsidiary to another subject . . .	46	8	8	74 19	25 81
5	a	Gymnasia	35	17	10	56.45	43.55
	b	Ball playing	45	9	8	72 58	27 42
	c	Boating	24	25	13	38.71	61.29
	d	Other methods[1]	35	10	17	56.45	43.55

[1] Among these, I find the following mentioned by various colleges: Military drill, at seven colleges; walking, or manual labor, in three; and calisthenics, "formerly" landscape gardening, farm labor, playing, jumping, boxing, Scotch games, games, wrestling, croquet, hunting, each in one college; and, finally, in one, is " an association to promote various physical exercises."

Considering the above table as fairly representing the amount of instruction afforded by the colleges of the country, we may say that —

1. Instruction in Public Hygiene and State Preventive Medicine is wofully neglected.
2. On Private Hygiene, only about one-third of the colleges give any instruction.
3. That a full *special* course of instruction on either of the above themes is almost unknown.
4. But *incidentally*, in connection with some other not necessarily allied subject, and therefore inefficiently, the topics are treated of by about three-fourths of the colleges, while one-fourth of them do not even perform this small duty in this most important matter. Meanwhile, although the instructors of the colleges thus neglect important duties, the youths, of their own free will, and at times, lately, with the aid and counsel of the college governments, have commenced athletic sports. This will gradually force the colleges to take, on their own parts, a higher position.

Among the results named by the writers, I find the following claims are made for physical culture of the students: The pupils gain "good" health, "better" health, "more vigor," "increased strength," "very high health rate," and "even correction of physical defects;" one says, "Dyspepsia, debility, formerly prevalent, have gone;" another, that "those exercising regularly, if well, keep well, if weak, get better, and escape diseases, usually incident to student life, coming out fresh and strong." "Physique of Western students almost always good." "Good incalculable." "Many students neglect exercise, and need hygienic advice." "Manly carriage and womanly grace, and agility in both sexes, promoted." "Military drill, especially for those last qualities, is good." "Students are *compelled* to exercise on the *campus*, with excellent effects." "Students frequently speak of good effects." "No one can study *hard*, except he exercise daily." The *morale* of the exercise is good, and the tone of the student is improved: in one "the moral effect was more marked than the physical." On the contrary, one says that the moral effect may be bad, with a low-minded superintendent. One claims the good effect on "brain workers."

One says he cannot say whether any good results have arisen; because, if exercise be optional, the strong tend to physical exercise, but the weak do not tend to the same.

In some cases, physical injuries have happened from overwork, — sprains. Boating has been specially blamed, in certain instances. (For further detail, see correspondence.)

With such an array of evidence of the excellent effects of this physical culture, one cannot but wonder that our returns (Table 1) show such meagre attention to the subject.

Very few of the colleges compel any kind of physical exercise, or encourage it, as any university should encourage every means tending to a perfect manly and womanly development. I can but hope that, during the coming century, a better course will be followed.

Extracts from Letters.

University of Alabama. — By military discipline, general good health, and manly, graceful port.

Southern University, Greenboro', Ala. — No regular gymnasium; but we are anxious to promote physical culture.

Trinity College, Hartford, Conn. — A subject of very great importance, and a college should care for the health of every student.

University of Chicago, Ill. — An unusually large number of our students are encouraged to labor on the college premises, and some outside. A military company has, much of the time, kept up drill exercise. Some have kept horses for riding. Walking, shooting, fishing, are in vogue. The habits of our students, during the eighteen years of our history, have been, by these various means, unusually active; and the health of the college, universally good, — much above the average health of one of the eastern colleges, where I was a student, or in any other college with which I am acquainted.

Knox College, Galesburg, Ill. — Those who exercise regularly, if well, keep well; if weakly, get well (as a rule); and escape, very noticeably, the diseases and weaknesses incident to student life, going through each term fresh and strong.

APPENDIX.

Southern Illinois College, Ill. — We think the health of the pupils much benefited, and we are sure that grace and ease of carriage have been promoted.

State Normal University, Ill. — The physical condition of the students is generally good. Most of them are accustomed to manual labor.

Franklin College, Indiana. — No student, who does not *exercise each day*, can study *hard* and *early*.

I wish to call attention to the two following: —

(From INDIANA STATE UNIVERSITY, Bloomington, Ind.)

BLOOMINGTON, IND., Feb. 24, 1876.

DEAR SIR, — The President and Faculty have requested me to answer your questions relative to the Hygiene of our college. I regret to say that, notwithstanding all my efforts, we have as yet done very little in that respect.

I lecture to the Freshmen once a week during one term, on Physiology and the Laws of Health. Formerly, it was in our Junior Year, because, without a pretty thorough acquaintance with them, they could not understand physiology. But we deemed it important that they should be warned, at an earlier period in their course, how to take care of their health; hence the change.

I have usually recommended them, also, to read Dr. Naphy's excellent work on the "Transmission of Life."

At one time, we had military exercises; but they became unpopular, and the military professor recommended discontinuing the exercises, which was done.

I earnestly and repeatedly urged the trustees to erect a gymnasium; and they always expressed their willingness, but were short of funds to do that, and other things which they considered more important. I even urged the students to attempt getting up a cheap gymnasium, and they seemed willing; but no one took hold of the matter, and it dropped.

As I was three years at Mr. Fellenberg's Institution (Hofwyl), in Switzerland, where we daily exercised in gymnastics, besides taking long walks, and spending our vacation in travelling on foot; also, bathing in the season, throwing lances,

and having many games, — I saw the great benefit of the system; and hence have contended that we are very deficient in our provision for physical training, as far as my observation has extended during forty-eight years in America, twenty-five of which I have spent in colleges. But there are always instructors, who adhere to the old-school system, and contend that students can walk, or chop or saw their wood, and thus have enough exercise. In practice, I find that the farmers' sons, of whom we have many, break down under the great change; unless they board out at some distance from town, or somewhat reduce their diet, and commence their mental labors gradually, in their Freshman Year, increasing the tension as they advance to the Senior Year.

Excuse my writing thus in detail; but I feel that we have not done what we know is necessary (at least, what some of us know), and yet I desired to show that we duly appreciate the value of hygienic lectures and exercises, and the importance of the statistics you are collecting and bringing to bear upon this subject.

If we fail to take heed, I fear we shall become a nation of dyspeptics, with overtaxed, nervous systems.

(From N. W. C. UNIVERSITY, Indianapolis, Ind.)

INDIANAPOLIS, February, 1876.

DEAR SIR, — I return your circular, not very satisfactorily filled, for the reason we have lately moved our school to this place, a suburb of Indianapolis, four miles out; have our main buildings completed, but not yet our gymnasium. In addition to ball-playing of various kinds, during the pleasant part of the year, we give a recess of one-half to three-quarters of an hour, and *compel* the students to play on the *campus* (twenty-five acres). The effect of this, specially upon the ladies, is very remarkable: instead of closing the summer term with faded cheeks, sunken eyes, curved spines, irregular menstruation, and ready to make their diplomas their winding-sheets, they close the year with as good health, if not better, than when they began it.

Gymnasium, boating, &c., will be added as rapidly as we can get our grounds and buildings in order.

Wabash College, Ind. — Better health and physique. We have experienced that the moral effects are good.

Bowdoin College, Me. — High average health rate. In special cases, great improvement in constitutional vigor, and even correction of physical defects.

Amherst College, Mass. — " In general terms, we seem to see a decided improvement in the physique." In connection with this college correspondence, I find the twelfth annual gymnastic exhibition held for the Washburn and Sawyer prizes, for various physical exercises.[1] With this programme, were given the maxima and minima of the "physical constants" of the students for fourteen years. I commend, most heartily, the care taken by Amherst for the proper development of the physique of its students. The exercises are required as much as those of an intellectual character are, and they are fully as well attended as the literary.

Harvard College, Mass. — Besides the gymnasium, ball-playing, and boating, there is an association which promotes walking, jumping, boxing, &c.; also, a small drill club, and another for rifle shooting. The average physique has distinctly improved during the last twenty-four years, especially among the city-bred young men. We have many students, however, who take no part in the above voluntary exercises, who are sorely in need of good hygienic advice and good training.

Phillips Academy, Mass. — Students who practise with regularity and moderation are, I think, uniformly benefited. Occasional accidents in the gymnasium and ball-field, and sometimes "vaulting ambition overleaps itself," *i.e.*, physical exercise is too severe or too prolonged; and thus, from want of method or prudence on the part of the pupil, accidents happen.

Williamstown College, Mass. — I think there has been some improvement, though it is not marked. Boating has been obviously injurious to some engaged in it.

Dartmouth College, N.H. — I present the following, from one of the catalogues of the institution: —

---

[1] See 1875. The twelfth autumnal gymnastic exhibition of Amherst College, held Dec. 18, 1875.

GYMNASIUM.

This edifice, erected by the munificence of George H. Bissell, Esq., of New York City, at an expense of $24,000, was opened for use in February, 1867. It is a tasteful and commodious structure, ninety feet in length, forty-seven in breadth, and two stories high. It has the most approved gymnastic apparatus and furniture, and affords ample opportunity for exercise, recreation, and the best physical culture. The students attend regularly upon the exercises, under an instructor, to such extent as to insure to each of them the benefit of the establishment; while the building is open at other times for voluntary practice. This department has been eminently successful. It has not only proved a source of constant gratification, but a great physical advantage. The following statement of the resident Medical Professor most frequently consulted by the students was embraced in a report of the President to the Trustees, in July, 1867: "Since the opening of the gymnasium, I have taken occasion to witness frequently the exercises, and the results have more than equalled my expectations. There has been no case of severe illness in the college during that time, and there have been fewer instances of slight indisposition, than I have ever known, in the same length of time before. Dyspepsia, debility, and similar affections incident to a sedentary life, and which have hitherto been frequent in the change of seasons from winter to spring, have, during the present season, been unknown. There has been a manifest improvement in the general physical tone of the college, and the increased muscular power and agility of the young men have forced themselves on the attention, even of unpractised eyes. I am fully satisfied that these exercises have greatly subserved the general health of the students."

Burlington College, N.J. — We have noticed more muscle, more agility, better carriage, and almost unvarying good health and spirits, with some slight accidents. I can hardly imagine a condition of things less favorable to study than a school without these (*i.e.*, military drill five days in the week, with gymnastics, ball, and boating), and other similar appliances.

The good order, improved feeling and morals, of the boys under such recreation and exercise as these facilities afford, deserve mention in their effect on the physique. We have had boys in college classes who used them with equal zest and benefit; and I should require them for the average American undergraduate.

Princeton College. — They promote the strength, health, and morality of the students. I can conceive evil to arise with a superintendent of low tastes.

Rutger's College, N.J. — The effects are good. The average health of the students is better than that of an equal number of young men of the same age, engaged in other pursuits.

Cornell University, N.Y. — We insist on military drill, and the effect is very perceptible on the carriage of the students.

Union College, N.Y. — For promoting physical culture among the students, there has been provided one of the largest and best equipped gymnasiums in the country. A competent instructor is constantly in charge to direct, and guard against overtraining. We have ball and boat clubs, and special prizes for encouraging physical culture, &c. For more than two years past, the college has engaged the services of a graduate from West Point, as professor of military drill; and in regular military drill exercise, as well as in other forms of physical culture, there has been constant advance, and a perceptible improvement in the physique of the students.

Antioch College, Yellow Springs, O. — 1. No instruction is given, except what I give on physiology, as one of the branches of natural science. I make it my aim to bring out, as far as possible, the physiological and hygienic bearings of every branch of the study of anatomy, of which regular dissection (animal) forms a leading feature. I also have always devoted one lecture a week to the subject mentioned in your first query. So that, in our six months' course in anatomy and physiology, I bring in a great many of them, and the students have the opportunity of becoming acquainted with the great laws of health, both relating to the individual and to the State.

2. There has been very great lack of physical exercise here in the past, and none too much exists, at present. As a partial remedy, but almost all that I can directly accomplish, I make

as much of my work, in the classes, lie out of doors as I possibly can; sending my students out for miles, sometimes on geological excursions, &c., to collect specimens in botany or zoölogy.

Our boys have lately established a small gymnasium, which time may develop into more; and last summer, for the first time, several of them built boats, and commenced a rowing club. I hope this will not quite die out during the winter; but our water here is not very well adapted for the purpose, being shallow in the summer time.

If there is any other information that I can give, I shall be happy to do so. I find your Massachusetts State Board of Health reports so useful that I willingly give all the help I can in furtherance of the work.

Oberlin College, Oberlin, O. — The importance of physical exercise has always been urged upon the students. We do not require it; but occasional lectures are given, by different members of the Faculty, on the subject. Base-ball is popular, and foot-ball. The gymnasium is patronized regularly by a large percentage of the college students, perhaps half. Manual labor has always been in good repute here, and some of our best students work every day, — saw wood, make gardens, do janitors' duties for the college, and for churches, &c. We aim to make labor honorable; and have succeeded, to a good degree, in maintaining that sentiment among students, and in the community.

Tennessee Agricultural College, Knoxville. — Gymnasium, ball, boating, and military drill, chiefly. Shoulders are drawn back, and the chest developed; the head is lifted up; the step steadied and made firm; and the general appearance and bearing, as well as the health of the students, are much improved.

University of Virginia. — For several years before the late civil war, there were adequate provisions for physical culture; the authorities having erected and equipped an extensive gymnasium, for the use of which, with *systematic instruction by an accomplished gymnast and instructor*, students were required to pay a small fee. The effect in producing a systematical muscular development, and in promoting the good health of the hard brain-workers, candidates for collegiate honors, was most manifest. In connection with a gymnasium was a house for giving

294 APPENDIX.

Russian or hot-vapor baths, open one day every week. During the war, the buildings, which were temporary wooden structures, were taken down, and the materials applied to other uses. Since the war, out-door gymnastic exercises have been practised by parties of the students, who have erected a modest apparatus at their own expense. Recently, a son of Dr. E. R. Squibb, of Brooklyn, himself a student, has presented, for the use of the students generally, a set of apparatus, which has been put up in a large hall provided by the authorities of the University.

Hygiene in Medical Colleges.

I sent out the same circular to various medical colleges throughout the country. The following (23) have kindly answered:—

Alabama	. . Medical College of Alabama,	. Mobile.
California .	. Med. Dept., University College,	San Francisco.
Connecticut	. Med. Dept., Yale College .	. New Haven.
Dist. of Col.	. National Medical College .	. Washington.
Georgia . .	. Atlanta Medical College .	. Atlanta.
„	Medical College of Georgia	. Augusta.
„	Savannah Medical College .	. Savannah.
Illinois . .	. Rush Medical College . .	. Chicago.
Indiana . .	. Indiana Medical College .	. La Porte.
Louisiana .	. Med. Dept., Univ. Louisiana	. New Orleans.
„	New Orleans School of Med. .	„

Massachusetts . Med. School, Harvard Univ. . Boston.

Michigan . . Med. Dept., Univ. Michigan . Ann Arbor.

N. Hampshire . Med. Dept., Dartmouth Coll. . Hanover.

New York . . Albany Medical College . . Albany.
"   Med. Dept., Univ. of Buffalo . Buffalo.

Ohio . . . . College of Med. and Surg.. . Cincinnati.
"   Medical College of Ohio . . "
"   Miami Medical College . . . "
"   Med. Dept., West. Reserve Coll., Hudson.

Pennsylvania . Jefferson Medical College . . Philadelphia.
"   Med. Dept., Univ. of Penn. . "

South Carolina, Med. Coll. of State of S.C. . Charleston.

TABLE II.

RESULTS OF CORRESPONDENCE WITH TWENTY-THREE MEDICAL COLLEGES, SHOWING THE AMOUNT OF INSTRUCTION IN PUBLIC AND PRIVATE HYGIENE AND PHYSICAL CULTURE GIVEN BY THESE INSTITUTIONS, EXISTING IN VARIOUS PARTS OF THE UNITED STATES.

No. of question.		Subject of question.	Attention paid.	No attention paid.	Doubtful, or no response.	Percentages of Colleges that pay attention to the subject.	Percentages of Colleges that pay no attention or make no reply.
1	a	Public Hygiene	9	10	4	39.13	60.37
	b	State Preventive Medicine . . .	7	12	4	36.43	69.57
	c	Private Hygiene	9	10	4	39.13	60.87
2		Special professorships	5[1]	18		21.73	78.27
3		Full course	5[2]	17	1	21.73	78.27
4		Subsidiary course	11	11	1	47.83	52.17

[1] See correspondence from Alabama, Buffalo, Harvard, and Miami Medical Colleges, and from Medical Department of University of Pennsylvania.
[2] See correspondence from Harvard Medical College.

A glance at the above data seems to show that, —

1. Only a little more than one-third of the colleges pay any attention to Public or Private Hygiene.
2. A still smaller proportion notice State Preventive Medicine.
3. Only about one-fifth have special professors and special courses of instruction in Hygiene.
4. About one-half say they have subsidiary teaching, given by various professors in other departments.

Facts and Extracts from Letters from the Medical Colleges.

Medical College of Alabama, Mobile. — A chair of Public Hygiene was established in this college in 1871. A professor was appointed. Medical jurisprudence "was added to, or made part of the same chair; but very nearly the entire course was taken up with lectures on *Public and Private Hygiene.*"

Medical Department of University College, San Francisco, Cal. — "A few lectures have usually been given on Hygiene during the preliminary course; but no special attention has been paid to the subject."

Medical Department of Yale College, Connecticut. — "Only in a superficial way," in connection with other professorships.

National Medical College, Washington D.C. — "We have no means of promoting physical culture in the Medical Department."

Atlanta Medical College, Atlanta, Ga. — "I am sorry to say that nothing has been done in our school. It is an important subject, and I am glad you are giving it attention."

Rush Medical College, Illinois. — Instruction on Hygiene given by professors of physiology and materia medica.

New Orleans School of Medicine, Louisiana. — Instruction in Hygiene, only subsidiary.

Medical Department of University of Louisiana. — "All the professors" lecture on hygiene.

Harvard Medical School. — Has a "lecturer" (not professor) on Hygiene, who delivers "a special course."

Medical Department of University of Michigan, Ann Arbor,

Mich. — Some years ago a special course of instruction in Hygiene, public, domestic, personal, and mental, was given to the students in the literary departments, and was appreciated by them; but was dropped, partly on account of funds, partly for want of time, and partly in deference to the prejudices of some who regarded it as an innovation, and who seemed to fear a materialistic tendency from the professor, who, though a believer in Orthodox Christianity, was not a *narrow* one.

We have no special professor on Hygiene in the Medical College, though a good deal of Hygiene is taught with other branches. The hygienic management of different diseases receives special attention; and, in the lectures on Pathology, etiology is made prominent. In the lectures on Physiology, too, the subject of food and drinks is discussed; and, in the lectures on Chemistry, the subject of ventilation is made a specialty, illustrated by models of houses; and disinfection, drainage, poisons, &c., are thoroughly taught: but there is no regular consecutive course on Hygiene in the medical course.

In the Medical Department, lessons are given by the Professor of Physiology and Pathology.

Medical Department of Dartmouth College. — Instruction in Private Hygiene; but no lectures on Hygiene, save in connection with other departments.

Albany Medical College. — " In the past, no chair of Hygiene; but Dr. I. S. Hooker has just been appointed to such a professorship, and probably a full course of lectures will be given."

Buffalo Medical College. — Hygiene, Private and Municipal, is taught in the "preliminary terms," from October 1 to November 1. Private Hygiene is the special type in this department (Materia Medica and Hygiene). During the regular term, Municipal Hygiene is taught in lectures, in connection (alternately) with therapeutics. This plan has been followed the past three years. I am very glad to find that a systematic effort to gain positive information is being undertaken.

Miami Medical College, Ohio. — Regular instruction is given in Public and Private Hygiene and State Preventive Medicine, during the spring session, which is naturally a prolongation of the winter or regular session. The course consists of about sixteen lectures, illustrated by diagrams. The chair proper is

that of Anatomy. The writer then continues as follows :[1] "In 1865, after my return from the army, I became Superintendent of Health of this city, which I held for eight years ; and I succeeded in placing the health department of this city on a permanent footing. I procured an Act from the Legislature, providing for the establishment of Boards of Health for all cities and larger towns in the State. I thus became much interested in sanitary science. I have learned its importance to the public, as well as to individuals. Hence the reason for my assuming the duty of an extra course of lectures on this subject. I am endeavoring to work up our State Medical Society to the necessity of having a State Board of Health."

Jefferson Medical College. — No *regular systematic* course of lectures upon Hygiene is delivered. Short practical courses have been, and are still, occasionally delivered during the spring, summer, and fall months. During the winter months, instruction upon Hygiene is given, more particularly by the Professor of the Institutes of Medicine. This is, however, incidental or subsidiary to the physiological course proper. The impurities of water and atmosphere, ventilation, and kindred subjects, are discussed in the course on Chemistry. Army, navy, and hospital Hygiene receives attention from the Professor of Surgery and Practice. By this division of labor, a great deal of practical information upon hygienic science is imparted to the class, although no special chair is devoted to the subject.

Medical Department of the University of Pennsylvania. — A three-months' course, of thirty-four to thirty-six lectures, is given in the Medical Department every spring, on Personal and Public Hygiene, by the Professor of Hygiene in the *Auxiliary Department.*

South Carolina Medical College, State of South Carolina. — Only in connection with general pathology and therapeutics.

[1] The remarks of my correspondent illustrate very well the truth of my statement in the address, of the influence of the war upon the private practitioner, by convincing him of the great value of preventive medicine. — H. I. B.

APPENDIX IV.

DIGEST OF AMERICAN SANITARY LAW.

By H. G. PICKERING,
COUNSELLOR-AT-LAW.

NOTE.

At the request of my friend Dr. Bowditch, I have prepared a digest of the sanitary laws passed by the several States, from the date of their admission to the Federal Union to the present time. So far as I was able, I have, in each case, brought the investigation to the present year. Where I have not been able to do so by notes of legislation and references to the statutes of the State, I have endeavored to supply the omission by correspondence furnished me by Dr. Bowditch, with local Boards and physicians. In this attempt, I have made no mention of the persistent but unsuccessful efforts made in several of the States to obtain sanitary legislation suited to their wants.

The establishment of State Boards of Health marks the highest point yet reached in the sanitary legislation of States. These now exist in the District of Columbia, and in fifteen of the thirty-eight States; viz., Alabama, California, Colorado, Georgia, Illinois, Louisiana, Maryland, Massachusetts, Michigan, Minnesota, Mississippi, New Jersey, Tennessee, Virginia, and Wisconsin.

The absence of all legislation on this subject in the States of Arkansas and Missouri, the primitive nature of the laws of Maine, New Hampshire, and Rhode Island, and the very inadequate provisions made by statute in Indiana, Iowa, Kansas, Kentucky, Nebraska, Nevada, and Vermont, — supply their own comment. A somewhat disproportionate space has been given to the State of New York, with the hope that the experience of a large State in its successive attempts to establish a satisfactory system of State sanitary law might prove instructive, and make amends for the minuteness of detail in this single instance.

H. G. P.

IV.

DIGEST OF AMERICAN SANITARY LAW.

UNITED STATES.

St. 1799 enacted that the quarantines and other restraints established by the health laws of any State shall be duly observed by the officers of the customs' revenue of the United States, by the masters and crews of the several revenue cutters, and by the military officers commanding in any fort or station upon the sea-coast; and all such officers of the United States shall faithfully aid in the execution of such quarantines and health laws, according to their respective powers, and within their respective precincts, and as they shall be directed, from time to time, by the Secretary of the Treasury.

It also provided for the discharge of cargoes in quarantine; the collector, after one report to him of the whole of the cargo, granting his warrant or permit for such discharge, under care of the surveyor, or one or more inspectors, at some place where health laws permit, and under the conditions and restrictions which shall be directed by the Secretary of the Treasury, or which such collector may, for the time, deem expedient for the security of the public revenue. This is where the vessel, arriving within a collection district, is prohibited from coming to the port of entry or delivery by the health laws of the State, and when such health laws require or permit the cargo to be unladen at some other place within or near to such district.

Suitable warehouses are to be purchased or erected, under orders of the President, with wharves and enclosures, where merchandise may be unladen and deposited in such cases, at

such convenient places therein as the safety of the public revenue and the observance of such health laws may require.

Cargoes unladen as aforesaid are to be deposited, at risk of parties concerned, in such public or other warehouses or enclosures as the collector shall designate, there to remain, under joint custody of the collector and of the owner, master, or person having charge of vessel, until unladen or discharged, and until they may be safely removed without contravening such health laws. Permits may, in such case, be granted by the collector to the respective owners or consignees, their factors or agents, to receive all merchandise which has been entered, and the duties accruing upon which have been paid, upon the payment by them of a reasonable rate of storage, to be fixed by the Secretary of the Treasury. The Secretary of the Treasury is authorized, when necessary, to extend the time for entry of vessels subject to quarantine, and also to direct the removal of revenue officers from ports where contagious disease prevails, to any other more convenient place; public notice of such removal to be given as soon as may be.

When contagious or epidemic disease prevails, the President may direct the removal of public offices from the capital; and, by law of 1867, in like case, the judges of the United States courts have power to direct their adjournment.

And (law of 1799) the judges of the district courts may direct the removal of prisoners, where contagious or epidemic disease prevails so as, in their opinion, to endanger their lives.

United States law of 1872 provides for the registration, under penalty for omission, in the log-book of every vessel required by law to keep such book, of —

(a) Every case of illness or injury happening to any member of the crew, with the nature thereof, and the medical treatment.

(b) Every case of death happening on board, with the cause thereof.

(c) Every birth happening on board, with the sex of the infant and the names of the parents.

(d) Every marriage taking place on board, with the names and ages of the parties.

DISTRICT OF COLUMBIA.

Law of United States, 1859, provides penalty for committing any act by reason of which the supply of water to the cities of Washington and Georgetown becomes impure, filthy, or unfit for use.

United States law of 1871 provided for the appointment by the President, by and with the advice and consent of the Senate, of a Board of Health for the District, to consist of five persons, whose duty it shall be to declare what shall be deemed nuisances injurious to health, and to provide for the removal thereof; to make and enforce regulations to prevent domestic animals from running at large in the cities of Washington and Georgetown; to prevent the sale of unwholesome food in said cities; and to perform such other duties as shall be imposed upon said Board by the Legislative Assembly.

The salary of the members was subsequently fixed at $2,000. By Act of 1874, it is made the duty of the Board to make and enforce regulations to secure a full and correct record of vital statistics, including the registration of deaths and the interment of the dead in said District.

ALABAMA.

The Act of 1807 provides penalty for introducing or spreading small-pox.

Governor is authorized to take means to prevent spreading of contagious diseases, and for aid and comfort of sick.

Persons wishing to be inoculated, to petition Governor, who shall appoint a place where public health will not be endangered.

Person having had small-pox shall obtain attendant physician's certificate of his recovery and being perfectly clean in person and clothes, before going abroad into company of people who have not had the disease, or going into any public road or highway where travellers usually pass, without retiring out of the same, or giving notice of the approach of passengers.

Then follow (1815) penalties for selling unwholesome provisions and liquors ; and on bakers, for selling bread not marked with their names, and on persons for counterfeiting bakers' mark.

By Code of 1852 (revised 1867), the corporate authorities of any town, or court of commissioners of any county, may establish hospitals in such town or county, and make regulations for them (not contrary to law).

On complaint of Health Officer of any town that there is good cause of suspicion or belief that any cause of disease or infection in any house, lot, or vessel, within town limits or vicinity, necessary to be destroyed or removed, or one or more persons, not in his own place of residence, infected with dangerous contagious disease, and that he has been refused admittance into such house, lot, or vessel, — any justice of the corporation or county may issue his warrant requiring sheriff or other executive officer to enter, and, under direction of such Health Officer, to remove such infected person, or to remove or destroy such source of infection or disease.

Quarantine Ground. — Any town may establish (with assent of county commissioners, if without limits of the town). Corporate authorities of town may, from time to time, prescribe quarantine regulations ; which regulations may extend to all persons, goods, and effects arriving in such vessels, and to all persons going on board of the same.

Persons violating, after notice, guilty of misdemeanor.

Health Officer of town, under direction of corporate authorities, may cause vessel arriving therein, or in vicinity, to go to quarantine ground, or other proper place, and be purified.

Refusal to answer inquiries of Health Officer, on oath, a misdemeanor.

Master of vessel ordered to quarantine to deliver to Health Officer his bill of health, log-book, &c.; and failure to do so, or to go to quarantine ground in proper time after notice, or departing thence without authority, a misdemeanor. Penalty not less than $200.

Persons ordered to quarantine, and escaping, to be arrested and delivered to quarantine officer, and may be detained by force by such officer if attempting to escape.

Travellers *by land* from infected place may be compelled by Health Officer to perform quarantine, and restrained from travelling till discharged; and any person thus restrained travelling before he is discharged is guilty of misdemeanor. Expenses to be reimbursed by person, or owner of vessel or goods. The word "town" includes city.

By Act of 1862, courts of county commissioners are given same powers with towns in respect to quarantine and hospital for contagious diseases, and may make such regulations, and appoint such guards and superintendents, as may be necessary.

In 1875, the following Act was adopted.

AN ACT TO ESTABLISH BOARDS OF HEALTH IN THE STATE OF ALABAMA.

SECTION 1. *Be it enacted by the General Assembly of the State of Alabama,* that the Medical Association of the State of Alabama, organized in accordance with the provisions of the constitution, which was adopted by said Association at its annual meeting, in the city of Tuscaloosa, in March, 1873, be and is hereby constituted the Board of Health of the State of Alabama.

SECT. 2. That the Board of Health of the State of Alabama, thus established, shall take cognizance of the interests of Health and Life among the people of the State; shall investigate the causes and the means of prevention of endemic and of epidemic diseases; shall investigate the influences of localities and employments upon the public health; shall, from time to time, make to the General Assembly such suggestions as to legislative action as in their judgment may seem advisable; and shall be, in all ways, the medical advisers of the State.

SECT. 3. That they shall make to the Governor and General Assembly of the State an annual report of their investigations and transactions; of which annual report they shall annually publish a sufficient number of copies for distribution among the members of the General Assembly, and, for such further distribution, among the physicians of the State, and in exchange for the reports and transactions of other Boards and Associations, as they shall think advisable; and, to defray the expenses of this publication, there shall be paid annually out of the Treasury of the State to the Treasurer of the said Board of Health of the State of Alabama, upon the requisition of the President and Secretary thereof, the sum of one thousand ($1,000) dollars.

SECT. 4. That the county medical societies, in affiliation with the Medical Association of the State of Alabama, and organized in accordance with the provisions of the constitution of the said Association, as described in the first section of this Act, be and are hereby constituted Boards of Health for their respective counties; and, as such, shall be

under the general direction of the Board of Health of the State of Alabama, created by the first section of this Act.

SECT. 5. That the County Boards of Health thus established shall have only advisory powers, and shall be conducted without expense to the State or to their respective counties, except under the conditions provided for under the sixth section of this Act, which here follows : —

SECT. 6. That the competent legal authorities of any county in this State, or of any incorporated town or city of any such county, shall, whenever in their judgment it becomes expedient to do so, proceed to invest the Board of Health of the county with such executive powers and duties for the public health, and under such rules and stipulations, as shall be agreed upon between the two parties.

SECT. 7. That, in any such agreement as is contemplated in section six of this Act, the right to elect or appoint the officers and servants employed in the administration of the sanitary regulations so agreed upon, shall, in all cases, be reserved to the Board of Health ; and, further, that all questions relating to salaries, appropriations, and expenditures, shall be reserved to the legal authorities of the county, town, or city, as the case may be.

SECT. 8. That no Board of Health, or advisory or executive medical body of any name or kind, for the exercise of public health functions, shall be established by authority of law in any county, town, or city of this State, except such as are contemplated by the provisions of this Act ; the object of this prohibition being to secure a uniform system of sanitary supervision throughout the State. But nothing in this article shall be so construed as to prevent any of the Boards of Health created by section four of this Act from accepting and executing any special powers that may be granted them by the General Assembly of the State.

ARKANSAS.

No legislation.

CALIFORNIA.

Act of 1850 created a Board of Health for San Francisco, to be composed of the Mayor, a Health Officer, Resident Physician, and Health Commissioner, who shall perform such duties as may be prescribed in this and all other acts relating to the public health. Mayor, *ex officio*, president. No person eligible unless a graduate of a regular medical institution, and with experience of three years' practice ; elected for two years, or until successors are qualified. Governor shall have power to fill vacancy for unexpired term.

Health Officer to perform duties specified in this or any other Act, and such other duties as Board shall lawfully require; may appoint assistant, to be approved by Board, for whose acts he shall be responsible, and who may perform all the duties of the Health Officer.

Resident Physician to reside at Marine Hospital, and shall be the consulting physician at the Hospital; and, further, shall visit all sick seamen on ships in the harbor, and all sailors and other persons in the city who have paid hospital money, and come properly under care of, and have been reported to, the Board of Health. All persons afflicted with any contagious or infectious disease shall, if it be deemed expedient by Board of Health, and life of the person not endangered thereby, be removed to the Marine Hospital.

Health Commissioner, under direction of Board of Health, shall assist Resident Physician in discharge of his duties, and receive and pay moneys for Marine Hospital.

Resident Physician and Health Commissioner to meet daily in San Francisco, at office of the Board of Health, during such part of the year and at such hours of the day as Board shall designate.

Board of Appeal from Health Officer to be the Mayor, Resident Physician, and Commissioner of Health, with power to grant relief as may seem to them proper.

Health Commissioner to be Secretary to Board of Health.

Master, owner, or consignee of vessel, at wharf or in harbor of San Francisco, shall report the name of every person on board who may be sick with contagious or infectious disease; and no such person shall be removed without written permit from Board of Health.

Penalties provided for obstructing Board of Health in execution of their duties; and on masters, for not complying with Act.

Health Officer, Resident Physician, and Health Commissioner are liable for wilful neglect or delinquency of duty, or for exercising powers not given to them, in damages to person injured thereby, and may be removed from office by Governor.

Act of 1850 provides for erection of a Marine Hospital for State of California in Bay of San Francisco, to be held by

Board of Health in trust for the people of the State, for purposes specified in this Act.

Health Officer is to reside there, and have charge, under superintendence of Board of Health.

Sick sailors, mariners, and other persons who shall have paid hospital money or given bond, shall be entitled to benefit of the hospital, free of charge; and also such other persons as authorities of city of San Francisco may request, provided such authorities pay therefor such charges as Board of Health may direct.

Such persons sent there are to be kept and attended to with necessary and proper care, and not to leave till Health Officer gives discharge in writing. Patients eloping therefrom may be apprehended.

Masters of vessels arriving at San Francisco to report within twenty-four hours, on oath, to Board of Health, name and number of cabin and steerage passengers, captain, mates, and sailors, and name and residence of owner and consignee.

Penalty for failing to report, or falsely reporting.

Owners or consignees to give bond to Board of Health to indemnify against charges for relief and support of persons named therein (for five years from date). Owner or consignee may commute.

Board of Health to report to Governor, as often as he may require, persons in such hospital affected with contagious or infectious diseases, and such as die or are discharged as cured; and shall also make annual report of number received, discharged as cured, and deaths, and moneys received and expended, and for what purposes.

Board of Health to keep office in San Francisco.

Quarantine anchorage to be fixed by buoys, and as near as possible to Marine Hospital.

Every vessel subject to quarantine to anchor there immediately on arrival; and remain there, with officers, passengers, and crew, during her quarantine, subject to examination of Health Officer and such regulations as Health Officer or Board of Health shall lawfully impose.

All vessels arriving in San Francisco Bay from sea are declared subject to quarantine regulations prescribed in this

Act; if steam vessels, only to such length of quarantine and other regulations as majority of Board of Health enjoin.

Quarantine of other vessels limited by discretion of Health Officer; and, unless under special circumstances, and with sanction of Board of Health, shall not exceed the time requisite for one examination of vessel and cargo and compliance with regulations of this Act.

Every vessel to be boarded by Health Officer immediately on arrival, and strict search and inquiry made into health of crew and passengers, and state of vessel and cargo.

He may question any one on board, who may be required to answer under oath. He is to report *directly* to Board of Health respecting vessels visited.

Board shall release vessel after regular period of quarantine, if Health Officer judge vessel and cargo free from infection. Quarantine flag in shrouds during quarantine.

Vessels not to load or unload while at quarantine, unless by permission, and under restrictions imposed by Health Officer.

No vessel to remove from quarantine ground during quarantine, without written permit from Health Officer.

A building to be provided, at safe distance from hospital buildings, on hospital grounds, for passengers not diseased who wish to go on shore.

Master to submit vessel, cargo, and passengers to examinations, and furnish all necessary information. Penalty for refusing, and for unloading before examination, and for obstructing Health Officer or pilot, and going on board without permit.

Pilots to hail vessels, and demand if any person has died within ten days, or been sick with malignant or contagious disease. If yes, pilots are to notify masters that their vessels are subject to quarantine, and shall conduct them into port, and bring them to anchor at quarantine. Shall prevent any boat coming alongside, or any thing from being thrown therefrom into any other boat. To give masters a printed copy of this Act; to take care that this Act is not violated by any person on board; and to report violations, as soon as may be, to Health Officer.

Vessel subject to regular quarantine to be purified, and released when free from infection.

Health Officer may destroy infected bedding, clothing, or cargo.

Misdemeanor (fine or imprisonment) to refuse to anchor at quarantine, to submit to examination, to remain at quarantine time assigned, or to submit to regulations while there.

There are also penalties for wilfully going into quarantine grounds without authority of Board of Health; for going on board, or holding intercourse with, vessel at quarantine, without authority; and for wilfully quitting quarantine without leave.

Violating, or neglecting to comply with, orders of Board of Health, made a misdemeanor.

By Act of 1868, amended 1870, the Board of Trustees of the city of Sacramento shall establish, by ordinance, a Board of Health for the city; to consist of five practising physicians, who shall be graduates of a medical college of recognized respectability. The President of the Board of Trustees shall be, *ex officio*, President of the Board of Health.

The Board shall have a general supervision of all matters pertaining to the sanitary condition of the city.

An Act of the year 1866 provided for a Board of Health in and for the city and county of San Francisco, to consist of the Mayor, and four physicians in good standing. It provided, also, for a Health Officer for the city and county and port, to be elected by the Board. Full powers are given to the Board and Health Officer in matters relating to sanitary condition of the city and county and to quarantine, respectively.

An Act of 1876 amended the foregoing, making the Deputy Health Officer Quarantine Officer, and providing for four health inspectors to be appointed by the Board. Notice of births is to be given to the Health Officer.

Sale of adulterated milk declared unlawful, and made punishable by fine.

Act of 1870. Governor shall appoint seven physicians; two from city of Sacramento, and the other five from different sections of the State, who shall constitute the State Board of Health and Vital Statistics. They shall hold office for four years, and until successors are appointed. All vacancies in the Board shall be filled by the Governor.

Duties.— They shall place themselves in communication with

the local Boards of Health, the hospitals, asylums, and public institutions, throughout the State, and shall take cognizance of the interests of health and life among the citizens generally.

They shall make sanitary investigations and inquiries respecting the causes of disease (especially of epidemics), the source of mortality, and the effects of localities, employment, condition, and circumstances on the Public Health; and they shall gather such information in respect to these matters as they may deem proper for diffusion among the people.

They shall devise some scheme whereby medical and vital statistics of sanitary value may be obtained, and act as an advisory board to the State in all hygienic and medical matters, — especially such as relate to the location, construction, sewerage, and administrations of prisons, hospitals, asylums, and other public institutions. They shall, at each biennial session of the Legislature, make a report of their doings, investigations, and discoveries, with such suggestions as to legislative action as they may deem proper.

To meet at capital at least once in every three months, and as much oftener as they deem proper. They shall elect, of their number, a president and permanent secretary, both to live at the capital, and be their executive officers.

No compensation except to Secretary; but travelling fees, while on duties of Board, paid out of general fund.

By Act of 1872, the Board of Health of the city of Sacramento is empowered and required to establish a dispensary for the sick poor of the city and county, and to exercise a general supervision over it.

COLORADO.

State Board of Health established Feb. 10, 1876.

CONNECTICUT.

In 1796 was passed "An Act providing, in case of sickness," with ordinary provisions against spread of contagious disease by persons coming from infected places, by removal and care.

Houses and nurses may be impressed, when necessary for the care of the sick.

Persons coming from infected places, Selectmen or Health Officers appointed by them, may examine on oath respecting the infection. And infected persons, and those coming from infected places, and those coming on ships coming from infected places, or having had contagious sickness on voyage, may be confined in such ships, or removed to proper places, by order of Selectmen.

Penalty provided for landing infected clothing. In case of great distress, application to be made to the Governor, who shall have power to make and give further orders and directions, with advice and consent of Council, such as they think fit to prevent spread of contagion or any thing relating thereto.

When contagious disease is prevalent, the civil authorities and Selectmen are to have general powers to make and publish regulations for preserving inhabitants, and persons transgressing are subject to penalty. Persons may be impressed to tend the sick, and, refusing, may be committed.

Further provisions for displaying signals and destroying dogs.

Duty of Selectmen, on application, to examine goods brought from infected places, and to decide whether it be necessary to air them; and, if not, they shall give certificate to that effect, with liberty to land them.

Master of vessel coming from infected place, to report to Selectmen, within twelve hours after his arrival, whence they come, and the circumstances of persons and cargo on board. Passengers are not to go ashore until after such information is given, and order made thereon.

There shall be no inoculation without certificate from the civil authority, based on the approbation of the town. Measures are enacted for relief of soldiers and marines, not inhabitants of this State but taken sick here, when they cannot be removed, nor provide for their own support, and are unable to procure the same from the United States Government.

Act of 1805 makes the civil authority and Selectmen of the several towns a Board of Health, with all such powers for preventing malignant or infectious disease as are given to civil

authorities and Selectmen, or to Selectmen alone, by former Act.

Such Board, or any officer or committee thereof, are to examine nuisances and sources of filth injurious to health, and cause the same to be removed; notice to be first given to the owner or occupier of the premises, who shall be fined if he neglects to remove the same within twenty-four hours thereafter, or such longer reasonable time as the Board shall direct.

The Board, or a committee thereof, or the Health Officer, shall have power to enter houses and places where nuisance or cause of filth is suspected to exist.

The Board may make regulations and rules, from time to time, and give the same effect within the limits of their town.

By Act of 1832, the Board shall assign quarantine ground; and vessels coming from foreign ports, or ports south of Delaware Capes, between June 1st and November 1st, in any year, are to anchor there until discharged. On notice of arrival, the Health Officer, or a member of the Board, shall visit the vessel without delay, and shall have power to examine and give certificate of health, and discharge or cause the vessel to continue subject to quarantine. Every vessel so subjected shall perform quarantine, under the restrictions and regulations of the Board. A penalty is provided if the master shall attempt to elude quarantine by false declarations, or land goods or persons, except as provided, or permit intercourse with his vessel before she has been visited.

A flag is to be hoisted while the vessel is cleansing, which is to be done by washing with a lye, or in such other method as the Board shall direct. And persons coming on board with malignant, infectious disease are to be removed and cared for. Board may seclude passengers on shore, and the latter shall continue in such confinement, and not depart without leave of the Board; and persons associating with them shall be deemed contaminated, and shall be subject to the same confinement and penalty. Vessels coming from north of the capes may be subjected to quarantine, by order of the Board, when they deem it expedient. Any physician, if requested by the Board, shall make to them a daily or weekly report of cases of malignant or pestilential

disease occurring in his practice. Innkeepers are to report within twelve hours, to the Health Officer or Board, any seafaring man or other lodger who becomes sick in their house.

Under the head of the internal police of towns, the civil authority and Selectmen of the several towns are to be a Board of Health in their respective towns, &c., as by Act of 1805; and the Board has power to appoint such Health Officers or Health Committees as they may deem expedient. The Board of any town may interdict communication with a town where contagious, malignant disease prevails. Between May 1st and November 1st, tavern-keepers are to give notice of lodgers sick at their house, with nature of disease.

The Board of Health may enforce their orders. Persons coming from places where small-pox or other contagious disease prevails, or has lately prevailed, may be confined in hospital, or elsewhere, as long as the Board think necessary to insure the safety of the town; and any person suspected to have been exposed to or infected with the small-pox, or such other disease, may have oath administered by the Board or Health Officer, whether he has come from an infected place, or has been exposed or infected; and, if he refuses to take it, he may be confined.

When contagious disease prevails in any town, the Board may make rules, orders, and regulations to preserve the inhabitants therefrom.

No person shall inoculate with small-pox, without permission of the Board.

Penalty provided for voluntarily taking or communicating small-pox.

Boards may adopt measures for vaccination; and penalty is provided (1828) for refusal to be vaccinated, on application of the Board of Health, or of physician employed by them for that purpose.

A certificate of health obtained by fraud or mistake is void.

By Act of 1866, the Board of Health in any town may appoint such Health Officers and Health Committees as it may deem expedient, and may delegate to them any powers that are now by law conferred on said Board of Health.

By Act of same year, vessels arriving in New Haven from

British North American provinces are declared not exempted from quarantine (Act of 1850 repealed).

Act of 1871 gives the Board of Health power to prohibit the introduction of cattle, or other domestic animals, into the State, at any time, for the purpose of guarding against the spread of contagious disease among neat cattle and other domestic animals.

Whenever contagious disease breaks out, or is known to exist in any part of the State, the Board may quarantine all infected animals, and may prohibit driving of animals on highways.

Three commissioners on diseases of domestic animals may be appointed by the Board of Agriculture.

The Revision of 1875 makes the justices of the peace and Selectmen in any town a Board of Health, with all the power necessary and proper for preserving the Public Health and preventing the spread of malignant diseases therein. Such Board may appoint its president, and such Health Officers or Health Committees as it may deem expedient, and delegate to them any of its powers; and the members present at any meeting, convened as the Board shall direct, shall be a quorum for business.

By Act of 1871, the State Board of Agriculture is empowered to make investigations and regulations necessary for the prevention, treatment, cure, and extirpation of disease among animals.

An Act of the same year prohibits the selling of diseased meat, knowingly, under penalty.

The law is the same in 1875 as in 1805, except additions, as follows: —

1874. That it shall be sufficient notice to all persons, of any regulation of such Board, if it be published in a newspaper published in the town, or posted for three days on each signpost in said town. Penalty of fifteen dollars for violating.

1828. Provisions as to compulsory vaccination.

In 1874 was re-enacted law of 1760, as follows: "The Board of Health in any town may order any person, whom they may have reasonable ground to believe to be infected with any malignant, infectious, or contagious disease, into confine-

ment, in any place to be designated by said Board, there to remain so long as said Board shall judge necessary."

Drains. — Commissioners appointed by Superior Court, in any county, as early as 1711, with power to contract, &c.

1728. Scavengers to be appointed to inspect and keep drains in repair.

By Act of 1846, each proprietor is to keep open and repair his part of the drain.

In 1861, proprietors of low lands may organize drain companies, by order of Superior Court, and have scavengers appointed. Such companies to hold annual meetings.

DELAWARE.

First sanitary legislation in 1797. — "An Act to prevent infectious diseases being brought into this State, and for other purposes." No vessel having on board more than forty persons, or any infected person,[1] or coming from sickly port or place, to come nearer than one mile to any port or place of landing.

Physician to be appointed, whose duty it shall be to board and examine ships and passengers.

Penalty if master conceals case of infectious disease.

Physician refusing permit to land persons or goods, or come into port with vessel, is to report to burgesses, justices of peace, or trustees of poor, who are authorized and required to give permit to master, under suitable regulations, to land such diseased persons as owner or commander can provide with suitable accommodations.

Penalty for going on board before permit granted.

Masters required to provide wholesome food for passengers, and to cleanse vessel, &c.

Physicians to inquire whether these directions have been complied with; if not, to make complaint to court.

Another Act was passed, in 1799, giving quarantine power, by sea and land, to the burgesses and assistants, with advice of

---

[1] Measles and small-pox are excepted.

Health Officer of borough of Wilmington, and certain commissioners and justices. Quarantine is to be performed when required or advised by the Health Officer.

Burgesses authorized to suspend intercourse by land with infected towns. Penalties on masters of vessels, owners, consignees, and persons on board, and on owners of carriages, or persons in charge, for contravening these regulations.

Health Officer is authorized to appoint deputies.

All civil officers to aid in the execution of powers enjoined by this Act.

Parts of former Act (1797), amended hereby, are repealed.

By Act of 1799, burgesses of Wilmington are given power over nuisances.

Some slight additions by law of 1800, a little more stringent.

Revised Statutes, 1852. An Act "to prevent the spread of contagious diseases."

The Governor shall appoint three physicians in each county to be Health Officers for such county.

"No master or person having charge of any vessel bound to any port in this State, having on board more than forty persons, or any one sick with any infectious disease, or coming from any sickly port, shall bring his vessel, or permit it to be brought, within one mile of place of landing; nor land, nor permit to be landed, at any place in this State, any person or any goods, until he obtains permit, in writing, from the Health Officer nearest place of landing. Penalty, $1,000."

It shall be duty of Health Officer to board vessels, and inspect vessels, persons, and cargo.

Master concealing infectious disease from Health Officer to forfeit $100.

Health Officer to give information of the penalty, and to put oath to any person on board to answer truly questions on the subject.

If Health Officer has occasion to refuse permit to land goods or persons, he shall report to Mayor of Wilmington, if the vessel is bound to that port; in any other case, to two justices of peace in place nearest where vessel is: and said Mayor, with advice of City Council, or said justices, with advice of nearest town commissioners, are authorized and required, under

such regulations as may seem most consistent with the public health and safety, to grant a written license to the owner, consignee, master, or person in charge of vessel, for landing of any of such sick persons as person to whom license is granted shall provide with suitable accommodations.

No master to bring more passengers than shall be well supplied with wholesome meat, drink, and other necessaries for the voyage, nor more than one passenger for every two tons. Health Officer to inquire into this, on visiting the vessel.

Mayor and City Council of Wilmington, with advice of nearest Health Officer, and two justices of the peace in any other town or hundred of the State, with the advice of the nearest town commissioners and Health Officer, are authorized and empowered, on receiving information of the prevalence of any infectious diseases in any port or place, to make that fact known by proclamation, and to order that no vessel bound from, or which may have touched at such infected place, shall be brought nearer to said city than the mouth of the Christiana River, or within one mile of port or place of landing in any town or hundred, and that no person or goods shall be landed from such vessel; and all persons on board shall be subject to such quarantine and other precautionary measures as the proclamation shall prescribe; and, after proclamation so issued, same officers shall have power, by further proclamation, to suspend intercourse by land between the infected place during prevalence of such infectious disorder, and their city, town, or hundred, or to impose such regulations and restrictions therein as may be deemed necessary to the public health and safety.

Penalty of $40 if any person, travelling afoot from any infected place, shall, after proclamation issued, enter any place in this State, contrary to such proclamation, or shall violate the regulations and restrictions thereby imposed.

All civil authorities in the State to assist in execution of the provisions of this chapter, and may command *posse comitatus* for the purpose.

Forfeitures and penalties recovered to go, one-fourth to the Health Officer at whose request the suit is brought, and the balance to the trustees of the poor of the county where suit is brought.

FLORIDA.

There was no sanitary legislation in this State, except that prohibiting the sale of unwholesome provisions, or spreading the small-pox, until the year 1869.

By Act of that year, the Mayor and aldermen of incorporated cities or towns, or, in the absence of any incorporated city or town, the justices of the peace of every justices' district where there is a port of entry, are made a Board of Health for such city, town, or district, and are authorized to take such measures as may be necessary to prevent the spread of contagious or malignant disorders or diseases.

They shall appoint a port inspector, who shall board and examine vessels coming from the high seas. If necessary, he shall order them to quarantine, and shall at once notify the Board of Health. They shall also appoint one or more port physicians to examine condition of such ships and health of persons on board; and such vessels shall not approach the town, unless with his certificate that no danger to the Public Health is likely to occur thereby.

Said Board may establish quarantine ground and hospitals, with physicians and nurses, and make regulations for the same.

They may cause infected vessels or cargo to be purified, if the same endangers the Public Health. The Governor or Adjutant-General may, by proclamation, declare a place infected, and forbid the landing of vessels therefrom until after quarantine.

A law has also been passed establishing a Board of Health for the city of Jacksonville.

GEORGIA.

1793. "An Act to oblige vessels and persons coming from places infected with epidemical distempers to perform quarantine, and to prevent the bringing into and spreading malignant and contagious disorders in this State."

Then follows common quarantine law, with penalty if master violates. Quarantine ground to be marked out, and intercourse forbidden with the shore.

320   APPENDIX.

Any officer of customs, or person appointed to see that quarantine is performed, to have power to seize boats of vessels under quarantine, and not to suffer seamen or passengers to leave ship during quarantine.

On proof made by master or by other person, before justice of the peace, that quarantine has been performed, the justice shall give certificate, and the vessel shall be freed from restraint. Goods imported in such vessels shall thereafter be aired.

Governor may, by proclamation, forbid intercourse between infected place and ports of this State not infected, by land or water; and appoint boats and sentinels to execute the law.

Duty of *pilot* to make strict inquiry of master as to health of persons coming into port; and master shall make true answer, under penalty.

Corporation of Savannah shall regulate quarantine in certain inlets and rivers; and, in others of the State, justices of the county, or commissioners of the town adjacent to such inlet or river, or commissioner of pilotage of such port, as the case may be. And such corporation, &c., is authorized to fix sentinels, guard boats, and to use all means in their power to enforce this law, for purposes intended.

Corporation, &c., after notifying people of their district of the necessity of ordering quarantine to be performed, shall forthwith transmit an exact account and statement to Governor or Commander-in-chief, who shall make proclamation of same; enjoining obedience to rules adopted for preventing contagious distempers being spread through the State and a due obedience of duties required by such regulations, accordingly.

Necessary expenses paid by State, and charged to contingent fund.

In 1803, jurisdiction of city of Savannah is extended, and Mayor and Aldermen are given power to take cognizance of, and inquire into all violations of, this Act, within certain limits; and may remove from city infected persons to such place without the limits as they may appoint for that purpose.

Corporation of city of Savannah may, by resolution or order, detain vessel suspected of being infected, till examination and purification.

Vessels arriving at Savannah, from July 1 to October 31,

from foreign country, or any other port of United States, shall make report in writing on oath, to Mayor (within twenty-four hours after entry), of age, name, and occupation of her passengers on last voyage. Seventy-five dollars forfeit for every alien neglected to be so reported. Mayor may require bonds to indemnify city for expenses incurred for maintenance and support of any persons so introduced, or their children, if at any time within six months they become chargeable to the city.

Vessel liable for penalties above, and householder for entertaining such alien without reporting to Mayor.

Mayor and Aldermen shall annually elect a Health Officer for port of Savannah, who shall be under direction and control of Mayor and Aldermen, and subject to such ordinances, rules, and regulations as they may make.

Penalty on physician for wilfully concealing, or not promptly reporting to Health Officer case of contagious disease in Savannah or vicinity.

Mayor and Aldermen may purchase land for a lazaretto, and to have jurisdiction over same while so used. Health laws of Savannah extended to Darien.

Justices of inferior court of any county, or corporate authorities of any city in the State, may provide suitable temporary hospitals, furnish with medicines, nurses, &c., and guard against communication of sick with others; and may order destruction of infected clothing, and interment of dead.

Vaccine matter to be furnished *gratis* throughout the State.

Punishments are provided for selling flesh of diseased animals, or other unwholesome provisions, bread or drink; for wilfully endeavoring to spread small-pox, and for violating quarantine regulations.

Nuisances abated on order of two or more justices of the peace, on verdict of twelve freeholders of the county; and, in cities, may be abated by order of Mayor or intendant or commissioner, with advice of aldermen, wardens, or council, or commissioners, after notice to parties interested.

Corporate authorities of cities and towns may establish hospitals and pest-houses, and make regulations. In other cases, justices of inferior courts of the county have the power. They may also prescribe quarantine, establish quarantine

ground, and cause Health Officer or visiting physician to have vessel removed there, if in the latter's opinion she or her cargo are infected so as to endanger Public Health; and master, seaman, or passenger refusing to answer questions of Health Officer as to disease, shall be guilty of misdemeanor.

Any person ordered to perform quarantine, and attempting to escape, may be forcibly detained.

Master of vessel ordered to quarantine shall deliver to Health Officer his bill of health, manifest, log-book, and journals; and, if he fail to do so, or to go to quarantine in proper time, after notice, or shall depart thence without authority, he shall be guilty of misdemeanor, and fined not less than two hundred dollars.

Inland travellers may be compelled by Health Officer to quarantine, under direction of corporate authorities.

Duty of *pilot* to inquire as to health of vessel, before going on board; and, if she is infected, he shall not go on board.

Master refusing to answer, liable to penalty.

Persons on board not to come ashore during quarantine.

Governor may, by proclamation, make orders as to contagious diseases; and any person violating shall be subject to fine or imprisonment.

Persons violating quarantine, or concealing case of small-pox, varioloid, or modification, may be indicted.

Health Officer or visiting physician shall give certificate to master after quarantine is performed.

By Acts of 1865-66, justices of inferior courts of each county, or corporate authorities in any town or city where small-pox appears, may provide suitable hospitals, and furnish them with medical and other attention; and may also make quarantine regulations to prevent spread of disease. But no person shall be forced to leave home to go to hospital aforesaid, when they are properly provided for and guarded at their own expense.

In 1875 was passed "an Act to create a State Board of Health, for the protection of life and health, and to prevent the spread of diseases in the State of Georgia, and for other purposes."

This Board shall consist of nine physicians of skill and ex-

perience, to be appointed by the Governor, who shall have been regular graduates of medicine, and practitioners of not less than ten years, together with the Comptroller-General and State Geologist.

Five shall be a quorum for the transaction of business.

The Secretary shall be the executive officer of the Board.

It shall be the duty of the Board to take cognizance of the interest of health and life among the people of the State. They shall make inquiries in respect to the causes of diseases, and especially of epidemics; and investigate the sources of mortality, and the effects of localities, employments, and other conditions upon the Public Health; and shall obtain, collect, and preserve such information relating to deaths, diseases, and health as may be useful in the discharge of its duties, and contribute to the promotion of health or the security of life in the State of Georgia; and it shall be the duty of all Health Officers and Boards of Health in the State to communicate to said State Board of Health copies of all their reports and publications; also, such sanitary information as may be useful: and said Board shall keep a record of its acts and proceedings, and send all proper information in its possession to the local health authorities, in any part of the State, which may request the same, adding such useful suggestions as the experience of the Board may supply; and said authorities shall supply like information and suggestions to the Board.

The Board may also require reports and information from public hospitals, prisons, dispensaries, and schools, and from managers of other public institutions and places of public resort; and shall, when requested by public authorities or when they deem it best, advise officers of the State, county, or local governments, in regard to sanitary drainage, and the location, drainage, ventilation, and sanitary provisions of any public institution, building, or public place.

It shall also be the duty of the Board to give all information that may reasonably be requested, concerning any threatened danger to the Public Health, to the Health Officers of the ports of Savannah, Darien, Brunswick, and St. Mary's, and to the Commissioners of Quarantine of said ports, and all other sanitary authorities in the State, who shall give the like informa-

tion to said Board; and said Board and said officers, said Quarantine Commissioners and said sanitary authorities, shall, as far as legal and practicable, co-operate to prevent the spread of diseases, and for the protection of life and the promotion of health, within the sphere of their respective duties.

The Board shall have the general supervision of the State system of registration of births, marriages, and deaths, and shall recommend such forms and amendments of law as shall be deemed to be necessary for the thorough organization and efficiency of registration of vital statistics throughout the State.

The Secretary of the Board shall be superintendent of registration.

The Board shall report annually to the Governor, who shall lay the report before the General Assembly. Such report shall be upon the vital statistics and the sanitary condition and prospects of the State; and shall set forth the action of the Board, of its officers and agents, and the powers thereof, for the past year, and may contain other useful information, and shall suggest any further legislative action or precaution deemed proper for the better protection of life and health.

The Board shall meet at least once in every twelve months, and may also hold special meetings as frequently as the proper discharge of its duties shall require.

Physicians are to report deaths and births, — parents to report deaths, when no physician attends, — and coroners to do the same, with statement of cause of death, to the Ordinary.

The Ordinaries in the several counties shall keep records, and report to the Secretary of the Board.

The law of 1875 was amended in 1876, by remitting the penalty imposed on parents, and by creating county Boards of Health, to consist of the Ordinary and two practising physicians.

The Ordinary is to be *ex officio* Secretary of the Board for his county; and said Board shall correspond with, and report statistics to, the State Board of Health, through its Secretary; giving special attention to gathering statistics, in accordance with the provisions of the Act of which this is amendatory. Said Boards shall have supervision of the sanitary condition of their counties, respectively, subject to the direction of the State Board of Health.

ILLINOIS.

Provisions as to removal of prisoners to safe place, in case of epidemic or contagious disease, and to prevent introduction of the same into insane hospital.

Also a provision that, in case of flowage of land, the jury shall inquire if it will injure the health of the vicinity.

By Act of 1865, it is enacted that the supervisors, assessors, and town clerk of every township shall constitute a Board of Health; and shall have power, on the breaking out of any contagious disease in their township or immediate vicinity, to make and enforce rules and regulations tending to check the spreading of such disease within the limits of such township; and, for this purpose, shall have power to shut up any house where any infected person may be, or remove such person to any pesthouse within the limits of the township.

The town-clerk is to keep a record of the doings of the Board, and report to annual town-meeting. This Act to be in operation only in counties where Board of Supervisors shall accept it.

Act of 1865 provides penalty for bringing (knowingly and wilfully) into State any sheep infected with contagious disease, or suffering them to run at large.

By Act of 1867, a Board of Drainage Commissioners is provided for, to whom application may be made by person desiring to make a drain. Owners of the land through which drain must pass are then notified, and a hearing appointed. If Commissioners are satisfied that, in order to drain the land of the applicant effectually, it is necessary to pass through the land proposed, they shall determine the direction and breadth. Depth always to be such as to produce a current. If owner of land refuses to do his part as directed, they shall cause drain to be made, and owner to be assessed his share.

Act of 1872 as to health in cities and incorporated villages. The city council in former, and board of trustees in latter, are given power to declare what shall be a nuisance, and abate the same, and to impose fine on parties who may create, continue, or suffer nuisances to exist; to appoint a Board of Health, and

prescribe its powers and duties; to erect and establish hospitals and medical dispensaries, and control and regulate the same; and to do all acts, and make all regulations, which may be necessary or expedient for the promotion of health or the suppression of disease.

This year (1877) was passed the following: —

A Bill for an Act to create and establish a Board of Health in the State of Illinois.

SECTION 1. *Be it enacted by the People of the State of Illinois, represented in the General Assembly,* That the Governor, with the advice and consent of the Senate, shall appoint seven persons, who shall constitute the Board of Health. The persons so appointed shall hold their offices for seven years: *Provided,* That the terms of office of the seven first appointed shall be so arranged that the term of one shall expire on the 30th day of December of each year; and the vacancies so created, as well as all vacancies occurring otherwise, shall be filled by the Governor, with the advice and consent of the Senate: *And provided, also,* That appointments made when the Senate is not in session may be confirmed at its next ensuing session.

SECT. 2. The State Board of Health shall have the general supervision of the interests of the health and life of the citizens of the State. They shall have charge of all matters pertaining to quarantine; and shall have authority to make such rules and regulations, and such sanitary investigations, as they may from time to time deem necessary for the preservation or improvement of Public Health; and it shall be the duty of all police officers, sheriffs, constables, and all other officers and employés of the State, to enforce such rules and regulations, so far as the efficiency and success of the Board may depend upon their official cooperation.

SECT. 3. The Board of Health shall have supervision of the State system of registration of births and deaths, as hereinafter provided. They shall make up such forms, and recommend such legislation, as shall be deemed necessary for the thorough registration of vital and mortuary statistics throughout the State. The Secretary of the Board shall be the Superintendent of such registration. The clerical duties, and the safe-keeping of the bureau of vital statistics thus created, shall be provided by the Secretary of State.

SECT. 4. It shall be the duty of all physicians and accoucheurs in this State to register their names and post-office address with the County Clerk of the county where they reside; and said physicians and accoucheurs shall be required, under penalty of ten dollars, to be recovered in any Court of competent jurisdiction in the State, at suit of the County Clerk, to report to the County Clerk, within thirty days from date of their occurrence, all births and deaths which may come under their

supervision, with a certificate of the cause of death, and such correlative facts as the Board may require, in the blank forms furnished as hereinafter provided.

SECT. 5. When any birth or death shall take place, no physician or accoucheur being in attendance, the same shall be reported to the County Clerk, within thirty days from date of their occurrence, with the supposed cause of death, by the parent, or, if none, by the nearest of kin not a minor, or, if none, by the resident householder where the death shall occur, under penalty as provided in the preceding section of this Act.

SECT. 6. The Coroners of the several counties shall be required to report to the County Clerk all cases of death which may come under their supervision, with the cause and mode of death, &c., as per forms furnished, under penalty as provided in section four of this Act.

SECT. 7. All amounts recovered under the penalties herein provided shall be appropriated to a special fund for the carrying out the objects of this law.

SECT. 8. The County Clerks of the several counties in the State shall be required to keep separate books for the registration of the names and post-office address of physicians and accoucheurs, for births, for marriages, and for deaths; said books shall always be open to inspection, without fee, and said County Clerks shall be required to render a full and complete report of all births, marriages, and deaths, to the Secretary of the Board of Health, annually, and at such other times as the Board may direct.

SECT. 9. It shall be the duty of the Board of Health to prepare such forms for the record of births, marriages, and deaths as they may deem proper; the said forms to be furnished by the Secretary of said Bo rd to the County Clerks of the several counties, whose duty it shall be to furnish them to such persons as are herein required to make reports.

SECT. 10. The first meeting of the Board shall be within fifteen days after their appointment, and thereafter in January and June of each year, and at such other times as the Board shall deem expedient. The meeting in January of each year shall be in Springfield. A majority shall constitute a quorum. They shall choose one of their number to be President, and they may adopt rules and by-laws for their government, subject to the provisions of this Act.

SECT. 11. They shall elect a Secretary, who shall perform the duties prescribed by the Board and by this Act. He shall receive a salary, which shall be fixed by the Board. He shall also receive his travelling and other expenses incurred in the performance of his official duties. The other members of the Board shall receive no compensation for their services; but their travelling and other expenses, while employed on business of the Board, shall be paid. The President of the Board shall quarterly certify the amount due the Secretary; and, on presentation of his certificate, the Auditor of State shall draw his warrant on the Treasurer for the amount.

SECT. 12. It shall be the duty of the Board of Health to make an annual report, through their Secretary or otherwise, in writing, to the Governor of this State, on or before the first day of January of each year ; and such report shall include so much of the proceedings of the Board, and such information concerning vital statistics, such knowledge respecting diseases, and such instruction on the subject of Hygiene, as may be thought useful by the Board, for dissemination among the people, with such suggestions as to legislative action as they may deem necessary.

SECT. 13. The sum of *five thousand* dollars, or so much thereof as may be necessary, is hereby appropriated to pay the salary of the Secretary, meet the contingent expenses of the office of the Secretary, and the expenses of the Board, and all costs for printing, which, together, shall not exceed the sum hereby appropriated ; said expenses shall be certified and paid in the same manner as the salary of the Secretary.

SECT. 14. The Secretary of State shall provide rooms suitable for the meetings of the Board, and office room for the Secretary.

SECT. 15. *Whereas*, Epidemics of scarlatina, diphtheria, and small-pox are now prevailing to an alarming extent in different parts of the State, and

Whereas, The co-operation, and prophylactic measures necessary to arrest their progress, cannot be well secured without the organization of such a Board; therefore an emergency exists, and this Act shall take effect and be in force from and after its passage.

INDIANA.

1867. Law to prevent diseased sheep running at large, or the selling the same.

And another providing that domestic animals dying of disease shall be burned or buried.

(This Act was passed in an emergency, to take effect immediately.)

1869. It is declared unlawful to bring into the State any cattle infected with the "Texas or Spanish fever," or liable to impart it to other cattle.

Parties violating, liable for damages resulting therefrom.

(This Act was passed, also, in emergency, to take effect immediately.)

By another Act (of same year), it is made a misdemeanor to bring Texas or Cherokee cattle into the State between March 1 and October 1.

This Act not to prevent transit, by railroad, of cattle to other States; nor to apply to cattle that shall have wintered, the previous winter, north of 38°.

IOWA.

Penalties enacted for importing or driving contagiously diseased sheep into the State, or turning out or suffering the same to go at large, or knowingly selling the same.

The same provisions are afterwards made as to horses and mules, and against bringing Texas cattle into the State (unless they have wintered for at least one winter north of the southern boundary of Missouri or Kansas), and against bringing diseased hop-roots or cuttings into the State.

Act of 1864, to amend ch. 173 of Revision of 1860 concerning offences against the Public Health, makes it punishable by fine or imprisonment to throw any dead animal into any river, well, spring, cistern, reservoir, stream, or pond.

The Code enacts penalties for selling diseased, corrupted, or unwholesome provisions, for adulterating food, liquors, drugs, or medicines, for neglect of apothecaries and others to label poisons sold by them, and for inoculating with small-pox with intent to cause its prevalence or spread.

Law of 1858 provides penalty for wilfully selling drugged liquors, or keeping the same for sale.

By law of 1866, the Mayor and Council of any incorporated town or city, or trustees of any township not incorporated, shall be and are hereby constituted a Board of Health, with power to make such regulations as they may deem necessary for the Public Health and safety respecting nuisances, sources of filth, and causes of sickness within their cities or towns.

They are also empowered to employ all such persons as shall be necessary to carry into effect their regulations, and to fix their compensation; to employ physicians in case of poverty; and to take such general precautions and actions as they may deem necessary for the Public Health.

KANSAS.

General Statutes, 1868. Mayor and council of cities with over 15,000 inhabitants shall have power to make regulations to prevent the introduction of contagious diseases into the city; to make quarantine laws for that purpose, and to enforce the same within five miles of the city; to erect, establish, and regulate hospitals, and provide for the government and support of the same; to make regulations to secure the general health of the city, and to prevent and remove nuisances,* and to make and prescribe regulations for the cleaning and keeping in order of all slaughter-houses, stock-yards, warehouses, stables, or other places where offensive matter is kept or liable to accumulate.

In cities having between 2,000 and 15,000 inhabitants, Mayor and Council have power, as in cities of first-class down to *, and, in addition, "to provide the city with water."

Law of 1868 provides for temporary removal of convicts (with care of sick), when contagious or pestilent disease breaks out in penitentiary.

KENTUCKY.

No legislation, except to prohibit the selling of poisonous drugs or medicines, or adulterating the same, until the Act of 1874, amended 1876, regulating the practice of pharmacy.

This law provides for the registration of pharmacists, who shall be either graduates from regularly incorporated colleges of pharmacy, or shall have practised for a certain number of years.

It also establishes a State Board of Pharmacy, to consist of seven persons, to be appointed by the Governor, and to be selected from among the most skilful pharmacists of the State. This Board shall examine all applicants for registration, and direct the registration of persons properly qualified, and shall report to each regular session of the General Assembly.

LOUISIANA.

By laws of 1848, the Board of Health of New Orleans consists of sixteen members, elected by City Council, not more than half to be practising physicians. Mayor is President; seven a quorum.

Duty of Board to designate hours at which offal and filth shall be deposited in the streets, and time when same shall be removed by contractor for cleaning streets.

Health Warden to report violation of regulations, promptly, to City Attorney, who shall institute suit in name of city, for penalty ($20 to $100).

Board have power to require sextons of cemeteries of parish of Orleans to make returns to them, and impose penalties for neglect to do so; and to require physicians, and others attending sick, at all times to transmit to them a statement of contagious maladies under their charge; and, during existence of epidemics or any alarming sickness, a daily statement of existence and locality of each and every case of disease; and for neglecting or refusing, physicians or other persons attending are subject to fine.

Board shall appoint one of its members (a physician) to visit ships arriving at New Orleans with sick on board; and physician shall take such steps in relation thereto as may be directed by the Board.

One shall be selected for each district, to perform duty in rotation, monthly.

Board shall declare vacant the seat of any member failing to attend their regular meetings, unless absent from city on leave from the Board, or unless on satisfactory explanation; and fill vacancy from his district.

Board may also fine commissioners of police, and contractors for removing filth from streets, for not conforming to requisitions of the Board. For incurring a third penalty, Board shall have power to remove.

Board shall appoint, annually, not less than two citizens, to be known as "Health Wardens," for each ward. Duty of these to visit from time to time, and inspect condition of houses

and lots in their several wards ; and to order removal of any nuisance likely to prove injurious to Public Health ; and, if order is disobeyed, to report to any two members of Board of Health. If latter approve the order, they shall direct the immediate removal of nuisance, at expense of tenant or owner of property.

Secretary of the Board shall publish weekly statements in the paper of greatest circulation in New Orleans, under direction of Board, stating cause of each death occurring during the week.

Regulations of the Board shall be published in official gazette of the Common Council.

Board shall make annual report to Common Council, as to health of city for preceding year, and suggest means for improving the same.

1856. Duty of practising physicians of the city, and families of deceased, to give certificate containing such facts as Board may require in relation to all persons dying within Parish of New Orleans, and duty of undertaker to receive and deliver this to sexton of cemetery to which he conveys the body.

Duty of sextons to keep their grounds in such cleanly and drained condition as may be required by the Board.

No person to be buried in New Orleans, out of limits of established cemetery, without previous authority of Board of Health ; and no burial shall take place within said cemeteries without such certificate as Board shall require.

Sexton to take name of each undertaker and driver who brings body for burial, and record the same.

Expense of Board (exclusive of Secretary's salary) not to exceed $500 annually, to be paid by Common Council.

Quarantine (1855). — Established at point not less than seventy miles below New Orleans, on the river Mississippi, to be located by Board of Health.

State Board of Health (1870). — Nine members, competent citizens of the State ; three elected by Council of New Orleans, six appointed by Governor, with advice and consent of Senate. The said members shall be selected with reference to their known zeal in favor of a quarantine system. Members to be commissioned by Governor, for one year, after taking oath " well and truly to

enforce and comply with the provisions of an Act entitled 'an Act to establish quarantine for the protection of the State;'" and, in case of neglecting or failing to comply with this oath within ten days after their appointment or election, their office shall be considered vacated.

Meetings of Board once a month, from November 1 to June 1; and once a week, from June 1 to November 1; and as often as they may deem necessary.

They shall elect, of their number, a President, who shall reside in New Orleans, and superintend the different quarantine stations of the State, and visit them as often as Board of Health shall deem necessary.

He shall have power to issue, during adjournment of Board, all orders and warrants provided by this Act to constables or sheriffs; and shall report to Attorney-General all violations of the same.

He shall lay before Board, at each meeting, the business to be transacted, and a book in which he shall enter copies of all letters written by him, orders and warrants issued, and a detail of all his acts.

He shall present, at each meeting, all communications forwarded to him, and a report of the resident physicians and treasurers, and perform such other duties as shall be assigned to him by Board of Health. To be removed only by impeachment. Four members of Board a quorum.

Board of Health shall authorize the resident physician to appoint, in case of need, an assistant physician at the quarantine ground on the Mississippi, who shall act as his deputy.

Board of Health. — Powers of: —

1. To employ nurses and assistants to attend sick, and such other persons as may be necessary to carry out proper quarantine regulations, and fix their compensation.

2. To fix number of days for quarantine (not less than ten), and determine how it shall be performed.

3. To make necessary legal regulations, not provided for by this Act, nor contrary to it, to carry out a proper system of quarantine, and enforce same by fine (not exceeding $500).

4. To make regulations for preservation of order and police within quarantine limits, and impose penalties for breach.

5. To contract for necessary buildings at quarantine grounds.

6. To appoint Secretary, who is to act as Treasurer. Latter is to keep minutes of proceedings of Board, and all vouchers and expenditures made by authority of said Board.

Board shall have power —

1. To remove, or cause to be removed, any substance they deem detrimental to the health of New Orleans; and commissioners of streets shall execute their orders when not in conflict with ordinances of the city or laws of the State.

2. To pass and enforce sanitary ordinances for the city, provided the same are approved by the Council and published as city ordinances.

3. To define duties of officers employed by them, and impose additional duties on officers appointed under this Act.

4. To issue warrant to any constable, police-officer, or sheriff in the State, to apprehend and remove any person who cannot otherwise be subjected to the provisions of this Act, or who shall have violated the same; and, when necessary, to issue warrant to sheriff of the city or parish where vessel may be which has violated provisions of this Act, commanding him to remove said vessel at quarantine grounds, and arrest the officers thereof; all which processes to be executed as if issued out of court.

Governor shall appoint a police-officer to be designated as Marshal, who shall be under control of the Board of Health, and reside at the Quarantine Station on the Mississippi River; whose duties and powers shall correspond to those of a sheriff or constable, so far as regards execution of warrant and arrest of person violating quarantine regulations. Quarantine station established at the Rigolet and on the Atchafalaya.'

Resident physician of quarantine ground to be appointed by Governor of State, by and with the advice and consent of the Senate, and removable at pleasure.

His duties. — 1. To visit every vessel coming from any port and entering mouth of Mississippi River.

2. To return to Secretary of Board of Health a weekly list of vessels inspected by him, with amount collected for inspection, which shall form a fund for support of quarantine.

Powers of. — To detain at quarantine ground, with cargoes,

crews, and passengers, all vessels coming from infected districts, or in foul condition, or having on board persons affected with pestilential, contagious, or infectious disease, during time he may deem necessary, — not less than ten days. To compel captain to land at quarantine ground, to fumigate and cleanse all such vessels, and to submit to such rules and regulations as will be hereafter provided by the Board of Health.

He shall have such other powers as may be delegated to him by the Board of Health, not contrary to provisions of this Act, and necessary to carry them into effect.

It shall be his duty to remain at the quarantine grounds, attend the sick, and perform all such other duties as may be required of him by the Board of Health.

Governor of State, on advice of the Board, shall issue proclamation, declaring place infected, and stating number of days for quarantine.

Resident physician shall give timely notice to the Board of the necessity of such proclamation.

Thereafter, all vessels arriving at New Orleans, or the Rigolet or the Atchafalaya stations, from such infected places, shall be subject to quarantine, and regulations of Board of Health, as provided by this Act.

Master of vessel subject to quarantine or visit, arriving at New Orleans, shall be guilty of misdemeanor who refuses or neglects —

1. To go and anchor at place designated for quarantine, at his arrival.

2. To submit to examination of physicians, and give information to enable physician to fix time of quarantine.

3. To remain with vessel at quarantine during period assigned; and, while there, to comply with directions and regulations of this Act or of Board, as prescribed for his vessel, &c., by resident physician.

Resident physician to report violation of this Act to Attorney-General.

Harbor-masters to demand of masters arriving from sea, at New Orleans, permit of resident physician, and report to Secretary of Board of Health all vessels having entered the port without such permit.

Tow-boats, between mouth of River and New Orleans, liable to inspection and quarantine from May 1 to November 1.

Extracts from this Act to be published by Board for information of masters of vessels arriving in the State, to be given to pilots to be distributed by them to masters.

Fine for going on board vessels performing quarantine.

Quarantine limits designated by large letters.

Buildings at quarantine on Mississippi River to consist of two buildings as hospitals for sick, a small house as residence for officers, and a well-ventilated store for reception of freight of such infected vessel as resident physician shall deem necessary to have unloaded.

Buildings at Rigolet Hospital for sick and store, as above.

At Atchafalaya, a good shade[1] to be provided for freight unloaded.

Board of Health and its successors is created a body corporate, under the name of " The Board of Health of the State of Louisiana."

1855. Authorities of incorporated towns and cities authorized to enact ordinances to protect them from the introduction of contagious and epidemic diseases.

By Act of 1835, police juries may enact ordinances and regulations, not inconsistent with laws and Constitution of United States, or of this State, to protect their respective parishes against introduction of all and every kind of contagious or epidemic disease.

Revised Statutes, 1870. Distance of quarantine from city of New Orleans made *seventy-five miles.*

Board shall have power to extend period of quarantine, if they deem necessary.

Resident physician at station on Mississippi River has power to grant permit, to persons acclimated and healthy, to go to the city. He may require the captain or owner of vessel to defray cost of purification; and to pay $5 for each sick person landed, to be appropriated to hospital expenses.

In cases of emergency, Board may issue proclamation of quarantine without reference to Governor, and enact needful regulations for its enforcement.

---

[1] Good " shade " reads good " shed."

Vessels, out ten days from infected ports, presenting clean bills of health, not having had any sickness on board, and which are not in foul condition, shall be permitted to pass to the city after thorough purification by disinfecting agents; to effect which, resident physician may detain vessel as long as he deems necessary. He shall require evidence, under oath.

By Act of March 16, 1870, the Board of Health have power to appoint sanitary inspectors, not to exceed six in number, one for each of the four districts of the city of New Orleans, one for the city of Jefferson, and one for the portions of the parishes of Orleans and Jefferson situated upon the right bank of the Mississippi River, which said inspector for the said four districts of the city of New Orleans shall be in place and in lieu of the four Health Officers now appointed by the Council of New Orleans.

And it is further enacted —

SECT. 6. That the Board of Health shall have power to employ nurses and assistants to attend the sick, and such other persons as may be necessary to carry out proper quarantine regulations, and to fix their compensation; to fix the number of days of quarantine for vessels liable to it under sections ninth and thirteenth of this Act, not to be less than ten days; to determine how said quarantine shall be performed, and to make all legal regulations not provided by this Act, nor contrary to the same, and necessary to carry out a proper system of quarantine, and to enforce the same by fine, not exceeding $500; to make rules and regulations for preserving good order and police within the limits of the quarantine ground, and to impose penalties for the breach thereof; to contract for the necessary buildings at the quarantine grounds; to appoint a secretary, who shall act as treasurer, whose salary shall be $1,500 a year, and who shall furnish security in the sum of $10,000. It shall be his duty to keep a minute of the proceedings of the Board, and all vouchers and expenditures made by authority of said Board. The said Board shall have the power to remove, or cause to be removed, any substance, matter, or thing which they may deem detrimental to health, whether such substance, matter, or thing be in the cities of New Orleans or Jefferson, or in the parishes of Orleans or Jefferson, on the right bank of the Mississippi River, and the respective street commissioners of said cities, and police juries of said parishes, shall, without delay, execute the orders of said Board with reference to the removal of such substance, matter or thing, and the expenses necessarily incurred in making such removal, as well as those incurred for purposes of disinfection and removal of sick persons, shall be borne respectively by said cities, and said portions of said parishes from which such removal, or

wherein such disinfection shall take place. The said Board shall have power to pass and enforce, by adequate fine, not in any case to exceed $50, sanitary ordinances for and within the cities of New Orleans and Jefferson, and the parishes of Orleans and Jefferson, on the right bank of the Mississippi River; and, for the purpose of enforcement of said ordinances, as well as of this Act, and the Act entitled "An Act to establish Quarantine for the protection of the State," and the amendments thereto, the said Board shall have power to sue, in its own name, in any civil court having competent jurisdiction, for any fines or pecuniary liabilities imposed by said ordinances, or by said Acts or amended Acts; and said fines or moneys so recovered shall become a portion of the funds of said Board.

And, should any street commissioner, or street contractor, or any person contracting or employed to clean the streets, after having been duly notified, neglect or refuse to obey any necessary sanitary order or ordinance of said Board coming within the purview of this Act, such street commissioner or street contractor, or person contracting or employed to clean the streets, shall be held personally liable, the same as if the matter or thing complained of was by his original fault. The Board shall have control of the sanitary police within the aforesaid cities, and the said portions of the aforesaid parishes where such sanitary police is upon duty; which force shall at all times consist of not less than one officer for each of the four districts of the city of New Orleans, one for the city of Jefferson, and one for the parishes of Orleans and Jefferson, on the right bank of the Mississippi River; and, in case of actual or threatened epidemic, said Board shall have power to call upon the Board of Metropolitan Police for such additional sanitary police force as said Board of Health shall deem proper. The Board of Health shall have power to define the duties of officers employed by them, and impose additional duties to officers appointed under this Act; to issue warrants to any constable, police-officer, or sheriff, in the State; to apprehend and remove such person or persons as cannot otherwise be subjected to the provisions of this Act, or who shall have violated the same; and, whenever it shall be necessary so to do, to issue their warrant to the sheriff of the city or parish where any vessel may be, having violated the provisions of this Act, commanding him to remove said vessel to the quarantine ground, and arrest the officer thereof; all which warrant shall be executed by the officer to whom the same shall be directed, who shall possess the like power in the execution thereof, and be entitled to the same compensation, as if the same had been duly issued out of any court of the State.

March 24, 1876, was passed

An Act

To authorize and empower the Board of Health of the State of Louisiana to detain and disinfect, and to pass after disinfection, vessels from infected ports, at and from quarantine stations, in lieu of a time of quarantine detention in certain cases, and to repeal conflicting laws.

SECTION 1. *Be it enacted by the Senate and House of Representatives of the State of Louisiana, in General Assembly convened,* That the Board of Health of the State of Louisiana be and is hereby authorized and empowered, at its discretion, at any time, to cause the detention at quarantine stations, for purposes of disinfection and purification, and to disinfect, fumigate, and purify any or all vessels from ports in which yellow fever usually prevails, or from ports where other contagious or infectious diseases are reported to exist ; and, after such disinfection, fumigation, and purification at quarantine, to permit the passage to the city of New [Orleans] of such vessel or vessels, without any prescribed time of detention, when it is satisfied that the same have been properly and sufficiently disinfected and purified, so that said vessel or vessels may safely be permitted to pass without damage to the public health, or risk of contagion.

SECT. 2. *Be it further enacted, &c.*, That all laws or parts of laws conflicting with this Act be, and the same are, so far as respects the operation of this Act, hereby repealed, and that this Act shall take effect from and after its passage.

EXTRA SESSION OF 1877.

An Act

To reorganize and render more efficient the Board of Health of the State of Louisiana ; to define its powers and prescribe its duties, and those of quarantine and other officers under its control ; to provide for its expenses, and for the recording of births, deaths, and marriages, in the parish of Orleans ; and to provide penalties for the enforcement of this Act, and for violation of the same, and for the ordinances and orders made in pursuance thereof.

SECTION 1. *Be it enacted by the Senate and House of Representatives of the State of Louisiana, in General Assembly convened,* That the Board of Health of the State of Louisiana shall hereafter consist of nine members, four of whom shall be appointed by the Governor, by and with the advice and consent of the Senate, and five of whom shall be elected by the Council of the city of New Orleans. They shall hold their office for four years, unless sooner removed for cause. The members first appointed shall be so designated that the term of two of those appointed by the Governor, and two of those elected by the Council of New Orleans, shall expire in two years from the 15th day of March, 1877,

and the term of the two others appointed by the Governor, and the three others elected by the Council, shall expire in four years from said date. At least, one of the members of said Board appointed by the Governor, and two of the members elected by said Council, shall be regularly licensed physicians, resident in New Orleans. And thereupon the Governor shall issue to each of them a commission for his respective term of office. At any meeting of said Board, five members shall constitute a quorum for the transaction of business.

SECT. 2. *Be it further enacted, &c.*, That the said Board shall proceed to organization at its first meeting in the month of April, of each alternate year, by electing one of its own number to be president, and a suitable person to be secretary and treasurer, whose powers and duties shall be those now prescribed by law for said officers, and such other powers and duties as may be herein devolved upon them. The president of said Board shall receive an annual salary not exceeding the sum of $2,400; and the secretary and treasurer shall receive an annual salary not exceeding the sum of $2,000, to be paid out of the funds of, or appropriations to, said Board. No other member of said Board shall receive any pay or compensation whatever.

SECT. 3. *Be it further enacted, &c.*, That said Board shall have power and authority to make all needful rules, regulations, and ordinances upon the subject of vaccination within the parish of Orleans: *provided*, that nothing in this Act shall be construed to render vaccination, in any case, compulsory. The said Board shall encourage vaccination, and shall furnish pure and fresh vaccine matter to the district sanitary inspectors and city physicians, for the purpose of gratuitous vaccination, and the furnishing of such vaccine matter shall be paid by the said Board of Health.

SECT. 4. *Be it further enacted, &c.*, That the said Board shall have power and authority, on the concurrence of the City Council, to provide for, protect, and preserve, by adequate means, the health and salubrity of the city of New Orleans; and, in the exercise of such power and authority, may, with the assent of the City Council, incur such necessary and reasonable expense as occasion may warrant, which expenses shall be paid by the city of New Orleans, after approval of the same by said Board, out of the budget appropriation, as hereinafter provided; and no expense beyond such budget may or shall be incurred, chargeable upon the city of New Orleans. It shall hereafter be the duty of said Board to forward to the Mayor and City Council, annually, and in time to be included in the budget of expenses of the City of New Orleans, an estimate of the probable sum required to meet the expenses aforesaid for the ensuing year, and other expenses provided for in this Act, to be paid by the city of New Orleans; and said estimate shall include the salaries of the sanitary inspectors appointed under existing laws for the different districts of said city, as well as the reasonable expenses of said sanitary inspectors for rent of office, and stationery for their official duties; and the said Board shall also, at the same time, make to the City Council a detailed statement (verified by the oath of

the president and secretary thereof) of all fees, fines, forfeitures, and sums of money which have been received by the said Board during the past year, as well as an estimate of the probable receipts for the ensuing year; and it shall be the duty of the Mayor and Council of the city of New Orleans, after considering such report and estimate, to make such appropriation as may be by them deemed necessary for the expenses of said Board, and place it on the annual budget of expenditures. And, should the fees, fines, forfeitures, and sums of money which have been received by the said Board, under the provisions of this Act, during the year, exceed the expenses of said Board, the said excess shall be paid to the Administrator of Finance of the city of New Orleans.

SECT. 5. *Be it further enacted, &c.*, That the Board of Health, through its president, or other proper officer, shall have power and authority to call upon the police authorities for necessary aid and assistance in enforcing any of the authority or powers conferred upon it by this Act, as well as enforcing any of its orders, rules, and regulations. And it shall be the duty of the police authorities to render to the Board of Health such necessary aid and assistance, when so called upon, by the use of the police force, as may effectually accomplish the intentions of this Act, and of the orders, regulations, and ordinances of said Board.

SECT. 6. *Be it further enacted, &c.*, That the said Board shall, in any civil suit or proceeding in which it may be a party, obtain all writs, appeals, or other process, without being compelled to furnish bond.

SECT. 7. *Be it further enacted, &c.*, That the said Board shall have power and authority to establish quarantine stations upon any of the approaches to the city of New Orleans, whenever, in its discretion, such stations may be rendered necessary to protect the heath of the city of New Orleans, or the State, and to make all needful rules and regulations with reference to the management and police of such stations. It shall regulate the duties and obligations of masters of vessels and other persons there arriving, and any master of a vessel or other person who shall violate any of the rules, ordinances, or regulations of said Board, made with reference to the management or police of such stations, or to vessels or other means of conveyance, or transportation at, or arriving at such stations, or shall evade or refuse visitation of the proper health or quarantine officer, or shall refuse to allow such quarantine officer to inspect, disinfect, or fumigate such vessel, or other means of conveyance or transportation, shall be liable to said Board in a sum not exceeding $500, for each and every offence, to be recovered by civil suit, wherever such offender, vessel, or means of conveyance may be found; and said Board shall have lien and privilege for the payment of said liability on such vessel, or other means of conveyance or transportation, to be conserved by writ of provisional seizure, in which case bond shall be given, in an amount to be determined by the judge issuing the writ, and the release bond shall be for an amount not exceeding $600. All quarantine physicians and other officers and employés for quarantine stations, both for those now existing or that may be established hereafter, excepting

the Mississippi Quarantine Station, shall be appointed, and their salaries fixed, by said Board.

Sect. 8. *Be it further enacted, &c.*, The president of said Board be, *ex officio*, the recorder of births, deaths, and marriages, for the parish of Orleans; but shall, as such, be under the general direction and control of said Board. All fees collected by him shall be paid into, and be a part of the funds of said Board. The said Board shall prescribe such blanks and forms as it may deem necessary for procuring vital statistics in said parish, and enforce the use of the same; and the president of said Board shall cause to be prepared, and shall keep, suitable books of record for said office, which shall be carefully preserved in fire-proof buildings or vaults.

Sect. 9. *Be it further enacted, &c.*, That it shall be the duty of the attending physician or midwife, at the birth of any child in the parish of Orleans, to report the same to the office of the Board of Health within twenty-four hours of the same; and it shall be the duty of the father, or, in his default, of any person present at the birth of any child, to report within twenty-four hours from the date of such birth, at the office of the Board of Health, such birth, which report shall be recorded in presence of two witnesses, and shall, as nearly as possible, show the date, hour, street, and number thereof of such birth, the sex of the child, and its name, the names of the father and mother, their nationality, age, occupation, and residence, and the names of said witnesses.

Sect. 10. *Be it further enacted, &c.*, That every death in the parish of Orleans shall be reported at said office within twenty-four hours after it has occurred: such report shall be made by the nearest relative, or the husband or wife of the deceased, if present in the parish; otherwise, by the executor, if designated, or landlord of the deceased, or the officiating undertaker. It shall be the duty of coroners to report all deaths coming to their official notice; and of the president, manager, or superintendent of any State, parish, municipal, charitable, or benevolent institutions; said report shall contain, as far as possible, the full name, sex, age, occupation, residence, color or race, and nativity of the deceased, the cause of the deaths, the street and number where it occurred; shall show whether the deceased was married or unmarried, the name of surviving spouse, if any, and where residing; also, the name, age, and residence of the declarant, and his relationship, if any, to the deceased, and such other particulars as may be required by said Board. No body shall be removed from said parish until a permit shall have been obtained from the president of said Board, under his official seal, showing that the requirements of this section have been complied with.

Sect. 11. *Be it further enacted, &c.*, That every marriage celebrated in the parish of Orleans shall be recorded in said office; such record shall show the full names of the contracting parties, their age, nativity, date of license of marriage, and by whom issued; the names of the parents or tutors of the contracting parties, the name of the officer, priest, or ecclesiastic celebrating the marriage, with the date of its celebration,

and the names of the witnesses thereto, and any such facts as the Board may judge necessary for vital statistics. It shall be the duty of the officer, priest, or ecclesiastic celebrating any marriage, to return the license authorizing such marriage to said office, after having indorsed on such license the date of such celebration; these licenses, so returned, shall be preserved among the papers of said Board.

SECT. 12. *Be it further enacted, &c.*, That it shall be the duty of the president of said Board to cause the registry of any marriage celebrated prior to the passage of this Act, on production of a certificate, duly attested, of the celebration of such marriage; and, in case of the loss of such original certificate, such registry shall be made on the production of the affidavits of the contracting parties, and at least one of the witnesses present, or of the officer, priest, or ecclesiastic celebrating such marriage; and a certified copy of such registry shall be *prima facie* evidence of such marriage.

SECT. 13. *Be it further enacted, &c.*, That there shall be collected for the recording under this Act of any birth or death the sum of fifty cents, and like fee for any certificate of such record; and, for recording any marriage, the sum of $1, and like fee for certificate of the recording of the same.

SECT. 14. *Be it further enacted, &c.*, That this Act shall not be construed so as to deprive the Board of Health of any powers or authority it has under existing laws, and that all acts and parts of acts in conflict with this Act are hereby repealed.

MAINE.

First sanitary legislation, 1821, provides against spread of contagious diseases, by requiring municipal officers to remove the person infected to separate house, providing nurses and attendants and necessaries, at his charge or that of parent or master, if able, otherwise, of the town to which he belongs.

Also, any person coming into the town from any infected place is to give notice to town-clerk, or one of the municipal officers, within two hours after arrival, or after actual notice, or forfeit $100 to use of town.

Such person may be forbidden to go to any part of the town where the officers think his presence would be unsafe for the inhabitants. If he refuses, they may order him to leave the State, as they may direct; if he neglect or refuses, a justice of the peace for the county may issue his warrant to have him removed; and he shall not return while distemper prevails

where he resides, without license of municipal officers aforesaid.

Special precautions are authorized for border towns, the municipal officers to appoint persons to attend at places where travellers may pass into such towns from infected places; to examine, and, if need be, restrain such persons from travelling, until licensed.

Any two justices may, by warrant, direct the removal of any person infected with contagious sickness, under direction of officer of the town where he is; and also the impressing and taking up convenient houses, lodgings, nurses, attendants, and other necessaries for the accommodation, safety, and relief of the sick.

Any justice may issue his warrant to secure and guard infected articles (baggage, clothing, or goods), and to impress men for the purpose, and houses or stores for their safe keeping; and all persons shall be prevented from removing or coming near such articles, till due inquiry is made; and the officers may detain such goods until, in the opinion of the selectmen, they are free from infection. Officers shall have power of entering in the execution of these orders.

Ch. 127, § 8, enacts: —

"That each town in this State may, at their meeting held in March or April, annually, or at any other meeting legally warned for the purpose, when they shall judge it to be necessary, choose and appoint a Health Committee, to consist of not less than *five* nor more than *nine* suitable persons, or one person to be a Health Officer, whose duty it shall be to remove all filth of any kind whatever, which shall be found in any of the streets, lanes, wharves, docks, or in any other place whatever, within the limits of the town to which such Committee or Health Officer belongs, whenever such filth shall, in their judgment, endanger the lives or the health of the inhabitants thereof; and also to require the owner or occupier to remove or discontinue any drain from which any such filth may proceed."

It is further provided that the expenses of such removal shall be paid by the person or persons who placed the filth there, if they are known, otherwise, by the town. If the filth or drain shall be on private property, the Committee or

Health Officer shall notify the owner or occupier thereof, who shall, after twenty-four hours' notice, remove or discontinue the same, at their own expense; and, in case said owner or occupier shall neglect so to do, at expiration of time aforesaid, he shall forfeit and pay one hundred dollars to the use of the poor of the town, and shall repay to the town the costs and charges incurred by the Committee or Health Officer in removal.

This is entitled "an Act to prevent the spreading of the small-pox and other contagious sickness," and was approved March 10, 1821.

Section 1 enacts: —

"That for the better preventing the spreading of infection, when it shall happen that any person or persons, coming from abroad, or belonging to any town or place within this State, which shall be visited, or shall lately before have been visited with the plague, small-pox, pestilential or malignant fever, or other contagious sickness, the infection whereof may probably be communicated to others, the Selectmen of the town where such person or persons may arrive or be are hereby empowered to take care and make effectual provision in the best way they can for the preservation of the inhabitants, by removing such sick or infected person or persons, and placing him or them in a separate house or houses, and by providing nurses, attendance, and other assistance and necessaries for them," at the charge of the parties themselves, their parents or masters (if able), or otherwise, at the charge of the town or place whereto they belong; and if such person or persons are not inhabitants of any town or place within this State, then at the charge of the State. When person or persons come into any town within this State from any place out of the State, where small-pox or other malignant distemper is prevailing, they shall, if thereto required by the Selectmen, within two hours after notice given them of the law, give notice of their coming, and of the place from whence they came, or forfeit one hundred dollars; and, if not disabled by sickness, shall depart (within two hours after warning given by Selectmen) from the State in such manner and by such road as the Selectmen shall direct; and, if they refuse, any justice of the peace for the county where the town lies may issue his warrant to a constable, or other proper officer,

and cause them to be removed into the State from which they may have come. And if, during the prevalence of the distemper, they shall return without liberty first obtained from such justice, they shall forfeit and pay not more than four hundred dollars.

Any person entertaining a person so warned to depart, for space of two hours after notice given him of such warning by the Selectmen, shall forfeit and pay two hundred dollars.

Section 6 provides for the examination (under oath) of masters, seamen, or passengers of vessels having or having had, or suspected of having or having had, infection on board, or coming from infected port, by Selectmen of town to which the vessel may come.

Vessels with infected persons on board are to anchor at safe distance from town, and no person or thing is to be brought on shore without written permit of municipal officers.

Quarantine. — Selectmen of any seaport town may establish regulations for, and may fix place. They are to give notice to pilots, who are to make known the order to masters of vessels which they shall board.

Penalties are provided for violation or evasion on the part of masters.

Persons going on board vessel at quarantine, in violation of this Act, are to be detained, and made subject to same regulations and restrictions as the vessel.

Health Officer, or Health Committee, where legally chosen as heretofore provided, in any seaport town, has powers and duties of Selectmen in relation to quarantine.

Hospitals. — Inhabitants of any town may establish, for reception of persons having small-pox, or other disease dangerous to the Public Health; or Selectmen may license any building for a hospital, such hospital or building to be under control of Selectmen.

Such hospital, with its physicians, patients, nurses, attendants, and all persons within its limits, and all furniture and articles used there, shall be subject to regulations made by Selectmen.

Immediately on the breaking out of infectious disease, the hospitals shall be provided for the reception of the sick, who shall be removed there, unless too sick to be moved, in which

case the house or place where they are shall be considered a hospital, for every purpose before mentioned; and all persons residing in or concerned with the same shall be subject to regulations of Selectmen. *In general*, Selectmen are to use all possible care to prevent the spread of the contagion, and to give notice of infected places to travellers by flags and other means.

Penalties are provided for violation of hospital regulations by persons subject thereto.

Householders and physicians are required under penalty to give immediate notice to Selectmen of cases of diseases under their care dangerous to the Public Health.

Towns, respecting which no provision is made by any special law, may choose a Board of Health, which shall have all the powers, discharge all the duties, and be subject to the same penalties or restrictions as are provided in this chapter, in relation to Selectmen, Health Committee, or Health Officer, of any town *not* electing to choose a Board of Health; and same penalties shall attach to persons disobeying their authority.

Plantations. — Provisions of this chapter in relation to towns extended to. — "*Assessors*" to have same duties and powers as Selectmen.

Vaccination may be provided for at expense of towns or plantations.

There are also provisions against the sale of unwholesome provisions, and the adulterating of food or liquors.

By Act of 1853, if any town, at its annual meeting, omits to choose a Health Committee or Health Officer, the municipal officers shall be a Health Committee, and have all their powers and perform all their duties.

By Act of 1855, towns may establish by-laws for the preservation of health, and for protection against infectious diseases.

There are also statute regulations prescribing what shall be deemed nuisances, and providing for the assignment, by municipal officers, of places for the exercise of unwholesome trade or employment.

In 1862 was passed an Act relating to infected cattle, providing for their isolation, &c., &c.

MARYLAND.

In 1796 was passed "an Act to appoint a Health Officer for the port of Baltimore town, in Baltimore County." "Whereas, to prevent the ingress of the plague, or other malignant, contagious diseases, is an object of great importance to the welfare and commerce of the citizens of the State: till, therefore, proper arrangements and establishments shall be made by Congress in the premises, the Governor is authorized, with advice of Council, to appoint physicians to examine foreign vessels, and those coming from suspected places, and, when necessary, to oblige them to perform quarantine, not less than ten days nor exceeding twenty; and, before end of quarantine, shall make a second visit, and may continue quarantine for not more than ten days. No vessel bound to Baltimore, having on board thirty persons disordered with any contagious disease, or coming from any sickly port or place, without a clean bill of health, shall come nearer than Hawkins' Point, nor land any of such infected persons, or any of their goods or effects, without license from the physician or assistant. Master subject to penalty for concealing infected persons ($300 for each offence).

By the Constitution, Governor is authorized to order and compel any vessel to perform quarantine, if such vessel, or the port from which she shall have come, shall, on strong grounds, be suspected to be infected with the plague.

And by Act of 1793, Governor is authorized, when he apprehends introduction of malignant, contagious disease, to compel any vessel coming into any port of the State to perform quarantine; and to forbid all communication, by land or water, between this State and place affected, or to lay such intercourse under such regulations and restrictions as he may think advisable; and to take all measures, and do all things which may appear to him necessary to give effect to objects of this Act.

Further penalty on pilots for conducting above Hawkins' Point vessels having infected persons on board.

Temporary hospital may be erected in such place as Governor, with advice of Council, may direct, for reception of such

sick persons as physicians may think proper to remove to shore for their better accommodation or cure, or to prevent the spreading of any malignant disease, or to shorten quarantine; and Governor, with advice, &c., shall prescribe rules and regulations for governing and managing said hospital.

Representatives and senators from this State are requested to state to Congress the necessity of the aforesaid arrangements, and to obtain consent of Congress to duty on all sea vessels above sixty tons, coming into Baltimore district, to defray expenses attending execution of this Act.

The Code of 1860 makes the President and visitors of the Maryland Hospital a body corporate, and provides that they shall admit into said hospital no person affected with any dangerous or contagious or infectious disease; but they may, in their discretion, build, or cause to be built, a separate and distinct house or establishment for such persons, on the grounds belonging to the corporation, which separate establishment shall be under the control, management, and direction of the said president and visitors, in the same manner as the hospital.

Law of 1872 established a "State vaccine agency."

Law of 1874 established a State Board of Health, to consist of five physicians, to be appointed by the Governor, by and with the advice and consent of the Senate. They shall take cognizance of the interests of health and life among the people generally; they shall make sanitary investigations and inquiries respecting the causes of diseases, — especially of epidemics, — the sources of mortality, and the effects of localities, employments, conditions, and circumstances on the Public Health; and they shall gather such information in respect to these matters as they may deem proper; they shall devise some scheme whereby medical and vital statistics of sanitary value may be obtained, and act as an advisory board to the State in all hygienic and medical matters; they shall make special inspections of public hospitals, prisons, asylums, and other institutions, when directed by the Governor or the Legislature, and shall, at each regular session of the Legislature, submit a full report of their acts, investigations, and discoveries, with such suggestions as they may deem proper.

They shall meet at least once in every three months, and as

much oftener as they may deem proper. Three shall be a quorum for business.

(This law is almost identical with that of Minnesota, passed in 1872.)

MASSACHUSETTS.

A law of 1784 prohibited, under penalty, the sale of any corrupted or unwholesome provisions, without notice to the buyer, and the fraudulent adulteration of food, liquors, drugs, or medicines.

Board of Health. — Every town may choose, annually, not less than three nor more than nine persons, to constitute a Board of Health, or any one person to be Health Officer. If the town does not so choose, the Selectmen shall be the Board of Health.

By Act of 1797, such Board may make regulations as to nuisances, sources of filth, and causes of sickness within their town and on board of vessels in their harbor; also, in relation to infected articles, and as to the interment of the dead, and burying-grounds in their town. They are to examine into nuisances, and destroy, remove, or prevent the same.

They may remove infected person to a separate house; and, if he or she cannot be removed, the persons in their neighborhood may be.

They may station persons on the borders of other States to examine persons suspected of bringing infection with them, and, if necessary, may restrain them from travelling until license is given to them by the Board of Health of the town to which they may come. Justices may issue warrants for removal of sick persons, to secure infected articles, and to take up houses and stores for the safe keeping of same. Officers may break open houses, shops, &c., and may command aid.

By Act of 1816, every Board may appoint its physician, to hold office during its pleasure.

Notice of their regulations shall be published. If the Board is refused admission to search premises, a justice may, on complaint, issue warrant.

The Board may grant permits for the removal of sick per-

sons or infected articles, when they think it safe and proper so to do, and may direct the removal of prisoners sick with disease dangerous to other prisoners.

By Act of 1821, the City Council in Boston is to have powers and perform duties of Board of Health.

By Act of 1827, the Court of Common Pleas may issue injunction to stay or prevent nuisances until the matter is decided by jury or otherwise.

Quarantine. — Any town may establish a ground, and any two or more may have, in common, at their joint expense. Board of Health in seaport towns may establish quarantine, and make regulations for, to extend to vessels and persons, goods and effects arriving in, and all persons visiting, or going on board.

These regulations to be binding on all persons after public notice given. Vessels may be ordered to quarantine ground by the Board, and persons arriving in, or going on board of, may be removed to hospital, under care of Board, there to remain under their orders.

Penalty ($200) if master, seaman, or passenger belonging to any vessel infected, or suspected of being infected, or coming from infected port, refuses to answer, on oath, questions put to him by Board of Health relating to such infection or distemper.

Small-pox and other dangerous diseases. — By Act of 1792, hospitals for may be provided by towns, to be subject to orders and regulations of Board of Health, or a committee of the town, appointed for the purpose, not to be within one hundred rods of houses in adjoining town, unless such town consents.

Penalty for inoculating without permission.

Physicians and others in these hospitals to be subject to Board of Health.

Hospitals to be *immediately* provided where small-pox breaks out unexpectedly, and persons sick removed thereto, unless too sick; in which case, the house where they remain shall be considered a hospital, subject to Board of Health. Selectmen and Board of Health to use all possible care to prevent the spreading of the infection, and give public notice of infected place, by displaying signals.

Penalty if physicians or others violate regulations.

Every householder and physician to give *immediate* notice to Selectmen or Board of Health of case of small-pox or other dangerous disease, under penalty not exceeding $100. (1792.)

Inoculation. — By Act of 1809, towns may provide for and defray expenses.

Offensive Trades. — By Act of 1785, Selectmen of towns, and Mayor and Aldermen of Boston, may assign places for. If place becomes a nuisance, Court of Common Pleas may revoke the assignment.

Gen. Stat. — Selling corrupt or unwholesome provisions, and adulterating food. Penalties against, re-enacted.

St. 1853 provides against adulteration of drugs and medicines.

St. 1843 punishes the wilful corrupting of springs, or injuring of aqueducts.

St. 1855 forbids adulterating of liquors used or intended for drink with substances poisonous or injurious to health.

Persons selling arsenic, strychnine, corrosive sublimate, or prussic acid, without written prescription of physician, to keep a record of sales, when and to whom sold, and in what quantity.

St. 1866 forbids the killing for sale, or selling of, calves less than four weeks old. Such meat exposed or kept for sale may be seized and destroyed by Board of Health, Health Officer, sheriff, constable, or police-officer.

Board of Health. — Act of 1849. Except where different provision is made by law, the city council of a city may appoint a Board of Health, may constitute either branch of such council, or a joint or separate committee of their body, a Board of Health, either for general or special purposes, and may prescribe the manner in which the powers and duties of the Board shall be exercised and carried into effect. In default of the appointment of a Board with full powers, the city council shall have the powers, and perform the duties prescribed to Boards of Health in towns.

By laws of 1849 and 1855, additional penalties are provided in case owners of property neglect to remove nuisance thereon.

By law of 1849, if owner does not comply, the Board may remove the nuisance, at his expense.

1850. The Board may require occupants of unfit dwelling-places to clean them; or, if necessary, to remove therefrom.

If, after notice, they refuse or neglect to comply with the order, the Board may have premises cleaned at expense of owners, or may forcibly remove the occupants and close the premises, which shall not be again occupied as a dwelling-place without written consent of the Board, under penalty.

By laws of 1837 and 1848, the Board of Health shall make provision for persons infected with sickness dangerous to Public Health, by removing them to separate house, or otherwise, and providing with nurses and necessaries.

By laws of 1838, if the infected person cannot be removed, persons in the neighborhood may be.

Last two sections do not apply to small-pox (Laws of 1838).

Vaccination. — Law of 1855 prescribes, before age of two years, and revaccination whenever the Selectmen or Mayor and Aldermen shall, after five years from the last vaccination, require it.

Five dollars penalty for every year's neglect.

Selectmen and Mayor and Aldermen to enforce.

Town to provide means to inhabitants unable to pay for same.

Inmates of manufactories, almshouses, of places where poor and sick are received, of prisons, &c., to be vaccinated.

By laws of 1837 and 1848, when a disease dangerous to the Public Health breaks out, the Board of Health shall immediately provide a hospital or place of reception for the sick and infected, and cause sick and infected persons to be removed thereto, unless too sick for removal, in which case the place where he is shall be considered a hospital, and be subject to regulation of Board, as before provided. (This is substantially a re-enactment, as well as the following, viz.: Selectmen are to give notice of infected places to travellers, by flags, &c., and use all possible care to prevent the spreading of the infection.)

Penalty on physicians and others in hospitals, for violating rules.

By laws of 1838, 1840, and 1848, the provisions of last three sections do not apply to small-pox.

By law of 1855, orders of prohibition from Board of Health, in case of offensive trades, are to be served on occupant or per-

son having charge of premises, who, if aggrieved, may appeal to Superior Court; but trade is not to be exercised pending such appeal.

Provisions of this chapter (26) of the General Statutes extend to cities, so far as the same are not inconsistent with their several charters or acts in amendment thereof.

By law of 1855, the owner of a tomb, aggrieved by the order of the Board of Health closing any tomb, burial-ground, or cemetery, may appeal therefrom to the Superior Court.

Law of 1866 provides for appeal to County Commissioners, when Board of Health neglects or refuses to abate nuisances.

By Act of 1866, Boards of Health may appoint "*agents*" to act for them in cases of emergency, or when the Board cannot be conveniently assembled; such agents to have all the authority which Boards appointing them had. They shall, within two days, report their action in each case to the Board of Health for their approval, and shall be directly responsible to, and under the control and direction of the Boards of Health from which they receive their appointments.

Act of 1869 established the State " Board of Health and Vital Statistics," — seven in number, — to hold office for seven years, term of one to expire each year; all vacancies to be filled by the Governor, with advice and consent of the Council.

The Board shall take cognizance of the interests of health and life among the citizens of the Commonwealth. They shall make sanitary investigations and inquiries in respect to the people, the causes of disease, and especially of epidemics and the sources of mortality, and the effects of localities, employments, conditions, and circumstances on the Public Health; and they shall gather such information in respect to these matters as they may deem proper for diffusion among the people.

They shall advise the government in regard to the location of any public institutions.

They shall report to the Legislature, in January of each year, their doings, investigations, and discoveries during the preceding year, with such suggestions as to legislative action as they may deem necessary.

They are to meet once in three months at the State House, and as much oftener as they may deem expedient. With ex-

ception of the Secretary, they are to serve without pay, their actual expenses while engaged in duties of the Board to be paid.

They are directed to examine into the effect of the use of intoxicating liquor, as a beverage, on the industry, prosperity, happiness, health, and lives of the citizens of the State; also, what additional legislation, if any, is necessary in the premises.

In 1868 was passed an Act "extending the provisions of chapter 26 of the General Statutes, relative to the preservation of the Public Health." It provides that lands which are wet, rotten, or spongy, or covered with stagnant water, so as to be offensive to persons residing in the vicinity thereof, or injurious to health, shall be deemed a nuisance; and the Board of Health or Health Officer of such city or town may, upon petition and hearing, abate such nuisance.

Persons injuriously affected may apply, by petition, to Board of Health or Health Officer, who shall view the premises and examine into the nature and cause of the nuisance; they are then to appoint a time and place for hearing, and notify all parties interested. After hearing, the Board or Health Officer may cause the nuisance to be abated, at their discretion; and, for that purpose, may enter and make such excavations, embankments, and drains, as may be necessary for such abatement.

They shall determine how the improvements shall be kept in repair, and shall estimate and award damages and benefits accruing. Return to be made within thirty days, to city or town clerk, for record.

If Health Officers unreasonably neglect or refuse to proceed on the petition, petitioner may apply to Superior Court, or any justice thereof, who may appoint three commissioners, who shall proceed in the manner hereinbefore provided.

Persons aggrieved in award of damages may complain to County Commissioners.

By Act of 1871, the State Board of Health are empowered to order persons carrying on any noxious or offensive trade to desist, under penalty, if in their judgment the Public Health or the public comfort and convenience shall require.

By Act of 1872, the owner of diseased or unwholesome meat or provisions, seized by inspector of provisions, may appeal to

the Board of Health, when said inspector shall cause said meat or provisions to be inspected by the Board, or a committee thereof, of not less than two members, who, if they find the same diseased or unwholesome, shall order them to be destroyed or disposed of otherwise than for food.

Act of 1873 (to amend Ch. 26 of General Statutes) provides for issuing of warrant by justice of any court of record, or two justices of the peace of the county, on complaint of member of Board of Health, or their agent, that they are refused entry into land, building, premises, or vessel, for purpose of examining into and destroying, removing, or preventing any nuisance, source of filth, or cause of sickness. This warrant is to be directed to sheriff or deputy, to the agent of the Board, or to any constable of the town, commanding him to take sufficient aid, and destroy, remove, or prevent the source of filth or cause of sickness, under directions of the Board.

Penalty is added for obstructing Selectmen, Board of Health, or their agent, in using means to prevent spreading of infection or wilfully removing, defacing, or handling flags or signals.

By Act of 1874, the Board of Health is to retain charge of any cases in which they have acted, to the exclusion of the overseers of the poor.

Reasonable expenses to be paid by the person infected, if able.

Also, by Act of 1874, State Board of Health is to establish regulations for business of slaughtering swine by corporations. Plans of the buildings to be used are to be submitted to the Board, or to some person designated by them, for approval.

By Act of 1875, the State Board of Health shall, by themselves or by agents appointed by them, investigate the subject of the correct method of drainage and sewerage of the cities and towns of the Commonwealth, especially with regard to the pollution of rivers, estuaries, and ponds by such drainage or sewerage, and to devise and report a system or method by which said cities or towns may be properly drained, and said rivers, estuaries, and ponds may be protected against pollution so far as possible, all with the view to the preservation of the health of the inhabitants of this Commonwealth, and the securing to the several cities and towns thereof a proper system of drainage

and sewerage, without injury to the rights and health of others; also, to report how far said sewage may be utilized and disposed of.

They are authorized to enter upon and make surveys of lands, and employ assistants. They are to report to the next Legislature not later than Feb. 1, 1876.

By Act of same year (1875), State Board of Health are given rooms in the State House, and $500 appropriated to their use, for books, journals, and maps.

By Act of 1876, State Board of Health is instructed to report to Legislature any additional facts in its possession in regard to subjects of drainage and sewerage, to be printed not later than Jan. 1, 1877.

By Act of 1877, in each of the several cities of the Commonwealth, except the city of Boston, the Mayor and Aldermen shall, in the month of January, in the year 1878, appoint two persons, not members of the City Council, who, together with the city physician, shall constitute the Board of Health of such city. The Board, so constituted, shall enter upon its duties on the first Monday of February then next succeeding. The terms of the two appointed members shall be so arranged that the term of one shall expire on the first Monday in February in each year, after the year 1878. All vacancies to be filled in each case by the Mayor, with the approval of the Board of Aldermen. The members so appointed shall be subject to removal by the Mayor for cause; and for their services they shall receive such compensation as the City Council may from time to time determine.

The Board may make rules for their own government and that of all subordinate officers in their department.

Boards of Health hereby constituted shall have and exercise all the powers vested in, and shall perform all the duties prescribed to, City Councils or Mayors and Aldermen as Boards of Health, under the statutes and ordinances now in force in their respective cities, and may appoint subordinate officers, agents, and assistants, as they may deem necessary. They are to report annually to the City Council, giving a comprehensive statement of the acts of the Board during the year, and a review of the sanitary condition of the city. Said Boards of Health and the

Board of Health of the city of Boston, in addition to the powers conferred upon them by existing statutes, are hereby authorized to prepare and enforce in their respective cities such regulations as they may deem necessary for the safety and health of the people, with reference to house drainage and its connection with public sewers, where such connection is made. This Act is made subject to acceptance by a majority of the legal voters in each city.

By Act of same year, the City Council of any city may, upon report of the Board of Health that the Public Health requires it, and after public notice and hearing, forbid future interment in any tomb or tombs within the city limits.

This is to be done upon a vote of both branches of the City Council, and with the approval of the Mayor.

The Board of Health may notify the owner of any tomb in the city that it is in need of repair, and require such owner to put it in proper state of repair; and, if he fails so to do, the Board may enter and repair at expense of the city, to be refunded by owner, — otherwise the tomb to be held by the Board until payment, with interest. Twenty years such possession shall vest all interest and right of burial therein in the city. Persons aggrieved by such action of the City Council or Board of Health may appeal to the Superior Court

MICHIGAN.

Rev. Stat., 1846. — Supervisor and justices of peace to be a Board of Health in every township, where no other provision is made by law, with power to appoint a physician to the Board, who shall be the health officer of his township, to hold office during pleasure of Board.

The Board shall make such regulations respecting nuisances, sources of filth, and causes of sickness, within their respective townships, and on board of any vessel in their ports or harbors, as they shall judge necessary for the public health and safety; to make regulations concerning articles capable of conveying contagion; to purchase, and hold in trust, land for burial of the dead; to give notice of their regulations, by pub-

lication or posting; to examine into all nuisances, sources of filth, and causes of sickness, that may, in their opinion, be injurious to the health of inhabitants of township, or in any vessel within port or harbor of such township, and destroy, remove, or prevent the same.

In case of nuisance on private property, the Board shall order the owner or occupant to remove the same, at his own expense, within twenty-four hours; and, in case of owner's or occupant's neglect, the Board may cause it to be removed, expense to be paid by owner or occupant.

When person convicted on indictment for common nuisance that may be injurious to Public Health, the court may order it removed or destroyed, at expense of defendant, under direction of Board. When entry of Board to building or vessel is refused, warrant may issue from justice of peace, directed to sheriff or constable, to destroy, remove, or prevent such nuisance, under direction of Board of Health.

Board may grant permits for removal of nuisance, infected article, or sick person, within limits of township, when they think it safe and proper to so do. Board shall make effectual provision to prevent spread of small-pox, by removing the sick to a separate house, and providing nurses and necessaries; if he cannot be removed without danger to his health, the Board shall make same provision for him in house where he is; and, in such case, may cause persons in neighborhood to be removed, and may take such other measures as they may deem necessary for the safety of the inhabitants of the township near to or bordering on either of neighboring States. Board may restrain persons coming from infected places in other States from travelling, till licensed by the Board. Warrant of two justices of the peace may remove, under direction of Board, persons infected with contagious disease, or take possession of convenient houses and lodgings, and provide nurses, attendants, and other necessaries for the accommodation, safety, and relief of the sick; and warrant of one justice of the peace enough to secure and guard infected clothing or goods, and impress house for their safe keeping.

Officer may break open houses and shops. Charges to be paid by owners.

Just compensation to parties interested for houses so taken.

Prisoners attacked with dangerous diseases to be removed to hospital, or place of safety, by order of Board.

Superintendents of poor may remove paupers when contagious disease breaks out in poor-house.

Quarantine. — Any township may establish, in any suitable place. Two or more may establish joint quarantine.

Boards of Health in townships on the lakes or principal rivers or straits connecting any of said lakes, or bordering on any navigable waters uniting with any of said lakes, rivers, or straits, may, from time to time, establish quarantine for all vessels arriving within limits of such townships, and may make such quarantine regulations as they shall judge necessary for the health and safety of the inhabitants. These regulations to extend to all persons and goods in such vessels, and to all persons visiting or going on board the same.

Vessels arriving within limits of townships above mentioned, if such vessel or its cargo be, in opinion of Board, foul or infected, may be removed by Board to quarantine ground, and thoroughly purified. All persons arriving in or going on board such vessel, or handling such cargo, to be removed to hospital, under care of Board, there to remain under their orders.

Masters, seamen, or passengers to answer Board, under oath, concerning infection at port of departure.

Inhabitants of any township may establish, and be constantly provided with, one or more hospitals for reception of persons having small-pox or other disease dangerous to the Public Health.

All such hospitals to be subject to orders and regulations of Board of Health, or committee appointed by them for that purpose. Penalty for inoculating with small-pox, unless at hospital licensed and authorized by law.

Physicians at such hospital, the sick, the nurses, attendants, and all persons approaching or coming within its limits, to be subject to regulations of Board or its committee.

When small-pox, or disease dangerous to Public Health, breaks out, the Board shall immediately provide hospital or place of reception, such as they shall judge best for accommodation and safety of inhabitants, to be subject to regulations of Board.

Person so sick or infected to be taken there; or, if too sick to be moved, the house or place where he remains shall be considered a hospital for every purpose before mentioned; and all persons residing in, or connected with the same, shall be subject to regulations of Board of Health.

Board shall use all possible care to prevent spreading of infection where it is found to exist, and give public notice of infected places to travellers, by such means as in their judgment shall be most effectual for the common safety. Householders to give immediate notice of dangerous disease in their house, and physician, when called to visit person so sick. Townships may provide for vaccination, under direction of Board of Health or Health Officer, at public expense.

Townships, villages, and cities, by their governing Boards, may assign certain places where alone offensive trades may be carried on; and, when places become nuisances, assignment may be revoked.

Mayor and Aldermen of each incorporated city, and the president and council, or trustees, of each incorporated village in the State, shall have and exercise all the powers, and perform all the duties, of a Board of Health, as provided in this chapter, within limits of cities or villages, respectively, of which they are such officers.

1863. Penalty enacted for importing diseased sheep, or allowing the same to run at large.

1869. Governor may appoint three commissioners, who shall have power to prevent spread of dangerous diseases among animals, and protect people of State from danger arising from consumption of diseased meat.

1869. Act to provide for the draining of swamps, marshes, and other low land. Drain Commissioner to be appointed by supervisors of each county. County Drain Law, and, also (1871), a Township Drain Law.

In 1867 was passed a law for the registration of births, marriages, and deaths, by clerks of counties, to whom returns are to be made.

Law of 1873 provides for the collection of statistical information of the insane, deaf, dumb, and blind, throughout the State.

Acts of the same year, and of 1875, give general powers and

authority to councils of cities and villages, in relation to Public Health, with authority in cities to establish Boards of Health.

Acts have also been passed at various times from 1863 to the present year, regulating the sale of poisons, providing against nuisances by burial of dead animals, directing the inspection of salt, and providing a penalty in case of the adulteration of milk and its products, and of alcoholic liquors.

There are also laws regulating the inspection of illuminating oils and explosive substances, and the keeping of gunpowder; and a general law relating to cemeteries, passed in 1869, with amendments.

An Act of 1865 prohibited the putting of offal, &c., into waters where fish are taken; and Acts of 1873 provided for the collection of statistics, as to the treatment and cure of inebriates, and prohibiting the sale of drugs for purposes of abortion.

By Act of 1873, the "State Board of Health" was established, to consist of seven members, six to be appointed by the Governor, with the consent of the Senate, and a Secretary to be elected by the Board, who shall be its executive officer.

The Board shall have the general supervision of the health and life of the citizens of the State. They shall especially study the vital statistics of the State, and endeavor to make intelligent and profitable use of the collected records of deaths and sickness among the people; they shall make sanitary investigations and inquiries respecting the causes of disease, and especially of epidemics, the causes of mortality, and the effects of localities, employments, conditions, ingesta, habits, and circumstances, on the health of the people. They shall, when required, or when they deem it best, advise officers of the government, or other State Boards, in regard to the location, drainage, water supply, disposal of excreta, heating, and ventilation of any public institution or building. They shall, from time to time, recommend standard works on the subject of hygiene, for the use of the schools of the State.

They shall meet quarterly, at Lansing, and at such other places and times as they may deem expedient. A majority shall be a quorum for the transaction of business.

They shall have authority to send their secretary, or a committee of the Board, to any part of the State, when deemed

necessary, to investigate the cause of any special or unusual disease or mortality.

The Secretary shall keep records, and shall, so far as practicable, communicate with other State Boards of Health, and with the local Boards of Health within this State, and file reports and correspondence received.

He shall prepare blank forms of returns, and such instructions as may be necessary, and forward them to the clerks of the several Boards of Health throughout the State. He shall collect information concerning vital statistics, knowledge respecting diseases, and all useful information on the subject of hygiene; and through an annual report, and otherwise, as the Board may direct, shall disseminate such information among the people.

It shall be the duty of the Health Physician, and also of the clerk of the local Board of Health in each township, city, and village in this State, at least once in each year, to report to the State Board of Health their proceedings, and such other facts as are required, on blanks, and in accordance with instructions received from said State Board. They shall also make special reports whenever required to do so by the State Board of Health.

In order to afford to this Board better advantages for obtaining knowledge important to be incorporated with that collected through special investigations, and from other sources, it shall be the duty of all officers of the State, the physicians of all mining or other incorporated companies, and the president or agent of any company chartered, organized, or transacting business under the laws of this State, so far as is practicable, to furnish to the State Board of Health any information bearing upon Public Health, which may be requested by said Board, for the purpose of enabling it better to perform its duties of collecting and distributing useful knowledge on this subject.

The Secretary shall be the superintendent of vital statistics; and, under the general direction of the Secretary of State, shall collect these statistics, and prepare and publish the report required by law relating to births, marriages, and deaths.

In 1875 was passed a joint resolution, providing for the publishing, in pamphlet form, by the Secretary of State, of all the laws of the State relating to the Public Health.

This year (1877), an Act has been passed, providing for the inspection of illuminating oils, and regulating the use and sale of the same; and also an Act " for the protection of guests in hotels from danger by fire."

MINNESOTA.

Penalties to prevent sale of diseased provisions, the fraudulent adulteration of food or drugs, and inoculation with small-pox, with intent to spread the disease.

Town Supervisors to constitute a Board of Health within their respective towns, to have and exercise all the powers necessary for promotion of Public Health.

Board may examine into all nuisances, sources of filth, and causes of sickness, and make such regulations respecting same as they judge necessary for Public Health and safety of inhabitants; and persons violating shall be punished by fine or imprisonment.

Board to give notice of their orders and regulations by publication or posting, to be deemed legal notice to all persons.

Board may order owner or occupant to remove nuisance, &c.; and, if he does not comply, may cause it to be removed at his expense.

They may enter building or vessel for purpose of examining and destroying, removing or preventing nuisance, &c.; and, if refused entry, justice of peace may issue warrant (on complaint) to sheriff or constable, who may destroy, remove, or prevent it, in presence of and by direction of members of Board.

Person coming from infected place, or who has been lately infected with contagious disease, dangerous to Public Health, Board of Health may cause to be removed to separate house, and provided with nurses and necessaries; and, if too sick to be moved, shall provide for him at house where he is, and may cause persons in neighborhood to be removed; and may take such other measures as they may deem necessary for safety of the inhabitants.

When disease dangerous to Public Health breaks out in any

town, Board shall immediately provide hospital or place of reception for sick and infected, such as they may judge best, which shall be subject to regulations of the Board; and Board may cause their removal thither, unless too sick, in which case, house where he is shall be considered a hospital, and, with all its inmates, be subject to regulations of Board.

Act of 1872 provided for a "State Board of Health and Vital Statistics," to consist of seven physicians, to be appointed by the Governor. The Board shall place themselves in communication with the local Boards of Health, the hospitals, asylums, and public institutions throughout the State, and shall take cognizance of the interests of health and life among the citizens generally. They shall make sanitary investigations, and inquiries respecting the causes of disease, especially of epidemics, the sources of mortality, and the effects of localities, employments, conditions, and circumstances on the Public Health; and they shall gather such information, in respect to these matters, as they may deem proper for diffusion among the people. They shall devise some scheme whereby medical and vital statistics of sanitary value may be obtained, and act as an advisory board to the State in all hygienic and medical matters, especially such as relate to the location, construction, sewerage, and administration of prisons, hospitals, asylums, and other public institutions. They shall, at each annual session of the Legislature, make a report of their doings, investigations, and discoveries, with such suggestions as to legislative action as they may deem proper. They shall also have charge of all matters pertaining to quarantine, and authority to enact and enforce such measures as may be necessary to the Public Health.

The Board shall hold regular meetings, at least once every three months, one of which meetings shall be held at the capital, during the session of the Legislature. Three members shall be a quorum.

By Act of 1873, "All incorporate towns, villages, boroughs, and cities shall have a Board of Health, who shall have and exercise all the powers necessary for the preservation of the Public Health, and who shall hold regular monthly meetings.

Said Board shall consist of not less than three members, one

of whom, when practicable, shall be a physician; and such physician shall be Health Officer, and, *ex officio*, president of the Board. It shall be the duty of the Health Officer to make, once in every three months, and oftener if necessary, a thorough sanitary inspection of said town, village, borough, or city, and present a written report of such inspection at the next meeting of the Board of Health; and he shall forward a copy of his monthly report, as soon as rendered, to the State Board of Health; and all local Boards of Health, and Health Officers, shall make such investigations and reports, and obey such directions as to infectious diseases, as shall be directed by the State Board of Health.

The Board shall be elected annually, by the council, or other body answering thereto, of each incorporate town, village, borough, or city, unless a different term or mode is now provided by law.

Act of 1875 requires druggists or other persons selling poison to keep a record of the name of the person to whom sold, the amount sold, and date.

MISSISSIPPI.

1822. Penalty for importing small-pox, or variolous or infectious matter of said disease, with design to spread the same, or inoculating after disease introduced, except under certain restrictions and regulations. Fine (not exceeding $2,000), and imprisonment (not exceeding twelve months), for each offence.

Governor authorized, from his own knowledge, or information given him, that contagious disease has been introduced into neighboring county or State, or found admittance into this State, or on board boat or vessel at or near shore, to take such measures as he deems meet to prevent communication of the infection, and for the aid and comfort of the sick within the State. Expense paid out of State Treasury on Governor's order, unless persons sick are able to pay.

Governor may allow inoculation for small-pox in certain cases, on petition. Persons petitioning shall be assigned to certain place.

Small-pox patients not to go abroad in company, or in public roads where travellers usually pass, without retiring, or giving notice, on approach of passengers, until certificate of recovery had from physician, Governor, or representative of county.

Court of government of incorporated city or town may appoint *inspector*, who shall inspect and brand flour and other provisions offered for sale, and inspect and gauge liquors.

Penalty for knowingly and wilfully selling, holding, or offering for sale any tainted, unsound, unwholesome, or unmerchantable flour, and marked as good flour, or for practising any fraud or deception in selling or offering the same.

Act of 1876 prescribed a Board of Health for the counties of Jackson, Harrison, and Hancock, to consist of one lawyer, one merchant, and not more than five physicians; the latter to be graduates of some medical college of good standing.

The Board shall select a physician to act as Quarantine Physician and Health Officer, at all ports of the State in said counties, and shall establish a quarantine at such ports.

Then follow the usual quarantine regulations, in detail.

This is entitled, "An Act more effectually to protect the health of the citizens of the State."

Feb. 1, 1877, was passed the following:—

An Act

To create a State Board of Health for the protection of life and health, and to prevent the spread of the disease in the State of Mississippi, and other purposes.

SECTION 1. *Be it [further] enacted by the Legislature of the State of Mississippi*, That, within ninety days after the passage of this Act, the Governor shall appoint twelve physicians, of skill and ability, upon the recommendation of the State Medical Association, two from each congressional district, who, for the time being, shall be sanitary commissioners for the said district; and the said sanitary commissioners, together with their [three] other physicians to be selected and appointed by the Governor, who shall be sanitary commissioners for the State at large, shall constitute a Board of Health, and shall be called "The Mississippi State Board of Health," five members of which shall constitute a quorum for the transaction of business: *provided*, four congressional districts are represented.

SECT. 2. *Be it further enacted*, That the said fifteen persons so appointed shall hold office respectively for the terms following, namely: six for two years, six for four years, and six for six years, and until

their successors are appointed and qualified. After the appointment of the said fifteen commissioners, they shall meet in the office of the Secretary of State, upon notice of the President of the State Medical Association of the day of said meeting, and shall proceed to determine, by lot, which of them shall hold for the respective terms of two, four, and six years, the said office as sanitary commissioners; but those appointed by the Governor, for the State at large, shall draw lots separately from those twelve physicians appointed upon the recommendation of the State Medical Association. Immediately, and before entering upon the duties of the office, they shall take the oath prescribed for State officers by the Constitution of the State, and shall file the same in the office of the Secretary of State, who, upon receiving the said oath of office, shall issue to each of said commissioners a certificate of appointment for his respective term of office, as determined as aforesaid; upon receiving which, they shall severally be and become sanitary commissioners, and shall possess and exercise the powers, and perform the duties of said Board, as defined in this Act.

SECT. 3. *Be it further enacted,* That the term of office of said sanitary commissioners, after the expiration of the terms aforesaid, shall be six years, and they shall be appointed by the Governor, as provided in section one of this Act. Any vacancies that may occur, by reason of death, removal from office, or otherwise, shall be filled in like manner.

SECT. 4. *Be it further enacted,* That immediately after the fifteen appointed sanitary commissioners shall have taken the oath of office, as above provided, they shall meet and organize a Board of Health, by electing one of said Board to be president, and by appointing a proper person, who shall be a physician, to be secretary of said Board; and the successive presidents of said Board shall be annually elected by said Board, from the members thereof. The secretary shall continue in office until removed by the election of a successor, or otherwise; and he shall be the executive officer of said Board.

SECT. 5. *Be it further enacted,* That the said Board shall take cognizance of the interests of health and life among the people of the State. They shall make inquiries in respect to the causes of diseases, and especially of epidemics, and investigate the sources of mortality and the effects of localities, employments, and other conditions, upon Public Health.

SECT. 6. *Be it further enacted,* That it shall be the duty of said Board to obtain, collect, and preserve such information relating to deaths, diseases, and health, as may be useful in the discharge of its duties, and contribute to the promotion of the health or the security of life in the State of Mississippi; and it shall be the duty of all Health Officers and Boards of Health in the State to communicate to said State Board of Health copies of all their reports and publications; also, such sanitary information as may be useful; and said Board shall keep a record of its acts and proceedings as a Board, and it shall promptly cause all proper information in possession of said Board to be sent to the local health

authorities of any city, village, or town in the State, which may request the same, and shall add thereto such useful suggestions as the experience of said Board may supply; and it is hereby made the duty of said health authorities to supply like information and suggestions to said State Board of Health, and said State Board of Health is authorized to require reports and information at such times, and of such facts, and generally of such nature and extent, relating to the safety of life and the promotion of health, as its by-laws or rules may provide, from all dispensaries, hospitals, asylums, prisons, and schools, and from the managers, principals, and officers thereof, and from all other public institutions, their officers and managers, lessees and occupants of all places of public resort in the State; but such reports and information shall only be required concerning matters and particulars in respect of which it may, in its opinion, need information for the proper discharge of its duties; said Board, when requested by public authorities, or when they deem it best, shall advise officers of the State, county, or local government, in regard to sanitary drainage and location, drainage, ventilation, and sanitary provisions of any public institution, building, or public place.

SECT. 7. *Be it further enacted*, That it shall be the duty of the State Board to give all information that may reasonably be requested concerning any threatened danger to the Public Health, to the Health Officers of the ports of Pascagoula and Ship Island, and the commissioners of quarantine of said ports, and all other sanitary authorities in the State, who shall give the like information to said Board, and said officers; said quarantine commissioners and sanitary authorities shall, as far as legal and practicable, co-operate to prevent the spread of diseases, and for the protection of life and the promotion of health, within the sphere of their respective duties.

SECT. 8. *Be it further enacted*, — That it shall be the duty of the Board, on or before the first Monday in December of each year, to make a report to the Governor of the State, in writing, who shall lay the same before the next legislature thereafter, upon the vital statistics and sanitary condition and prospects of the State; and such report shall set forth the action of said Board, of its officers and agents, and the names thereof, for the past year, and may contain other useful information, and shall suggest further legislative action or precaution, deemed proper for the protection of life and health.

SECT. 9. *Be it further enacted*, That said Board shall meet at least once in every twelve months, and may also hold special meetings as frequently as a proper discharge of its duties shall require; the same to be convened by order of the president; and its by-laws shall provide for the giving of proper notice of all such meetings to the members of the Board.

SECT. 10. *Be it further enacted*, That all **Acts** in conflict with this Act are hereby repealed, **and that this Act** take effect and be in force after **its passage.**

MISSOURI.

No legislation.

NEBRASKA.

Act of 1867 provides penalty for allowing diseased or distempered cattle to go at large. Justice of peace shall order constable or sheriff to impound.

Act of 1873. In cities of first class (*i.e.* more than 15,000 inhabitants), Mayor and Council shall have power "to make regulations to prevent the introduction of contagious, infectious, or malignant diseases into the city; to create a Board of Health; to make quarantine laws, and enforce the same within the corporate limits, or within three miles thereof; to erect, establish, regulate, and maintain hospitals; to make regulations to secure the general health of the city; to provide for the prevention, abatement, and removal of nuisances, and to make and prescribe regulations for the location, construction, and keeping in order of all slaughter-houses, stock-yards, warehouses, stables, or other places where offensive matter is kept, or is liable to accumulate.

Cities of second class (more than 500 and less than 15,000 inhabitants, Act of 1871) in their corporate capacity may enact ordinances " to make regulations to prevent the introduction of contagious diseases into the city; to make quarantine laws for that purpose, and enforce the same within five miles of the city; to erect, establish, and regulate hospitals, and to provide for their government and support; to make regulations to secure the general health of the city, and to prevent and remove nuisances, and to provide the city with water.

Penalties are also provided for knowingly selling unwholesome provisions, and for permitting stagnant water, injurious to public health and safety; for putting carcass or other filthy substance into well, spring, brook, or any running water of which use is made for domestic purposes, or for putting or leaving offensive matter, or contents of privy vault, in any field, road, creek, river, bay, pond, &c.; for keepers of distilleries, suffering sties to become unclean between April 1 and October 1, to annoyance of citizens.

Certain things declared nuisances, and penalties provided; *e.g.*, erecting or maintaining building for trade or business, which by occasioning noxious exhalation, noisome or offensive smells, becomes injurious and dangerous to health, comfort, or property of individual or the public, the obstructing, without legal authority, of any navigable water, or corrupting any water-course, or diverting same to injury or prejudice of others, &c.; for knowingly selling "*skimmed*" or adulterated milk, or milk diluted with water, or milk the product of diseased animal, or knowingly using any deleterious matter in manufacture of cheese or butter, fine $25 to $100, and liability in damages besides.

Unlawful to transport nitro-glycerine, except under certain conditions; and it is never to be carried with passengers.

Canada-thistle to be cut by land-owners, or others may enter for purpose, without trespass; fine for knowingly vending seed of the same.

NEVADA.

1869. Act to prevent the spread of contagious diseases.

Any person knowingly having, or using, or conveying into any neighborhood, any clothing, bedding, or other substance, used by, or in taking care of any person afflicted by small-pox or other infectious or contagious disease, or infected thereby, or doing any other act with intent to, or necessarily tending to, spread such disease into any neighborhood or locality, is guilty of misdemeanor, and liable to fine or imprisonment; and court trying such offender may order such clothing or property destroyed, and shall have power to carry order into effect.

Persons violating liable, in addition, to damages.

NEW HAMPSHIRE.

Act of 1789 was "an Act to prevent the spreading of the small-pox, for allowing hospitals to be erected under certain restrictions, and to repeal an Act entitled 'an Act providing, in

case of sickness,' and also an Act entitled 'an Act to prevent the spreading of the small-pox in this State.'"

The justices of the inferior court of common pleas, in the respective counties, on proper application, to grant license for hospitals for inoculating for the small-pox, provided consent of town or place be first obtained.

They shall also, from time to time, license physicians to take care of and superintend the same.

If small-pox at any time breaks out, the Selectmen may remove any infected persons to hospital or place remote from inhabitants, unless such removal be dangerous to life.

Penalty is provided for communicating small-pox, and for inoculating without license.

Act of 1792 provides that whenever any vessel arrives at any port in the State, having on board any person infected with the plague, small-pox, pestilential or malignant fever, or shall have been so infected during the voyage, or having on board any goods which may be reasonably apprehended to have any infection of such disease, it shall be the duty of the master or commander to immediately notify the Selectmen of Portsmouth thereof, who are empowered immediately to take such prudential methods and precautions as to them appear necessary, to prevent the spreading of such infection.

The Selectmen further have power to appoint the distance at which such vessel shall lie from shore, and to remove such vessel at expense of owner or master, if they refuse or neglect when ordered by Selectmen; and to prevent persons or goods being landed until such precautions be taken as public safety may seem to them to require.

Justice of peace may confine person coming on shore from such vessel without leave.

Selectmen have full power to seize and keep any goods landed from such vessel without such leave, until same are cleansed at expense of owner.

It shall be part of the condition of the physician's bond that he will use every precaution to prevent the spreading the small-pox, and will not suffer any person to depart from the hospital until he be effectually cleansed, and will then give such person a certificate thereof, under his hand; and penalty is provided

for leaving hospital without such certificate, or being found without it within one month afterwards.

Proviso. —When any person shall break out with the small-pox in the natural way, in any town in this State, and, in the opinion of the Selectmen, he may without danger remain, without communicating the disorder to any but his own family; if the family, or any other person, has been exposed to the danger of taking said disorder, the Selectmen may grant license for any such person to be inoculated, who, with the physician, shall not in such a case be liable to the penalties of this and the aforementioned Act.

June 15, 1799, was passed an Act empowering inhabitants of town of Portsmouth to appoint Health Officers, and for preventing nuisances in said town.

Three persons to be chosen annually by ballot, to be Health Officers.

Duty. — To search for and examine into all nuisances or other causes injurious or dangerous to health of inhabitants.

On oath made to magistrate, warrant shall issue to Health Officers to examine premises, with powers of entering.

Owners and occupiers to be notified to remove nuisances; and, in default by them, officers may enter and remove.

Provisions against throwing or leaving filth in highway or streets.

Vessels arriving at Portsmouth between May 15 and November 1, from any place subject to malignant, pestilential, contagious disorder, or where same usually or often prevails, shall be examined by Health Officers, and may be ordered to remove to place of safety and be cleansed, for time not exceeding thirty days.

By Act of 1803, the Health Officers have power, from time to time, to make rules and regulations for health and safety of town and people, and for removing and preventing nuisances; and also to make orders and regulations, from time to time, respecting quarantine, and shall cause vessels having infection on board, or justly suspected of endangering health of town, to perform quarantine under such restrictions and regulations as they may judge expedient.

Pilots to give notice of such order to masters of vessels which they shall board or can communicate with.

Health Officers to notify commanding officer at New Castle, and request his co-operation.

Penalty on masters evading or landing contrary to law.

Diseased mariners and others provided and cared for on shore.

By Act of 1807, fort at New Castle may fire on vessels subject to quarantine, and attempting to pass, after being hailed.

By the Revised Statutes of 1843, any town may choose Health Officers by major vote. If such officers are not chosen, the Selectmen shall discharge the duties, and have the powers of that office.

The Health Officers may make regulations for the prevention and removal of nuisances, and such other regulations relating to the Public Health as in their judgment the health and safety of the people may require, which shall take effect when approved by the Selectmen, recorded with such approbation by the town-clerk, and published in some newspaper printed in the town, or copies thereof posted in two or more public places in the town.

They are to inquire into all nuisances, and other causes of danger to the Public Health, and make complaint to a justice of the peace, who shall issue his warrant to them to search any building, vessel, or enclosure where they know, or have cause to suspect, such exists. After notice to owner, and neglect on his part to remove, they may enter forcibly, and remove or destroy.

They may employ assistants, and, if resisted, shall have the power of sheriffs to command assistance.

Penalties are enacted in case of any person's placing or leaving any substance liable to become putrid, or offensive, or injurious to the Public Health, in or near any highway, street, alley, or public place, or wharf, or in any water where the current will not remove the same; and the Health Officers shall remove it.

And in case of any person's using or occupying any building in the compact part of any town, for a slaughter-house, or for certain other unwholesome occupations, without the written permission of the Health Officers.

And, also, if any person erects or continues a privy within

forty feet of any street, or of the dwelling, shop, or well of any other person, unless the same is vaulted six feet deep, and sufficiently secured and enclosed, or shall erect or keep any pen or sty for swine so near the dwelling-house of another as in the judgment of the Selectmen shall be a nuisance.

Any town may appoint an agent for vaccination, who shall at all times be provided with suitable matter for communicating the kine-pox, and may vaccinate all persons at the expense of the town, who have not had the small-pox or the kine-pox.

Such agent may be appointed by the Selectmen of the town, whenever in their opinion the health of the inhabitants of said town, by reason of the spreading of the small-pox, shall require.

Health Officers may remove persons infected with malignant, pestilential disease to some suitable house, to be provided by them for the purpose, if it can be done without endangering the life of such person, and make regulations respecting such house, and for preventing unnecessary communication with such persons or their attendants.

Inoculation for small-pox is prohibited.

Court of common pleas, on application, may license any physician to establish a house for inoculating persons for the small-pox, in any town which shall consent thereto, under such regulations as they may prescribe; and such physician shall give a bond to the county treasurer, conditioned that he will use every means and precaution in his power to prevent the spreading of the disease, and will not inoculate except in said house, and will not suffer any person to depart from such house until he is effectually cleansed, and will give to such person a certificate thereof, under his hand.

If any person breaks out with the small-pox in the natural way, and the Health Officers judge that he may remain without endangering others than his own family, they may give license to any persons who have been exposed to the danger of taking the disease, to be inoculated, and to remain in the same house; and the provisions of this chapter, and all regulations of the Health Officers in relation to other licensed pest-houses, shall apply to such house and its inmates.

Quarantine. — The Health Officers may, from time to time,

make regulations respecting, to be approved, recorded, and published, as other regulations made by them.

They shall require vessels infected, or suspected of being so, to perform quarantine at such place as they shall appoint.

They may seize any goods landed from such vessel without their permission, and remove and keep the same until they shall have caused the same to be thoroughly cleansed.

Penalty provided, if orders and regulations are disobeyed; and for landing without permission.

Any person going on board to be deemed infected, and detained.

Quarantine signal to be displayed.

Penalties for knowingly bringing such vessel to or near wharf, dwelling-house, or store, without permission; and Health Officers may have such vessel removed.

Penalties also provided for making false declaration as to place from which the vessel came, or for aiding or permitting the landing of any person or property from such vessel without permission of the Health Officers.

Master and officers to give notice immediately on arriving, to the Health Officers or Selectmen, of any infection on board.

The Health Officers shall notify pilots, and the latter shall notify the masters of vessels, of quarantine regulations.

These regulations shall also be communicated to the commander of any fort near such port, and his co-operation be requested in stopping all vessels subject to quarantine, attempting to pass into the harbor.

These same enactments appear unchanged in the Compiled Statutes of 1853, and the General Statutes of 1867.

An Act of 1867 gave the Mayor and Aldermen of Portsmouth full, exclusive power to appoint annually a Board of Health for Piscataqua Harbor, who shall carry out the ordinances of the City Council in reference to the harbor, and to quarantine. The Board shall consist of not less than three persons, one at least of whom shall be a physician.

They shall be independent of the Mayor and Aldermen, and shall continue in office until a new Board is chosen and qualified, unless removed for due cause shown on due notice and hearing, or by death.

In 1875 was passed an Act to prevent incompetent persons from conducting the business of druggists and apothecaries, and also the following: —

An Act to regulate the Practice of Medicine and Surgery in the State of New Hampshire.

Be it enacted by the Senate and House of Representatives in General Court convened: —

SECTION 1. Each and every medical society organized under a charter from the Legislature of the State of New Hampshire, shall, at each annual session thereof, elect a board of censors, consisting of not less than three members, who shall hold their office till others are elected; which board shall have authority to examine and license practitioners of medicine, surgery, and midwifery, as provided in subsequent sections of this Act.

SECT. 2. Every practitioner of medicine, surgery, or midwifery, including all persons who, by sign or advertisement, or by any means whatever, offer their services to the public as practitioners of either medicine, surgery, or midwifery, or who, by such sign or advertisement, assume the title of doctor, shall be required to obtain a certificate of some one of the chartered medical societies of the State — either from a county, district (embracing more than a county), or State society, — which certificate shall set forth that said censors have found the person to whom it is given qualified to practise all the branches of medical art mentioned in it; and the certificate shall be substantially in the following form: —

CERTIFICATE.

No.　　　State of New Hampshire, county of　　　This may certify that the undersigned Board of Censors have found　　of　　　in the county of　　and State of　　qualified in the following branches of the medical profession:
and therefore license him to practise said branches within the State of New Hampshire.

　　　　　　　　　　　　　　　　{ Board of Censors
　　　　　　　　　　　　　　　　{ of　　Medical Society.

SECT. 3. Such certificate shall be recorded in a book provided and kept for the purpose by the county clerk of each county in the State, which book shall bear the title and inscription, and shall be styled, the Medical Register of　　county; and the fee for recording the same shall be twenty-five cents.

SECT. 4. Any person to whom a certificate is issued by a board of censors, as herein provided, shall cause the same to be recorded in the medical register of the county in which he actually resides, if a resident of the State; if not a resident of the State, in the county where he obtains such certificate; and, for failure or neglect to record the same within thirty days after its issue, the person so neglecting shall be liable

to a fine of twenty-five dollars; and any person who shall practise medicine, surgery, or midwifery in this State, or who shall sign a certificate of death for purposes of burial or removal, whose aforesaid certificate is not recorded in the manner aforesaid, shall be liable to the same penalties provided in section eight of this Act, for the punishment of persons who shall practise without a certificate.

SECT. 5. The censors of each medical society aforesaid shall, in their discretion, notify all practitioners of medicine, surgery, or midwifery in this State, of the terms and requirements of this Act, and shall require such person so notified to comply therewith within thirty days after such notification, or within such further time as may be allowed by special permission of such censors, not exceeding ninety days.

SECT. 6. Any person, not a resident of this State, shall be required to obtain a certificate from some board of censors in this State, and cause the same to be recorded, as herein provided, before he shall be permitted to practise the medical art within this State.

SECT. 7. Each board of censors shall issue certificates, without fee, to all physicians and surgeons who furnish evidence by diploma from some medical college or university, or by certificate of examination by some authorized board, which shall, after due investigation, satisfy said censors that the person so presenting such credentials has been, after due examination by a legally authorized board, deemed properly and adequately qualified to practise the branches mentioned in such diploma or certificate. Any certificate issued by any board of censors, as herein provided. shall be valid throughout the State, after being duly registered. Said censors shall also have power to revoke or annul any certificate, if, in their judgment, the person holding it has obtained it fraudulently, or has, by crime or misdemeanor, whereof such person shall have been duly convicted, forfeited all right to public confidence.

SECT. 8. It is hereby declared a misdemeanor for any person to practise medicine, surgery, or midwifery, in this State, unless authorized so to do by a certificate as herein provided. And any person found guilty of such misdemeanor shall, for the first offence, be fined not less than fifty nor more than two hundred dollars; for any subsequent offence, not less than two hundred nor more than five hundred dollars; which fine may be recovered by an action of debt for the use of any person who shall sue therefor, or by an indictment.

SECT. 9. No person practising either of the branches of medicine, surgery, or midwifery, within this State, without a certificate as provided in this Act, shall be permitted to enforce, in any of the courts of this State, the collection of any fee or compensation for any services rendered, or medicine or material of any kind furnished, in the practice of any of the branches not mentioned in such certificate.

SECT. 10. This Act shall not be so construed as to apply to the practice of dentistry, nor to those practitioners of medicine who have resided five years in the town or city of their present residence.

SECT. 11. This Act shall take effect from its passage.

[Approved July 2, 1875.]

NEW JERSEY.

Law of 1799, entitled "an Act to provide for the security of the citizens of this State against the introduction of contagious diseases." To prevent evasion of Pennsylvania and New York laws for preventing contagious diseases, Governor shall have power, on complaint of New York or Pennsylvania authorities of vessel infected with malignant disease, and performing quarantine under laws of Pennsylvania or New York, being then in rivers Delaware or Hudson, or waters adjacent to New York City, by proclamation, to forbid all communication by citizens of New Jersey with such vessel, or bringing any goods, merchandise, bedding, or clothing from such vessel to the shores of the State, under penalty of $300 for each offence. And, in 1812, an Act was passed "to prevent the introduction of malignant and other infectious diseases into the city of Perth Amboy," providing for the anchoring of any vessel arriving between last of May and first of October, from ports or places south of a certain line, or from place where yellow or pestilential fever prevails, or on board of which any person shall have died while at a foreign port or on the homeward passage, to be subject to examination and regulations of the Health Officer; and, when latter judges necessary, such vessel shall be unloaded, cleansed, and purified, and may be detained for this purpose twenty days at quarantine after cargo is unloaded, and shall not be permitted, till thus cleansed, to approach nearer to Perth Amboy.

Mayor, Recorder, Aldermen, and Commonalty shall have power to appoint Health Officer or Visiting Physician, whose duty it shall be to visit all vessels arriving from places or under circumstances mentioned in this Act, and report same and condition thereof to the Health Committee; and to direct cleansing, ventilating, and purifying of vessel, at expense of master; and, when so done, to certify same to Health Committee.

Mayor, Recorder, and Aldermen of City of Perth Amboy, for the time being, shall constitute a health committee, and shall perform such duties as shall be necessary to carry this Act into effect; and, on the report of the Health Officer, may grant permit to vessels aforesaid to proceed to Perth Amboy. And the

Board shall have power to forbid intercourse with any such vessel arriving and having on board persons sick of a pestilential or yellow fever, and to prevent persons landing from such vessel.

By Act of March 19, 1874, a commission was appointed " to examine into the present sanitary needs of this State, into any deficiencies in existing laws as to the securement of vital statistics, the abatement of nuisances, or whatever concerns the prevention or mitigation of disease, and also to report such form of general State law as to health as may seem to them desirable."

That the commission be instructed, through a secretary appointed from one of their number, to inquire into the present construction of Health Boards, and as to local health laws, so as to know what general legislation may be needed. "This commission to report to Governor on or before December 1st."

This report has been filed. This year (1877) were passed Acts regulating the practice of pharmacy, the return of statistics of births, marriages, and deaths, to the county Boards of Health; and also the following: —

An Act to establish a State Board of Health.

1. Be it enacted by the Senate and General Assembly of the State of New Jersey, That the Governor shall appoint seven persons, who, together with the Secretary of State and Attorney-General, as *ex officio* members, shall constitute the Board of Health of the State of New Jersey; the persons so appointed shall hold their offices for seven years: provided, that the terms of office of the seven first appointed shall be so arranged that the term of one shall expire each year; and the vacancies so created, as well as all vacancies occurring otherwise, shall be filled by the Governor.

2. And be it enacted, That the Board shall take cognizance of the interests of health and life among the citizens of this State; they shall make sanitary investigations and inquiries in respect to the people, the causes of disease, and especially of epidemics and the sources of mortality, and the effects of localities, employments, conditions, and circumstances on the Public Health; and they shall gather such information in respect to these matters as they may deem proper for diffusion among the people; they shall also make inquiries and reports in reference to diseases affecting animals, and the methods of prevention; they shall appoint a chairman, who shall call meetings as often as every three months, or when requested to do so by three members of the Board; they shall, in the month of December, make report to the Governor of their investigations and opinions during the year ending December 1st,

with such suggestions as they may deem necessary: provided, that the provisions of this Act shall not apply to any city, borough, or township, in which there is a local Board of Health.

3. And be it enacted, The Board shall elect a secretary from their own number, who shall superintend the work prescribed in the law, as the Board may require; the entire expense in prosecuting inquiries and securing the desired information shall not exceed one thousand dollars; and said amount shall be payable by the comptroller on account rendered, and signed by the President and Secretary of the Board, and approved by the Governor.

4. And be it enacted, That this Act shall take effect immediately.

Approved March 9, 1877.

NEW YORK.

The first sanitary legislation in this State was in 1784, — "an Act to prevent the spreading of infectious distempers in this State." This related to quarantine, and was followed by Acts of 1794, 1796, 1797, 1798, and 1800. In the same years, and also in 1799, were passed Acts relating to the port of New York, respecting masters, wardens, pilots, and pilotage, and the landing of foreign poor.

Act of 1801, "to provide against infectious and pestilential diseases," enacts "that there shall continue to be a health office in the city of New York, under the superintendence of three commissioners, who shall consist of a Health Officer (to reside at Staten Island), a resident physician (to reside in city of New York), and one other person (at or near either of said places), as a majority of said commissioners may deem most proper; these commissioners to be appointed by the person administering the government of this State, by and with consent of council of appointment."

The Act provides for the quarantine of vessels, inspection by Health Officer, and affixes penalties, &c. (general quarantine laws).

It provides, further, that physicians shall report cases of pestilential or infectious diseases to Commissioners of Health Office. Latter may order persons so infected to marine hospital.

Hospital at east end of Staten Island to be held by the Commissioners in trust for use of the people of the State and the

purposes specified in this Act. Commissioners to make rules for this hospital, and superintend it.

Commissioners to be compensated, and to account annually to the Comptroller.

They may also make and execute rules and orders for cleansing and scouring the streets, alleys, passages, curtilages, sewers, yards, cellars, vaults, sinks, and other places where filth and corruption collect within said city; and for removing all offensive, noxious, or putrid articles or substances which may be stored or otherwise collected within the said city; all such rules and orders to be reported to, and may be suspended or repealed at any time by, the person administering the government of this State.

The Act further provides, that, "whenever the city of New York, or any part thereof, shall be annoyed or rendered foul by any manufactory, trade, work, or business, producing noxious vapors or highly offensive smells, or by any places where noxious or putrid substances shall be stored or collected within the said city, it shall be the duty of the Commissioners, if in their opinion the Public Health or that of individuals shall be endangered thereby, to go to such place or places, and make due inquiry and strict examination respecting the same; they may have assistance of justice of the peace and constable, who are authorized and required to break open, whenever admittance cannot otherwise be obtained, the doors of such place; and, if the Commissioners shall judge such trade or manufactory or repository to be a *nuisance*, they shall declare it in writing to the owner thereof, and require its removal, abatement, or discontinuance, within a limited time; and, if the order is not complied with, the Mayor or Recorder shall issue warrant to sheriff, commanding him forthwith to cause such nuisance to be removed, abated, or discontinued.

Persons coming from infected places, into any town in the State, to be detained; and, on cause to suspect such persons infected, they may be sent out of the State (not being inhabitants thereof), or kept in such place as will not expose inhabitants.

In cities of Albany and Hudson, the person administering the government of the State, or, in his absence, the Mayor, and in his absence, the Recorder, to be assisted by physician ap-

pointed by "person administering government of State, and council of appointment," shall have jurisdiction in cases of quarantine and infectious diseases; in other towns, two justices of the peace shall have jurisdiction.

Feb. 28, 1804, a supplemental Act was passed, with some additional quarantine regulations; and also certain provisions relating to the packing of salted provisions, and the bringing of cotton in bales into the city of New York, during certain months.

By Act of April 9, 1804, the persons specified in Act of March 30, 1801, in Albany and Hudson, are required to execute that Act.

By Act of April 2, 1806, the Common Council of Albany may appoint so many of their number as shall be thought necessary, to form a Board of Health, to aid the Mayor and Recorder to carry into effect the provisions of the several statutes which are or may be passed, to preserve the health of said city, and to prevent the introduction and spreading of infectious and pestilential diseases in the same; said Board, in conjunction with Mayor and Recorder, to have like powers and authority, for purposes aforesaid, as are possessed by the Mayor and Recorder, and Board of Health, of city of New York.

By Act of March 9, 1805, the powers granted to Commissioners of the Health Office, in regard to cleansing streets, &c., and removing or abating noxious trades, &c., are transferred to the Mayor, Aldermen, and Commonalty; who shall have power to remove all infected persons and things within the city, to such place as may, in their opinion, most conduce to the preservation of the city's health. Penalties to be fixed by by-laws and ordinances.

Said Mayor, Aldermen, and Commonalty may, from time to time, institute a Board of Health for said city, consisting of the Commissioners of the Health Office, and such other persons as they may think proper; and invest said Board with such of the powers of said Mayor, &c., in relation to the Public Health, as they may judge proper; and to enforce compliance with orders of the Board, by infliction of penalties.

Revised Statutes, ch. 14 (1829): "There shall *continue* to be a Board of Health in the city of New York, of which the

Mayor shall be *ex officio* President; and members to be, from time to time, appointed by the Common Council.

Commissioners of Health, as heretofore, are the Health Officer, resident physician, and Health Commissioner of the city.

The Board of Health may, from time to time, appoint consulting physician, and also an "inspector of vessels."

Quarantine provisions enacted; Health Officer to visit vessels, &c.

The Mayor of New York, or President of the Board for the time being, may, by proclamation, declare any place to be infected, and thereafter all vessels from such place shall quarantine for thirty days; and the Board may, in their discretion, prohibit or regulate intercourse between such place and New York City.

This proclamation shall fix period when it shall cease to have effect, which period the Board of Health may extend, if they think the Public Health requires.

Then follow penalties on masters and pilots for violation of quarantine laws.

Board of Health. — Powers of: —

1. To appoint Health Wardens and other officers, to carry law into effect, and rules and regulations of the Board.

2. To authorize such officers to enter and examine buildings, lots, &c., and ascertain condition thereof, and report.

3. To give directions and adopt measures for cleansing and purifying all such places; and to do, or cause to be done, every thing in relation thereto, which, in their opinion, may be proper to preserve the health of the city.

4. To fence up or close streets, passages, &c., if they think the Public Health requires it; and to adopt suitable measures for preventing persons going to part so enclosed.

Duties of: —

1. To adopt measures to prevent spread of contagious disease when resident physician, or Health Commissioner, or consulting physician, reports a case in the city.

2. To forbid communication with house or family so infected, except as necessary through physicians, nurses, &c.

3. To adopt such measures to prevent communication between part of the city infected with fever of malignant or

contagious character, and all other parts, as shall be prompt and effectual.

4. To exercise all such other powers, whenever contagious disease appears in the city, as in their judgment the circumstances of the case and the public good shall require.

The Board, or the Mayor and Commissioners of Health, may, when they judge necessary, cause any cargo, or part of cargo, or any thing within the city that may be dangerous to the Public Health, to be destroyed or removed (to the quarantine ground, or where Board may direct); and may also send person sick of any malignant or contagious fever to the marine hospital, or such other place as Board of Health shall direct.

Commissioners of Health are, from time to time, to communicate to President of Board all reports made to them, and give all information to enable Board to preserve health of the city.

Practising physicians are to report to Mayor, Board, or Commissioners, between May 31 and November 1, in each year, all cases of yellow, bilious, malignant, or other pestilential or infectious fever, under their care, within twenty-four hours after they shall ascertain or suspect the nature of the disease; and, if required by Board of Health, all cases of fever, with specific names and types, and death by fever, within forty-eight hours after such death (with name and type).

Keepers of lodging or boarding houses in New York City, between same days, are to report the name of any one sick in their house with fever, within twelve hours after each case occurs.

The master, owner, or consignee of vessel at wharf shall make like report, within same period, of name of every sick person on board; and no sick person shall be removed therefrom without written permit from Mayor, &c.

Consulting physician and Commissioners shall make report to Board of any practising physician who violates these provisions, on penalty of being suspended.

Then follow provisions as to not packing or repacking certain salted provisions, rags, hides, and skins, south of a certain line in the city, at certain time of the year, under penalty of destruction or seizure and sale. Damaged cotton to be reported.

"Marine Hospital" on Staten Island to be held by Commissioners of Health in trust for the people of the State.

Provisions of this chapter as to time of year may be extended by Mayor, if Board recommend.

It is made the special duty of magistrates, civil officers, and all citizens of the State, to aid the Board and all Health Officers in the performance of their duties.

Then follow provisions for Albany, Troy, Hudson, and the "village" of Brooklyn.

† Revised Statutes (2d ed.), 1836, make it the duty of the Common Council of cities, and trustees of incorporated villages, to appoint Board of Health, and of supervisors, overseers of poor, and justices of the peace of towns, to constitute a Board of Health, and to appoint a competent physician for Health Officer.

These boards are to fix quarantine regulations, to prescribe duties of Health Officer, regulate intercourse with infected places, treatment of emigrants and persons having no residence in the State, and the suppression and removal of nuisances, and make all such other regulations as they shall think necessary for the preservation of the Public Health ; and are to procure suitable places to receive persons under quarantine, and sick of malignant disease, and procure proper attendance, &c., and to publish their regulations.

N. B. These last provisions from † relate to cities, towns, and villages in counties bounded by the Lakes and the Hudson and St. Lawrence, or on any canal.

Other villages and towns may appoint Boards of Health and Health Officers. And the same powers shall belong to them.

Governor may employ agents to go to any part of the State, or the Canadas, to procure information relative to progress of disease and the prevention or treatment thereof, or for any other purpose conducive to the Public Health.

Up to this date, the whole title is superseded by ch. 275, Laws of 1850. See Rev. St. (4th ed.) p. 816, vol. i.

Revised Statutes, New York (4th ed.), ch. xiv. Legislative powers heretofore vested, by any existing law of this State, in the Board of Health of the city of New York, other than as the same are hereinafter modified or altered, shall be vested in the

Mayor and Common Council of the said city of New York; the Mayor and Council so acting to be known as the "Board of Health of the City of New York," ten members necessary for a quorum. Mayor shall be President.

President of Board of Aldermen, President of Board of Assistant Aldermen, Health Officer, Resident Physician, Health Commissioner, and City Inspector shall be Commissioners of Health.

Mayor and Commissioners shall advise Board of Health and City Inspector in regard to matters connected with Public Health.

Health Officer may appoint assistant.

Resident Physician shall visit all sick persons reported to the Board, or to Mayor and Commissioners, and perform such other duties as Board enjoins.

Health Commissioner shall, under direction of the Board, assist the Resident Physician.

Mayor and Commissioner shall meet daily at office of Board of Health, during such part of the year, and at such hours of the day, as Board shall designate.

Board may, from time to time, appoint so many visiting, hospital, and consulting physicians as they may deem necessary, designate their duties, and fix their compensation.

With advice and consent of Aldermen, they may appoint an Inspector of Vessels, who shall, under direction of Mayor and Commissioners of Health, or of Board of Health, perform the duties required of him, and report to Board of Health, or to Mayor and Commissioners of Health.

Article 4 regulates intercourse with infected places.

Mayor of New York may, by proclamation, declare any place infected. Such proclamation shall fix the period when it shall cease to have effect, which period the Board of Health may extend, and publish notice thereof in one or more papers.

Thereafter, vessels from such place shall quarantine for thirty days, or until end of period fixed by proclamation; and Board of Health may prohibit or regulate intercourse by land or water with such infected place; and provide that persons coming into the city contrary to their prohibitions or regulations, shall be conveyed to the vessel, or place whence they last

came, or, if sick, to the Marine Hospital, or such other place as Board of Health shall direct.

Penalties in case masters violate these regulations or persons obstruct the Health Officer, or trespass on quarantine grounds, or hold intercourse with vessel at quarantine, without authority or permission of Health Officer.

Internal regulations to preserve Public Health of city of New York, as follows, viz : —

City Inspector shall have power to appoint, with advice and consent of Board of Aldermen, from time to time, all and so many Health Wardens and other officers as Common Council or Board of Health shall direct, to carry into effect the provisions of this title, and rules and regulations of the Board of Health, the laws and ordinances of the Common Council of said city, and the laws of this State, relating to the Public Health; such Health Wardens and officers to be subject to the supervision and control of City Inspector; and the Inspector shall have power to authorize such officers, at such times as he shall think fit, to enter into, and examine in the day, all buildings, lots, and places within the city, and to ascertain and report condition thereof (as far as public may be affected thereby) to Mayor and Commissioner of Health.

On complaint made to him, Inspector shall notify persons carrying on trade, business, or profession, detrimental to Public Health (or, if he shall so deem, complaint not being made), to show cause before Board of Health, why the same be not discontinued or removed ; this notice to be of not less than three days, except that, in case of epidemic or pestilence, the Board may direct a shorter time, — not less than twenty-four hours. Cause may be shown by affidavit, and order of Board shall be final and conclusive thereon.

Inspector is to give directions and adopt measures for cleansing and purifying all such buildings, lots, and other places; and cause to be done every thing in relation thereto which, in the opinion of Mayor and Commissioners of Health, shall be necessary.

Any person disobeying is liable to arrest, and fine or imprisonment, or both.

Inspector shall also adopt such prompt measures to pre-

vent the spreading of any contagious, infectious, or pestilential diseases, as shall be directed by Mayor and Commissioners of Health, when it shall appear to them that any person within the city is afflicted with disease of that character.

Mayor, Aldermen, and Commonalty of New York City shall have full power and authority to make and pass by-laws and ordinances for the preservation of the Public Health of the city, and for abatement and removal of nuisances.

Board of Health. — Duties of : —

1. To close up streets, &c., if they think the Public Health requires, and prevent persons going within the enclosure.
2. To forbid and prevent communication with house or family infected, except by physician, nurses, &c.
3. To adopt such measures to prevent communication between infected and non-infected parts of city as shall be prompt and effectual.
4. To procure suitable places for the reception of persons sick of any pestilential, contagious, or infectious disease, or procure proper attendance and provision for them (medical and otherwise).
5. To publish and make public their regulations, from time to time.
6. To issue warrants to apprehend and remove persons who cannot otherwise be subjected to their regulations.

Board, or Mayor and Commissioners, may cause any cargo, part of cargo, matter or thing within the city, putrid or dangerous to Public Health, to be destroyed or removed at expense of owner.

Board may send to Marine Hospital, or other places, non-residents sick of such diseases; and shall have power to take possession of, and occupy for temporary hospitals, any building or buildings in the city, during the prevalence of epidemics, paying just compensation for private property so taken.

Mayor and Commissioners shall, from time to time, communicate to Board of Health all reports made to them, and further communicate all information in their power that may better enable Board of Health to preserve the health of the city.

Practising physicians shall, whenever required by Board of Health or Mayor and Commissioners, report to City Inspector

the number of persons attacked with pestilential, contagious, or infectious disease, attended by him for the twenty-four hours next preceding, and number of persons who have died of such disease under his care during the twenty-four hours next preceding, report; and shall report in writing to City Inspector, Board of Health, or Mayor and Commissioners of Health. every patient he has sick with such disease, within twenty-four hours after he ascertains or suspects the nature of the disease.

Keepers of boarding or lodging houses are to report, when required by Mayor and Commissioners of Health, in writing, to City Inspector, Board, or Mayor and Commissioners, the name of every person sick in their houses, within twelve hours after each case shall have occurred.

Masters, owners, or consignees of vessels at wharf to make like report within like time; and no person shall be removed from such vessel without permit from the Board, or the Mayor, or one of the Commissioners.

It shall be the duty of each Commissioner of Health, and of each visiting, hospital, and consulting physician, to make immediate report to the Board of Health, of every practising physician who he has reason to believe violates the above provisions. If such practising physician shall neglect or refuse to perform his duty, the Board shall suspend him from his office, and may affix further penalty. The Board has also certain powers in regard to the packing of provisions, skins, hides, and damaged cotton. Generally, whenever it shall appear to the Board that the provisions of this Act, limited to a certain period of the year, ought to be extended, the Mayor may extend the same by proclamation; and may revoke such extension, if it appears to the Board that the necessity for it has ceased.

Cities and Villages. — The Common Council of any city, and trustees of incorporated village where a Board of Health is not now organized, shall appoint, once in each year, a Board, to consist of not less than three nor more than seven persons, and a competent physician to be Health Officer thereof. Any two justices of the peace, in any town of this State, may, by order in writing, cause non-residents sick of such diseases to be removed to such place of safety within the town as they shall deem necessary for the preservation of the Public Health.

The Supervisor and justices of the peace, or the major part of them, of each town in this State, shall be a Board of Health for such town, for each year, whenever, in the opinion of the majority of such Board, the public good requires it; and they shall appoint some competent physician to be the Health Officer for such town.

Quarantine. — Anchorage near the Marine Hospital, marked by buoys, under direction of the Health Officer. All vessels coming direct from infected place, or on board of which any case of pestilential, infectious, or contagious disease has occurred during the voyage, arising between May 31st and October 1st in any year, shall perform quarantine for at least thirty days after arrival, and at least twenty days after the cargo shall have been discharged; and shall perform such further quarantine as the Mayor and Commissioners of Health may prescribe. The Board of Health, or the Mayor and Commissioners of Health, whenever in their judgment the Public Health shall require, may order any vessel at wharf, or in vicinity, to the quarantine ground or other place of safety, and may require all persons or things introduced into the city from such vessels to be seized, returned on board, or removed to quarantine ground or other place. No infected vessel shall approach within three hundred yards of the city, without consent of the Mayor and two of the Commissioners. Every vessel with passengers is to be detained and examined by the Health Officer; but not to be detained beyond the time necessary for such examination, unless she has had infectious, contagious, or pestilential disease on board during the voyage; and the Health Officer may, in his discretion, cause the persons on board to be vaccinated. The master of every vessel released from quarantine, and arriving at the city of New York, shall, within twenty-four hours thereafter, deliver the permit of the Health Officer at the Mayor's office.

Nothing contained in this Act shall prevent any vessel arriving at the quarantine from again going to sea before breaking bulk.

Pilots to hail vessels entering port, and ascertain as to deaths or sickness on board, and whether contagious or infectious disease existed at port from which she sailed. If yea, pilot is to notify master that his vessel, crew, passengers, and cargo are subject to examination of Health Officer, and to direct him to

anchor at quarantine anchorage, to await further directions of the Health Officer.

Every pilot conducting vessel subject to quarantine into port shall bring her to anchor within the quarantine buoys, and prevent any vessel or boat coming alongside, and prevent any thing on board from being thrown into any other vessel or boat; and give the master a printed copy of this title, when such copy shall have been delivered to him for that purpose; and shall take care that no violation of this title be committed on board, and report such as may be committed, as soon as may be, to the Health Officer.

Health Officer to board vessel subject to quarantine or visitation by him, immediately on her arrival; to inquire as to health of persons on board, and condition of the vessel and cargo, by inspection of the bill of health, manifest, log-book, or otherwise; to examine on oath when vessel is suspected of coming from a sickly port, or having had sickness on board, and report facts and conclusions, and especially the number sick and nature of disease, to the Mayor and Commissioners of Health, in writing.

He shall reside within the quarantine grounds, and have power to —

1. Remove vessel to south of quarantine buoys, and inside Sandy Hook.
2. Cause discharge of cargo.
3. Purify vessel.
4. Prevent persons leaving quarantine, or taking their goods or baggage away within a certain time.

Cargoes judged free from infection may be removed.

Vessel at quarantine shall be designated by colors in her main shrouds.

Mayor and Commissioners of Health of said city shall constitute a Board of Appeal from the Health Officer, with power to grant relief. Their decision to be final.

Internal Regulations (city of New York). — City Inspector shall have power, —

(1.) To appoint (with advice and consent of Aldermen) Health Wardens and other officers; they shall be subject to his supervision and control; they are to carry into effect the provisions of this title, the rules and regulations of the Board of

Health, the laws and ordinances of the Common Council of the city, and the laws of the State, relating to the Public Health.

(2.) To authorize such officers to enter and examine lots, buildings, and places, and ascertain and report to Mayor and Commissioners of Health the condition thereof, so far as the public may be affected thereby, &c., as *ante*.

Commissioners of Emigration. — By Act of 1847 (amended 1851), the masters of vessels arriving at port of New York, from any place out of the State, are to make report to the Mayor, within twenty-four hours after their arrival; stating name, place of birth, last legal residence, age, and occupation of any person, not a citizen of the United States, who shall have landed from such vessel on her last voyage to said port, and who shall have within last twelve hours arrived from any country out of the United States, at any place within United States, and who shall not have paid the commutation money or been bonded, as required by law. The report shall also give statement of all persons landed or permitted to land during last voyage, or put on board any other vessel or boat with intention of landing at New York, or elsewhere within the limits of this State.

Report is to specify particularly the condition of families and individuals, with names, last places of residence, and ages of any who may have died during said last voyage, and also the names and residences of the owner or owners; also, whether any are deaf, dumb, &c., or widows with families and with no means of support, &c.

Mayor, by indorsement on this report, is to require owner or consignee to give a several bond to the people of the State, in a penalty of $300 for each passenger in the report, conditioned to save harmless the Commissioners of Emigration and each and every city, town, or county in the State, from cost incurred for relief or support of the person named in the bond, within five years from date of bond, and for support or medical care of the persons named therein, if received into Marine Hospital or any other institution under their charge; each bond to have two sufficient sureties.

Owner or consignee may commute, by paying $1.50 for every person reported, — the Health Commissioner to pay the money

directly to Chamberlain of New York City; but shall not commute in cases of persons sent from shipboard to Marine Hospital, by Health Officer or Board of Health, for ship fever.

Latter cases Health Officer shall report without delay, to Commissioners of Emigration.

Commissioners of Emigration are to examine condition of passengers arriving in any ship or vessel; and if they find any unable to take care of themselves, and likely to become a care to them or to the city, town, &c., to which they may go, they shall report to the Mayor; and, unless bond has been given as required in previous section, a joint and several one shall be required from owner or consignee.

Penalty for refusing to give bond.

Six Commissioners appointed, — two for two, two for four, and two for six years; with Mayors of New York and Brooklyn, and Presidents of German Emigrant Society and Irish Emigrant Society, *ex officio.*

They shall provide for maintenance of such of the persons for whom commutation money has been paid, or on whose account bonds have been taken, as would otherwise become a charge on any city, town, or county of this State; and shall appropriate the money paid as aforesaid to Chamberlain of New York, which is to be paid out on their warrant, to indemnify, as far as may be, the several cities, towns, and counties proportionably for expenses incurred. And they may, in their discretion, use any part of said moneys to remove said persons to another part of the State, or to another State, or to assist them in getting employment, so as to prevent their becoming a public charge.

Chamberlain to report to Commissioners annually, and latter annually to Legislature.

Marine Hospital is hereby vested in Commissioners of Emigration, for the purpose of receiving persons for whom bonds may be required, or for whom any bond or bonds may have been given, required, or commuted, suffering under any contagious or infectious disease, or other disease preventing immediate removal to more distant hospital, and who shall be sent to such hospital by direction of Health Officer, or under his authority.

Commissioners are authorized to employ a superintendent physicians, nurses, &c., for Marine Hospital, and other hospitals used for quarantine purposes.

Commissioners may require Health Officer to act as physician to the Marine Hospital.

Superintendent of Marine or other hospital to report to Commissioners all cases in hospital of contagious or infectious disease and deaths, or those discharged as cured; to be countersigned by agent of Board of Health. And no such patient shall be discharged or removed without permit in writing from Health Officer.

Commissioners shall receive into Marine Hospital, or other hospital for quarantine purposes, all alien passengers, for whom bonds shall be given or commutation paid, affected with any contagious or infectious disease, and sent to such hospital by authority of Health Officer.

Also, cases of contagious or infectious disease directed to be received by Health Officer, or Board of Health, receiving for latter three dollars per week, to be paid by owner or consignee of vessel in which they shall have arrived, or from which they shall have landed.

In Brooklyn, the Aldermen, or such a number of their body as Common Council shall designate, shall be Board of Health.

Duties. — To consider and act upon any matter requiring their action.

Power and Authority. — Same as New York Board of Health.

Quarantine. — Vessels subject to examination of New York Health Officer not to approach Brooklyn beyond quarantine limits, without such officer's permit, countersigned by President of the Board of Health.

Physicians to report cases of malignant, infectious, or contagious disease to Board, with certificate of name and residence of patient. Board may require affidavit of physician.

Boarding-house keepers may be required to report sick persons.

Permit required from President or one of members of Board for removing sick person into city.

General powers: —
Shall have charge of city hospitals.
1. May prohibit intercourse with infected places.
2. May require vessel suspected of contagion to remove from wharf.
3. May cause infected persons or things to be removed to hospital.
4. May destroy bedding, clothing, putrid meat, &c.

Health Officer. — Shall visit all sick persons reported to Board, and report to Board his opinion of their sickness. Shall visit and inspect vessels coming to city, or within three hundred yards of it, suspected of having infectious or contagious disease on board, or likely to communicate same; and all places in city suspected of containing putrid or unsound provisions, or article likely to communicate disease to inhabitants; and report in writing as to the same, with his opinion as to probability of disease being communicated by them, and file report in office of Board of Health; and shall discharge other duties prescribed by Board.

Other cities and villages: —

Boards of Health. — Same as ch. 324 Laws of 1850, entitled, "An Act for the preservation of the Public Health," with section added, as follows: —

"Any two Justices of the Peace in any town in this State may cause all persons who shall be sick of any infectious or pestilential disease, and not being residents of such town, by an order in writing, to be removed to such place of safety within the town as they shall deem necessary for the preservation of the Public Health."

Passengers arriving at Ports of Entry northerly of Albany. — Same as ch. 431 of Laws of 1847.

Of passengers arriving at ports of entry northerly of Albany (including those on River St. Lawrence, Lake Ontario, Niagara River, and Lake Erie) from any other of United States or foreign country, master is to report within twenty-four hours to Trustees of village, or Mayor or Aldermen of city, or one of Overseers of Poor in care of town; giving name, place of birth, &c., of passengers by his vessel on his last trip, emigrating to States or Territories, not citizens thereof, and who shall not

have executed bond or paid commutation money mentioned in next section.

Master is to give $500 bond, conditioned to pay charges for maintaining such person within five years from date of bond.

Master may commute by paying one dollar for each person.

Superintendents of Poor of counties shall provide for support of persons for whom commutation money is thus paid, and appropriate moneys so received to indemnify cities, towns, and counties of the State for expense incurred for support of said persons.

Statute of 1850, ch. 324, entitled, "An Act for the preservation of the Public Health," supersedes all previous legislation on this subject.

In 1866 was constituted "The Metropolitan Sanitary District of the State of New York," its bounds to be those of the Metropolitan Police District of the State of New York.

Board of Health. — The Governor shall nominate, and, by and with the consent of the Senate, shall appoint four suitable persons, residents of said district; three of whom must be physicians, and one of whom shall be a resident of the city of Brooklyn, who, with the Health Officer of the port of New York for the time being, shall be Sanitary Commissioners in and for said district; and the said Sanitary Commissioners, together with the Commissioners, for any time being, of Metropolitan Police (not exceeding four, and being the present four and their successors), shall constitute a Board of Health for the said Metropolitan Sanitary District, to be denominated "The Metropolitan Board of Health;" any five members of which, at any regularly called or adjourned meeting, shall organize and constitute a quorum for the transaction of business.

This Board shall have power to appoint a "Sanitary Superintendent — to be an experienced and skilful physician — and two Assistant Sanitary Superintendents;" one of the latter to be a resident of Brooklyn, and to principally perform his duties in that city. These officers are to cause the orders of the Board to be executed, and to exercise a practical supervision in respect to inspectors, agents, and other persons exercising authority under this Act. The Superintendent is to make weekly reports of the condition of the Public Health in the district, and of any

causes endangering life or health that have come to his knowledge during the week.

The Board may also appoint and commission such number of "Sanitary Inspectors" as the Board may deem needful, not exceeding fifteen, and from time to time prescribe their duties and fix their salaries. At least ten of these Inspectors shall be physicians of skill and of practical, professional experience in said district; and the others shall be selected with reference to their practical knowledge of scientific or sanitary matters which may especially qualify them for such Inspectors.

Each Inspector shall report twice a week to the Board, in writing, stating what duties he has performed and where; and also such facts as have come to his knowledge, connected with the purposes of this Act, as are deemed by him worthy the attention of the Board, or such as its regulations may require of him.

All the powers heretofore given to any Board of Health or Health Officer, within the said district, are by this Act exclusively conferred upon "the Metropolitan Board of Health," and the members and officers thereof; and no municipal body or other authority in said district shall hereafter create or employ any officer or agent, or incur any expense, under any health laws or ordinances, or in respect of any matter concerning which said Board is by this Act given control or jurisdiction.

The powers of the Board extend to, —

1. The ordering and enforcing repairs of buildings, houses, and other structures.

2. The regulation and control of all public markets (so far as relates to the cleanliness, ventilation, and drainage thereof, and to the prevention of the sale, or offering for sale, of improper articles therein).

3. The removal of any obstruction, matter, or thing in or upon the public streets, sidewalks, or places, which shall be, in their opinion, liable to lead to results detrimental to the public, or dangerous to life or health.

4. The regulation and licensing of scavengers.

5. The prevention of accidents by which life or health may be endangered; and, generally, the abating of all nuisances;

DIGEST OF AMERICAN SANITARY LAW. 399

e. g., the purifying, cleansing, disinfecting, altering, or improving any excavation, erection, vehicle, vessel, water-craft, room, building, place, sewer, pipe, passage, premises, ground, matter, or thing (in said district or adjacent waters), regarded by said Board as in a condition dangerous or detrimental to life or health, and the removal of any substance, matter, or thing being or left in any place (whether public or private), which said Board may regard as dangerous or detrimental to life or health.

The Board is to possess all the authority and be charged with all the duties conferred or imposed on the City Inspector of the City of New York by Act of April 2, 1853, or by any and all Acts relating to births, deaths, or marriages.

The Board shall execute its orders through its own officers, or persons and means engaged by them, or through the Board of Police.

It shall be the duty of the Board to give all information that may be reasonably requested concerning any threatened danger to the Public Health, to the Health Officer of the port of New York, and to the commissioners of quarantine of said port, who shall give the like information to said Board; and said Board and said officer and said quarantine commissioners shall, so far as legal and practicable, co-operate together to prevent the spread of disease, and for the protection of life, and for the promotion of health, within the sphere of their respective duties.

Certain extraordinary powers are conferred upon the Board, as follows, to wit: They shall use all reasonable means for ascertaining the existence and cause of the disease or peril to life or health, and for averting the same throughout said district; and shall promptly cause all proper information in possession of said Board to be sent to the local health authorities of any city, village, or town in this State which may request the same, and shall add thereto such useful suggestions as the experience of said Board may supply. And it is hereby made the duty of said health authorities to supply the like information and suggestions to said Metropolitan Board of Health.

They are also to provide for general and gratuitous vaccination and disinfection, and afford medical relief to and among the poor of said district; and in the presence of great and immi-

nent peril to the Public Health, by reason of impending pestilence (as declared by proclamation of the Governor of the State, and the Board), it shall be their duty to take such measures, and to do and order and cause to be done such acts, and make such expenditures, for the preservation of the Public Health as they may, in good faith, declare the public safety and health to demand, and the Governor of the State shall, in writing, approve.

It shall be the duty of the Board, so far as it may be able without serious expense, to gather and preserve such information and facts relating to deaths, diseases, and health, from other parts of this State, — but especially in this district, — as may be useful in the discharge of its duties, and contribute to the promotion of health or the security of life in the State of New York. And it shall be the duty of all Health Officers and Boards of Health in this State to communicate to said Metropolitan Board of Health copies of their reports, and also such sanitary information as may be useful in said district.

The Board is to keep records, and report in writing to the Governor on or before the first Monday of December in each year, upon the sanitary condition and prospects of said district; and shall hold regular and special meetings as frequently as the proper and efficient discharge of its duties shall require.

It shall be the duty of the Board to aid in the enforcement of, and, so far as practicable, to enforce, all laws of this State applicable in said district to the preservation of human life, or to the care, promotion, or protection of health; this section to include all laws relative to cleanliness, and to the use or sale of poisonous, unwholesome, deleterious, or adulterated drugs, medicine, or food.

The Board is authorized to require reports and information from dispensaries, hospitals, prisons, schools, and all public institutions, and from proprietors and managers of theatres and other places of resort or amusement in said district, concerning matters in respect of which it may need information for the better discharge of its duties in said district.

The "City Inspectors' Department" is abolished.

By Act of 1870, the Metropolitan District Act was repealed, and a Health Department and Board of Health for the metrop-

olis was constituted, which replaced the Metropolitan Sanitary District Board; and, by charter of 1873, a new department was established. Although the Metropolitan Act was repealed in terms, the powers and duties embraced therein were applied to these latter departments, within the city limits.

"Whenever, in any law of this State, any power or duty shall be conferred or enjoined upon any Board of Health, or in relation to the Board of Health of the Metropolitan Sanitary District, except as herein provided, the same shall be applicable to the department hereby created."

The Health Department shall consist of the President of the Board of Police, the Health Officer of the port, and two officers to be called "Commissioners of Health," one of whom shall have been a practising physician for not less than five years preceding his appointment. They shall constitute a Board, which shall be the head of the Health Department.

There shall be two bureaus in this department. The chief officer of one bureau shall be called the "Sanitary Superintendent," who, at the time of his appointment, shall have been for at least ten years a practising physician, and for three years a resident of the city of New York, and he shall be the chief executive officer of said department. The chief officer of the second bureau shall be called the "Register of Records." And in said bureau shall be recorded, without fees, every birth, marriage, and death, and all inquisitions of coroners, which shall occur or be taken within the city of New York. The Board may delegate any portion of its powers to the President or Sanitary Superintendent, to be exercised when the Board is not in session; and may appoint an attorney, at a salary not exceeding $2,500 a year.

The "Sanitary Code" is to be made to conform to this article, and the Health Department may add thereto provisions for the security of life and health in the city of New York. Violations of this Code to be punished as misdemeanors.

By law of 1873, a Department of Health was created in and for the city of Brooklyn, to be known as the "Board of Health of the City of Brooklyn." The management and control of said department shall be vested in a Board of Health, to be composed of the President of the Board of Police, and two practis-

ing physicians who shall have been ten years in practice. They may appoint a Sanitary Superintendent and Sanitary Inspectors, and shall have the powers of the old Board; and shall possess, within the city of Brooklyn, the authority, and be charged with the duties, conferred or imposed on the Metropolitan Board of Health under Act of February 26, 1866, and Acts in amendment thereof, also of two Acts passed May 14 and April 23, 1867, relating to lodging and tenement houses and the abatement of nuisances, respectively.

By Act of 1871, Boards of Health are provided for in Westchester County, and provisions of Metropolitan District Act repealed, so far as relates to towns in that county.

By Act of 1872, a Board of Health and Vital Statistics is established in the county of Richmond.

The law of 1850 (as given *ante*) provides for the creation of Boards of Health in ports and places other than the City of New York; and, as amended by Act of 1867, prescribes their duties as follows, to wit: —

1. To determine the period of quarantine for vessels.

2. To prescribe the duties and powers of the Health Officer, to direct him from time to time in the performance thereof, and to fix his compensation.

3. To make orders and regulations, in their discretion, concerning the place and mode of quarantine, the examination and purification of vessels, boats, and other craft not under quarantine; the treatment of vessels, articles, or persons; the regulation of intercourse with infected places; the apprehension, separation, and treatment of emigrants and other persons who shall have been exposed to any infectious or contagious disease; the suppression and removal of nuisances; and all such other orders and regulations as they shall think necessary and proper for preservation of the Public Health.

4. To regulate and prohibit or prevent communication with infected tenements, places, and persons.

5. To procure suitable places for the reception of persons under quarantine, and those sick with malignant, infectious, or contagious disease; and, where they cannot otherwise be provided for, to procure for them proper medical and other attendance and necessaries.

6. To publish from time to time all such orders and regulations of general obligation as they shall have made, in such manner as to secure early and full publicity thereto; and to make, without publication thereof, such orders and regulations in special or individual cases as they may see fit, concerning the suppression and removal of nuisances, and concerning all other matters in their judgment detrimental to the public health.

7. To issue warrants to sheriff and constables to apprehend and remove such persons as cannot otherwise be subjected to the orders and regulations by them adopted, and, when necessary, to bring to their aid the power of the county.

8. To employ all persons necessary to enable them to carry into effect the orders and regulations they shall have adopted, published, and made, and the powers vested in them by this Act; and to fix their compensation.

By law of 1860 (amended 1865), the trustees of common-school districts and local boards of common school government in the several cities are directed and empowered to exclude children not vaccinated from common schools, until such time as they shall be vaccinated, and may appoint competent physician to vaccinate.

Quarantine, and regulations in the nature of quarantine, in the port of New York, established by law of 1863. The Quarantine Establishment to consist of —

1. Warehouses, wet-docks, and wharves.
2. Anchorage for vessels.
3. Floating Hospital.
4. Boarding Station.
5. Burying-ground.
6. Residence for officers and men.

The only diseases to which quarantine shall apply are yellow-fever, cholera, typhus or ship fever, and small-pox, and any new disease not now known, of a contagious, infectious, or pestilential nature, at the discretion of the Quarantine Commissioners and Health Officer.

Time and manner of quarantine prescribed.

A Health Officer for the port of New York to be nominated by the Governor, and appointed by him, with consent of the Senate, to hold office for two years, and until a successor shall

be duly qualified. He shall be a Doctor of Medicine, of good standing, and of at least ten years' experience in the practice of his profession, and shall also be practically familiar with the diseases subject by this Act to quarantine. It shall be the duty of such officer to reside at place convenient for the boarding of vessels, as the Commissioners of Quarantine may determine, and to have the general superintendence and control of the Quarantine Establishment and the care and treatment of the sick, and to carry out all the provisions of this Act. He may appoint two Assistant or Deputy Health Officers.

The Health Officer, in the presence of immediate danger, shall take the responsibility of applying such additional measures as may be deemed indispensable for the protection of the Public Health. Appeal lies from the decision or direction of the Health Officer to the Commissioners of Quarantine. The Health Officer is to report annually to the Commissioners of Quarantine the condition of the Quarantine Establishment, with the statistics of the institution in detail, and such other information and suggestions in regard to the same as he may deem advisable.

The Commissioners of Quarantine shall be three discreet persons, citizens of the State and residents of the Metropolitan Police District, to be appointed by the Governor, by and with the advice and consent of the Senate, to hold office for three years, and until their successors shall be appointed and qualified. They shall meet daily from May 1 to November 1, in each year, and as often in the other months as, in their judgment, may be necessary. They shall make annually to the Legislature a report of their proceedings and of the condition of the Quarantine Establishment.

By Act of 1866, the Commissioners of Quarantine, in conjunction with the Mayors of New York and Brooklyn, shall constitute a Board of Commissioners to perform the duties and exercise the powers imposed and conferred by this Act. They shall erect a hospital for quarantine purposes, with all necessary docks, wharves, and appurtenances. By Act of 1867, a special port warden is to be appointed, every two years, by the Governor, by and with the advice and consent of the Senate, to act as warden in and for the City of New York in regard to vessels under or subject to quarantine. He shall discharge his duties

under and subject to such regulations as the Health Officer shall see fit to impose for the protection of the Public Health. Parts of Act of 1866 inconsistent with the provisions of this Act are repealed.

The law of 1847 relating to emigrants was amended in some of its details by laws of 1849, 1850, 1851, 1856, and 1869, and some further changes made by laws of 1855 and 1865.

Act of 1856 prescribed the powers and duties of the " Physician of Marine Hospital."

Law of 1873 provided for the appointment by the Governor of six Commissioners of Emigration for the State of New York, — two to hold office for two years, two for four years, and two for six.

The Mayor of New York and the Presidents of the German and Irish Emigration Societies of the city of New York are made additional Commissioners, *ex officio;* but the two last named have no power to vote on the appointment or removal of subordinates.

The said Commissioners shall have all the powers and perform all the duties now imposed upon the Commissioners of Emigration by the Act of 1847 and the various Acts supplementary to and amendatory thereof.

Their successors shall hold office for six years, and until their successors shall be appointed in like manner and qualified. They may appoint an agent in all incorporated cities.

Revised Statutes New York (ed. of 1875), note : " The original title of the Revised Statutes has been entirely abrogated, and various laws have been enacted relative to the Public Health. Ch. 74 Laws of 1866 created a Metropolitan Sanitary District and Board of Health, including the city and county of New York and other counties. Ch. 636 of Acts of 1874 gave powers of this District and Board to a new " Health Department," which is a department of the government of New York City. The situation in which the laws are left by the Acts above referred to is simply deplorable. Nothing less than a systematic compilation and revision can remedy the confusion into which the law has been thrown." A thorough revision of the law on this subject was completed last year (1876.)

NORTH CAROLINA.

1783, 1793, 1802. "Commissioners of Navigation, or any three Justices of the Peace where there are no such commissioners, shall appoint place for vessels to perform quarantine; and the master of vessel having infectious disease on board, or coming from infected port, is to anchor there, and inform the commissioners or justices, who shall direct examination by at least one competent physician; and, on his report and other information, vessel may be required to perform quarantine, and persons on board are to obey orders of the commissioners or justices respecting victualling, purifying the vessel, &c., and intercourse of persons on board with inhabitants of the State.

Property of captain, with vessel and cargo, liable to forfeiture for failure to perform, if failure was by consent of owner or consignee; otherwise, only master to be liable.

Master shall declare, on his arrival, the state of health of himself, crew, and passengers, and of place from which he comes, to commissioners or justices, if they require it.

Commissioners or justices empowered to furnish vessel at quarantine with good, wholesome provisions, for which master, vessel, and cargo shall be liable.

Revised Statutes, 1837 : Vessel coming from infected place, or having infectious disorder on board, or having had such on her passage to this State, shall anchor at quarantine, and there remain till permitted by commissioners or justices to depart; and master or pilot bringing such vessel into port without permit is liable to indictment.

Commissioners may use necessary force to remove to quarantine vessel arriving in violation of this chapter.

Commissioners are authorized to appoint port physicians to attend quarantine station, to inspect vessels, and give certificate of their situation and condition in regard to health of crew and passengers.

Penalties prescribed for passenger or crew breaking quarantine, for persons going on board without permission, and on master for permitting it. Such persons may be ordered to

remain on board by commissioners or justices as long as they think proper.

Persons breaking quarantine may be arrested and sent back, and penalty exacted for landing articles.

Master may be required to declare on oath, on his arrival, the state of health of himself, crew, and passengers, and of place from whence he came.

Commissioners of Navigation of the several seaport towns shall have power to appoint a Harbor Master and Health Officer, and prescribe their duties and authority, and shall have power to make by-laws (not inconsistent with laws and Constitution of State and United States) for better regulation of quarantine.

Commissioners of the several seaport towns, and towns having port of entry where there are no Commissioners of Navigation, shall have powers of latter, and be subject to same duties in relation to quarantine of vessels in the ports of their respective towns.

In seaport towns, all pools of stagnant water and cellars and foundations of houses containing stagnant and putrid water; dead and putrefied animals lying about docks, streets, alleys, vacant lots, &c.; privies with no wells under them; slaughter-houses; docks whose bottoms are alternately wet and dry by ebbing and flowing of the tide; all accumulations of filth in streets, lanes, alleys, and gutters; and all accumulations of vegetable and animal substances undergoing putrefactive fermentation; are declared common nuisances, provocative of offensive vapors and noxious exhalations, the causes of diseases, and ought to be restrained, regulated, and removed.

Owners of lots in seaport towns shall keep them drained from June to October; and Commissioners may remove nuisances at expense of owner, if latter fails to.

Officers of police in incorporated towns shall adopt precautionary measures to prevent introduction of contagious disease raging elsewhere.

Powers of Commissioners of seaport towns or of Navigation not impaired by latter provisions.

County Commissioners and Commissioners of incorporated towns may establish hospitals for the county and towns, respectively, and make new regulations and by-laws to prevent

spread of contagious and infectious diseases, and for taking care of the afflicted, (not inconsistent with laws of the State).

By Act of 1868, quarantine is established at mouth of Cape Fear River.

Governor is to designate some physician of experience as Medical Quarantine Officer for this station, who shall prescribe regulations, and advertise them, make monthly report of receipts and disbursements, and pay over all moneys to State Treasurer. He shall be removable at pleasure of Governor.

A hospital shall be established at nearest convenient station on the shore, for accommodation of sick persons directed to be removed there by the Medical Quarantine Officer, from vessels, for better nursing and attendance. Medical Officer shall employ attendants and purchase food.

Vessel subject to inspection shall pay fee of $5, and for sick persons taken to hospital not exceeding $3 per day.

Duty of pilots to bring vessels to the visiting station, as required from time to time by the Quarantine Officer; and they shall not take any vessel subject to quarantine or visitation past the station, till released by the Quarantine Officer. Penalty on pilot and master for disobeying quarantine regulations.

Quarantine Medical Officer may issue warrant for arrest of any person violating quarantine; and have him, without delay, before competent jurisdiction for trial.

OHIO.

Law as amended by Act of May 1, 1854.

City Council had power to establish a Board of Health; to invest it with such powers and impose upon it such duties as shall be necessary to secure the city and the inhabitants thereof from the evils of contagious, malignant, and infectious diseases; provide for it proper organization, and the election or appointment of the necessary officers thereof; and make such by-laws, rules, and regulations for its government and support as shall be required for enforcing the prompt and efficient performance of its duties and the lawful exercise of its powers.

City Council also had power to seize and destroy any tainted

or unsound meat or other provisions. (The above appears to have been the first legislation on the subject in this State.)

By Act of 1867, entitled "An Act to create a Board of Health in any city, and to prevent the spread of diseases therein," the City Council has power to create such board, to be composed of seven (7) members; viz., the Mayor, who shall be President *ex officio*, and six (6) to be appointed by Council.

Term of office, three years. Members to serve without compensation.

Majority a quorum.

Board shall have power, —

To appoint a Health Officer, clerk, as many ward or district physicians as they may deem necessary for the proper care of the sick and poor, and such other persons as are needful; and to define their duties and salaries. Such appointees to serve during pleasure of the Board.

Council may grant to Board power to abate and remove nuisances, assessing cost and expense on the property (assessment to become a lien); or cause owner of premises to remove same.

To regulate construction and arrangement of water-closets and privy-vaults, and the emptying and cleansing of such vaults.

To create a complete and accurate system of registration of births, deaths, and interments occurring in or near the city, for purposes of legal and genealogical investigation; and to furnish facts for statistical, scientific, and, particularly, for sanitary inquiries; when complaint is made, or reasonable belief exists, that infectious or contagious disease prevails in any locality or house, to visit and make all necessary investigation by inspection, and, on discovering such disease to exist, to send person or persons so diseased to the pest-house or hospital.

Council may grant power to make and pass all such orders and regulations as they from time to time deem necessary and proper for Public Health and prevention of diseases, which, when adopted, shall have force and effect of city ordinances.

What may be declared a Nuisance. — Any building, erection, excavation, premises, business, pursuit, matter, or thing, or the sewerage, drainage, or ventilation thereof, whenever in opinion

of the Board it is, in whole or in part, in a condition or in effect dangerous to life or health.

Board may order it to be removed, abated, suspended, altered, or otherwise improved or purified; such order to be served on owner, agent, occupant, or tenant: and parties interested may have hearing, when Board may make a new or modified order, or reaffirm the old, and require its execution.

Mayor may detail policemen as the "Sanitary Squad," whenever, in opinion of the Board of Health, the Public Health and sanitary condition of city require. This squad shall be subject to exclusive control and direction of said Board, for enforcement of proper sanitary measures and promotion of the Public Health.

Board may take measures, and supply agents, and afford inducements and facilities for general and gratuitous vaccination and disinfection; and may afford medical relief among poor of city, as in its opinion protection of Public Health may require; and, during prevalence of any epidemic disease, may provide temporary hospitals for such purposes.

Board shall make annual report, in writing, to City Council, on the sanitary condition and prospects of the city; and such report shall set forth generally the statistics of deaths, and the action of the Board, its officers and agents; and may contain other useful information; and shall suggest any further legislative action deemed proper for the better protection of life and health.

Any persons violating provisions of this Act, or order of Board, or Law or Ordinance therein referred to, or who shall obstruct or interfere with execution of order of Board, or wilfully and illegally omit to obey such order, shall be deemed guilty of misdemeanor, and subject to fine or imprisonment, or both.

All authorities, duties, and powers heretofore given for preserving or protecting life or health, or preventing disease, conferred on Board of Health.

By Act of April 13, 1867, provisions of this Act are extended to any incorporated village, whenever the council of such village shall by ordinance adopt said Act and agree to be governed by its provisions.

By Act of 1869, the Board is empowered to restrain person of liberty who is found afflicted with infectious or contagious disease, and send to pest-house or hospital until danger of infection or contagion has ceased.

By Act of 1872, Boards of Education have authority to make and enforce rules for vaccination in public schools, and to prevent spread of small-pox therein; and Board of Health, Town Council, or trustees of township, on application of Board of Education, are to provide means, at public expense, without delay.

Act of 1874 gives Boards of Health powers in abating nuisances, and over the registration of births, marriages, and deaths. Physicians and householders are to give notice to the Board of cases of infectious or dangerous disease.

The Board may appoint "sanitary police," and inspectors of milk and meat, and market-masters, and as many persons as are necessary to carry out the provisions of this Act, and define their duties.

By Act of 1875 (amending Act of 1869), cities and incorporated villages may establish Boards of Health, may invest them with powers, and prescribe their duties.

OREGON.

1872. Bringing animals infected with contagious disease into State forbidden. Animals so infected to be kept within enclosure, secure from contact with other domestic animals. (Does not repeal Act of 1862, amended 1865).

Act of 1864. Any person wilfully and wrongfully committing act which grossly disturbs Public Health, if no punishment is expressly prescribed therefor, shall, on conviction, be punished by fine or imprisonment.

Quarantine (Act of 1870). — Governor to appoint Health Officer, to live at Astoria, who shall be a graduate of a medical college, and whose duty it shall be to board and take charge of every ship and vessel arriving from sea, which shall have on board any person or goods infected with contagious disease, or shall have had any such infection on board during the voyage, or which

shall be in such condition by reason of bad health of passengers on board, or filthiness of ship, or decaying state of cargo, or other cause, as to endanger health of inhabitants of State.

Pilot to anchor vessel in bad sanitary condition, or which he suspects capable of propagating disease, below Smith's Point, and give immediate notice to Health Officer.

Health Officer, when he goes on board, shall raise red flag at mainmast, which shall suspend all intercourse with shore, except by his permission.

He shall then proceed, by personal inspection and examination of witnesses sworn by him, to ascertain if there be cause for detention. If he finds contagious disease or infected persons or cargo, or believes vessel likely to propagate disease if allowed to go into port, he shall cause her to anchor at safe and convenient place, to be designated by him; and to be subjected to such cleansing and renovation, and cargo and hold to such ventilation and other treatment, as he deems necessary for their purification; and shall cause sick or infected people to be subjected to such sanitary treatment, on ship or shore, as he thinks necessary for their speedy recovery.

While under his flag, he shall give all his time and care to ship without charge.

Health Officer also appointed at Coos Bay, with same duties.

PENNSYLVANIA.

Act of 1818 established quarantine regulations, providing for anchoring and examination of vessels arriving in the river Delaware from foreign port or place, and bound for Philadelphia, between June 1 and October 1; prohibiting communication with shore before health certificate is obtained.

The lazaretto physician and quarantine master are to board ship, and examine ship, crew, passengers, cargo, and baggage; putting questions, and demanding answer under oath, if necessary.

Health certificate given, if ship has not come from infected place, nor had the disease on board on last voyage, and if cargo does not appear infected.

This certificate to be presented at Health Office in Philadelphia within twenty-four hours after arrival.

But, if it appears that she has come from infected place, she may be required to perform quarantine, in discretion of Board of Health, for not more than twenty days.

Letters, when purified, to be transmitted to Health Officer in Philadelphia, who is to deposit them in post-office.

Board of Health shall thereupon determine on measures of purification, which shall be carried on under inspection of lazaretto physician and quarantine master.

At expiration of quarantine, certificate to be given.

Vessel may be detained longer time, if Board of Health deem necessary.

Penalties enacted for deceiving Health Officers, neglecting to present certificate, or refusing to comply with quarantine regulations.

Vessels from foreign port, having touched at domestic port, subject to same regulations.

Persons and goods from foreign ports where plague or malignant disease prevails, not to enter county of Philadelphia or Delaware without permission of Board of Health.

Board of Health to regulate communication with places where malignant disease prevails.

Port physician to examine suspected cases of infection on ships or vessels at port of Philadelphia; and may order them removed to lazaretto, or other safe place specified by Board of Health; and shall report state of vessel, cargo, and crew to the Board, who shall direct measures for their purification and restoration of health.

He shall also examine vessels not previously examined at the lazaretto, and report to Board in cases of suspicion.

Health office to be kept open daily to receive certificates and bills of health.

Sick persons to be maintained at the lazaretto; and persons escaping to be apprehended, and confined for not more than three months.

Penalty for refusing to obey directions of physician or quarantine master.

Board of Health may order vessel appearing to be infected

414   APPENDIX.

and dangerous, to the lazaretto, notwithstanding its certificate of health.

Pilots bringing up infected vessels, to remain at lazaretto.

Communication with infected places in America to be regulated by the Board.

By Act of 1821, from June 1 to October 1, vessels laden with vegetables, fish, or hides, not to be unloaded at Philadelphia without permit from Board of Health.

Master or owner of cargo discharged at Philadelphia to give notice within forty-eight hours to Board, that they may examine condition of hold, ballast, and limbers of the vessel, and shall permit such examination

Board may direct her to be cleansed.

By Act of 1824, ships arriving at Philadelphia with small-pox on board, subject to same rules as provided by Act of 1818 in relation to contagious diseases.

General Health Law of 1818 (*ante*) shall be taken and construed as if the words "small-pox" had never occurred therein.

By Act of 1848, vessels not to leave lazaretto without security for expense.

By original Act (1818), penalties are enacted for obstructing (wilfully or knowingly) the Board of Health, or any of its members, and for assaulting members or officers.

By Act of 1852, removal of church burial-grounds, or remains of deceased persons, is made subject to approbation of the Board of Health.

By Act of 1830, it is made the duty of Board of Health to file claims for removal of a nuisance, in District Court of city and county of Philadelphia.

Acts of 1860 and 1870 provide for registration of births, marriages, and deaths in cities of Philadelphia and Pittsburg, respectively, and making it the duty of clergymen, magistrates, physicians, undertakers, sextons, &c., to report the same to the Health Officer.

St. 1867 prohibits occupants of houses in Philadelphia, other than the owners thereof, from throwing rubbish into privy-wells.

St. 1869 regulates the practice of medicine in certain counties.

By Law of 1872, Board of Health appointed for city of Harrisburg, whose duty it shall be to have all objects which may have a tendency to endanger the health of the citizens removed or corrected, as they shall deem necessary for the health of the citizens; and the City Council may provide by ordinance for the carrying into effect of the orders and regulations of the Board.

Duty of the police to inquire into nuisances, and report to Board.

All matters relating and appertaining to the health of the city to be referred to this Board.

By Act of same year (1872), Health Law of city of Pittsburg is revised and amended, so as to authorize Board to provide lazaretto and hospital, to make rules and appoint physicians, officers, and servants; and making it the duty of the Board to visit persons infected with contagious diseases, and remove them to hospitals, and to place notice in large letters on houses where there is small-pox.

Persons are prohibited from throwing filth or offensive matter into streets, or allowing same to remain on their premises.

Physicians to report to Board cases of infectious disease under their care.

Persons sick with contagious disease not to be turned into street, but reported to Board of Health.

The physician of the Board shall, —

1. Report to Board the prevalence of any epidemic, contagious, or infectious disease, or other causes, which, in his opinion, are likely to be detrimental to the general health.

2. To keep sufficient supply of vaccine, and see that all persons, so far as he has it in his power, are vaccinated; especially those in the vicinity of small-pox.

3. On being informed of introduction or existence of any contagious or infectious disease in the city, to inquire immediately into the facts, and report them to Board, and see that orders of Board are obeyed so far as practicable.

4. To attend meetings of Board, and report all cases where sick person has not been properly attended to, and all other matters which he may deem important, and give such informa-

tion as Board may desire in relation to the sanitary condition or regulation of the city, so far as he is able to do so.

5. To examine, at request of Board or Health Officer, boats, vessels, cars, and other vehicles coming into city of Pittsburg, supposed to have infected persons on board, and advise the Health Officer what disposition shall be made of the same; and perform such other duties as Board of Health shall hereafter prescribe; and make a monthly report to Board of Health of his transactions, together with such suggestions as experience may point out as calculated to promote the general sanitary condition of the city.

Board may order vaccination, and in case of pestilence or epidemic existing or impending, or when sanitary condition of city warrants it, shall " take such measures, and do and order and cause to be done such acts for the preservation of the Public Health (though not herein or elsewhere authorized) as it may, in good faith, declare the public safety and health demand."

Board shall make rules and regulations for government of quarantine or health of city as they, from time to time, shall deem necessary; and physician or Health Officer in charge of any quarantine shall have power to make and enforce necessary regulations for its management, and persons in quarantine, and police and others in and about quarantine, shall carry out and obey the same.

Masters of vessels, railroad conductors, &c., shall not knowingly bring into the city any person having contagious disease; and all vessels, cars, and public conveyances shall stop at quarantine station, and not leave without permit of Board of Health.

Penalty for aiding in violating Act or resisting Board, and on captains of vessels and others for violating Act.

Health Officer to carry out orders of Board, to examine city thoroughly from time to time, and cause nuisances to be abated; and shall have power to enter.

Further, to visit and examine persons reported to him as sick or supposed to be sick with infectious or pestilential disease; and, with advice of physician of Board and consent of attending physician, cause them to be removed to hospital, or other safe and proper place, as directed by said physician, and provide them

with proper nurses and attendance, at their own expense, if they can pay, if not, at expense of the city.

Regulations as to keeping vaults clean, and removing dead animals within a specified time (six hours).

Board to elect meat-inspector each year.

"Rendering" establishment not to be in city, unless measures are adopted for preventing unwholesome and disagreeable odors, as Health Officer may direct.

All dwellings to be provided with sufficient drain and privy by the owner or occupant.

Penalty for exposing to sale unwholesome meat, and permitting establishments or premises to become offensive.

Board shall employ sufficient force, under control of Health Officer, to carry out this Act, and thoroughly examine city, and report violation of health laws.

Board may cause nuisance to be summarily abated, as they may direct, and may employ scavengers to collect offal and swill.

Same year (1872). City Council of Williamsport shall annually appoint a Board of Health, — one person from each ward, at least two of them to be practising physicians. It shall have power, and it shall be their duty, to make all needful regulations to prevent introduction and spread of infectious or contagious disease, by regulation of intercourse with infected places, and separation and treatment of persons who have been exposed, and by abating and removing nuisances prejudicial to the Public Health; and Board shall have power to make all such other reasonable regulations as they think necessary for preservation of the Public Health.

Board may have person sick with contagious or infectious disease sent to city hospital, if attending physician certifies it is necessary for preservation of Public Health.

Practising physicians to report forthwith to Board all cases of contagious or infectious disease coming under their care.

Board may enter premises and examine nuisances, and abate the same.

Persons not to clean cesspool or privy without permit.

Board has power to register deaths and burials, and employ persons to carry this Act into effect.

It shall publish regulations from time to time.

Penalty for violating regulations of Board or obstructing it in performance of duties.

Laws of 1873. — Town Council, borough of Carlisle, shall establish Board of Health of five (5) members; a majority to be a quorum.

The Board shall have power, and it shall be their duty, to make all needful regulations to prevent introduction and spread of contagious or infectious diseases, by the apprehension, separation, and treatment of infected persons, and those who shall have been exposed thereto; to abate and remove nuisances or causes deemed prejudicial to health of borough; to provide and fit up public hospitals; and to make such rules, orders, and regulations as may be deemed proper for the controlling government and management of said hospital, and appoint such physicians, officers, and servants as may be necessary to attend the same; and to appoint a Health Officer to visit and examine all sick persons reported to him or to Board, and laboring or supposed to be laboring under any infectious or pestilential disease; and under advice of Board and attending physician, if any, cause their removal to hospital, and provide with attendance at their own expense, if they can pay, and, if not, at expense of county.

Board shall publish its rules and regulations, from time to time, in such manner as to secure early and full publicity thereto: and shall employ persons to carry this Act and their rules and regulations into effect.

Penalties for violating Act, or orders of Board.

Same year. Common Council of Harrisburg to elect four members of Board of Health. Repealed.

Vacancies to be filled by majority of remaining members.

The Board shall establish such regulations for promoting and preserving the health of the inhabitants, and obtaining information and statistics relative thereto, as they may deem necessary; and shall provide all books, blanks, &c., and cause to be inflicted such fines for non-compliance with their rules as they may deem proper, and shall appoint a secretary and agent to enforce the regulations of the Board.

Expense to be paid out of city treasury.

Same year. Council of borough of Lebanon shall appoint Board of Health, — one citizen from each ward, majority a quorum.

Duties and Powers of Board. — To have all objects which may have a tendency to endanger the health of the citizens removed or corrected, as they shall deem necessary; to mark infected houses with flags; to provide for the burial of persons deceased with infectious or contagious disease; to cause any person infected with contagious or infectious disease to be removed to a hospital to be provided by the directors of the poor of the county, at expense of county, away from the borough limits, provided such removal can be made without danger to life of patient; to provide regulations imposing on physicians practising in the borough the duty of reporting to the Board all persons (with residence) afflicted with contagious or infectious diseases, and to make all such other reasonable regulations as they shall think necessary for preservation of the Public Health; and, in order to carry regulations of Board into practical operation, the council of the borough shall pass all ordinances necessary, and shall have power to impose penalties for violation or neglect.

Board of Health shall report to the Council at least every three months (oftener, if requested by Council) the sanitary condition of the borough, and such other matter as Council may request.

By Act of same year, Board of Health of the city of Reading established and made a body corporate, seven in number; no member to be member of Council of city. No limit of years as to eligibility.

Board shall annually appoint a Health Commissioner, who shall perform all services required of him by Board, and in manner required by Board, and shall attend all meetings of said Board.

They may make all needful rules and regulations to prevent introduction and spread of infectious and contagious diseases, by regulation of intercourse with infected places, by arrest, separation, and treatment of infected persons, and persons who have been exposed to infectious or contagious disease, and by abating and removing all nuisances which they

shall deem prejudicial to the Public Health; they shall enforce vaccination, mark infected houses or places, and make all such other regulations as they shall deem necessary for preservation of the Public Health.

They shall have power, with consent of Council, in case of prevalence, or reasonable ground to apprehend prevalence, of any contagious or infectious disease in the city, to establish one or more hospitals, as they shall deem circumstances to require; and to make provisions and regulations for such hospitals.

All physicians practising in the city shall report to Secretary of Board name and residence of all persons coming under their professional care, afflicted with such contagious or infectious disease as Board may, in their rules and regulations, designate, under penalty.

Board may enter on premises to examine and abate nuisances; and Health Commissioner and his subordinates and workmen shall execute orders of Board, under penalty.

Board may employ persons to carry Act and their rules and regulations into effect.

Board to report to Council, at least every three months (and oftener, if required), the sanitary condition of the city, and such other matters as Council may request.

Board may cause registration of deaths (with causes) and burials; and may enforce rules regarding same, by penalties.

Cesspools not to be cleansed without license from Board.

Penalties for violating, or refusing or neglecting to obey, any regulation or order of Board made in pursuance of powers conferred by this Act, and for obstructing Board or Commissioner or servants in performance of duties.

Board shall publish regulations, from time to time, so as to secure early and full publicity.

Act of same year as to city of Pittsburg. Penalties provided for neglecting to provide dwellings with drains and privies; and for selling meat unfit for food, and adulterated milk, or milk from diseased cows.

By law of 1873, Chief Burgess and Town Council of borough of York are authorized to appoint a "Health Officer" of borough, to be a competent person and educated physician.

He shall exercise a general supervision over health of bor-

ough, advise Chief Burgess and Town Council in regard to measures which he shall deem it advisable to adopt to preserve health of borough, and perform all duties properly belonging to his office which shall be imposed on him by the Chief Burgess and Town Council.

Duty of Burgess and Council, under his advice or otherwise, to have all objects which have a tendency to endanger health of the citizens removed or corrected; to mark in which contagious or infectious disease exists; to provide for burial of dead from such disease, and separate treatment of those sick therewith, and provide for removal to county hospital (directors of poor to receive and provide for such, under supervision and by order of Health Officer); to enact ordinance requiring physicians to report; to provide vaccine for Health Officer, and for free vaccination of poor when deemed advisable by Health Officer; and, generally, to make such ordinances and regulations as may be deemed by Health Officer, Burgess, and Town Council necessary or proper for preservation of health of people of borough.

Burgess and Council shall have power to enforce obedience to all orders, regulations, and ordinances adopted by them in pursuance of this Act, by imposing fine.

Act of 1873 provides for a Board of Health in the city of Allegheny, to be appointed by the presidents of councils; and for a City Physician and Health Officer, to be elected by the councils and Board respectively.

By Act of the same year (1873), the City Councils of any city of the third class, in which there does not now exist a Board of Health organized according to law, shall have power to create a Board of Health, which shall, in their turn, have power to appoint a Health Officer, clerk, and ward or district physicians. The Board has general powers in the matter of nuisances, construction of water-closets, registration of births, &c. Mayor shall detail "sanitary police" whenever deemed necessary by the Board.

In 1876 was passed an Act requiring registration of births and marriages; making it the duty of clergymen, magistrates, physicians, and midwives to report the same, and of the Boards of Health in cities to furnish books for registration, with penalties for neglect.

The Boards of Health have power to make all rules and regulations for carrying the provisions of this Act into effect.

RHODE ISLAND.

As early as 1743 and 1748, and again in 1798, was re-enacted " An Act to prevent the spreading of the small-pox and other contagious sickness in this State, by which no vessel infected shall anchor within one mile of any landing-place, without license from Governor or Lieutenant-Governor; or, in their absence, from one or more assistants of this State; or, in his or their absence, from two or more justices of the peace or wardens of town where vessel arrives."

Master of such vessel to hoist and keep his colors in his shrouds.

Person coming on shore from such ship, without license, may be sent back or confined on shore.

And the officers aforesaid (Governor, &c.) are to send a physician or suitable person to examine state of vessel and report; and Town Council are empowered and directed to send suitable persons on board to secure such vessel, and effectually prevent any communication therewith.

Infected persons to be sent to hospital, or confined on board.

Goods imported in such vessel to be cleaned at expense of owners.

Also, all goods imported *by land* from infected place.

Such goods clandestinely imported, and not cleansed or aired by order of Town Council, are to be forfeited.

Persons coming from infected place in Massachusetts or Connecticut into this State, within ten days after leaving such place, subject to penalty.

Town Council may appoint person to guard ferries and places; " to examine on oath all persons suspected to transgress this law; and, on reasonable cause of suspicion, to bring such offenders before justices of the peace or wardens, that they may be dealt with according to law."

Tavern-keepers are to give notice of infected lodgers to next assistant, justice of the peace, or warden of town where they

dwell; and if the disease be pronounced contagious, after examination by physician or other skilful person, they are immediately to set a proper guard to prevent the spreading of the infection, and to summon the Town Council, who are authorized to remove the sick person, and to confine all persons suspected of having taken the distemper until they are recovered and cleansed, or have performed a suitable quarantine.

Assistants, justices, or wardens, with the Town Council, are empowered, when contagious disease breaks out in any family or house, to remove the sick to the hospital or other convenient place, in order to prevent the spread of the infection, or to place a guard round the house, as to them shall seem necessary.

Infected houses not to be entered without license.

Penalty for wilfully spreading contagious disease. Persons suspected of so doing may be committed.

Penalty on physicians, surgeons, and other officers for refusing or neglecting to perform his duty.

Town Councils may permit inoculation in their towns, under regulations and restrictions to be made by them.

They are also fully authorized to make and prescribe such orders and regulations as they may deem prudent and advisable for the preservation of the health of the inhabitants, and annex penalties for breach. They may adopt such measures as they shall deem effectual for the removal of nuisances or other causes injurious to the health of the inhabitants; and sheriff, town sergeants, and constables are to execute their orders.

Health Officer. — Governor may appoint, when occasion may require, a Health Officer at every port where he thinks necessary, whose duty it shall be, under the direction of the Governor, to visit all vessels suspected of having contagion on board, and to carry into effect the provisions of this Act.

1822. If person sick with malignant or infectious disease cannot be removed without danger to his life, or if the disease has so spread, that, in judgment of the Town Council, the atmosphere has become so contaminated as to endanger the lives of persons in neighborhood, Town Council may notify latter to remove within three days, and Council may remove any person remaining.

St. 1806, 1816, 1822. Town Councils, *ex officio*, made Boards

of Health, with power to make orders and regulations to protect towns from contagious and infectious disease, to make regulations relative to quarantine, to appoint place where vessels shall anchor, and appoint a sentinel to hail vessels arriving; and, if he finds it subject to quarantine, to direct commander to come to anchor within quarantine limits, and to remain there till visited by the Health Officer.

Penalty for refusing to anchor there, and for leaving vessel subject to quarantine, without permission of Health Officer or Town Council.

Special penalties as to entering town of Providence or village of Pawtuxet, from vessel under quarantine, until visited, and permission given by Health Officer or Town Council.

Towns and Town Councils may appoint Health Officer for purposes aforesaid, to be accountable to Town Council.

Quarantine rules to be published.

Town Council of Newport may appoint a Board of Health to have duties and exercise powers of Council during period for which Council is appointed, for preservation of the health of the inhabitants.

Whole subject re-enacted in 1844 and 1872, with the addition of an Act relating to contagious disease among cattle; providing for appointment by the Governor of a Board of Cattle Commissioners, who may prohibit introduction of cattle into the State, and shall endeavor to acquire full information in regard to any contagious disease among cattle near borders of State, and publish and circulate the same at their discretion, and shall examine particular cases and report for benefit of the public. They may make regulations for prevention, cure, and extirpation of such disease.

Regulations of Commissioners to supersede those of towns.

Penalty for selling diseased cattle, or milk from the same.

By General Statutes (1872), Town Councils and Aldermen are *ex officio* Boards of Health. They may make regulations for the preservation of health, the prevention and abatement of nuisances, the promotion of cleanliness, and the removal of causes and prevention of contagious disease, by removing inhabitants, or forbidding or regulating ingress and egress, and, in case of seaports, by prescribing and regulating quarantine.

Town Council to provide for removal of nuisances; may designate places for slaughtering animals.

No boiling of bones, depositing filth, keeping swine, or slaughtering cattle, except in places designated by Town Council; nor expressing oil from fish.

Town Councils may prohibit burials in thickly populated or compact parts of any town, and may make by-laws and ordinances relating to the same; may designate places for manufacture of articles deleterious to health of neighborhood, and have power to regulate and control construction and location of places for keeping swine, privy-vaults, sinks, sink-drains, sink-spouts, cesspools, stables, and time and manner of removing manure therefrom, or from privy-vaults or slaughter-houses, and for driving animals through the highways.

Quarantine. — Penalty for coming by land from infected places.

Town Councils to appoint persons to examine those so coming.

Housekeepers to give notice of small-pox in their houses; and the Town Council shall thereupon make examination, and guard the house, or remove the sick, and subject suspected persons to quarantine.

Penalty enacted for spreading infectious disease, and for neglect of duty by physicians, surgeons, and others.

Persons residing near infected place may be removed.

The Town Council shall provide for gratuitous vaccination.

SOUTH CAROLINA.

1784. No vessel coming into harbor or port to pass the forts or places appointed by the Governor for examination of such vessels; nor shall any person be suffered to land from any such vessel before she shall be examined by some person to be appointed for that purpose. Pilots subject to penalty of £100 for violating these rules. Commanding officer of fort, or other person appointed by the legislature or executive, shall cause captain of vessel to declare on oath concerning condition of vessel, health of place sailed from, and condition of crew since

leaving port. And if he apprehends, or has reason to believe, that any infectious distemper (except small-pox) is on board, or that crew are, or place sailed from was, infected with any such malignant disorder, he shall stop such vessel from proceeding further into port, and prevent any of her crew from landing, until the pleasure of the Governor or Commander-in-chief is known, who shall thereupon cause vessel and crew to be examined by one or two experienced physicians, and, if deemed necessary, shall cause them to perform quarantine, to prevent such distemper from spreading in this State.

Crews performing quarantine to obey orders of Governor or Commander-in-chief in regard to victualling, purifying, and cleansing ship, and intercourse with mainland. Penalty for going on board without leave.

Vessels arriving from Mediterranean and Levant, and places where plague is frequent, shall exhibit proper bill of health, and shall be admitted after performing quarantine for such time as Governor or Commander-in-chief shall direct, and, after examination, prescribe.

Governor is to have pest-houses and warehouses erected on Sullivan's Island, and on some island adjacent to each trading port in this State, for purposes mentioned in this Act; and to erect small fort in each harbor of the State, to stop and examine vessels.

Warehouses to be used for airing cargoes, when required.

In consequence of removal of seat of Government from Charleston to Columbia, powers vested in Governor relating to quarantine are vested in intendant and wardens of city of Charleston, at all times when Governor shall be absent from the city, and in Commissioners of Streets in Beaufort and Georgetown.

Then follow enactments relative to pest-houses and Commissioners appointed to erect the same.

Officers intrusted with the execution of quarantine laws to have power to board by force and detain any vessels used in violating or attempting to violate any of said laws.

Such vessels may be fired upon and detained by force of arms.

1797. Governor or Commander-in-chief authorized to provide

boats and men to enforce quarantine laws, and to arm men (if requisite) with State firearms.

Quarantine (1869). — Governor and Health Officer of Charleston authorized to establish quarantine hospital on Morris Island.

Health Officer and deputies to be stationed at Sullivan's Island or Fort Johnson; anchorage ground at Georgetown, Charleston, and Hilton Head (including Beaufort), fixed.

All vessels subject to quarantine to anchor there immediately on arrival, subject to examination.

Vessels subject to *quarantine* are: those arriving from any place where pestilential, contagious, or infectious disease existed at time of departure, or those which shall have arrived at such place and come thence to either of said ports; or those on board which, during voyage, any cases of such disease shall have occurred between May 1 and November 1. Quarantine to continue thirty days after arrival, and at least twenty after cargo discharged, and such further quarantine as Health Officer may prescribe.

Subject to *visitation* are: vessels arriving from Asia, Africa, the Mediterranean Sea, or any of West Indies, Bahamas, Bermudas, or Western Islands (or any place in America in ordinary passage from which they pass south of Hilton Head); and all vessels on board which, during voyage or at point of departure, any person shall have been sick, arriving between May 1 and November 1; and all from foreign ports, and not embraced in first subdivision of this section.

These shall be detained only for time requisite for due examination, unless they have had on board, during voyage, case of infectious, contagious, or pestilential disease; in which case, they shall be subject to such quarantine and regulations as Health Officer prescribes.

Health Officers, intendant, and wardens, or Mayor and Aldermen, as case may be, whenever in their judgment Public Health requires it, may order vessels at wharves or their vicinity to quarantine grounds or other place of safety, and require persons and things introduced into such ports from such vessels to be seized, returned on board, or removed to quarantine ground or other place. And if master or consignee cannot be found, or refuses,

they may cause such removal at expense of master, &c.; and such vessel or person shall not return to the port without written permission of the Health Officer.

Vessel subject to quarantine, and *bound North*, may pass after examination; but shall not anchor off either of said ports, nor hold communication with the shore.

Pilots to hail vessel entering port, and endeavor to ascertain whether she is subject to quarantine on examination. If she is, pilot shall notify master to proceed to quarantine ground.

Directions given to pilots as to bringing vessel into quarantine and preventing communication with other vessels or boats, and as to cleaning and purifying himself after having boarded such vessel.

Health Officer shall visit such vessel immediately on her arrival, inquiring as to health of persons on board and condition of vessel and cargo, by examination of bill of health, manifest, log-book, or otherwise; he shall examine persons, to determine length of quarantine, and regulations, and shall report facts and conclusions (particularly as to number sick and nature of disease) to Mayor or intendant, in writing.

Health Officer, Duties of : —

To reside in or near quarantine grounds.

To remove vessels from quarantine grounds to place south or east thereof, inside the bar, if he deems necessary.

To cause vessel to discharge cargo, passengers, or crew, if necessary for purposes of purification.

To cause vessel or cargo, bedding and clothing, to be ventilated and purified; and, if necessary, any part (of cargo) destroyed, with concurrence of Mayor or intendant.

To prevent persons leaving quarantine, or removing goods or baggage, until fifteen days after last case of contagious disease has occurred on board, and ten days after arrival in quarantine, unless sooner discharged by him.

To permit cargo, when he judges it free from infection or contagion, to be conveyed to landing.

To cause persons under quarantine to be vaccinated, when he deems necessary.

To administer oaths and affidavits in examinations prescribed, and in relation to any alleged violation of quarantine law or regulation.

May cause arrest of any person eloping from quarantine, or violating quarantine laws or regulations, or obstructing Health Officer.

Vessels in quarantine to be distinguished by colors.

No vessel or boat to pass through range of vessels at quarantine without permission of Health Officer.

No lighters to load or unload vessels at quarantine without his permission.

Health Officer may enforce his orders, and expense of this shall be a lien on the vessels.

Made a misdemeanor, punishable by fine or imprisonment, to violate quarantine regulations.

Governor may, by proclamation, declare place infected, and fix time, which may be extended from time to time.

It is made a misdemeanor in master, —

To refuse or neglect to proceed, and anchor at place assigned for quarantine.

Not to submit vessel, cargo, and passengers to examination; nor remain at quarantine during period assigned, and comply with directions and regulations.

To give false information to pilot as to condition of vessel, &c., or of places from which he comes, or to refuse to give information lawfully required.

To land any one, or permit any one, except pilot, to come on board, or unload or transship any part of cargo before visit and examination of Health Officer, or to approach with his vessel nearer wharves than place of quarantine.

Health Officers. — One at Georgetown, one at Charleston, and one at Hilton Head. Appointed by the Governor to hold office for two years. They are to keep record of their doings under this chapter, and report to Governor at end of each month.

"Health Officer" to include deputies, provided latter are graduates of regular medical schools.

Penalty of $500 if pilot violates the law.

Quarantine officers may employ force in execution of the quarantine laws, and may fire on vessel violating.

Act of 1876 amended the quarantine law as to length of quarantine, and place whence vessels come that shall be subject, and prescribed that Health Officer shall in all cases be a graduate of a regular medical school.

TENNESSEE.

Act of 1849–50, " Of preventing the spread of disease."

County Court may adopt measures to prevent spread of small-pox or other contagious disease, and to put a stop to the same. Necessary expenses to be a county charge. Judge or chairman of the County Court may adopt measures in vacation.

Selling, offering or exposing for sale, of unwholesome provisions, or drugged or manufactured wines or adulterated spirituous liquors, is made a misdemeanor; adulteration of liquors by poisonous ingredients, a felony. Manufacturer or rectifier of spirituous or alcoholic liquors to take oath not to adulterate before manufacturing or rectifying. (Exception in favor of druggists and physicians.)

Acts of 1849–50. Municipal corporations have full power and authority to enact laws and ordinances necessary and proper to preserve health, quiet, and good order of town, and to prevent and remove nuisances.

By Act of 1866–67, unhealthy trades, collections of filth and rendering water unwholesome, are declared nuisances, to be abated at the defendant's expense.

This year (1877) was passed the following: —

An Act

To create a State Board of Health for better protection of life and health, and the prevention of the spread of diseases, in the State of Tennessee.

SECTION 1. *Be it enacted by the General Assembly of the State of Tennessee,* That there is hereby created and established a State Board of Health, to be denominated " The State Board of Health of the State of Tennessee," and to be constituted as follows : —

SECT. 2. *Be it further enacted,* That, within twenty days after the passage of this Act, the Governor shall appoint five physicians of skill and experience, regular graduates of medicine, who have been engaged in practice not less than ten years, — one from East Tennessee, three from Middle Tennessee, and one from West Tennessee Three members of this Board so appointed shall constitute a quorum for the transaction of business at any regular, called, or adjourned meeting. All vacancies occurring by death, resignation, or otherwise, shall be filled by the Board, with the advice and consent of the Governor, and commissioned as hereinafter provided.

SECT. 3. *Be it further enacted,* That immediately, or as soon as expedient, after the appointment of said five physicians as aforesaid, they shall meet at the office of the Secretary of State; and, having taken the oath prescribed for other State officers, the Secretary of State shall issue to each of said members of the aforesaid State Board of Health a certificate of appointment, upon receiving which they shall severally be and become members of the "State Board of Health of the State of Tennessee," and shall possess the power and perform the duties of said Board, as defined by this Act: and they shall hold their office respectively for the terms following; namely, one for one year, one for two years, one for three years, one for four years, and one for five years, or until their successors are appointed and qualified. They shall next proceed, under the direction of the Secretary of State, to determine by lot which of them shall hold their office for the respective terms of one, two, three, four, and five years; which being determined, the Secretary of State shall enter upon their certificates of appointment the term of office thus fixed each member. The term of office of members of the Board after the expiration of the terms aforesaid shall be five years.

SECT. 4. *Be it further enacted,* That immediately after determining the term of office, as hereinbefore provided, the Board shall proceed to organize by electing one of their number to be President of the Board, and by electing a proper person, who shall be a regular physician of skill and experience, to be the Secretary of said Board; and, in case the Board shall elect one of their number Secretary, then, upon his acceptance of that position, there shall be a vacancy in the Board, which shall be filled as other vacancies are filled. The Secretary shall continue in office as such for a term of five years, unless removed by a majority of the whole Board by the election of a successor or otherwise, and shall be the executive officer of said Board. He shall give bond, with security, in the sum of ten thousand dollars ($10,000), conditioned for the faithful and impartial performance of his duty; which bond, when accepted by the Board, shall be made of record with the proceedings of the Board, and placed on file with the Secretary of State. He shall keep his office at some central and convenient place in the State, and shall perform the duties prescribed by this Act or required by the Board.

SECT. 5. *Be it further enacted,* That the Secretary shall receive an annual salary, which shall be fixed by the Board, and the Board shall quarterly certify the amount due him; and, on presentation of the certificate, the Comptroller shall draw his warrant upon the State Treasurer for the amount. The members shall receive no *per diem* compensation for their services; but their travelling and other necessary expenses while employed in the business of the Board shall be allowed and paid.

SECT. 6. *Be it further enacted,* That the State Board of Health shall have the general supervision of the interests of health and life of the citizens of this State. They shall especially study the vital statistics of this State, and endeavor to make intelligent and profitable use of the records of sickness and death among the people. They shall make sanitary investigations and inquiries respecting the causes of disease, espe-

cially epidemics; the causes of death; effects of employments, habits, localities, and circumstances upon the health of the people. They shall, when they deem it necessary, advise in reference to location, water supply, drainage, and ventilation of any public institution. They shall, from time to time, recommend works upon the subject of hygiene for the use of schools of the State.

SECT. 7. *Be it further enacted*, That, in order to afford to this Board better advantages for obtaining knowledge important to be incorporated with that collected through special investigations and from other sources, it is hereby made obligatory upon every municipality throughout the State having five thousand and over inhabitants to organize, within sixty days after the passage of this Act, provided said municipalities have not already done so, a properly constituted Board of Health, which, in addition to their duties as such local Boards, shall also make monthly, quarterly, semi-annual, and annual reports, to and in accordance with such form and instructions as said State Board of Health may prescribe, and also shall make special reports whenever required.

SECT. 8. *Be it further enacted*, That the Board shall meet quarterly at Nashville, and at such other places and times as they may deem expedient. A majority of the Board shall constitute a quorum. The Board may adopt rules and by-laws, subject to the provisions of this Act.

SECT. 9. *Be it further enacted*, That this Act take effect and be in full force from and after its passage, the public welfare requiring it.

TEXAS.

By Act of 1856, person carrying on trade or business injurious to health of vicinity, or suffering any substance which shall have that effect to remain on his premises, punished by fine.

Also, knowingly selling flesh of diseased animals, or unwholesome or adulterated food, or liquor for drink, injurious to health, or medicines fraudulently adulterated, so that operation is changed, or rendered worthless, or injurious to health.

Also (1860), polluting or obstructing any water-course, lake, pond, marsh, or common sewer, or continuing such obstruction or pollution, so as to render the same unwholesome or offensive to the county, city, town, or neighborhood thereabouts, or doing any other act or thing that would be deemed and held to be a nuisance at common law, — is made a misdemeanor.

1852. — If irrigation or damming up of water injures the Public Health, the county courts shall decree the discontinuance thereof.

In 1870 was passed "An Act authorizing quarantine on the coast of Texas, and elsewhere within the State."

Governor may declare quarantine by proclamation; and, as soon thereafter as practicable, the corporate authorities of every town and city on the coast shall establish a quarantine station, and appoint a competent physician as Health Officer, and furnish him with things necessary for proper and efficient discharge of his duties; and shall have power to provide for quarantine, and enforce by ordinance.

Health Officer to stop and rigidly examine every vessel from infected port or district, notwithstanding she may have a clean bill of health; and, if necessary, to take affidavit of master as to health of self and crew at time of sailing from infected port; and shall detain such vessel at quarantine for time designated by Governor's proclamation, and may use force, if necessary.

Where on the coast there is no corporate power, Governor shall have power to appoint Health Officer, and make regulations for quarantine.

This Act is amended so as to make master punishable for misdemeanor, in not having clean bill of health, Health Officer to take possession of and hold vessel till master's fine is paid; but payment of fine shall not release the vessel, but same rule shall apply as in case of other vessels.

And master passing or attempting to pass quarantine without permission from Health Officer, guilty of felony, and punished by fine or imprisonment.

Persons belonging to and going ashore from, or landing goods from, vessel at quarantine, without written permission of Health Officer, guilty of misdemeanor.

City authorities to keep account of receipts and expenditures. Excess of latter to be paid by State. Excess of former to maintain marine hospitals in towns and cities.

Cities and towns may establish quarantine.

And further amended by Act of 1871.

In 1874 was passed an Act authorizing counties, cities, or incorporated towns, on the gulf coast of Texas, to establish quarantine rules or regulations, not in conflict with State or United States laws.

The city of Galveston has a Board of Health, consisting of

three physicians and six laymen, who derive their powers from the Act incorporating the city. Power to create like boards is given to certain other cities by their several acts of incorporation.

VERMONT.

Revised Statutes, 1840, prescribe penalties for knowingly selling diseased or unwholesome provisions (the same not being fully known to the buyer) ; and for fraudulently adulterating liquors, drugs, or medicines, for purpose of sale.

They further prescribe the duties of Selectmen as to removal of sick when small-pox breaks out, and preventing the spread of the disease; also, their duties when the disease appears in an adjoining town.

The Selectmen of any town may, from time to time, grant license for erecting or using houses for inoculating with smallpox, under regulations to be made by them, and may license physicians to superintend, and shall make and cause to be posted suitable regulations to prevent the spreading of the infection.

They are also to provide physicians, nurses, and attendants for the sick.

A penalty is enacted in the case of any person coming into a town when infected, or communicating the infection.

No butchering shall be carried on in any building, without the approbation of the town in writing, describing the building and limiting the time.

The Selectmen are to make regulations generally concerning nuisances, sources of filth, and causes of sickness.

They may destroy or remove nuisances: the owner of any premises on which nuisance exists shall be directed to remove the same within twenty-four hours after notice ; and, if he neglects to do so, the Selectmen may remove it at his expense.

By Act of 1852, a penalty was enacted against any one putting any dead animal or animal substance into rivers, ponds, springs, &c., or on the premises of another, or allowing the same to remain unburied on his own, between March and December in any year.

General Statutes, 1863, regulate the sale of poisons and anæsthetic agents.

VIRGINIA.

By Act of 1831–32, the Council of any town, or the court of any county, may establish in such county, or in or near such town, hospitals, which shall be subject to regulations, not contrary to law, made by such Council or court. The cost of establishing and maintaining such hospital shall be chargeable to the town or county, as the case may be.

By Act of 1852–53, the above powers are conferred on any three justices of the peace in and for any county.

Any justice may issue warrant requiring two physicians whom he may designate to examine persons reported to him, or who he has reason to think are infected with small-pox or other dangerous disease.

The physicians shall report to him in writing their opinion of such disease, and whether the public interest requires any action by the justices under this Act.

By Act of 1856, the circuit and county courts are authorized to incorporate companies for hospitals.

Inoculation forbidden, except at hospitals established by law.

The Council or Health Officer of a town, or any two justices of a county, may cause any person in said town or county, infected with any infectious disease, dangerous to the Public Health, to be removed to a hospital or other place of reception for the infected, unless such person be sick in his own place of residence, or cannot be removed without danger to his life.

If Health Officer of any town is refused admittance to any lot, house, or vessel, where there is good cause of suspicion or belief that there is any nuisance, source of filth, or cause of sickness, proper to be destroyed or removed, or one or more persons, not in his or their own place of residence, infected with contagious disease, any justice of the corporation or county may issue warrant to the sheriff, sergeant of the corporation, or constable, requiring him to enter, and, under direction of such Health Officer, remove or destroy any such nuisance, source of filth, or cause of sickness.

Vaccine agents to be appointed by the Governor.
Overseers of the Poor have power to compel vaccination.

Quarantine. — The Council of any town may establish a ground for, and two or more towns may have in common. Said Council may, from time to time, prescribe quarantine and regulations therefor, to extend to all persons, goods, and effects arriving in vessels coming within the harbor or vicinity of such town, and to all persons who may go on board of the same.

Health Officer may cause foul or infected vessel or cargo to be removed to quarantine ground or other proper place, and to be purified.

Penalties are enacted in case master neglects to comply with regulations, or any person ordered to perform quarantine shall escape.

By Act of 1847–48, penalties are enacted in case of knowingly selling unsound provisions, without making the same known to the buyer, and in case of the fraudulent adulteration of provisions or medicines.

Statutes 1871–72. — Persons suffering with contagious disease shall be excluded from the public free schools while in that condition; and teachers shall require of the pupils cleanliness of person, and good behavior during their attendance at the schools, and on the way thither and back to their homes: and no pupils shall be admitted unless they have been vaccinated: provided, that the operation of this clause concerning vaccination may be suspended, in whole or in part, by the school board of any city or county.

Statutes 1871–72, ch. 91. — " Governor to appoint seven physicians, — three from Richmond, and other four from different sections of the State, — who shall constitute a State Board of Health and Vital Statistics; to hold office four years, and until successors appointed; vacancies to be filled by Governor."

This Board shall place themselves in communication with local Boards of Health, hospitals, asylums, and public institutions, throughout the State, and take cognizance of interests of health and life among the citizens generally.

For duties, see ch. 84, § 2, Virginia Code, 1873, p. 729.

Board of Health to meet at capital of State, at least once every three months.

Person entering and coming out of infected house to be carried to hospital, — not to be discharged until he has physician's certificate that he may, without danger of spreading contagion; and person recently infected, and not cleansed, shall not expose himself on highway, without warning approaching person.

Citizens to be furnished with vaccine matter free of charge.

Quarantine. — If vessel or cargo be infected, Health Officer may quarantine and have it purified, and cause persons arriving in or going on board such vessel, or handling such cargo, to be removed to hospitals.

Master, seamen, and passengers shall answer, on oath, inquiries of officer as to infection or disease, under penalty; and master shall deliver to quarantine officer his bills of health and books.

Persons arriving *by land* from infected places may be compelled to perform quarantine by Health Officer.

Quarantine expenses to be reimbursed to town by the person, or owner of vessel or goods; and town may detain vessel or goods till such expenses are paid.

Word "town" in this Act includes "city," and "council" includes any body authorized to make ordinances for a town.

1875.

CHAP. 157. AN ACT to amend and re-enact Section 10 of Chapter 84 of Code of Virginia, edition of 1873, in reference to the propagation of small-pox.

(Approved March 11, 1875.)

SECTION 10. Any person who shall inoculate himself or another, or suffer to be inoculated, for the small-pox, unless at a hospital established by law, shall forfeit, for every such offence, not exceeding three hundred dollars; and if any person shall bring into this State the small-pox, or any variolous matter thereof, with the intent of propagating such disease, he shall be deemed guilty of a felony, and shall be punished by confinement in the penitentiary not less than one nor more than five years. And if any person shall wilfully abandon or desert, or cause to be abandoned or deserted, any person who is sick with the small-pox, upon the shores of this Commonwealth, he shall be deemed guilty of a felony, and shall be confined therefor in the penitentiary not less than three nor more than ten years; and if such abandoned person shall die, by reason of such wilful abandonment and desertion, the person who abandoned or caused him to be abandoned shall be deemed guilty of murder, and shall be punished accordingly.

AN ACT in relation to cemeteries and cemetery associations.

(Approved Feb. 10, 1876.)

SECTION 5. No land shall be condemned under the provisions of this Act within the corporate limits of any city or town, or within four hundred yards of any residence outside of the corporate limits of any city or town, without the consent of the owner of such residence.

CHAP. 259. AN ACT to incorporate the Consolidated Abattoir Company of Alexandria, Washington, and Georgetown.

(Approved March 29, 1876.)

SECTION 9. That the Governor shall appoint a competent person as inspector of all live stock and meats slaughtered by this company, which is intended for sale and consumption; said inspector to be empowered to condemn all live stock or slaughtered animals, the meat of which is unfit for food; said inspector to be required to give bond in the sum of ten thousand dollars for the faithful and impartial discharge of his duties, and to be subject to the rules and regulations governing inspectors in the State of Virginia. . . .

SECT. 10. . . . That said inspector may appoint as many deputies as may be necessary; that, for dereliction of duty on the part of said inspector or his deputies, a fine of fifty dollars for each neglect shall be imposed on said inspector, to be collected (as all other fines are) for the benefit of the State.

WEST VIRGINIA.

By the Code, on condemnation of the land for mill-dam, &c., inquiry is to be made whether health of neighborhood will be endangered by the stagnation of the water or otherwise.

The Code also provides against selling unsound provisions, and the adulteration of provisions, drink, or medicine.

By law of 1861, the Governor shall appoint annually an agent to furnish vaccine matter.

Act of 1866 amends and re-enacts provision of Code as to restraint of distempered cattle.

To knowingly sell any diseased, corrupted, or unwholesome provisions, whether meat or drink, without making the same known to buyer, is an offence punished by fine and imprisonment. Also, to adulterate, for the purpose of sale, any article intended for food or drink, or to drug any medicine with any substance injurious to health, is an offence punished by fine and

imprisonment, and forfeiture of the article. There are no other sanitary regulations prescribed by law, except such as are vested in the chartered towns and cities. Any trade, occupation, or other thing injurious to health may be enjoined or removed as a nuisance.

WISCONSIN.

Revised Statutes, 1858, provide that "the justices of the peace of every town, the president and trustees of every incorporated village, and the Mayor and Aldermen of every incorporated city, in this State, shall be Boards of Health; and as such shall exercise all the powers and perform all the duties provided in this chapter, within the limits of their respective towns, villages, and cities.

Every Board may take such measures and make such rules and regulations as they may deem most effectual for preservation of Public Health; and for that purpose may appoint a physician, who shall be the Health Officer of the territory within the jurisdiction of the Board, to hold office during their pleasure; and may appoint so many persons to aid them in the execution of their powers and duties as they may think proper; and shall regulate the fees and charges of every person so employed by them.

The Board shall examine into all nuisances, sources of filth, and causes of sickness, and make such regulations respecting same as they may judge necessary for the public health and safety of the inhabitants. Person violating is guilty of misdemeanor.

Notice to be given by Board of their rules and regulations, by publication or printing; this to be legal notice to all persons. Nuisance on private property to be removed by owner or occupant, on order of Board, at his own expense, within twenty-four hours. Owner or occupant not complying, Board may cause it to be removed, at his expense.

When entry into building or vessel is refused to the Board, on complaint to justice of peace, warrant shall issue to sheriff or constable to destroy, remove, or prevent the nuisance, in presence and under direction of the Board.

Person infected or who has lately been infected with small-pox or other contagious disease, dangerous to the Public Health. Board shall cause to be removed to separate house, and provide nurses and necessaries, at his charge or that of person liable for his support. If he cannot safely be removed, Board shall make provision for him in house where he is, and may cause persons in neighborhood to be removed, and may take such other measures as they may deem necessary for safety of the inhabitants.

Warrant to remove and care for infected person may be issued by two justices.

Penalties enacted for selling unwholesome provisions, fraudulently adulterating food, liquors, drugs or medicines, or inoculating with small-pox with intent to spread the disease; in case of physician prescribing when intoxicated; and of apothecary selling poison without labelling.

Some amendments were made in 1862, 1868, and 1871: *e.g.*, providing against erection of slaughter-houses on banks of any river, stream, or creek, or throwing any carcass or offal therefrom in or upon the bank of any such river, &c., which shall flow through any city or incorporated village in this State; and against erection of slaughter-houses within limits of village of not less than one hundred inhabitants, and within one-eighth mile of any dwelling-house, or building used as place of business; and making more stringent rules as to putting up of medicines, and penalties for adulterating.

In 1876 was created the "State Board of Health and Vital Statistics," to consist of seven persons, to be appointed by the Governor, with the advice and consent of the Senate.

They shall meet in June and January of each year, and at such other times as the Board or President of the Board shall deem expedient.

The rest of the Act, except as regards appropriations for expenses, is identical with the Michigan Act of 1873, with this added clause: "The Board shall have charge of all matters pertaining to quarantine; and shall have authority to make such rules and regulations as they may, from time to time, deem necessary for the preservation or improvement of the Public Health."

APPENDIX V.

LOUIS AND PIERSON ON DR. JAMES JACKSON, JR.

V.

(Page 15.)

Louis' Estimate of James Jackson, Jr., and the Relations of the Master and Pupil.

From the interesting memoir[1] of Dr. James Jackson, Jr., written by his father, and from an obituary of the same by the late Dr. Pierson, of Salem,[2] I make the following extracts. They will confirm the views expressed in the memoir of the influence exerted in America by that young physician, immediately on his return, after his long student life under the eye of Louis. I think no one can read them without feeling the loss which our profession sustained by Dr. Jackson's early death. They will enable the reader, also, more fully to appreciate the close relations which existed between Louis and his favorite pupil; while at the same time they show some of the traits, moral and intellectual, of both teacher and pupil. Young Jackson died only about six months after his return to America: —

M. Louis to Dr. James Jackson, Sr.

My dear Sir, — I have received, with gratitude, the letter you did me the honor to write me in regard to your son, and his memoir upon cholera. I give you special and hearty thanks for having afforded me so good an opportunity for speaking of one, toward whom I entertain sentiments of real friendship, as well as of esteem. It did not require much time

[1] Memoir of James Jackson, Jr., M.D., with Extracts from his Letters to his Father, and Medical Cases collected by him. By James Jackson, M.D., Professor of the Theory and Practice of Medicine in Harvard University, and Physician of the Massachusetts General Hospital. Boston: I. R. Butts, 1835.

[2] Medical Magazine, April 15, 1834.

for me to appreciate fully the sagacity and talents, which your son possesses for the observation of nature. I had noticed these characteristics in him, before I knew who he was. Soon afterwards, learning that he would ere long return to Boston, I pointed out to him the advantage it would be for science and for himself, if he would devote several years exclusively to the observation of disease. I now retain the same opinion of him, and am strengthened in it; for the more I become acquainted with him, and the more I have watched him applying himself to observation, the more I have become persuaded that he is fitted to render real service to science, and promote its progress. I find that he would be well pleased to follow, for a certain period, that vocation for which nature has fitted him. He has, however, stated to me that there are many difficulties, which would prevent his devoting himself, for many years, exclusively to observation. But are these difficulties insurmountable? Must we compel ourselves to believe that a man, whom nature has peculiarly qualified for observation, cannot be permitted to exercise the peculiar talents bestowed upon him? For my own part, I cannot admit the belief. I hope and trust that the difficulties, of which Mr. Jackson has spoken, will disappear. Let us suppose that he should pass four more years without engaging in the practice of medicine, what a mass of positive knowledge will he have acquired! How many important results will he have been able to publish to the world during that period! After that, he must necessarily become one of the bright lights of his country: others will resort to him for instruction, and he will be able to impart it with distinguished honor to himself. If all things be duly weighed, it will appear that he will soon redeem the four years, which men of superficial views will believe him to have lost. It is with the utmost seriousness, sir, that I write to you thus. It would not be without the deepest conviction of the advantages of the plan I propose, that I should offer my advice on a subject, on which I have not been consulted. It is not for the sake of making to a parent some grateful remarks about his son, that I have pointed out to you how much may, in my opinion, be hoped from the talents for observation which belong to Mr. Jackson, but simply to render homage to truth. Excuse me, then, for the

step I have ventured to take: and believe that, if I had not felt that I had, in this case, a duty to fulfil, I should not have offered to you my advice, nor addressed to you my petition; for it is rather a petition I have addressed to you, than advice that I have given you.

How could I venture to do the latter? Nevertheless, in reading over my letter, it seems to me to betray the tone of an advocate, who is pleading a cause; and I would willingly begin it anew, were I not afraid that, from my deep conviction of the truth of what I have stated, I should relapse into the same fault. Accept it then, sir, such as it is, with indulgence; and believe that no one here is more sincerely attached to your son, or entertains for him a higher esteem than I do. Above all, listen to the suggestions which I have ventured to make; and may my wishes that your son may devote himself exclusively to observation be ultimately realized; for it is to that point I constantly return.

I conclude by renewing to you my thanks, and beg you to be assured of my sentiments, &c., of respect.

(Signed)   LOUIS.

PARIS, Oct. 28, 1832.

LOUIS TO DR. JAMES JACKSON, SR.

DEAR SIR, — My respected brother, I thank you most sincerely for your last letter, and particularly for the details, into which you were kind enough to enter with regard to your son. Nothing certainly could be more grateful to my feelings; for it is almost a mark of affection for myself, and I feel almost worthy of it, from the strength of that which I bear your excellent son. He will soon leave us; but his name will long be mentioned among us, and I hope that the ocean, which is to separate us, will not be a complete barrier to our intercourse. I feel more than any one else how much you must long to see, as soon as possible, a son whose profession is the same as your own, and with whom it will be so delightful to converse respecting it. Indeed, I never thought of inducing you to leave him with us in Europe for four or five years. I love in Mr.

Jackson the man and the physician: but he is a son, and you are a father; and, though I have never known the delight of paternal affection, I should not have regarded as possible the sacrifice, which you understood me to propose to you. My only wish was that you should allow your son to devote himself exclusively to observation, for several years, in Boston. I recommended this to you, because no one is more capable than he is of cultivating science, and consequently of promoting the progress of our professional practice. For what is practice, but science brought into daily use? Think, for a moment, sir, of the situation, in which we physicians are placed. We have no legislative chambers to enact laws for us. We are our own lawgivers, or rather we must discover the laws, on which our profession rests. We must discover them, and not invent them; for the laws of nature are not to be invented. And who is to discover these laws? Who should be a diligent observer of nature for this purpose, if not the son of a physician, who has himself experienced the difficulties of the observation of disease, who knows how few minds are fitted for it, and how few have, at once, the talents and inclination, requisite for the task? The inclination, especially, for this requires that the observer should possess a thorough regard for truth, and a certain elevation of mind, or rather of character, which we rarely meet with.

All this is united in your son. You ought, — for in my opinion it is a duty, — you ought to consecrate him, for a few years, to science. This, sir, is my conviction; and I hope it will be yours also. I know very well that every one will not be of the same opinion; but what matters it, if it be yours, — if you look upon a physician (as I do) as holding a sacred office which demands greater sacrifices, than are to be made in any other profession? Believe me that I do not forget in all this the force of established usages. I think of all this; but I am none the less convinced that Mr. Jackson, entering into practice, after three or four years, with the esteem of all his professional brethren, and surrounded, as it were, with their respect, will very rapidly regain all which he may have sacrificed, and much more.

At all events, my best wishes, and those of all his friends here, will follow him, whatever may be his course; and I shall

always esteem myself happy in having known him. Permit me, sir, to assure you of this, and of the sentiments of respect and affection with which I am, &c.

(Signed)   LOUIS.

PARIS, March 22, 1833.

DR. JAMES JACKSON, JR., TO HIS FATHER.

PARIS, July 13, 1833.

MY DEAR FATHER,— In two hours, I am out of Paris. I will not attempt to describe to you the agony it gives me to quit Louis. He is my second father, and God knows that is a name I, of all men, cannot use lightly. I may not persuade you to look upon him with my eyes exactly, as a scientific man; but in your heart he must have the share of a brother, for he almost shares my affection with you. From one upon whom I had no claims, but those which my life and mind and habits gave me, I have experienced a care, an affection, which I never could dare expect from any but my dear father, and which I shall ever feel to be the most honorable and truly worthy prize of my life. To meet with satisfaction in the eyes of such a man, and to hold a place in his heart, as I do, I allow I am proud of. But, my dear father, I cannot write. I am sitting here, expecting to see Louis for the last time in my life; and it is only upon the occasion of quitting yourself, whom I have ever felt to be a part of me, that I have suffered as I do at present. The ties of relationship are strong: the strongest when that relationship is close and dependent, especially if it be mingled with the strongest and warmest sympathies. But one's mind's friends, — the hearts which not nature, but our own characters have given us, — the friend who, not father to our bodies, has yet been, and is ever to be, the source, fountain, and direction of the dearest thoughts of our minds, — that friend and that relationship is also dear. It is that friendship I must now quit, probably for ever; it is that relationship that in the person I must now break, though in the mind and in the heart it can never be broken. Till now, I knew not how I loved my French master. I know well I shall rarely be called to such trials: they can occur but few times in life. Thank God

that with me grief is as short as it is poignant, and that in a few days nought will occupy my mind but the anticipation of the joys of home! Once more in the arms of my beloved family, and under the wing of my dear father, and I can imagine no higher joy.

DR. PIERSON'S ESTIMATE OF JAMES JACKSON, JR.

I quote the following from Dr. Pierson's Obituary, in order to show the position which Jackson held among his elders. It is simply the introductory sentences of a brief biography: —

"It is seldom that the death of a junior member of the profession has called forth so general a voice of sympathy and regret, as has been heard among us, since the death of this estimable and talented young man. There were circumstances in his private life, which warranted the high expectation of the community in which he lived; and, in venturing to allude to these circumstances, it is in the hope that his example may speak to us in the tones of that voice, we are destined to hear no more.

"In our profession, the paths of mediocrity are crowded. There are multitudes among us who feel, perhaps, some aspirations to benefit mankind, by researches which would carry us a little beyond the circle of our common duties, and yet who are conscious of a thousand deficiencies of time, opportunity, and education, which fetter us in our daily task. It is, therefore, a public loss, in which the interest and honor of the profession are largely concerned, when one is taken away from us, who has been eminently qualified by disposition, by mental endowments, by zeal and opportunity, to shed lustre upon a useful and honorable pursuit. Yet such was James Jackson, Jr. His profession was that of his only, his earliest choice; his mind was of good material, well nurtured, mature for his years, and peculiarly adapted to the nature of his occupation; his opportunities had been, and continued to be, most improving; and his constitutional zeal and ardor, directed (as they were) singly to the science of medicine, were calculated to surmount every difficulty, and to remove every obstacle, which would be likely to

intimidate and deter less gifted minds. It was a pure zeal: it was ardor in the cause of truth. It was like the zeal and ardor that actuated the mind of John Hunter, and filled that of the youthful Bichat. It was an unceasing prompting, which always is and must be connected with generous and noble sentiments, — which carries men to the highest ends, by the most virtuous means. If this be deemed the language of friendship, be it so. We know that it is the language of truth; and we record it to excite those among us, who are capable of it (for even our partiality will allow that there are many such) to devote themselves to those noble purposes in the art of healing, to which our lamented friend had devoted the best energies of his cultivated mind."

APPENDIX VI.

LAW OF SOIL MOISTURE.

VI.

(PAGE 119.)

LAW OF SOIL MOISTURE AND LAND DRAINAGE, AND THEIR INFLUENCE ON CONSUMPTION.

On the 28th of May, 1862, in a public address before the Massachusetts Medical Society, at its annual meeting, I gave the first detailed statement of the Law of Soil Moisture, as a cause of consumption in Massachusetts, and probably elsewhere. In 1855, and again in 1856, I had previously made partial reports on the same subject. Before the announcement in 1862, pulmonary consumption had been supposed to be everywhere, if not equally prevalent, throughout the globe. Keith Johnston,[1] in his chart on the " Geographical Distribution of Health and Disease," had, however, marked New England as especially liable to it, compared with other places. When I commenced my investigations under the sanction of the Society, I held the same opinion. It was, I believe, the opinion of the profession generally. No one admitted that a residence on a damp soil begets consumption. But I was compelled by the force of facts, presented by my correspondents from all the towns of Massachusetts, and from some towns in other New England States, to alter my opinion. The following is the synopsis of the data and argument on which that change is based. I laid down the two following propositions, as containing the essential points I hoped to prove:[2] —

"*First.* A residence on or near a damp soil, whether that dampness be inherent in the soil itself, or caused by percolation from adjacent ponds, rivers, meadows, marshes, or springy soils, is one of the primal causes of consumption in Massachu-

[1] Geographical Distribution of Health and Disease. By W. Keith Johnston. Edinburgh, 1854.

[2] Topographical Distribution and Local Origin of Consumption in Massachusetts. Read at the Annual Meeting of the Massachusetts Medical Society, May 28, 1862. By Henry I. Bowditch, M.D., of Boston.

setts, — probably in New England, and possibly in other portions of the globe.

"*Second.* Consumption can be checked in its career, and possibly — nay probably — prevented, in some instances, by attention to this law."

After a few remarks in regard to my confidence in the truth of these two propositions, I laid down the following, as among my medical axioms drawn from my investigations : —

"1st. *Consumption is not, as some writers have contended, endemic equally in every part of New England;* but there are some localities where it is very rife, and others where it is vastly less destructive than in the States at large.

"2d. *There is a law,* hitherto scarcely noticed, or but vaguely hinted at by one or two individual writers, but (as I believe) *never proved* until now, *which is one of the main causes, if not the sole cause, of this unequal topographical distribution of consumption in New England.*

"3d. *This law is intimately connected with, and apparently dependent on, the humidity of the soils on or near which stand the towns, villages, or even single houses, where consumption prevails.*

"4th. *The existence of this law of soil moisture, as one of the prime causes of consumption in New England,* can be proved, as I think, by several lines of argument, resting on actual facts obtained either from public or private records, statistical data, or the opinions of physicians, practising medicine in various parts of New England."

These lines of proof or of argument are drawn from the following sources : —

"I. Massachusetts State Registration Reports.

"II. Medical opinion of Massachusetts, as embodied in the returns made to me as a committee of this Society; these returns consisting of written reports from resident physicians of one hundred and eighty-three towns.[1]

"III. Actual statistics of deaths by consumption, received from such correspondents. Some of these statistics are but

[1] Returns, more or less detailed, were finally procured from all the three hundred and twenty-five towns, into which Massachusetts was divided at that time.

incidentally mentioned, while others are from towns districted, and carefully examined with reference to the relative prevalence of consumption in the different districts. In some of the most important of these, the examination was made without my correspondent or myself being aware of the existence of any law, such as that which I shall present at this time.

"IV. Peculiarities of certain towns, and of villages in the same townships, in some of which consumption is quite prevalent, and in others much less so; these differences being connected most closely with corresponding differences in the amount of moisture of the soil of said places.

"V. Certain well-known houses, which, in various towns, are known by the inhabitants and physicians to have been long noted as the abode of consumption, and in some of which several families have been, during the past fifty years, cut off by the disease, without the least suspicion, on the part of the occupants, of the fatal position in which the houses were placed.

"VI. Confirmatory facts, statistics, and opinions from Rhode Island, Maine, and New Hampshire.

"VII. The medical statistics given in the report on the health of the United States Army, strongly supporting the idea of the existence of the same law, and the operation of it over the whole of the United States.

"VIII. Results of my own practice since I first became convinced of the truth of the law, said results consisting of (*a*) Statistics from my private medical records; (*b*) Results actually derived from my choice of localities for consumptive patients, based on a belief in the law.

"IX. Apparent exceptions to the law."

From these various lines of argument, I obtained as follows: —

"I. *The registration reports of deaths in Massachusetts seemed to indicate* (a) *that consumption had not been equally prevalent in all parts of the State; and* (b) *that probably the disease had prevailed more on the coast than in the interior.*"

"II. *Medical opinion in Massachusetts, as deduced from the written statements of resident physicians in one hundred and eighty-three towns, tends strongly to prove, though perhaps not affording perfect proof of, the existence of a law in the develop-*

ment of consumption in Massachusetts, which law has for its central idea that dampness in the soil of any township or locality is intimately connected, and probably as cause and effect, with the prevalence of consumption in that township or locality."

Medical opinion is deemed almost valueless by some. But by combining the returns of many witnesses, all bearing testimony upon the simple question as to where in a town consumption had prevailed, and those where it had not, I arrived at the significant fact; viz., that, in those spots where consumption prevailed, the proportion inclined to moisture was more than twice as great as those, which were either dry or insular in their situation.

I could assert that —

"III. (a) *Statistics gathered incidentally from my correspondents sustain, as far as they sustain any opinion, on the question before us. the views we have drawn from Medical Opinion.*"

"(b) Some of the towns present, in their data, a *more or less regular gradation in the prevalence of consumption, according to the amount of moisture in or near the various localities.*"

"(c) By the *statistics from one town, which had been examined very carefully by a correspondent, I found, much to my surprise, that the relative proportion of deaths by consumption could be classified according to the amount of soil moisture in each district.*"

IV. I found two villages in the same township, "*in one of which consumption is quite prevalent, and in another much less so; these results being connected most closely with corresponding differences in the amount of moisture of the soil of said villages.*"

On these points I presented undoubted statistical facts sustaining the law of soil moisture.

"V. *Certain houses which, in various towns, have been long known, by the inhabitants and by resident physicians, as the abodes of consumptive patients, and in some of which several families have been, during the past fifty years, cut off by consumption.*"

While examining this part of the subject, I was able to give evidence going strongly to prove, that "*even some houses may become the* foci *of consumption, when others but slightly removed from them, but on a drier soil, almost wholly escape.*"

The various facts under this head indicated that certain houses, built long ago, had proved to be *pest-houses* and consumption-breeders for two or three generations. These houses rested on a wet foundation, and were constantly exposed to dampness from all sides.

"VI. *Confirmatory opinions, facts, and statistics from Rhode Island, Maine, and New Hampshire.*"

The facts reported by my correspondents in other States were very significant. One house, washed daily by the tide, had witnessed the loss of a whole family of children by consumption. The childless parents left the house, and the children of the second occupants were beginning to fall in the same way, when my correspondent wrote. In another case, members of the family, becoming alarmed, had removed, and had escaped the disease.

I closed this portion of the argument with these words:—

"May I not say that these data from Maine, New Hampshire, and Rhode Island afford nearly as certain evidence of the operation of this law of dampness throughout New England as we have for its prevalence in Massachusetts? *A priori*, we must admit that *any* etiological climate-law acting in Massachusetts must extend over the New England States, so entirely analogous are they in their characteristics."

"VII. *Medical statistics, given in the report on the health of the United States Army intimate the existence of this law, and of its wide operation over that part of this continent, contained within the limits of the United States.*"

From this report, I adduced the testimony of Dr. Coolidge.[1]

Dr. Coolidge writes: "The most important atmospherical condition for a consumptive is *dryness*."

Similar testimony is given from the dry and equable climate of Fort Clark in Texas, by Surgeon Norris; and from Camp Scott, at Utah, by Surgeon Bartholow. The latter

[1] Statistical Report on the Sickness and Mortality in the Army of the United States, compiled from the Records of the Surgeon-General's Office; embracing a period of sixteen years, from January, 1839, to January, 1855. Prepared under direction of Brevet Brigadier-General Thomas Lawson, Surgeon-General, by Richard H. Coolidge, M.D., Assistant-Surgeon U.S.A. Washington, 1856. Also, Second Report, from 1855 to 1859.

says: "All who came hither, laboring under incipient or well-established symptoms of consumption, speedily improved." The *dryness* and equableness of the climate is noted as the most important element in the cure.

In common with this part of the subject, I draw attention to the fact, that most of those places in different parts of the globe said to be favorable to consumptives are, so far as I could learn, *dry;* while other spots, unfavorable to such patients, were *moist.*

In 1859, during a visit to Europe, I brought my investigations to the knowledge of M. Louis (who was deeply interested in my communication), and I presented them before the Society for Medical Observation at London. Still later, I sent a communication on the subject to the International Medical Congress held at Paris, over which the celebrated Bouillard presided. To all these individuals and societies the subject was new. I urged upon the Congress to appoint a committee to carry out a world-wide investigation, but my efforts were vain. Only one physician, whom I accidentally met, a resident among the hills of Scotland, said, after hearing my statements, that they would explain the different prevalence of consumption in two valleys, which before he could not understand; but the fact was that one was dry and the other wet.

VIII. *Results of my own practice since I first became convinced of the truth of this law.* (a) *Statistics from my private records of cases.*

They gave, as final results, the following: " *Three-quarters of all these patients have resided where dampness of the soil is a prominent characteristic. Somewhat less than one-quarter have resided in dry places.*"

(b) *As the results of my practice, when applying this law to the prevention or cure of consumption,* I state as follows: —

"*First.* Persons having had hæmoptysis and irritation of the lungs, and who have apparently been threatened with phthisis, but without physical signs, have been completely restored to health by going to live in a dry locality, and leading more active lives. These patients have considered the change of residence the *prime cause* of their improved health, although other remedies were not neglected."

"*Second.* I have had patients in whom physical signs of an undoubted character existed, — such as crackling under the clavicle, diminished vesicular murmur, and some dulness on percussion, — who, by removal from towns and localities lying under or near the influence of dampness of the soil, to another town very dry, have experienced immense benefit."

"In one young lady, crackling disappeared almost wholly from the entire upper lobe of one lung, after a residence of six months in a very dry town, selected for the purpose, because the resident physician assured me that the town was very dry, and that cases of hæmoptysis that would, he thought, have terminated in fatal phthisis in a town on the coast, where he previously resided, got well in his actual abode."

Other cases of similar character had occurred.

"*Third.* I have had another and equally significant class of cases, in which undoubted and more extensive rational and physical signs of consumption have existed for a year or more, and in whom, even now, the physical signs are sufficiently well marked, though showing less irritation of the lungs; while the constitutional symptoms are very much better, under similar changes of residence."

Finally, I stated that, "to sum up the results of my experience, and my present judgment, on this subject, as a matter of therapeutics, I dare not neglect the abundant evidence of the influence of locality; and that I deem a residence on a damp soil one of the great causes of consumption in Massachusetts."

Wishing, however, to look fairly at all the evidence, *pro* and *con*, I next considered some of the

IX. *Apparent exceptions, taken by different physicians, to the view of the subject presented in this address.*

From only two had I procured statistics; viz., Dr. Alden, of Randolph, and Dr. Benjamin E. Cotting, of Roxbury. Both of these writers stated simply the number of deaths by consumption in a place, and failed to give either the population or the whole number of deaths in the districts, alluded to as dry or moist: hence, no inferences could be justly made from them. Dr. Cotting is very earnest, however; and declares, in the following language, his belief that "from the East Indies and the West, from the isles of the ocean and those in the Mediter-

ranean, from the Western prairies and from Italian skies, we hear the same story of the universal existence, prevalence, and inexorable progress, of pulmonary consumption." This, of course, expressed Dr. Cotting's opinions very fully; but I do not see that they *prove* any more than his statistics, — any thing against the facts I had given.

After some remarks upon places in Massachusetts, fitted or unfitted for consumptives, under the guidance of the principles laid down in the address, I declared my firm belief in the following: —

"*First.* Consumption is not equally distributed over New England.

"*Second.* Its greater or less prevalence depends very much upon the characteristics of the soil on or near which the patients affected with it have resided.

"*Third.* Moisture of the soil is the only known characteristic which, so far as our present investigations have gone, is connected with the consumption-breeding districts.

"*Fourth.* An attention to this law in the development of consumption in New England (now first nearly,[1] if not quite, proved to be true, by the analysis of the data which your courtesy has afforded me), I have found of great advantage in my professional practice."

As practical measures, legitimate outgrowths of the investigation, I urged: (*a*) The establishment of a State Board of Health to investigate all such subjects. (*b*) The proper selection of sites for villages. (*c*) The underdrainage of wet towns and villages. (*d*) I warned private individuals not to reside in houses subjected to dampness.

Finally, I urged the Society to impress upon the public conscience the truth of the law, and "thereby cut off one of the principal roots of consumptive tendencies in New England."

The views advocated in that address were received openly by

[1] By this term I meant to intimate a deference to the general opinion among all classes in Europe and America, which was, at the time of the address, the very reverse of my own. But I did not mean to admit that I myself had doubts. In fact, I was already practising upon my own estimate, and in opposition to public medical opinion.

a few only. Europe ignored them. America, generally, waited for England to rediscover the law.

Soil Moisture as a cause of Phthisis in England. — In the Ninth Report of the Medical Officers of the Privy Council (for 1866), on p. 49, Appendix No. 2, Dr. Buchanan writes thus: " Taking all the towns below Stratford, on the foregoing list, as having been unimproved in their rate of mortality from consumption, there is seen a large and pretty constant connection between the fluctuations of this disease and the changes effected on the subsoil water, and the two have varied very closely to the same degree."

Mr. Simon, in summing up the general results of the year's investigations, says : " The novel and most important conclusion suggests itself, that *the dryness of soil, which has in most cases accompanied the laying of main sewers in the improved towns, has led to the diminution, more or less considerable, of phthisis.*" And he adds, " This, should it be substantiated, will constitute a very valuable discovery, evolved by Dr. Buchanan from the inquiries here reported."

He closes that part of his report by stating that, deeming the subject so important, he had requested the Council to authorize Dr. Buchanan to make further inquiries, and he hoped at a future time to " bring other facts into evidence on the subject."

In the Tenth Report, for 1867, Mr. Simon refers to Dr. Buchanan's investigations under the direction of the Privy Council, in order to settle more definitely the exact influence of soil moisture as a factor in consumption ; and Mr. Simon states that Dr. Buchanan presents " an elaborate examination of the distribution of phthisis, as compared with variations of the soil, in the three south-eastern counties of England ; and it confirms, without any possibility of question, the conclusion previously suggested, *that dampness of soil is an important cause of phthisis to the population living upon the soil.*"

Having seen, in the Ninth Report, that Mr. Simon, thinking that Dr. Buchanan was on the verge of a discovery in regard to the etiology of consumption, and, in consequence of that opinion, he had requested the Privy Council to allow Dr. Buchanan to make definite inquiries, as above stated, I immediately for-

warded my address to him and to the members of the Privy Council. It arrived after Dr. Buchanan's report was written; and therefore the law of soil-moisture in regard to phthisis may be said to have been settled, by two perfectly independent observers, in two widely different portions of the earth's surface.

The knowledge we have since gained of various places in different parts of the world — Switzerland, Scotland, Mexico, Peru, and Colorado and California of this country, &c. — all now make the law of soil moisture, as a cause of consumption, as certain as any medical opinion, which the profession holds.

Questions of priority of discovery have been mooted. I prefer to say nothing, having given the above facts. Let us rather all rejoice that this great fact has been made known to us; and let all of our energies be directed to the instilling of that truth into the mind of every community throughout the globe: for thereby we shall hasten the day when they will more or less carefully obey the law, and thus save many from premature death.

APPENDIX VII.

MASSACHUSETTS LAW ON NOXIOUS AND OFFENSIVE TRADES.

VII.

(PAGE 51.)

AN ACT CONCERNING SLAUGHTER-HOUSES AND NOXIOUS AND OFFENSIVE TRADES.

Be it enacted, &c., as follows: —

SECTION 1. Whoever in any city or town containing more than four thousand inhabitants,[1] erects, occupies, or uses any building, for carrying on therein the business of slaughtering cattle, sheep, or other animals, or for melting or rendering establishments, or for other noxious or offensive trades and occupations, or permits or allows said trades or occupations to be carried on upon premises owned or occupied by him or them, without first obtaining the written consent and permission of the mayor and aldermen or selectmen of such city or town, shall forfeit a sum not exceeding two hundred dollars for every month he or they so occupy or use such building or premises, and in like proportion for a longer or shorter time: *provided*, that the terms of this section shall not apply to any building or premises now occupied or used for the trades or occupations before described; but no person or persons or corporation now occupying or using any buildings or premises for the trades or occupations aforesaid shall enlarge or extend the same, without first obtaining the written consent and permission of the mayor and aldermen or selectmen of the city or town in which such building or premises are situated, in the manner provided in this section.

SECT. 2. Whenever, in any city or town containing more than four thousand inhabitants,[1] any building or premises are occupied or used, by any person or persons or corporation, for carrying on the business of slaughtering cattle, sheep, or other animals, or for melting or rendering establishments, or for other

---

[1] Amended, chapter 308, Acts and Resolves, 1874, by striking out the words " containing more than four thousand inhabitants."

noxious or offensive trades, the State Board of Health may, if in their judgment the public health or the public comfort and convenience shall require, order any person or persons or corporation carrying on said trades or occupations, to desist and cease from further carrying on said trades or occupations in such building or premises, and any person or persons or corporation continuing to occupy or use such building or premises for carrying on said trades or occupations, after being ordered to desist and cease therefrom by said Board, shall forfeit a sum not exceeding two hundred dollars for every month he or they continue to occupy and use such building or premises, for carrying on said trades or occupations, after being ordered to desist and cease therefrom by said Board, as aforesaid, and in like proportion for a longer or shorter time: *provided* that, on any application to said Board to exercise the powers in this section conferred upon them, a time and place for hearing the parties shall be assigned by said Board, and due notice thereof given to the party against whom the application is made; and the order herein before provided shall only be issued after such notice and hearing.

SECT. 3. The Supreme Judicial Court, or any one of the justices thereof, in term time or vacation, shall have power to issue an injunction to prevent the erection, occupancy, use, enlargement, or extension, of any building or premises occupied or used for the trades or occupations aforesaid, without the written consent and permission provided in section one of this act being first obtained; and also in like manner to enforce the orders of the State Board of Health, issued under section two of this act. [*Approved April* 8, 1871.]

APPENDIX VIII.

EUROPEAN SANITARY WORK.

VIII.

EUROPEAN SANITARY WORK.

In the following pages, I have, of course, not undertaken to go into minute details. I could not have done so without making a volume. My object has been simply to suggest to the reader the great imperfections of sanitary law everywhere, — in some countries by the want of law upon the subject, and still more significantly by the neglect of carrying out laws which have been enacted. These facts seem to prove that America, notwithstanding her shortcomings, as proved in the address, is, however, quite equal to the majority of other countries; and her cities are not in a worse plight than most of the cities of the Old World, while, in the fact of their more recent growth, they have not to contend with the accumulated filth of centuries.

ENGLAND.

In the address, I have alluded to the influence of England, as shown by the acts of her citizens and her government, in behalf of Public Hygiene. For years, Mr. Simon has labored, and especially in his admirable reports presented to the Privy Council and Local Government Board.[1] He has had under him an able and trained corps of observers. These, with private investigators, medical and laity, have made great advances in our knowledge of the special causes of disease.

But, undoubtedly, one of the most important acts of modern times, made by a nation, was the passage by the British Parliament of the "Public Health Act of Aug. 21, 1875." It was

[1] See p. 33 of Address, and Appendix VII., Soil Moisture in England.

for "consolidating and amending the Acts relating to public health in England."[1]

A friend, formerly a member of the House of Commons, who had much to do with the preparation of the Act, writes as follows: "It is a most important Act. It repeals a whole mass of statutes, and reproduces what is in them, with amendments and corrections. Redundancies and repetitions have been struck out. This Act, taken together with the Act of 1871,[2] constituting the Local Government Board the central authority, contains all the public general law upon these matters.

These new enactments may not run easily at all times. The recent resignation of the veteran and singularly clear-headed, wise sanitarian, Mr. Simon, and the complaints lately and loudly made by the English medical press seem to indicate that such is indeed the fact. Nevertheless, I think that there can be no doubt that these two Acts have contributed mightily to the advance of England in sanitary matters.

What are needed in England and America, and, in fact, in all nations, are ministers or secretaries of health, members of the imperial or national cabinets.

FRANCE.

From "Le Dictionnaire de la Politique," by M. Block,[3] under the heading "Régime Sanitaire, Hygiène Publique," we find the following: "The administration of sanitary matters throughout Europe may be included under three distinct systems; viz., the French, English, and German methods. All the other States may be classified with one or the other of these three.

"The French system is characterized by the institution of authorities, under the names of Councils of Public Health, and their powers are simply for consultation. The executive power resides in the Prefect, who is, *ex officio*, president of each council.

[1] 38 and 39 Vict., ch. 55.
[2] 34 and 35 Vict., ch. 70.
[3] 3 Rue des Beaux Arts, Paris.

"At the period of the new organization of the police of the city of Paris, in 1667, the chief magistrate requested a commission of physicians to consult upon the subject of the proper preparation of bread. The opinions of this commission being very divergent, he appealed to the medical faculty; which, at that time, embraced the whole body of physicians. There was not less divergence of opinion in this body. Then a commission, consisting of six physicians and six citizens, *well known and experts*, was requested to decide the matter. Recourse was subsequently had, more than once, to the advice of this commission; and, toward the end of the last century, the sanitary police of the French capital had such a relative superiority that it excited the enthusiasm of J. P. Frank, who may be considered as the founder of scientific hygiene. . . .

"The Royal Society of Medicine was, moreover, religiously faithful to this same object. The usefulness of its labors in behalf of the public health extended far beyond the limits of Paris, and has even survived the existence of this famous society itself. Whoever has been called upon to treat of the subject of hygiene, especially of epidemics and of epidemiology, must have felt a profound gratitude for the memoirs, published by the Society from 1779 to 1790, for the instructive character of its plans, and the richness of the materials it has left for subsequent laborers in the same field.

Mons. Dubois, Prefect of the Police, revised and renewed these admirable traditions when, July 6, 1802, he, by decree, appointed a council of health, composed of four salaried officers. From that period, the council, consulted as it has been on all matters pertaining to the Public Health, must have found the number and importance of the questions submitted to it increase with the increasing size of the city. Its organization was made permanent by a decree of the Prefect, 24th December, 1832; somewhat modified in 1838 and 1844. Finally, the decree of 15th December, 1851, only confirmed the institution now in existence. The Council has powers only over the city of Paris; but there is in each one of the arrondissements (districts) of Paris, and in those of Sceaux and of St. Denis, similar commissions, but of less extensive authority.

The example of the capital was slowly followed by the

principal cities of France. From 1822 to 1832, Lyons, Marseilles, Lille, Nantes, Troyes, Rouen, Bordeaux, Toulouse, and Versailles were supplied with Health Councils. In 1836, the governments thought of preparing a general and definite sanitary organization for the whole of France. The Academy of Medicine earnestly supported this plan, by means of a long and remarkable report by Dr. Marc; but the project failed. The effort was renewed during the revolution of February. In the midst of the ardent aspirations for the public good of the masses, which agitated this epoch, Public Hygiene, which touches them by so many points, could not be forgotten. A plan, elaborated under the direction of Mons. Tourret, then minister of agriculture and of commerce, was decreed Dec. 18, 1848. This act not only applies to the departments, but it organizes commissions of hygiene in each department, arrondissement and canton. They are composed of physicians, pharmacists, architects, and special experts.

Their duties extend to the care of the salubrity of all public ways, dwellings, shops, schools, &c., of the abattoirs, factories, and other industrial establishments; all depots of filthy matters; dangerous animals; cemeteries; epidemics and endemics, epizoötics. They have surveillance as to the quality of foods, drinks, condiments, and medicines. The decree mentions several other points; but, as they are wholly neglected, we need not mention them. In fact, the work of health councils consists in examining into all requests for removal of or revoking of permissions in regard to all dangerous, unhealthy, or inconvenient establishments, which have been recorded from Oct. 15, 1816, to Dec. 31, 1866.

Health committees have formed, at times, useful auxiliaries among the district physicians, and those appointed to supervise in case of epidemics occurring. These were first instituted in May, 1805; and, the moment that they are called upon by the Prefect, it is their duty to visit the localities where the epidemic has broken out, and to learn all the circumstances, and the habits of the people, which may have caused it to break out, or which favor its spread; to say what measures are proper to take to arrest its progress, and also to suggest its treatment. The district physicians date from April 13, 1835; and

they are to be found only in a certain number of the departments.

The organization of the Consulting Committee of Public Health was regulated by a decree dated Aug. 16, 1848; Oct. 23, 1856; and Nov. 5, 1869. It is composed of physicians, of a chemist, an engineer, an architect, and several public officers. The power of the Committee extends to quarantine, and the service of sanitarian physicians, established in the East; to the measures necessary to take to prevent and contend against epidemics; to the improvement of Public Health; and to the means necessary to make them more and more accessible to the sick poor.

The law of April 13, 1856, has also instituted, in each district where the Council of Health has declared it necessary, certain committees to supervise unhealthy residences. They are armed with power to clean all such dwellings.

Finally, the Academy of Medicine completes the full number of institutions bearing upon this subject. It encourages the study of epidemics, by offering rewards of honor. It brings together the works which this study produces, and annually, in its scientific transactions, a well-arranged and appropriate account is given of the diseases which have prevailed in the various parts of France. The diffusion of the knowledge of vaccination, and the collecting of observations made at the various bathing establishments and mineral springs, are given to it.

Italy, Belgium, and Spain have generally followed the French. But it would not be true, if we placed them all in the same rank. Even during the Middle Ages, Italy was in advance, in this respect, of other countries. At the present time, Italy holds an honorable rank among those countries which cultivate Public Hygiene.

In the London "Lancet's" report on the present working of sanitary law in France ("Lancet," Dec. 23, 1876), we find the following facts: —

"As at present constituted, the government of Paris has two heads, and both have sanitary powers. They are the Prefecture of Police, and the Prefecture of the Seine. That these

two must sometimes clash is evident, when, as sometimes happens, the inspectors from each department meet in the same house, at the same time, to investigate the same grievance. The Prefect of the Seine nominates a committee for the inspection of unwholesome dwellings. The Prefect of Police appoints a sanitary committee, under the title of Conseil d'Hygiène Publique et de Salubrité. Each arrondissement has its own sanitary organization. These are under the control of the above-named Conseil, and all are under the control of the Minister of Agriculture and of Commerce. It would appear, moreover, that, although by means of the police power the Conseil has a wide control, its action is very lax."

From the above it would seem that France, like all other countries, is deficient in its *administration* of sanitary laws.

Like England and America, it needs a minister of Public Health.

GERMANY.

Through the kindness of James M. Barnard, Esq., of Boston, I am able to present the following sketch — by one most fitted to give it — of the present condition of Public Hygiene in many of the German States. Everywhere there, as in this country, sanitary science is merely in the initiative: —

FRANKFORT, May 17, 1876.

JAMES M. BARNARD, ESQ.

SIR, — I have written to some friends in several places in Germany, in order to get more exact information in regard to the organization of Public Health in the different States of Germany. But the result is very poor. We are, in fact, more in a discussion of the way how to organize than in any practical execution of a good organization.

Seven years ago, a number of physicians, engineers, town councils, &c., addressed a petition to the Nord Deutsche Bund, and repeated the same, two years later, to the German Empire, in order to ask for a general board of health for Germany (published in the "Deutsche Vierteljahre Schrift für öffentliche

Gesundheitspflege, vol. i. pp. 132 and 284" *et seq*.[1] There was great opposition in the beginning, from local points of view. Quite recently, such a Board has been organized, but on a miserable scale (a medical man, a veterinarian, and a statistician). It will, in the beginning, do nothing but collect medical statistics, and study the organization in other countries.

In *Saxony*, the central Board of Health is pretty well organized. It publishes a yearly report (till now, 5). You will find an abstract of the 1st Report in Deutsche Vierteljahre Schrift, vol. i. p. 628 *et seq.*: 2d Report in vol. iv. p. 270; 3d Report in vol. ii. p. 96; 4th Report in vol. vi. p. 631, of the same journal.

In *Bavaria*, this body is organized in intimate relations with commissions, elected by the medical societies of the eight different provinces of the kingdom. You will find the statistics of this organization, vol. iii. 580–3; and the rules for the preceding, in vol. v. 477; vii. 764 *et seq*.

In *Würtemberg*, just now, a very similar organization has been formed, or is to be formed immediately.

In the same way, nearly, the *Grand duchy of Baden* is working. You will find an abstract of its doings in vol. iv. p. 278.

In the province of *Schleswig Holstein*, an organization of a more local character is existing. You will find an account of its mode of action in vol. vii. p. 396.

The two republics of *Hamburg* and *Bremen* have quite recently organized their Boards of Health. *Vide* vol. iii. 368; vol. vi. 440.

For the last five or seven years, in many towns, Public Health Societies have been formed; engineers, teachers, town councilmen, and, above all, physicians, being members. Some of them are very active; for example, those of Halle, Hanover, and Magdeburg. They publish reports, not exactly annual. Above all others, the Niederslandische Verein für öffentliche Gesundheitspflege is to be mentioned. It comprises, in the Prussian Rhineland and Westphalia, the representatives of

[1] A complete set of this trimestrial journal of Public Health, edited by myself, is in the hands of (*a*) Dr. Edward Jarvis, of Dorchester, Mass.; (*b*) D. Edwin Snow, City Registrar, Providence, R.I.; (*c*) Metropolitan Board of Health, New York.

more than fifty-six towns, and has more than one thousand members. It holds several meetings a year, and publishes a trimestrial journal of Public Health, which is particularly remarkable for its articles on the medical statistics of the towns of this region.

Basel, though not in Germany, may be mentioned. It has, I think, the best organized Board of Health on the Continent, which is vested with the greatest powers. You will find its regulations in my journal, vol. ii. 356, 366.

As to the prevention of infectious diseases among the children in schools, we have, so far as I know, no exact laws upon the subject. There is much discussion about it amongst the physicians of the country. The opinion is, I believe, prevailing, that children affected with diphtheria, scarlatina, and whooping-cough should be prevented from returning to school too early. Some say their brothers and sisters should be prevented from visiting; and some even say that if scarlatina, and especially diphtheria, has affected a pretty large number of children of one class, this class should be suspended for some time. *Measles* are rather too mild in our country, and are communicated particularly during the prodromes of the disease. So one is not inclined to order any thing in regard to them.

There exists nearly everywhere a certain hygienic inspection of schools; but a very insufficient one. I may say that, in the last year, nearly every government and municipal central school-board has had a medical man as one of the committee. But its duties are not very carefully defined. Nearly everywhere, the Kreis-medicus, *i.e.* the public officer on matters pertaining to medical jurisprudence and Public Health, has the duty of making a certain inspection of the schools. In Saxony, the school boards have the power of keeping from school diseased children, in whose families diseases are prevailing. In the villages, even those children who are living in a house where certain diseases — such as cholera, typhus petechialis, scarlatina, and measles — prevail, may, on order of the Kreis-physicus, be kept from school. In Saxony, there is no medical inspector. The powers of the Kreis-physici are regulated by the law, April 26, 1873, &c., §§ IV. 37, and by the regulations.

For *Würtemberg*, please consult Deutsche Vierteljah., vol. iii. 490.

I am sorry not to be able to give you a more satisfactory answer. In fact, all is in preparation: very little is already done or organized.

I add a report I had to make, several years ago, on the organization of local Boards of Health, particularly in Frankfort. It had no real or full effect, because the political position of Frankfort has been entirely changed since.

I have the honor to be, sir, your obedient servant,

DR. GEO. VARRENTRAPP.

NORWAY.

While these pages are passing through the press, I find the following in the London "Lancet," Dec. 17, 1877, p. 251:—

"We have received a copy of the first of a new series of weekly returns for the city of Christiania, which bears unmistakable evidence that the capital of Norway is considerably in advance of the capital of England, in the organization of its Public Hygiene. Christiania is a city with an estimated population, not exceeding 79,000 persons. The weekly return, in question, records, however, the number of living and still births, distinguishing the legitimate and illegitimate; and, as regards the deaths, shows the ages of the deceased in eight groups, and the diseases under sixteen headings. Beyond this, the return records the number of *new* cases of epidemic diseases, reported by the medical practitioners during the week; and a note, appended to these figures, states that it is compulsory upon a medical practitioner to report to the sanitary authorities all cases of infectious diseases, occurring under his notice. With reference to the causes of death, it is stated that they are generally reported by the medical practitioner; but, in cases where no medical practitioner has been in attendance, they are verified by professional certifiers. It appears, therefore, that in two important essentials of effective sanitation, Christiania is far ahead of London, or, indeed, of any large town of the United Kingdom. Not only is scientific evidence forthcoming

of the cause of every death, but every *case* of infectious disease is compulsorily reported to the sanitary authority. It is far from satisfactory to find that, while such important sanitary progress is being made abroad, sanitation is standing still at home, for want of a minister of health, and of a capable central health authority."

INDEX.

ABBREVIATIONS, &c.

L. . . . stands for . . . . . Letter.
H. . . . ,, ... Hygiene.
S. B. of H. ,, ... State Board of Health.
D. of S. L. ,, ... Digest of Sanitary Law.
P. H. . . ,, ... Public Hygiene or Public Health.

N. B. References made, in Mr. Pickering's Digest, to special diseases are omitted in this index, because they would have made it too long and confused; but, as the States are arranged alphabetically, a person can easily refer to the laws of each State on any special diseases which have not only called for the interference of Government, but which have been, at least, partially restrained by legal enactments.

A.

ABATTOIR, Brighton, 51; Philadelphia, 228, 229.
Academy (Phillips), Massachusetts, Hygiene in, 290.
Adulteration of food, prevention of, by States, 43; prevention of, 51; Pennsylvania, 234; liquors, 234.
Alabama, State Board of Health, 54; early established, why, 55; County Health Board, 61; malarial hæmorrhagic fever, 95; typhoid, 95; general powers of Board of Health, 100; registration, 113; L. Drs. Cochran and Johnson, 135, Scales, 136; Hygiene in Colleges of, 283; in University of, 287; in Medical Colleges of, 296; D. of S. L. in, 303; S. B. of H. laws, 305.
Albuminuria, 146.
Alden's, Dr., opinion on the law of soil moisture as a cause of consumption, 459.
Alexandria, Va., changes in diseases owing to changes in locality, 264, 265; more salubrious than formerly, less malaria, 265; more phthisis, 265.
Allen, Dr. Nathan, Massachusetts, L., 171.
"Allopathy," a nickname, not to be used by physicians, 23.
America, influence of other countries upon it, 4.

American Medical Association an aid to preventive medicine, 37.
Amherst College, Hygiene in, 290.
Anderson, Dr. E. A., Wilmington, N. C., bilious and pernicious fever less, 92; diphtheria, 96; drainage laws, 99, 100; L., 216.
Anderson, Dr. W. F., Utah, small-pox quarantine, 101; L. on Utah, 262.
Andral, Louis, Chomel, the great French teachers of former days, 15.
Antioch College, Hygiene in, 292.
Apothecaries' Act, Pennsylvania, 232.
Appropriations for State Boards of Health, 44, 45, 56.
Arizona, 47; land irrigation in, 71.
Arkansas, drainage of land, 70; irrigation in, 71; levees, 72; Public Health measures, 99; registration, 113; L. on, from Drs. Lawrence, Linthicum, 136; want of sanitary legislation, 136; D. of S. L., 306.
Army itch, 160.
Army Medical Library, 147; Museum, 151.
Army publications, list of, relative to prevailing diseases, barracks, hospitals, Hygiene, sickness, and mortality in, 148-150.
Arnold, Dr. R. D., Savannah, cholera and yellow fever, 96.
Arnold, Dr. S. T., Newport, R.I., sewerage of Newport, 239; his own method, 240.

Artesian wells at Fond-du-Lac, Wis., 278.
Arthritic diseases in New York, 197.
Asheville, N.C., Table of Temperature and Rainfalls, 214, 215.
Association, American Medical, 37.
Association, Public Health, 37.
Atlanta Medical College, Hygiene in, 296.
"Atlantic Monthly" discusses sewerage, 38.

B.

BADEN, Grand Duchy, P. H., 475.
Bailey, Dr. F. K., Knoxville, Tenn., L. 257.
Baker, Dr. H. B., Lansing, Ill., scarlet fever, 118; croup, pneumonia, 119; L. on sanitary inspection, scarlatina worse than small-pox, 175; influence of present knowledge of disease as a preventive, 176.
Baldwin, Dr. A. S., climate in relation to medicine, 152.
Baldwin, Dr. W. O., Ala., Health Boards, 100.
Ball-playing in Universities, Table, 285.
Bard, Dr. Samuel, diphtheria in New York, 1789, 212.
Barnard, J. M., Esq., letter from Dr. Varrentrapp, on sanitary law in Germany, 474-477.
Barracks, army report, 149.
Bartlett, Dr. Elisha, 19; his wide influence, 25; admires Louis, 26; condemns Rush, 26; defends the Observation School; satirizes heroic medication, 26, 27.
Baruch, Dr. Simon, Camden, S.C., L, 241.
Basel (Switzerland), P. H., 476.
Bates, Charles B., Santa Barbara, Cal., L. 138.
Battle-field succor, North, 242-246; battle-field succor, South, 246-255.
Bavaria, P. H. in, 475.
Beauregard, Gen., "Wayside Home," 249.
Beech, Dr. J. H., drainage on pernicious fevers, 91; L. 176; drainage, laws in Michigan, 177.
Belgium, P. H. in, 473.
Bell, Dr. A. N., Brooklyn, N.Y., L., journals devoted to sanitary work, 190.
Belton, George W., Tallahassee, Fla., L., 152.
Bemis, Dr., vital statistics of Kentucky, 172.

Benham, Gen., U.S.A., construction of Quarantine Islands, N.Y., 210.
Bigelow, Jacob, 6; life, 19, 20, note; reminiscences of Rush, 20; interview with, 20; great influence of, 20; "self-limited diseases," 20; advocate of Louis and of his method, 21; scepticism increased by, 22; "Nature in disease," 21; opposed to Rush and Broussais, 21.
Bilious remittent, 90, 91.
Billings, Dr. J. S., U.S.A., Washington, D.C., L., lessons from war on P. H., 147; army publications, 149.
Births. See Registration, 63, 66, et cet.
Black jaundice, in Texas, 97, 259.
"Black tongue," 90, 94; among the wild deer of Louisiana, and said to have infected human beings, 164.
Blodget, Lorin, Esq., Philadelphia, 80; L., house-building for the poor in P., 216-220.
Boards of Health, 43; willingness to spend money for do., 43, 44; few States have one, 44; States unwilling to spend money for, 44; no State fully aroused to their value, 45; County Boards, 61; Town Boards, 62; number of State Boards, 45; correspondents of S. B. of H., 58; no State has a perfect system of, 59; considered a place of honor in Massachusetts, 59; also, Pickering's Digest of Sanitary Law, App. IV., 300.
Boating in Universities, Table I., 285.
Boerhaave, a leader, a system-maker, influence on America: disease in the fluids, 7.
Boston, imperfect registration, 67, note; Co-operative Building Co., 79, 81-89; "Crystal Palace" experiment, 83-89; sewerage very imperfect, 105; proposed improvement, 105; site of hospitals, 106; Homes for the poor 219.
Bowdoin College, H. in, 290.
Bowles, S. W., Colorado, "the Switzerland of America," 140.
Brandon (Vt., registration, 114.
Breed, Dr S. P., Princeton, Ill ; cattle disease, 78; L. cattle epidemic, 155-158; land drainage, benefits of, 159.
Bremen, P. H. at, 475.
Bridgeton, registration, 114.
Bright, Dr. J. W., Kentucky, scarlatina, fever, diphtheria, 96.
Brighton, Mass., its disgusting condition before the abattoir was built, 49; excellent results of abattoir, 51.

INDEX.

Bronchitis in Colorado, 143.
Brooklyn, registration, 114.
Broussais, leader of medical thought, 5; wide influence in Europe and America, 10; his fall, 11; termination of medical system-making, 5.
Brown, Bedford, Dr., Alexandria, L., 264; experience as an army surgeon, 264, 265.
Brown, successor of Cullen: sthenic or asthenic states, 7.
Bryce, Mrs., Wayside Home, 247.
Bryce, Miss, Wayside Home, 247.
Buchanan, Dr., on consumption in England, as influenced by soil moisture, 461.
Building companies, 80, 81; in Philadelphia, 216, 220; Boston, 81-89.
Bund, Nord Deutsche, P. H. in, 474.
Burch, Dr. J. D., malaria lessened, 91; L., 178.
Burials in Pennsylvania, 233.
Burlington (Vt.), registration, 114.
Burlington College, N.J., H. in, 291.
Bush, Dr. L. P., L. on malaria in Delaware, 90.
Butler, Dr. J. S., on diphtheria and cerebro-spinal meningitis, Connecticut, 95.
Butler, Dr. L. C., Vt., no disease has disappeared, 93; compulsory vaccination, 101; typhoid fever developments, 118.

C.

CABELL, Prof. J. L., of University of Virginia, L., 264.
California, appropriations for S. B. of H., 45, 47; S. B. of H. established, 54, 310; County Boards, 61; vital statistics neglected, 66; registration laws, 68; land drainage, 70; laws against cholera, 75; yellow fever left to local boards, 77; overcrowding of Chinese, 80; registration, 112, 113; L. from Drs. Bates, McKee, 138; Hygiene in University (Medical) College, 296; D. of S. L., 306-311.
Campbell, Dr., on Georgia State Hospitals, 250.
Canada, cattle disease in, 78.
Carleton, Dr. C. M., Norwich, Conn., L., 145.
Carn, Dr. J. M., Florida, health laws, 99.
Carpenter, Dr. A. M., Keokuk, Iowa, L., 162.
Catarrh, chronic, Colorado, 141, 143.
Catarrhal diseases in Illinois, 160, 161.
Catarrhal zone, 160.

Catlin, Dr. Benjamin H., W. Meriden, Conn., cerebro-spinal meningitis, 96; L., 144, 145.
Cattle disease, prevention of, 43, 52, 78; advantages of co-operation between States, 78; convention of American and Canadian cattle dealers, 78; Massachusetts' doings, 52, 78, 157; Dr. Breed, 155; convention in regard to, 157; in Virginia, 269, 270; Hamburg, 78; commissioner's report on, of Illinois, 78, 157; department of agriculture of the United States, New York, Massachusetts, 78, 157.
Cattle transportation in Pennsylvania, 233.
Causes of disease, investigations by the States, 43.
Cemetery, effect of, on typho-malarial fever, 277.
Census, United States, imperfection of, 115.
Centenary, natural division of, into three epochs, 4.
Cerebro-spinal meningitis, in Connecticut, Indiana, and Michigan, 96; increased of late, 97; newly introduced into Michigan, 98; New Hampshire, 189; Connecticut, 145; New York, 212; Vermont, 263.
Cesspools, influence of on workman, 106.
Chadwick, Edwin, pioneer of State Preventive Medicine in England, 6, 30.
Chaillé, Dr. Standford E., typhoid fever in Louisiana, 90, 98; smallpox, 100; yellow fever in New Orleans, 166; L. Revised Statutes of Louisiana, 169, 170.
Chandler, Prof. C. T., analysis of waters of New York City, 203.
Charity to an enemy, in letters from a Southern to a Northern lady, 252.
Charleston, S.C., yellow fever, 77; registration, 114.
Chattanooga, registration in, 114.
Chemical examination of soils, law for in Pennsylvania, 222.
Chicago, registration, 113; water supply, possible pollution of, 162; Hygiene in University of, 287.
Cholera, prevention of, 75; imperfectly done; United States report on, 75; in Georgia, 96; Kentucky, 97; Louisiana, 97; California, Connecticut, Nebraska, Texas, Utah, Virginia, Iowa, North Carolina, Oregon, 75; need a central power to give notice of the approach of such epidemics, 75; stamped out in Chatta-

nooga, 256; in Knoxville, 257; laws in Connecticut, 144, 146; District of Columbia, 147, 149; Illinois, 155; Kansas, 163; Kentucky, 164; Louisiana, 165; New York, 201, 207, 209, 212; Pennsylvania, 226; Tennessee, 256-258; Virginia, 272, 275.
Cholera infantum, District of Columbia, 90; Nebraska, 182.
Cholera morbus, District of Columbia, 90.
Chomel, 15.
Christian Commission, 35, 244.
Christiania (Sweden), P.H. 477.
Cincinnati, registration, 114.
Circular to correspondents, 39, 125
Civil war, our late, a teacher of Hygiene, 34; promoter of beneficent actions, 242-255; hospitals at Richmond, 250, 251; spirit of self-sacrifice on both sides, 251; incident during, 252.
Claiborne, Dr. J. H., Petersburg, Va., L., 266.
Cochran, Jerome D., L., Mobile, 135.
Colleges, Hygiene in, App. III.; circular to, 281, 282; list of those who replied to circular, 283, 285; table showing amount of Hygiene taught in them, 285; medical colleges, list of, 294, 298; table, 295; replies from, 296, 298; Hygiene in Trinity, Hartford, Knox, Ill. 287; Southern Illinois, Franklin, Ind., 288; Wabash, Ind., Bowdoin, Me., Amherst, Mass., Harvard, Mass., Williamstown, Mass., Dartmouth, N.H., 290; Burlington, N.J., 291; Princeton, N.J., 292; Rutgers, N.J., Union, N.Y., Antioch, O., 292; Oberlin, O., Tennessee Agricultural, 293; (medical), *see* Medical Colleges.
Colorado, appropriation for S. B. of H., 45, 47; S. B. established, 54, 311; County Boards, 61; land irrigation, 71; yellow fever never in, 77; phthisis in, 95; Public Health measures, 99; registration, 112, 113; L., Dr. Denison, 139; Dr. Mack, 139; temperatures, January and February, 1875, 143; Dr. Mack's description of the Los Pinos County (temperature, dryness, &c., variable climate), influence of height on man; Indians, 139-144; D. of S. L., 311.
Columbia, District of, appropriations for B. of H., 45, 47; S. B. of H. established, 54; ample powers for nuisance removal, 60; law for registration, 68; registration in, 112.
Columbia (S. C.), registration in, 114.

Commissions, Christian; United States Sanitary; Western Sanitary, as promoters of private and public munificence, 35, 244.
Confederate States, battlefield succor in, 246-252.
Congestive fever in Illinois, 160.
Conjunctivitis in Colorado, 143.
Conn, Dr. G. F., Concord, N. H. L.,182.
Connecticut, no S. B. of H.; but partial powers in cities, 60; law for registration, 68; "vaccination and red flag," 74; cholera, local laws, 75; diseases more manageable, 90; diphtheria and cerebro-spinal meningitis, 95; registration, 113; L. Dr. Catlin, 144, Drs. Carleton and Hubbard, 145; Woodward, 146; D. of S. L., 311-316.
Constipation in Colorado, 143.
Consumption, Fisher on, 195; soil moisture, as a prominent cause, 119; in Connecticut, 145; Illinois, 160; Vermont, 233; Virginia, 265, 266; residence on a damp soil one of the primal causes of, in Massachusetts, 455; not equally distributed in New England, 46); Mr. Simon's view of soil moisture as cause, 461
Contagious diseases, prevention of in the various States, 73; Illinois, 161; Louisiana, 135, 170.
Contagious and infectious diseases in New Hampshire, 189; New York, 194, 195, 199, 206-209, 212; Pennsylvania, 225, 226, 228, 229, 238; Tennessee, 257; Virginia, 267, 271, 272.
Cook, Dr. John L., milk-sickness and malaria in Kentucky, 90; L., 163.
Co-operative building companies, 80; rare, 81; Boston Co-operative Building Company, experience of, in their trial on the "Crystal Palace," 81, &c.; in Philadelphia, 216, 220.
Corbin, Dr. G. E., 177; malarial diseases in Michigan more prevalent on east than west banks of swamp, 177.
Cornell University, Hygiene in. 292.
Correspondents, character of, 40; list of, from each State, 129-134; L. from correspondents, App II. 135-278; L. Alabama, 135; Arkansas. 136; California, 138; Colorado, 139-143; Connecticut, 144-146; District of Columbia, 147, 152; Florida, 152; Georgia, 152-154; Illinois, 155, 162; Iowa, 162; Kansas, 162; Kentucky, 163; Louisiana, 164-170; Maine, 171; Massachusetts, 171-174; Michigan, 174-178;

INDEX.   483

Mississippi, 178; Missouri, 180; Nebraska, 181; Nevada, 182; New Hampshire, 182–189; New Jersey, 190; New York. 190–213; North Carolina, 216; Pennsylvania, 216, 239; Rhode Island, 239; South Carolina, battle-field succor at, 246; Tennessee, 256–258; Texas, 258–262; Utah, 262; Vermont, 262–264; Virginia, 264–276; Wisconsin, 277; Wyoming, 278.
Cotting's, Dr. B E., opinion on the law of soil moisture as cause of consumption, 459.
County Boards of Health, Alabama, California, Colorado, Georgia, 61; future value, though rare now, 61.
Cowan, Dr. G., Danville, Ky., L., 163.
Cow-pox in Virginia, 271.
Coxe, Dr., vital statistics, Washington, 173.
Crimean war, lessons in Public Hygiene, 34.
Crockwell, Dr. J. D., Salt Lake, L., 262.
Croup, in Connecticut, 90, 146; Michigan, 119, 176.
Cullen, influence in America, opposed to Boerhaave; all disease in the solids, 7.
Cullen, Dr. J. D., Richmond, Va., diphtheria, 96.

D.

DABNEY, Dr. W. C., Virginia, compulsory vaccination, 101.
Dakota, no yellow fever, 77.
Dalton, Dr. John C., New York, on trichina spiralis, 213.
Dancy, Dr. F. W., Holly Springs, Miss., L., 180.
Dartmouth College, Hygiene in, 290.
Darwin, successor of Brown, 7; Linnæan classification, 7.
Davis, Dr. N. S., Chicago, L., 161.
Death rate in New York, 194; higher where filth, 276.
Deaths. *See* Registering of, 63, 66 *et seq.*
Delaware, vaccination in, 74; less malarious disease, 90; drainage in Wilmington, 100; registration, 113; D. of S. L., 316–318.
Denison, Dr. Charles, Denver, Col., phthisis perhaps introduced into Colorado, 95; L., 139.
Denver as a residence for consumptives, 95; registration, 113; Dr. Denison, L., 139; Dr. Mack, L., 139–143.

Diathetic diseases of localities in New York, 197.
Diphtheria, Connecticut, 95; North and South Carolina, Vermont, Virginia, 96; last century in England, 96; Kentucky, 97; more severe than formerly, 97, 98; Connecticut, 146; Florida, 152; Illinois, 160; New York, 192, 202, 203; Albany, 202; Elmira, 212, 213; Virginia, 275.
Diseased or tainted flesh, Pennsylvania, 234; Virginia, 269.
Diseases, preventable, large number, 42; contagious, prevention of, 73 *et cet.*; formerly prevalent, which have ceased, 89; crushed (?), 94; no evidence to that effect, 94; a new disease generated, 94; typhoid in Alabama, 95; new in State. 98; zymotics *de novo*, 264; modified, 274.
Disinfection of streets, Louisiana, 167.
District of Columbia, building company for tenements for the poor, 81; lessening of malarial diseases, 90; L., Dr. Toner, 150; D. of S. L., 305 *et seq.*
Downes, Dr. Charles L., Nottingham, N.H., general statutes, *et cet.*, 183–185; evil influence of bad sanitary arrangements of a house, 186, 187; cerebro-spinal meningitis, 189.
Drainage of land, 63, 69; good effects, Illinois, 70; New Jersey, Pennsylvania, 70; Illinois, thousands of acres improved, 159; in Michigan, good effects, 177, 178; New York, 205; St. Albans, 263; as a preventer of consumption in England, 461.
Duncan, Dr. William, Savannah, Ga., cholera, yellow fever, 96.
Duration of life, 67, 115; do we live now longer than a century ago? no facts to enlighten us, 115; Dr. Jarvis's opinion, 116.
Dysentery fatal in Coldwater, Mich., till a dam was destroyed, 177; malignant in Virginia, 275.
Dyspnœa in Colorado, 141.

E.

ELLIOT'S Approximate Life Tables, 115; United States' Census, 115.
Endemic disease, Nebraska, 182; New York, 193.
England, influence of, 33, 469; Artisans' and Laborers' Dwelling Improvement Act, 79; soil moisture as

484   INDEX.

a cause of consumption, 461; sanitary work in, 469; Public Health Act, importance of, 469.
Epidemics, Mississippi, 179; Nebraska, 182.
Epizoötic among horses, Virginia, 269.
Epochs, centennial period divisible into three, 4.
Epoch; First, 1776–1832, 5; polypharmacy and medical system-making, 5; influence of preceding century, Boerhaave, Cullen, *et cet.*, 7; Rush, 8; Broussais, 10; characteristics of, 11.
Epoch, Second, 1832–69, 5; observation, enumeration, scepticism, reverence for nature, 6. *See* Louis, 14; Forbes, Bigelow, Bartlett, Gerhard, J. Jackson, Jr.; results of, 28; chiefly destructive and sceptical, 28.
Epoch, Third, State Preventive Medicine, 6. *See* Lemuel Shattuck, Edwin Chadwick, 30; State Preventive Medicine, 30; grand ideas underlying this epoch; to be hereafter permanent, 121.
Erysipelas, epidemic of, in New Hampshire, 188; malignant. *See* Black Tongue, Louisiana, 164.
Europe, sanitary work in, App. VIII. 469–478.

F.

"FAMILY doctor," 13.
Farcy in horses in V rginia, 270.
Fassett, Dr. O. F., St. Albans, Vt., L., 262.
Fellenberg's institution at Hofwyl, 288; advantages, 289.
Fever: —
 Congestive, rare in Illinois since clearing of land, 160.
 Intermittent, recently in Connecticut, 146; prevalence in Florida in the autumn, 152; common in Nebraska, 182; formerly pernicious in New York, now rare, 198, 202; pernicious, occasional in Norfolk, Va., 274.
 Malarial, in Arkansas, 137; less in Alexandria, Va., than formerly, owing to drying up of marshes, 265; do. Michigan, 176; common in Arkansas, 137; more on east than west banks of rivers in Michigan, 177; at one time extinct in New York, and relapse, from neglect of culture, 197; formerly frequent in Alexandria, Va; now, under changes of soil, &c., rare, 265; in Charleston, S.C., controlled, 242; malignant from obstructed drainage in the Southern States, 268; frequent among negroes in Norfolk, Va., 275.
 Malarial hæmorrhagic, in Alabama since the war, 95; a new? disease in Mississippi, 179.
 Mountain, or typho-malarial, in Nevada, 182.
 Paludal, in Arkansas, 137.
 Pernicious malarial, less in the North than formerly, 93.
 Remittent, common in Nebraska, 182.
 Spotted, in Connecticut, 1807–1813, 146; ? or cerebro-spinal meningitis, in New Hampshire, 189.
 Swamp, in Arkansas, 137.
 Typhoid, in Alabama "since the war," 95; almost the sole disease at Santa Barbara, Cal., 138; rare in Camden, S.C., 241; originates at times, '*de novo*," in Vermont, 264; traceable to impure water in Warrenton, Va., 269; beginning to appear in Kentucky, 164; rare in Nebraska, 182; in New Hampshire, from water? 185-187; in Vermont, 263; as typhus in Norfolk, Va., 275; Dr. John Warren on, 195.
 Typho-malarial, in Viroqua, Wis., apparently caused by disturbing of an old grave-yard, 277.
 Typhus, originating, "*de novo*," in Vermont, 264.
 Yellow, has left the North, still at the South. 93; one or two epidemics formerly in Connecticut, 146; yellow, in the army, 1867, 149; recent epidemic of in Savannah, Ga., 153, 154; correspondent thinks it only a paludal fever in Louisiana, and could be prevented, 165; not endemic in Louisiana, 166; "germ theory" in, 168; formerly prevalent in New York, now rare, 198, 205; terrible epidemics of in New York, 1719 and 1809; laws against in, 205-208; treatment of in, 209, 210; law against in Pennsylvania, 226; not prevented by quarantine in Charleston, S. C., 242; but thought to be kept out by quarantine in Memphis, Tenn., 256, 257; rarer than formerly in Norfolk, Va.; minny epidemics formerly, rarer now, in Virginia, 275.
Field, Cyrus, Atlantic telegraphy, 4.

Field, Dr. N., Indiana, cerebro-spinal meningitis, 96.
Finfrock, Dr. J. H., inefficient laws in Wyoming Territory, 100.
Fish culture in Pennsylvania, 222.
Fisher, Dr. J. D., consumption in Massachusetts, 195.
Fisher, Mrs. J., "Wayside Home" in the South, 247.
Flint, Dr. Austin, yellow fever at Staten Island, but not at New York, 92.
Florida, P. H. in, 99; L., Dr. Belton, 152; D. of S. L., 319.
Folsom, Dr. C. F., river pollution in Massachusetts, 57.
Food adulteration, prevention of, 51, 52; New Hampshire, 183; Pennsylvania, 221, 234.
Forbes, John, 6; leader of modern thought, 19; "Homœopathy, Allopathy, and Young Physic," 22; polypharmacy deprecated, 23; nature glorified, 24; his influence needed for the evolution of the 2d epoch, 23; suggestion of preventive medicine, 24.
Ford, Dr. William, Philadelphia, tenement houses, 80; L. 220-231; sanitary laws on P. H., 232, 236.
France, P. H in; influence of, 32; characteristics of its sanitary system, 472; influence of the Royal Society of Medicine; per cent of health, 473; in various cities, 474; health committees, 472-473; Academy of Medicine, 473; "Lancet's" report on; deficient in administration of sanitary law, 473.
Frankfort (Germany), P. H. in, 477.
Franklin (Conn.), registration, 113.
Franklin College, Indiana, hygiene, 288.
Frankness to patients, 14.
French, Dr. George F., Portland, Me., L., 171.

G.

GALVESTON (Texas), registration, 114.
Georgia, appropriations for S. B. of H. 45, 47; S. B. of H. established, 54; why early established, 55; county boards, 61; law for registration, 68; registration, 113; letters from "Daily Constitution" on yellow fever, 152; State hospitals at Richmond during the civil war, 250; D. of S. L., 319-324; S. B. of H., 322.

Gerhard, Dr., influence on second epoch, 15; a pupil of Louis, 15.
Germ theory in contagious disease, 168.
Germany, public hygiene in, letter from Dr. Varrentrapp to James M. Barnard, Esq., 474-477; Nord Deutsche Bund, 474; Saxony, Bavaria, Würtemberg, Grand Duchy of Baden, Schleswig Holstein, Hamburg, Bremen, Halle, Hanover, Magdeburg, Prussian Rhineland, Westphalia, 475; Basel, 476; Frankfort, 477.
Glandered horses, 270.
Gött, Dr. Wm. A., Viroqua, Wis., L., effects of open cemetery, 277.
Grants of money by various States, for special sanitary work, 57.
Green, Dr. John, St. Louis, Mo., L.; "spasmodic sanitation and patronage," 180.
Grindley, T. R., Esq., Carson City, Nevada, L., 182.
Griscom, Dr. John, on prevention of disease, 195.
Gymnasia in universities, table 1, 285; at Hofwyl, Switzerland. 288; Amherst College, Mass., Harvard, Phillips Academy, 290; Dartmouth, Burlington, N.J., 291; Union, 292; Oberlin, Tennessee Agricultural, Virginia, 293.

H.

HÆMATURIA miasmatica, or black jaundice, in Texas, 259; Virginia, 268.
Hæmorrhagic fever, malarial, 95. See Hæmaturia.
Halle (Germany), P. H., 475
Hamburg (Germany), P. H., 475.
Hamilton, Alexander, quarantined at Albany, 207.
Hampton Falls, registration, 114.
Hanover (Germany), P. H. in, 475
Harris, Dr. Elisha, tenement houses, 80; malaria less, 91; typho-malaria, 118; scarlatina and diphtheria more fatal, 97; on topographical and hydrographical survey of the State, 204; New York, L., history of sanitation in America, 191; laws of New York, 192; State, city, 193; death rate, 194; quarantine, &c., in Mass., 194.
Hartford, registration, 113.
Harvard College, Hygiene in, 290.
Health, Boards of, history of, 194; action, 54; reports, published by

States and towns, list of, 113, 114; S. B. of H., action thereon in various States, 43–47; appropriations for, 45, 56; when established in twelve States, 54; correspondents, 58; powers, 59; county, 61; town, 62.
Health council, 76.
Health, a national secretary of, 76; and imperial, needed, 470, 474, 478.
Heard, Dr. T. J., Texas, typhoid, diphtheria, cerebro-spinal meningitis, malaria, 97; drainage, 100.
Henderson, Ky., registration, 113.
Henshey, Dr. D. W., Nebraska City, Neb., L , 181.
Herrick, Dr. S. S., New Orleans, La., yellow fever might be crushed out, 97; L. yellow fever, 166; plan of disinfection of streets, 167; germ theory, 168.
Hill, Miss Octavia's, plan for improving the houses of the poor, impossible, probably, under any committee, 88.
Hoffman, precursor of Cullen, 7.
Hog cholera, 269.
Homes for the people, 89; Blodgett on, 216–219; in Philadelphia, 227; Boston, 81, &c.
Horner, Dr. F., Jr., Virginia, L., typhoid, cattle plague, hog cholera, 269.
Hosack, Dr., yellow fever in New York, 76.
Hospitals, sustained by Southern States at Richmond during the late civil war, 248.
Hubbard, Dr. Stephen G., New Haven, Conn., diphtheria, 96; L. 145.
Huger, Dr. William H., Charleston, S.C , L., 241, 242.
Hun. Dr. E. A., on trichina spiralis, 213.
Hygiene (public), neglected, 1; duty of all to urge attention to it, 117; legitimate growth of late, 122; within the domain of modern science, 122; neglected in the universities, 286; at Hofwyl, Switzerland, 288; private; in universities, table 1, 285–294; good effects of attention to, in universities, 286; in medical colleges, 294–298; in universities and colleges: Univ. of Ala., Southern University, Ala., Chicago, Knox College, 287; Southern Ill , State Normal Ill , Franklin, Indiana State Univ., 288; N. W. Christian, 289; Wabash, Ind., Bowdoin, Me., Amherst, Harvard, Phillips, Williamstown, Mass., Dartmouth, N.H., 290; Burlington, 291; Princeton, Rutger's, N.J., Cornell, Union, N.Y., Antioch, O., 292: Oberlin, O., Tenn. Agricultural, Univ. of Va., 293, 294; table 2, shewing amount of attention paid to, in medical colleges, 295; results of table, 296; letters from Med. Col., Ala., Med. Dep. Univ. Col., San Francisco, Yale, National, Washington, D.C., Atlanta, Ga., Rush, Ill., New Orleans School of Med., Med. Dep. Univ., La., Harvard, Univ. Michigan, 296; Dartmouth, N.H., Albany, Buffalo, N.Y., Miami, Ohio, 297; Jefferson Med. Col., Univ. Pennsylvania, S. Carolina Med. Col., 298; in universities and colleges, 283–294.
Hygiene in universities and colleges: Alabama, Southern University, Ala.; Trinity, Conn.; Chicago; Knox; Southern Illinois and State Normal, Ill. ; Franklin; N. W. Christian; N. W. Christian and Wabash, Ind.; Bowdoin, Me.; Amherst, Harvard, Phillips Academy, and Williamstown, Mass.; Dartmouth, N.H.; Burlington, Princeton, and Rutger's, N.J.; Cornell, Union, N.Y.; Antioch; Oberlin, O.; Tennessee Agricultural, Tenn.; University of Virginia, Va., 283–294.

I.

IDAHO, local statistics, record marriages only, 66, 112.
Illinois, drainage of land, interesting results of, 79; water in cities, 72; Chicago, purity of water, 73; cattle disease, 78; registration, 113; L. Dr. Breed, 155–161; Davis, Johnson, 161; D. of S. L. 325, 328; S. B. of H. 326.
"Il vomito." See "Yellow Disease," 268.
Immigrant's law, Pennsylvania, 228. See Vanderpoel.
Indiana, water in cities, 72; small-pox in, 74; registration, 113; State University, hygiene in, 288; inadequate sanitary legislation, 300; D. of S. L., 328.
Indianapolis, registration, 113.
Indigestion, common among North American Indians, 143.
Infectious diseases in Virginia, 271 (see Contagious); in Germany, 476.
Influence of certain men upon various States, 69.

INDEX. 487

Inoculation in Virginia, penalty for, 271.
Inspection of schools, hygiene in Germany, 476.
Inspectors, English, sanitary, admirable, 33.
Intermittent fever, New York, 92, 198, 202, 212; Vermont, 93; Connecticut, 146; Florida, 152; Nebraska, 182; pernicious, New York, 198; Virginia, 274.
Iowa, vaccination compulsory, 74; quarantine and hospitals for cholera, 75; yellow fever, 77; registration, 113; L. Dr. Carpenter, 162; inadequate sanitary legislation, 300; D. of S L , 329.
Irrigation of land, 70, 71; Arizona, Colorado, New Mexico, Utah, Washington Territory, Arkansas, 71.
Islamism and Mormonism, 71.
Italy, war in, a teacher of hygiene, 34; P. H. in, 473.
Itch, army, 160.

J.

JAUNDICE, Black. *See* Hæmaturia miasmatica, 97, 259.
Jackson, Dr., Jr., influence on second epoch, 15; a pupil of Louis, 15; his influence in New England, 15; Louis's estimate of, as a scientific observer, 443-447; letters to his father, 447; Dr. Pierson's obituary remarks on, 448.
Jackson, James, Senior, views of bloodletting, influence in New England, 11, note; Louis's letters to, App. V. 443-447; L. from son. 447; experience of yellow fever, 76.
Janes, Dr. E. H., New York, intermittent less, 92; nomenclature of diseases, 97; L., pernicious intermittent and yellow fever almost extinct; formerly prevalent, 198.
Janeway, Dr., on New York sanitary laws, 198, 199.
Jarvis, Dr Edward, a pioneer in sanitary work in America, 32, 68, 116; on registration in the States, 172, 173; duration of life, 174; Report to the Massachusetts Legislature, 196.
Jefferson, Thomas, his low estimate of the medical profession, 9.
Jenckes, Dr. G. W., Woonsocket, R.I., L., 241.
Jennings, Dr. R. G., Little Rock, Ark., sanitary survey of the city. 137.
Johnson, Hosney A , Chicago, Ill., L.,
possible pollution of water supply, 162.
Johnson, Dr. J. B., St. Louis, Mo., L., 180.
Johnston, William Henry, Dr., Selma, Ala., hæmorrhagic fever since the war, 95; L., 135.
Johnston, Dr. Wirt, Jackson, Miss., L., 179.
Journals, sanitary, list of in U. S., 190.
Joynes, Dr. Levin S., Richmond, Va., L. sanitary laws, 269-273.

K.

KANSAS, Dr. Sinks, 162; inadequate sanitary legislation in, 300; D. of S. L., 330.
Kedzie, Dr. R. C., malaria lessened, 91; cerebro-spinal meningitis, 96; sanitary inspection of Michigan, L., 178.
Kentucky, vital statistics, law defective, 66; bilious remittents less, 90; milk-sickness, 90; cholera, scarlatina, typhoid fever, diphtheria, 97; registration, 113; L., Drs. Cowan, Cook, 163; milk-sickness, typhoid fever, cholera, 164; inadequate sanitary laws in, 300; D. of S. L., 330.
Keokuk, registration, 113.
Kilpatrick, Dr. A. R., Texas, black jaundice and neuralgia more common, 97; B. of H. given up, 100.
Kinloch, Dr. Robert A., Charleston, S.C., L., 242.
Kirkwood, James P., river pollution, 57
Knox College, Hygiene in, 287.
Knoxville, registration, 114.

L.

LABOR, regulation of in Pennsylvania, 235
Laity, union with the profession to promote sanitary measures, 29, 38, 121.
Land drainage in the various States, 60; California, 138; Illinois, 155, 158-159; Louisiana, 167; Michigan, 177; New Hampshire, 184, 188; New York, 199, 205; Pennsylvania, 225, 230; Rhode Island, 239, 240; Virginia, 273. *See* Drainage.
Land irrigation, 70. *See* Irrigation.
Lawrence, Dr. G. W., L., Hot Springs, Arkansas, 136.
Laws of development of disease, 118; views of Drs. Harris, Plummer, Oregon, Butler, Vt., Stewart and To-

ner, Washington, D.C., Baker, 118; results of investigation in Massachusetts, 119.
Le Conte, Dr. J. L., Philadelphia, L., 236.
Legislation, history of sanitary in United States, 194.
Letters: circular letter to correspondents, 125; colleges, &c., 281, L.; from a lady in the Confederacy to one in the North, on the death of her son, during the late civil war, 252.
Levees, River, 71; in Arkansas and Louisiana, 72.
Library and Museum, United States, must be sustained, 34.
Life, duration of, 116, 174.
Life, value of, 194.
"Lincoln Building," history of experiment of, 83-89.
Lindsley, Dr., New Haven, on S. B of H., 145.
Linthicum, Dr. D. A., L., Helena, Ark., health laws, 99; L., 136.
Little, Dr. George, on yellow fever in Savannah, 154.
Little Rock, registration, 113.
Local Government Board (English), 33.
Lodging houses for the poor. *See* Boston, 81, &c.; Brooklyn, New York, 201; England, 79; Philadelphia, 81; Blodgett's letter on, 216, &c.
Logan, Dr. J. P., yellow fever in Savannah, 154.
Los Pinos Agency (Col.), table of temperature, 143. *See* Mack.
Louis's numerical method, influence of, 14; Louis's life work, 14; Broussais's opponent, 15; Louis's pupils, 15; contempt for the past by his school, 16; scepticism in medicine, 16; his school needed for reform in medicine, 17; numerical method adopted by modern sanitarians, 17; has made many observers, 18; his mottoes, those of modern science, 18; sustained by Bigelow, 20; and Bartlett, 26; estimate of Dr. J. Jackson, Jr, 443-447.
Louisiana, appropriations for S. B. of H, 45, 47; investigations for public health, 53; S. B. of H. established, 54; why early established, 55; vital statistics only in New Orleans, 66; laws for registration, 68; land drainage, 70; vaccination in, 74; quarantine for yellow fever, 77, 97; typhoid fever less prevalent, 90, 98; smallpox, 100; registration, 113; L. Dr. Milner, 164; black tongue, 164; cholera, yellow fever, small-pox, 165;
medical department, University of, hygiene in, 296; Dr. Herrick, yellow fever and Board of Health, water supply, 166; sewage, 167; germ theory? 168; Dr. Chaillé, Louisiana laws, 169, 170; State Hospital at Richmond, 243; D. of S. L., 331-343; S. B. of H., 339-343.
Louisville, registration, 113.
Lung fever, Colorado, 143; Connecticut, 145; Vermont, 263. *See* Pneumonia.

M.

MACK, Dr. David, Jr., Los Pinos Agency, Col., L., 139; Indians, diseases, &c., recorded temperature, &c., 143; climate, &c, of the Rocky Mountains, 140; its influence, snow blindness, moonlight, difficult to exercise, effect on pulmonary difficulties, 141; menstruation, Indians, half civilized, &c., their diseases, 142, 143.
Magdeburg (Germany), P. H. in, 475.
Malarial disease, District of Columbia, 90; in Henderson, Ky., 90; less since filling pond, 90; lessened by drainage in Michigan, 91; after clearing of swamps and drying of soil in Mississippi, 91; and in Massachusetts, 91; lessened generally in Northern States, 93; malarial hæmorrhagic fever, since the war, in Alabama, 95; precursor of typhoid in New York, 97, reports on, 193; typhoid has replaced them, 198; more common than formerly, Texas, 97; Arkansas, cursed with malaria, 137; Illinois, less common than formerly, 160; Michigan, much less prevalent, 176; more on east than west banks of rivers in Michigan, 177; Nevada, a prevailing disease, 182; legal measures in 1800 about dam said to cause, in New York, 195; extinction and reproduction of in do., 197; in connection with wet soil in New York, 205; controlled in Charleston, S.C., 242; Virginia, lessened by disappearance of marshes, 265; malignant, while typhoid is rare, 268; intermittent fever rare in Norfolk, Va., except in those exposed to malarial influence, 274; among negroes, 275; Wisconsin, owing to disturbance of an old and offensive cemetery, 277.
Malarial hæmorrhagic fever in Alabama, 'since the war," 95; query

INDEX.

if not a new disease in Mississippi, 179.

Malignant congestive fever less in New York, 91; malignant intermittent fever in New York, formerly prevalent, now nearly gone, 198; dysentery rarer than formerly in Virginia, 215.

Maine, vital statistics, only marriages, 66; registration law, 68, 112; Dr. French, 171; primitive sanitary legislation, 300; D. of S. L., 343-347.

Mange. See Army itch, 160.

Marriages. See Registration, 63, 66-69.

Maryland, appropriations for S. B. of H., 45, 47; S. B. of H. established, 54; correspondents of, 58; registration laws, 68; vaccination and quarantine, 74; quarantine for yellow fever, 77; D. of S. L., 348-350; S. B. of H., 349.

Massachusetts, sanitary report, 31; S. B. of H., 43, 45; special appropriations, 47, 48; noxious and offensive trades law, 50, 463; influence of that law on Brighton, 49, 51; pollution of rivers, 57; correspondents of S. B. of H., 58; powers of S. B. of H., 59; registration law, 68 of H., 53; registration law, 68; Boston and Charlestown, impurity of water supply, 73; no person unvaccinated allowed to attend school, 74; yellow fever, 76; cattle disease, 78; co-operative building companies, 81; intermittent fever formerly, 91; health laws inefficient, 100; registration, 113, 116; L., Dr. Allen, preventive medicine, &c., 171; Jarvis on registration in the various States, 172-174; Jarvis on the increased length of life in modern days, 174; law on slaughter houses, noxious and offensive trades, 463; recommended to other States, 51; D. of S. L., 330-338; S. B. of H., 334-337.

McFie, Mrs., "Wayside Home" hospitals in South Carolina during the civil war, 247.

McKee, Dr. J. H., L., Los Angelos, Cal., L., 138.

McMaster, George, Wayside Home Hospital at Richmond during the civil war, 248.

Mears, Dr. George W., Indiana, trichiniasis, 96.

Measles in Florida, 152.

Medical colleges, Hygiene in, circular to, 282; list of those which replied to it, 294; table 2, showing average amounts of instruction in hygiene given by the colleges, 295; of Alabama, of University California, Yale, Ga., Rush, Ill., New Orleans, La., University of La., Harvard, Mass., University of Michigan, 296; Dartmouth, N.H., Albany, N.Y., Buffalo, N.Y., Miami, O., 297; Jefferson, Pa., University Pennsylvania, South Carolina, 298.

Menstruation, said to be more profuse in Colorado, 142.

Metropolitan Board of Health, New York, 34; doings on cattle disease, 78; tenement houses, 79.

Metuchen, N.J., registration, 114.

Miasmatic diseases, Louisiana, 166; Nebraska, 182.

Michigan, appropriations for S. B. of Health, 43, 47; investigations for Public Health, 53; S. B. established, 54; correspondents, 58; registration laws, 68; no yellow fever, 77; malarial diseases less since drainage of swamps, 68; cerebro-spinal meningitis, 98; registration, 113; L., Dr. Baker, 175; Dr. Beech, 176; Dr. Kedzie, 177; D. of S. L., 358-364; S. B. of H., 362.

Milk-sickness, Illinois, common, years ago, 160; in Kentucky, less, 90; lessened by cultivation of the soil, 164.

Milner, Dr. U. R., New Orleans, La., black tongue, 90; cholera, 97; L., 164, 165.

Milwaukee, Mich., registration, 114.

Minneapolis, Minn., registration, 114.

Minnesota, appropriations for S. B. of H., 43, 47; S. B. established, 54; powers of, 60; sanitary survey of State, 65; registration, 68, 114; leaves yellow fever to General Statutes, 77; D. of S. L., 364-366; S. B. of H., 365.

Mississippi, vital statistics, law for, now pending, 67; "vaccination before the war," 74; malaria less since swamps dried up, 91; registration, 114; L., Dr. Burch, 178; Wirt Johnson's, 179; Dr. Whitehead's, 179; Dr. Dancy's, 180; D. of S. L., 366-369; S. B. of H., 367-369.

Missouri, vital statistics, imperfect, 66; registration laws, 68; registration, 114; L., Dr. J. B. Johnson's, 180; Dr. John Green's, 180, 181; Dr. R. W. Oliphant's, 181; want of sanitary legislation, 300; D. of S. L., 370.

Mobile, registration, 113.

Moisture of soil as cause of consump-

490 INDEX.

tion in America, 453-460; England, 461, 462.
Money, amounts paid by States for Public Eygiene, small, 46; by Massachusetts, 46, 47; large salaries demoralize.
Montgomery, Ala., registration, 113
Moore, Dr. P., C.S.A. State hospital at Richmond, during the late war, 251.
Mormons, land irrigation with them a necessity, 71.
Morse electric telegraph, 4.
Mortality reports in different States, summary of by Dr. Edward Jarvis.
" Mountain (typho-malarial) fever," chief disease in Nevada, 182.
Museum, army, medical and surgical, should be amply sustained by Government, 151.

N.

NASH, Dr. H. M., Virginia, L., 274-276.
National Medical College, Washington, D.C., Eygiene, 296; Medical Library, importance of, 148, 151; Medical Museum, importance of, 150, 151; National Sanitary Conventions, 35, 36.
Navasota (Tex.), registration, 114.
Nebraska, vital statistics imperfect, 66 ; registration law, 68; small-pox, 74; cholera laws, 75; L. Dr. D. W. Henshey, 181; J. H. Peabody's, 181; inadequate sanitary laws in, 300; D. of S. L. 370, 371
Nervous fever (typhoid), Virginia, 275.
Neuralgia in Texas more common of late years, 97; more common in Navasota, Tex., than elsewhere, 259.
Neuralgic diseases, Dr. Harris on the "equivalents," or local causes of, 197; very prevalent in Navasota, Texas, 259.
Nevada, Public Health wholly neglected, 67; small-pox, laws against, good, but imperfect execution of, 74; T. R. Grindley, Esq., L. 182; inadequate sanitary laws in, 300; D. of S. L. 371.
New Hampshire, vital statistics, imperfect, 66 registration laws, 68; registration, 114; L. Dr. G. P. Conn's 182; Dr. G. B Twitchell, 183; Dr C. L. Downes, 183-189; Dr. J. W. Parsons, 189; inadequate sanitary legislat on in, 300; practice of medi-

cine, law regulating, 377-378; D. of S. L. 371-378.
New Haven, Conn., registration, 113
New Jersey, registration law, neglected, 67; land drainage, 70 registration, 114; L. Dr. E. Warman's, 190; D. of S. L., 379-381; S. B. of H., 380.
New Mexico, land irrigation, 71.
New Orleans, registration, 113
New Orleans School of Medicine, Hygiene in, 236.
New Orleans, yellow fever, 77; endemic or imported ? 77; Dr. Herrick thinks might be extirpated, 77.
New York, registration law, 68; land drainage, ' for crops, not for health," 70; impure water in Albany, 73; yellow fever, occasionally at quarantine ground, never now epidemic, 76 homes for the cattle disease, 78; malarial disease lessened, 80, 219; diphtheria, Dr. Harris thinks more fatal formerly, 97; scarlatina, 97; registration, 114; L. Dr. A. N. Bell, 191; Dr. Elisha Harris, 191-198; Dr. E. H. Janes, 198; Mr. Janeway's report to Dr. Austin Flint, 198, 199; Dr. W. H.Thayer, 200-205; Dr. S. O Vanderpoel, 205-211; Dr. W. O. Wey, 212; inspection by Citizens' Committee, 197; quarantine, 205; Health Laws, 198, 199; Dr. Thayer's account, 200-204; confusion of laws, ' deplorable " (Pickering), 405; D. of S. L., 381-403.
Nomenclature of diseases, Dr. E. H. Janes on, change of, effects of, 97.
Norcom, Dr. W. A. H., Edenton, N.C., health laws, 99; L. 216.
Norfolk, Va., malignant dysentery less than formerly, 275; health measures, 275.
North, battle-field succor in, 242-243.
North Carolina, " cholera," " left in United States hands," 75; yellow fever, 77; bilious, remittent, and pernicious fever almost wholly gone, 92; diphtheria, possibly a new disease, but probably known long ago in England, 96 ; Public Health measures, " none important," 99; L. Dr. Anderson's, 216; Dr. W. A. B. Norcom, 216; hospitals at Richmond, 210; D. of S. L., 406-408.
Hygiene in, 289.
Norway, P. H., in, 477.
Norwich (Conn), registration, 113.
Nostrums in Pennsylvania, 233.
Noxious and offensive trades, repres-

sion of by the States, 48; difficulties of regulating them in crowded parts, 48; experience in Brighton, Mass., 49-51; law against in Massachusetts, App. VII, 465.
Numerical method, Louis, 14; basis of modern medicine and Public Hygiene, 17; its wide-spread influence, 18; Dr. Bigelow's opinion on, 20, 21; Dr. Bartlett's, 26.

O.

OBERLIN COLLEGE, Ohio, Hygiene in, 213.
Observation School of Medicine, contempt for the past, and resulting scepticism, 16; its watchwords, those of the present times, 16.
Offal, disposal of, in the various States, 108-110; wretched arrangements, almost everywhere, 109.
Ohio, registration law, 68; billious, remittent, and intermittent fever much less than formerly, 92; Public Health measures, 99; registration, 114; D. of S. L., 408, 411.
Oregon, vital statistics, marriages only, 66; water in cities, 72; small-pox, only certain towns provide against it, 74, 99; law insufficient against cholera, 75; inefficient laws against yellow fever, 77; probable rare occurrence of, 77; quarantine against yellow fever, 77; overcrowding of the Chinese, 80; Public Health measures, 99; special nuisances, 100; D. of S. L., 411, 412.
Organization (sanitary) of the nation and of the States our first duty, 121.

P.

PALPITATION, liability to, in Colorado, 141.
Paludal fever, Arkansas, 137; Louisiana, 140; yellow fever a species of (Dr. Miner), 165; New York, Dr. Harris on, 192-197.
Parent Duchatelet, his great labors for Public Hygiene, 33.
Parsons, Dr. J. W., Portsmouth, N. H., 189
Peabody, Dr. James H., Omaha, Neb., good health prevalent, L., 181, 182.
Pennsylvania, vital statistics for Philadelphia, not for the State, 67; land drainage, 70; water in cities, 72; in Philadelphia, 73; no compulsory

INDEX.   491

vaccination in, 74; building associations, advisable, 79, 80, 81; have any diseases ceased? 92; registration, 114; L. Lorin Blodgett, 216-220; Dr. W. Ford, 220-231; Dr. Ford, 232-36; Dr. J. L. Le Conte, 236; Dr. J. T. Rothrock, 237; Dr. Ruschenberger, 238; D. of S. L., 412-422.
Pernicious intermittent fevers, 274; formerly prevalent in New York, now have nearly ceased, 198; rare in Virginia, 274.
Pestilent diseases, laws to prevent in New Hampshire, 184-183; do. in New York, 199; do. in Pennsylvania, 238.
Petersburg, Va., powers of Board of Health, "almost despotic," 266; water supply, 267; new disease since the war (see "Yellow Disease," it Vomito), 268; "no typhoid," 268. Petenkofer, of Munich, his labors for Public Hygiene, 33.
Pettersen, Dr., of San Antonio, Tex., rainfall and temperature, 260, 261. Pettigrew, Dr., Wayside Home; hospitals in Georgia during the civil war, 250.
Philadelphia, yellow fever terrible formerly, 76; house-building corporations, 79; model city in this respect, 81; registration, 114; Mr. Blodgett's letter on homes for the people, 216-220.
Phillips Academy, Hygiene in, 230.
Phthisis in high lands of Colorado, 95; influence of soil moisture in Massachusetts, 119; a most frequent cause of death in Connecticut, 143; increasing in Virginia, 263; proofs of existence of law of soil moisture as a permanent cause of, in New England, 453-460; do. in England, 461, 462.
Physical culture, school for, 237; good effects of, in the universities and colleges of the country, 286.
Physical exercises, various methods in universities, table 1, 283; replies from universities and colleges to circular, 283-294.
Physician, relations to the community in former times and now, 12; relations to patient, 13, 14; Dr. Bigelow's account of, 12, 13.
Pickering, H. G., Esq., Digest of Sanitary Laws, App. IV., 300-440.
Pierson, A. L., Dr., obituary notice of Dr. James Jackson, Jr., 448.
Pleuro-pneumonia in cattle in New York, legislative acts, 198, 201, 202;

492 INDEX.

do. in Pennsylvania, 226; none since 1871 in Virginia, 269.
Plummer, Dr. J. P. S., Oregon, health laws, 99; special nuisances, 101; law of development of typhoid fever, 118.
Pneumonia, 182 (see Lung Fever); may possibly be prevented by attention to sleeping-rooms, &c. (Dr. Baker), 119; Michigan, 176; common in Nevada, 183.
Policing of camps as a means of eradicating disease, 36; good policy of frequent changes of position of tents during war, as shown by facts in the Confederate army, 264.
Politics, deleterious influence of, in selection of sanitary agents, 274.
Pollution of streams used for culinary purposes, general results from the various States, 101-103; only about one-third of them seem to care any thing about the matter, 102.
Polypharmacy, Dr. Bigelow, Rush's, 9, 10; former notions thereof in New England, 13; Dr. Bigelow's opposition to, 20-22; Dr. Forbes's, 23, 24; Dr. Bartlet's, 26.
Poor, tenements for, regulations for, 79; Boston, 82-83; Miss Hill's method in possible, with a committee as superintendents, 82, 88.
Powers of Sanitary Boards grow slowly, under fear of dangerous diseases, 60; and from necessity of quarantine in infectious diseases, as seen in great cities on Gulf of Mexico, 55-60.
Preston, Gen., Wayside Home, 247.
Prevention of disease in camp, 264.
Preventive medicine, State, 29; its destiny to be coeval with civilization, 30; the noblest form of Public Hygiene, 3.
Prince George (Va.), registration, 114.
Princeton College, Hygiene in, 292.
Providence (R.I.), registration, 114.
Public Health Associations, 37; measures for improvements, in Arkansas, Colorado, Florida, North Carolina, Ohio, Oregon, 99; South Carolina, Texas, Wyoming Territory, Massachusetts, 100; laws inefficiently used, 100; England's Public Health Acts, 187; importance of, 469, 470.
Public Hygiene, founded on natural law, greeted by modern science, 122; in universities, table 1, 283; colleges, table 2, 235. See Hygiene.
Pulmonary diseases probably cause one-half of the deaths in Illinois, 161.

Putnam, Dr. Sumner, Montpelier, Vt., L., 263.
Putrid sore throat, probably the modern diphtheria, Virginia, 275.

Q.

QUARANTINE, necessity of, originates health boards, 60; history of, in New York, Dr. Harris, 195; do. Vanderpoel, 203, 208; Vanderpoel, plans of, 208-211.
Questions, analysis of, replies from all the States to the: first, 41; second, 43; third, 54; fourth, 61; fifth, 62; sixth, 63; seventh, 89; eighth, 94; ninth, 98; tenth, 99; eleventh, 101; twelfth, 101; thirteenth, 101; fourteenth, 101; fifteenth, 103; sixteenth, 107; seventeenth, 108; eighteenth, 111; nineteenth, 112; twentieth, and test question of the century, 117.
Questions, list of, addressed to correspondents, 125-128.
Quetelet, of Belgium, well known, 33.

R.

RAMSAY, DAVID, high estimate of Dr. Rush, 8, note.
Reed, Dr. J. H., Colorado Health Laws, 99.
Reeves, Dr. J. E., thinks diphtheria not seen in Virginia before 1844, 96.
Registrar, a national, needed, 120.
Registration of births, deaths, marriages, 66; very imperfectly done throughout the various States, 66, 116; period of existence of law for, in several States, 68; any law drawn from, 69-111; California, District of Columbia, Pennsylvania, Louisiana, South Carolina, Colorado, Idaho, Maine, Texas, Virginia, 112; number of years published in various States and towns, 112-114; in Massachusetts, 116; national, needed, 120.
Registration of births, &c.: Nebraska, Missouri, New Hampshire, California, Kentucky, Louisiana, Maine, Oregon, Colorado, Idaho, New York, 66; Pennsylvania, Nevada, New Jersey, South Carolina, Texas, Virginia, Mississippi, West Virginia, Wisconsin, Massachusetts, Boston; an efficient State preventive medicine impossible without it, 67.

Russell, Dr. G. H., Wyoming Terri-
Ruschenberger, Dr. S. W., Philadelphia, L., 238, 239.
Rush Medical College, Chicago, Hygiene, 296.
Rush, Benjamin, great leader in American medicine, 5; life, 8; influence as
professor, 9; statesman, 10; medical
system-maker, 10; a political colleague with Jefferson, 10; superseded
by Broussaisism, 10; heroic method
of treatment, 10; inordinate use of
calomel, jalap, and the lancet, 10;
Bigelow's estimate of, 20-22; Bartlett's, 26; yellow fever in Philadelphia, 76.
Rothrock, Dr. J. F., Wilkesbarre, Pa.,
compulsory vaccination, 101; L.,
school for physical culture, 237.
River pollution, in Massachusetts reports, 57.
River levees, analysis of questions to
the States, 71, 72.
Richmond (Va.), registration, 114; L.,
Dr. Levin S. Joynes, sanitary laws,
269-274.
Rhode Island, D. of S. L., 422, 425.
Arnold, 239-240; Dr. G. W. Jencks,
241; primitive sanitary legislation
in, 300; D. of S. L., 422, 425.
vital statistics in, 114; E. S. F.
from, coped with "indirectly," 77;
Rhode Island, 41; yellow fever deaths
Rhineland, Prussian, P. H., 475.
Rheumatism in Colorado, 142; com-
mon among the Indians, 143.
Reports of deaths, &c., 111; one-half
of States make none; in California,
District of Columbia, Pennsylvania,
Louisiana, South Carolina, Colorado,
Idaho, Maine, Texas, Virginia, 112;
Alabama, Arkansas, Colorado, Con-
necticut, Delaware, Georgia, Illinois,
Indiana, Iowa, Kentucky, Louisiana,
Massachusetts, Michigan, 113; Min-
nesota, Mississippi, Missouri, New
Hampshire, New Jersey, New York,
Ohio, Pennsylvania, Rhode Island,
South Carolina, Tennessee, Texas,
Utah, Vermont, Virginia, Wisconsin,
114; United States censuses "grossly
incomplete," 115; opinion of experts,
115; not a single State in the United
States has such as will be event-
ually required, 117.
Religious bigotry, influence of, in preventing the teaching of hygiene,
297.
Remittent fever, light in Nebraska, 182.
Relief societies, Northern and Southern,
during the late civil war, 35, 242-
255.

S.

Rutger's College, N. J., Hygiene in,
292.
L., 278.
tory, quarantine in, small-pox, 101;
St. Louis, registration, 114.
St. Paul, registration, 114.
Salem, Va., Dr. Frederick Horner, Jr.,
L., 269; cattle plague, hog cholera,
269.
Salt Lake City, registration, 114.
San Antonio (Tex.), registration, 114;
rain-fall and temperature, 260, 261.
Sanitary boards spring up under the
influence of fear, and finally become
permanent, 60.
Sanitary Commission, 35; amounts
spent by it during the civil war, &c.,
244, 245.
Sanitary Conventions in various cities,
35.
Sanitary inspection of State institu-
tions, Michigan, 178; New York
City, 197.
Sanitary investigations, by the different
States of the Union, analysis of, 53.
Sanitary journals, list of, 190, 191.
Sanitary Law, Digest of, by H. G. Pick-
ering, Esq.; in United States, 301;
District of Columbia, 303; L., Ala-
bama, 303-306; copy of Act to estab-
lish State Board of Health, 305;
Arkansas, no legislation, 306; Cali-
fornia, 306-311; Colorado, 311; Con-
necticut, 311-316; Delaware, 316
Florida, 319; Georgia, 319; Illinois,
325; law to create State Board of
Health, 326, &c.; Indiana, 328; Iowa,
329; Kansas, 330; Kentucky, 330;
Louisiana, 331-343; law relative to
State Boards of Health, 332, 339-343
Maine, 343-347; Maryland, 348-350;
Massachusetts, 350, 358; Michigan,
358, 364; Minnesota, 364, 366; Mississippi, 366-369; Act relative to
State Board of Health, 367-369; Missouri, 370; Nebraska, 370-371; Nevada, 371; New Hampshire, 371-
377, 378; Act relative to medical practice,
379; New Jersey, 379; Act
relative to State Board of Health,
380, 381; New York, 381 405;
North Carolina, 406, 408; Ohio, 408,
411; Oregon, 411; Pennsylvania,
412, 422; Rhode Island, 422, 425;
South Carolina, 425, 429; Tennessee,
430-432; law on State Board of
Health, of, 430; Texas, 432, 434;
Vermont, 434; Virginia, 435, 435;

494 INDEX.

State Board of Health, 436; West
Virginia, 439; Wisconsin, 439.
Sanitary legislation, absence of, in
Arkansas, Missouri, 300; primitive
nature of, in Maine, New Hampshire,
and Rhode Island, 300; inadequate
provisions by statute in Indiana,
Iowa, Kansas, Kentucky, Nebraska,
Nevada, Vermont, 300; successive
attempts in New York instructive,
as showing the experience of a large
State, 300.
Sanitary survey of a State, 64–66; petition for in Massachusetts, 196; analysis of answers from various
States, 65; no State has made one, 64;
except Minnesota, perhaps, partially,
65; a most important matter, 66.
Sanitary work during the late war, 36;
experience gained by army surgeons,
86; public interest in, 38; amount of
sanitary work lately done, 38; neglected by majority of the States, 39,
42.
Santa Barbara, registration, 113.
Savannah, Ga., yellow fever, 77.
Saxony (Germany), P. H. in, 475.
Scales, Dr. T. S., L. from Mobile, 136.
Scarlatina, Kentucky, 97; more severe of late, 97; in Michigan, 118;
Florida, 152; Illinois, 160; New
York, 192; Vermont, 263, 264; Saxony, 476; more dangerous in Michigan than sr all-pox, 175; do. New
Hampshire, 184.
Scepticism in medicine, 22; of the
present epoch, 28, 23; and in all the
domain of modern thought, 120, 121;
eventually good to result, 121.
Schleswig Holstein, P. H. in, 475.
Scientific investigations as to causes of
disease, 47; by various States, 47;
most of them, small, 47.
Sewerage, discussion by literary journals, 38; methods in various States,
analysis of replies, 108; chaotic in
most of them, 109; Boston, 105–108;
Albany, Chicago, Philadelphia, 108;
Alabama, California, Dist. Columbia, Louisiana, Florida, North Carolina, Indiana, Minnesota, Washington Territory, Massachusetts, New
York, Rhode Island, Kansas, 104;
Newport, 239.
Sewers, primitive view, evils of not
having them, 103; outlets of, analysis of replies from various places,
107; distances from water supply,
107; Boston, 103; Philadelphia, Chicago, 108.
Shattuck, Lemuel, 6; a pioneer of
State Preventive Medicine in America, 6; his Massachusetts Sanitary
Report, 31; calmness, 31; his propositions were neglected, 31; but
became the inspiration of Dr. Derby,
32; Dr. Harris on, 191; do. on Mr.
Shattuck's Report to the Massachusetts Legislature, 196, 197.
Ship fever, New York, 207, 209.
Sickness in camp, summarily stopped
by frequent change of place and by
the policing of camp sites, 264–266.
Simon, Mr., of London, filth diseases,
33; trained inspectors, 33; views on
soil moisture as cause of consumption, 461; admirable reports to the
Privy Council, 469, 470.
Sinks, Dr. Tiffin, Leavenworth, Kan.,
L., 162.
Slaughter houses, Massachusetts law
on, 465.
Slops, disposal of, analysis of answers
from the various States thereupon,
101–111.
Small-pox, imperfect law for prevention, 73; a national vaccination law
needed, 73; very prevalent formerly,
93; in Canada now, 93; quarantine
against, 101; Boston, Maine, 73;
Delaware, Louisiana, Nebraska, Oregon, Wisconsin, Utah, Indiana,
South Carolina, Texas, Nevada,
Mississippi, Iowa, Virginia, Pennsylvania, Connecticut, Massachusetts, Maryland, Tennessee, 74; Connecticut, 90, 144–146; Rhode Island,
92; Florida, 152; Illinois, 155; Louisiana, 165; New Hampshire, 184;
New York, 194, 199, 209, 212, 213;
Pennsylvania, 226; Tennessee, 256;
Virginia, 271, 273.
Snow, Dr. E. M., small-pox in Providence, R.I., 92; vital statistical reports of do., 173.
Snow blindness in Colorado, 141.
Soil moisture, law of, as a cause of
consumption, discovery of, App. VI.,
452–462; confirmed by registration,
medical opinion, and statistics, 453;
peculiarities of towns, houses, by
facts from other States, army statistics, medical practice, 457–460; apparent discovery in England, 461, 462.
South, battle-field succor, 246–251.
South Caroli a, vital registration, "before the war and since," 67; small-
pox in, 74; cholera quarantine, 77;
diphtheria, 96; Public Health measures, 100; registration, 114; Dr. Simon Baruch, 241; Dr. W. H. Huger,
241; Dr. R. A. Kinloch, 242; bat-

INDEX.

tle-field succor, South, Dr. Turnip-
seed, 246, 248, 249; D. of S. L., 425-
429.
Southern Illinois College, Hygiene in,
288.
Southern University, Hygiene in, 287.
Spain, P. H. in, 473.
Spotted fever, formerly very severe
epidemics in Connecticut, 145, 146;
lately in New Hampshire, 183; in
New York, 213.
Squire, Dr. T. H., Elmira, N. Y., on
cerebro-spinal meningitis, 213.
Stark, Miss Mary, "Wayside Home"
in the south during the war, 247.
State Boards of Health, 34; reports of,
34; money to support? 43 45; of
Massachusetts, its influence, 49-51;
last decade includes all lists of,
54; imperfectly supported in some
States, 56; yellow fever epidemics
influenced the establishment of
Boards of Health in Louisiana, 56;
annual appropriations for, 45, 56,
57; extra grants, 57; correspondents,
58; executive powers, 59; list of
States having them, 84; do. in Pickering's Digest, 300; in Louisiana,
Mississippi, Michigan, Minnesota, Wyoming, 60; establishment
of, marks highest ground reached in
sanitary law, 300; in Alabama, 305;
California, 310; Colorado, 311; District Columbia, 54; Georgia, 51, 322;
Illinois, 326; Louisiana, 339-343;
Maryland, 349; Massachusetts, 45,
54, 354-356; Michigan, 362; Minnesota, 365; Mississippi, 367; New
Jersey, 380; Tennessee, 430; Virginia, 436.
State Normal University, Ill., Hygiene
in, 288.
State Preventive Medicine, 2; noblest
phase of Public Hygiene, 3; culmination of the Centenary, 6; Dr.
Forbes's allusion to it, 24; results of
third epoch, 29; influence of American Medical Association upon, 37;
present status of the country on, 39;
circular relative thereto, to the States,
39; replies from every State, 40; no
State has as yet entered fully on it,
55; small advances as yet, 58; its
influence on future centuries, 122;
growing in these States, 55; aroused
by suffering in the South, less so in
North, 55; Griscom on, 193; in universities, see table 1, 283; medical
colleges, table 2, 235.
Stephenson, of England, steam locomotive, its civilizing influence, 4.

Stewart, Dr. W. D. L., 90; prevention
of zymotics in District of Columbia,
118.
Stille, Charles J., story of U. S. Sanitary Commission, 243; perforation applicable North and South, 255.
Strong, Dr. C. C., Oregon, small-pox,
99; special nuisances, 101.
Survey, sanitary, of a State, 63; mistakes from not having it, 64; no
State has made one, 65; but it will
eventually be made, 66.
Sutton, Dr., Kentucky, vital registration, 172.
Swamp fever, in Arkansas alluvial regions, 137.
Syphilis, among Indians in Colorado,
143.

T.

Temperature in January and February, 1873, at Los Pinos Agency, Colorado, table of, 143; do. for Asheville,
N. C., 214; do. for San Antonio, Tex.,
260.
Tenement houses, law regulating, analysis of answers from the States, 79
Philadelphia English in advance, 79;
better than all others, 79; importance
of regulating them, 80; experience
in Boston, 81-83; some are nuisances,
and should not be allowed by law, 87;
death rate reduced even in the worst
by sanitary regulations, 87; common
corridors and common house conveniences a nuisance, and promotive of
crime, 82 et seq.; Lorin Blodgett on
Philadelphia, 216, l.; effect on population, 219; by becoming property
owner, 218, 219; Ford on, 227.
Tennessee Agricultural College, Hygiene in, 293.
Tennessee, "small-pox" under County
Judges" in, 74; registration, 114;
1. Dr. J. H. Van Deman, 256; Frederick Bailey, 257; D. of S. L., 430-
432; S. B. of H., 430.
Texan cattle disease, doings in regard
to in Illinois, 135-137; do. New York,
198; has not appeared since 1871,
Virginia, 269.
Texan fever in animals, 155.
Texas, small-pox in, 74; cholera laws,
75; quarantine for yellow fever, 77;
cattle disease, 78; Public Health measures, 100; registration, 112, 114; L.
Dr. A. R. Kilpatrick, 258; Dr. Peter-
sen, 259-261; D. of S. L., 432-434.
Thayer, Dr. W. H., Brooklyn, tenement houses, 80; intermittents less,

496 INDEX.

92; diphtheria, 97, 98; New York, health laws of, New York L., 200–204.
Toner, J. M., Dr., prevention of zymotics, 118, Washington, D.C., L., 150.
Town Boards of Health, natural growth of, from right of self-defence, 62.
Trades, noxious and offensive, law on, in Massachusetts, 465.
Trees, good e'tects of cutting down, in Virginia, 255.
Trichiniasis, Indiana, 96; Steuben County, N.Y., 212; Dr. Dalton and Dr. Hun on, 213.
Trinity College, Hartford, Hygiene in, 287.
Tuberculosis, 160, 193 (see Consumption and Phthisis); from bad surroundings in homestead, 186.
Turnipseed, Dr. E. F., Columbia, S.C., diphtheria, 93; battle-field succor organized in the Confederate States during the civil war, 246–251; political influences on sanitary measures, 100; names of various persons connected with sanitary relief societies in the South during the war, 246.
Typho-contagia, Dr. Harris on, 118, 192; in New York, 192.
Typhoid fever Kentucky, 97; Virginia, 98; of malarial fever, 97; Virginia, 98; investigated in New Orleans, 98; typho-contagia and their factors, 118; investigations in Vermont, 263; not very common in California, 138; beginning to appear in Kentucky, 164; Nebraska, rare, 182; by bad drainage in New Hampshire, 185–188; New York, 213; rare in South Carolina, 241; investigated by medical society, in Vermont, 263; from Petersburg, Va., 268; in cattle, 269; bad hygiene, 264; very rare in met with in Norfolk, Va., 275.
Typho-malarial fever caused by the breaking up of an old cemetery, in Wisconsi 1, 277.
Typhus, during 1806–7 in Connecticut, 145; in Massachusetts, 1796, 195; originating, "de novo," in a lone quarantine for in New York, 209; house in the woods of Vermont, 264.
Twitchell, Dr. G. B., Keene, N.H., L., 183.

U.

UNION COLLEGE, Hygiene in, 292.
United States, various army publications, 34; library, museum, 34; in-

completeness of census, 115; D. of S. L., 301.
United States Christian Commission, Sanitary do., Western Sanitary do., 248: estimated expenditures of each during the civil war, 245.
Universities, hygiene in, 281; of Alabama, Southern, Chicago, 287; State Normal, Ill., Indiana State, 288; N.W.C., Indianapolis, 289; Cornell, 292; of Virginia, 293 (see Colleges).
Unvaccinated children not allowed to attend school in Massachusetts, 74; do. in New York, 199; unvaccinated from Maine, cause of small-pox in Boston? 73.
Utah, land irrigation, 71; a necessity; analogy between Mormons and Moors, 71; small-pox in, 74; cholera laws, 75; registration, 114; L. Dr. W. F. Anderson; Dr. J. D. Crockwell, 262.

V.

VACCINATION, national law on, needed, 74; summary of returns from twenty-one States, 74; gratuitous in Virginia, 74; in public schools in New Hampshire, 184; law absolute to promote vaccination, but not executed, in New York, 192, 193; gratuitous by do., 193; do. Pennsylvania, 226; "vaccine agent," for free vaccination in Virginia, 270, 271; in Richmond, 272.
Vaccination in various States, 74; vaccination, compulsory, Iowa, 74; Pennsylvania, Virginia, Vermont, Tennessee, 101; Chattanooga, Tenn., 257; do. in city of Chester, Pa., 226; failure to get a law for it in Arkansas, 137.
Van Denman, Dr. J. H., Tennessee, compulsory vaccination, 101; L., 257.
Vanderpoel, Dr. S. Oakley, L. on New York quarantine, 205–208; plan of quarantine, 208–211.
Warrentrapp, Dr., on sanitary law in the different States of the German Empire, 474–477.
Venereal disease among the Colorado Indians, 143.
Venesection, absurd pretensions by Rush, 10; neglect of, at present, 16. Vermont, no former disease has ceased, Fassett, 262; neglect of sanitary matters in, 262; Dr. S. Putnam, 93; registration, 114; L. Dr. O. E. 263, 264; inadequate sanitary laws in, 300; D. of S. L., 434, 435.

INDEX. 497

Vicksburg, Miss., registration, 114.
Viél, General, on drainage, 205, note.
Vienna School of Medicine, 15.
Virchow, as a sanitarian, 33.
Virginia State Board, established, 54;
vital statistics imperfect, not of
births, 67; gratuitous vaccination,
74; quarantine in, cholera, 75; diphtheria, 96; typhoid fever, endemic
since 1814–15, 98; registration, 112;
114; Dr. Claiborne, 268; Dr.
Frederick Horner, Jr., 269; Dr. Levin
S. Joynes, 269; D. of S. L., 435–439;
S. B. of H., 436.
Virqua, Wis., typho-malarial fever,
from disturbing a cemetery, 277.
Vis medicatrix naturæ, contempt for, in
first epoch, 6.
Vital statistics, see Registration, 65–69.
see Jarvis's letter, registration in the
various States, 172–174; no State, nor
the United States government, has a
proper system, 116.
Voorhies's Civil Code of Louisiana, 170.

W.

Wabash College, Ind., Hygiene in,
290.
Walker, Gen. Francis A., 68; statement in reference to United States
census, 115.
War, influence of, on Public Hygiene,
34, 147; sanitary work during the
civil war, 35; battle-field succor,
North and South, during late war,
242–235.
Warman, Dr. D., Trenton, N.J., L,
190.
Warren, Dr. John, opinion of origin
of typhoid, 195.
Washington Territory, irrigation, 71.
Water, introduction of, into cities, 72;
imperfectly done, 73; questions of
purify, 101; rivers, wells, purify of,
102; most people of United States,
neglectful of, 102; Indiana, Pennsylvania, Oregon, Illinois, 72; want
of perfect care in Boston, Charlestown, Chicago, Albany, Philadelphia,
73; supply at Fond-du-Lac from
deep artesian wells, and, of course,
free from surface pollution, 278.
Watt, steam-engine, an aid to civilization, 4.
Wayside hospitals in the South, 35,
246, &c.
Wells (" driven "), in Arkansas, 137;
Wells, Dr. Frank, intermittents less
in Cleveland, O., since drainage, 92;

Western Sanitary Commission, 35;
amount of money expended by,
land, 99.
Westphalia (Germany), P. H. in, 475.
West Virginia, vital statistics imperfect, 67; law, 68; diphtheria, not seen
before 1844, 96; D. of S. L., 438.
Wey, Dr. W. C., Elmira, N.Y., L,
212.
Williamstown College, Hygiene in,
290.
Wild deer; " black tongue " epidemic
among them, said to have extended
to human beings in Louisiana, 164.
Willis, Major E., " Wayside Home,"
249.
Wilmington (Del.), registration, 113.
Winona, registration, 114.
Winsor, Dr. F., river pollution in Massachusetts, 57.
Wisconsin, appropriations for State
Board of Health, 45; special grants,
47; State Board of Health, 54; law
for collection of vital statistics neglected, 67; law, when enacted, 68;
small-pox guarded against by laws
in certain towns, 74; registration,
114; L. Dr. W. A. Gott, 277; E.
Griffin, 277; D of S. L., 439, 440.
Woodward, Dr. Ashbel, Franklin,
Conn., L. on small-pox and croup,
as being more manageable of late,
90.
Woodward, Dr. A. T., intermittent
gone, 93.
Woodward, Dr. J. J., Washington,
D.C., L. Army Medical Museum
and Library, influence on Public
Hygiene, 130, 152.
Woodhull, Dr. A. A., Assistant Surgeon United States Army, on uniform
and clothing of army, 149.
Würtemberg, Germany, P. H. in, 475.
Wyoming, no State Board; city marshals have powers, 60; Public
Health measures, 100; law on professional practice, 278.

Y.

Yale College, Medical Department,
Hygiene in, 296.
Yandell, Dr. L. P., bilious remittent,
in Kentucky, formerly annual; it is
very rare now, 90.
" Yellow disease," " a new disease,"
Virginia, 268.
Yellow fever, prevention of, 76;

INDEX.

Charleston, Savannah, New Orleans, 77; present doubt as to cause, as formerly, 77; never seen in Colorado, Dakota, Michigan, 77; left to local boards in California, 77; inefficient laws in Iowa, Louisiana, Maryland, Oregon, South Carolina, Texas, 77; General Statutes in Minnesota, 77; in United States hands in North Carolina, 77; "indirectly" met in Rhode Island, 77; gone from the North, 76; still prevails South, 77; doubts about its nature, as in Rush's time, 77; endemic in Georgia, 96; Connecticut, earlier laws on, 144, 146; in army, 149; epidemic in Savannah, 153½ L., report of State Board of Health on same epidemic, 154; "paludal" in Louisiana, 165; begun in last decade of last century; not strictly endemic now, 166; gone from New York, 198; quarantine acts from 1784 to 1823, 201; devastated New York in the last century, 203; quarantine, as made now, 210; in Chattanooga, 256; germ theory in, 163; South Carolina, periodical, and not kept out by quarantine, 242; prevented in Chattanooga, 256; Virginia, 275; Vanderpoel on, 92; has left the North, still prevails South, 93; might be crushed in Louisiana, says Dr. Herrick, 97; formerly prevalent in New York, not now, 198; quarantine of Hamilton at Albany for yellow fever at Philadelphia! 207; in Pennsylvania, laws against, 226; "interior yellow fever," a new disease, 268.

Z.

Zymotics: Drs. Plummer, Butler, Stewart, Toner, views of, Dr. Harris, opinions on, 118; in Michigan, 91; universal formerly in do., 177; in animals, 269.

Cambridge: Press of John Wilson & Son.

Medicine & Society
In America

An Arno Press/New York Times Collection

Alcott, William A. **The Physiology of Marriage.** 1866. New Introduction by Charles E. Rosenberg.

Beard, George M. **American Nervousness: Its Causes and Consequences.** 1881. New Introduction by Charles E. Rosenberg.

Beard, George M. **Sexual Neurasthenia.** 5th edition. 1898.

Beecher, Catharine E. **Letters to the People on Health and Happiness.** 1855.

Blackwell, Elizabeth. **Essays in Medical Sociology.** 1902. Two volumes in one.

Blanton, Wyndham B. **Medicine in Virginia in the Seventeenth Century.** 1930.

Bowditch, Henry I. **Public Hygiene in America.** 1877.

Bowditch, N[athaniel] I. **A History of the Massachusetts General Hospital: To August 5, 1851.** 2nd edition. 1872.

Brill, A. A. **Psychanalysis: Its Theories and Practical Application.** 1913.

Cabot, Richard C. **Social Work: Essays on the Meeting-Ground of Doctor and Social Worker.** 1919.

Cathell, D. W. **The Physician Himself and What He Should Add to His Scientific Acquirements.** 2nd edition. 1882. New Introduction by Charles E. Rosenberg.

The Cholera Bulletin. Conducted by an Association of Physicians. Vol. I: Nos. 1-24, 1832. All published. New Introduction by Charles E. Rosenberg.

Clarke, Edward H. **Sex in Education; or, A Fair Chance for the Girls.** 1873.

Committee on the Costs of Medical Care. **Medical Care for the American People: The Final Report of The Committee on the Costs of Medical Care, No. 28.** [1932].

Currie, William. **An Historical Account of the Climates and Diseases of the United States of America.** 1792.

Davenport, Charles Benedict. **Heredity in Relation to Eugenics.** 1911. New Introduction by Charles E. Rosenberg.

Davis, Michael M. **Paying Your Sickness Bills.** 1931.

Disease and Society in Provincial Massachusetts: Collected Accounts, 1736-1939. 1972.

Earle, Pliny. **The Curability of Insanity: A Series of Studies.** 1887.

Falk, I. S., C. Rufus Rorem, and Martha D. Ring. **The Costs of Medical Care: A Summary of Investigations on The Economic Aspects of the Prevention and Care of Illness, No. 27.** 1933.

Faust, Bernhard C. **Catechism of Health: For the Use of Schools, and for Domestic Instruction.** 1794.

Flexner, Abraham. **Medical Education in the United States and Canada: A Report to The Carnegie Foundation for the Advancement of Teaching,** Bulletin Number Four. 1910.

Gross, Samuel D. **Autobiography of Samuel D. Gross, M.D.,** with Sketches of His Contemporaries. Two volumes. 1887.

Hooker, Worthington. **Physician and Patient; or, A Practical View of the Mutual Duties, Relations and Interests of the Medical Profession and the Community.** 1849.

Howe, S. G. **On the Causes of Idiocy.** 1858.

Jackson, James. **A Memoir of James Jackson, Jr., M.D.** 1835.

Jennings, Samuel K. **The Married Lady's Companion, or Poor Man's Friend.** 2nd edition. 1808.

The Maternal Physician; a Treatise on the Nurture and Management of Infants, from the Birth until Two Years Old. 2nd edition. 1818. New Introduction by Charles E. Rosenberg.

Mathews, Joseph McDowell. **How to Succeed in the Practice of Medicine.** 1905.

McCready, Benjamin W. **On the Influences of Trades, Professions, and Occupations in the United States, in the Production of Disease.** 1943.

Mitchell, S. Weir. **Doctor and Patient.** 1888.

Nichols, T[homas] L. **Esoteric Anthropology: The Mysteries of Man.** [1853].

Origins of Public Health in America: Selected Essays, 1820–1855. 1972.

Osler, Sir William. **The Evolution of Modern Medicine.** 1922.

The Physician and Child-Rearing: Two Guides, 1809–1894. 1972.

Rosen, George. **The Specialization of Medicine: with Particular Reference to Ophthalmology.** 1944.

Royce, Samuel. **Deterioration and Race Education.** 1878.

Rush, Benjamin. **Medical Inquiries and Observations.** Four volumes in two. 4th edition. 1815.

Shattuck, Lemuel, Nathaniel P. Banks, Jr., and Jehiel Abbott. **Report of a General Plan for the Promotion of Public and Personal Health. Massachusetts Sanitary Commission.** 1850.

Smith, Stephen. **Doctor in Medicine and Other Papers on Professional Subjects.** 1872.

Still, Andrew T. **Autobiography of Andrew T. Still,** with a History of the Discovery and Development of the Science of Osteopathy. 1897.

Storer, Horatio Robinson. **The Causation, Course, and Treatment of Reflex Insanity in Women.** 1871.

Sydenstricker, Edgar. **Health and Environment.** 1933.

Thomson, Samuel. **A Narrative, of the Life and Medical Discoveries of Samuel Thomson.** 1822.

Ticknor, Caleb. **The Philosophy of Living; or, The Way to Enjoy Life and Its Comforts.** 1836.

U.S. Sanitary Commission. **The Sanitary Commission of the United States Army: A Succinct Narrative of Its Works and Purposes.** 1864.

White, William A. **The Principles of Mental Hygiene.** 1917.